Electronic Commerce

Wiley Series in Information Systems

CURRENT VOLUMES IN THE SERIES

Electronic Commerce

B2C Strategies and Models

Edited by

STEVE ELLIOT

University of Newcastle, Australia

JOHN WILEY & SONS, LTD

658.84
E38

Other Wiley Editorial Offices

John Wiley & Sons, Inc., 605 Third Avenue,
New York, NY 10158-0012, USA

WILEY-VCH Verlag GmbH, Pappelallee 3,
D-69469 Weinheim, Germany

John Wiley Australia Ltd, 33 Park Road, Milton,
Queensland 4064, Australia

John Wiley & Sons (Asia) Pte Ltd, 2 Clementi Loop #02-01,
Jin Xing Distripark, Singapore 129809

John Wiley & Sons (Canada) Ltd, 22 Worcester Road,
Rexdale, Ontario M9W 1L1, Canada

British Library Cataloguing in Publication Data

A catalogue record for this book is available from the British Library

ISBN 0-471-48705-8

Typeset in $10\frac{1}{2}/12$ pt Palatino by C.K.M. Typesetting, Salisbury, Wiltshire.
Printed and bound in Great Britain by T.J. International Ltd, Padstow, Cornwall.
This book is printed on acid-free paper responsibly manufactured from sustainable forestry,
in which at least two trees are planted for each one used for paper production.

Wiley Series in Information Systems

Editors

RICHARD BOLAND   Department of Management Information and Decision Systems, Weatherhead School of Management, Case Western Reserve University, 10900 Euclid Avenue, Cleveland, Ohio 44106-7235, USA

RUDY HIRSCHHEIM   Department of Decision and Information Systems, College of Business Administration, University of Houston, Houston, Texas 77202-6283, USA

Advisory Board

For Jenny, Chris and the Curry Club

Contents

Foreword

This book is research at its best. It's a systematic and highly reliable comparative analysis of the patterns of e-commerce experience in many countries, large and small. The cases alone would be of value in expanding our understanding of the dynamics of e-commerce retailing; they cover Australia, Denmark, Greece, Hong Kong (China), the UK, and the USA, and provide five in-depth examples in each marketplace. But what makes *Electronic Commerce* a significant and very practical contribution to management knowledge and methods, is the extent to which it so clearly demonstrates that the dynamics of success are absolutely independent of specific national context – that there are common structural forces at work, regardless of whether this is an online retailer of CDs in Hong Kong, an e-mall in Greece, or a grocery startup in Australia.

Steve Elliot and his co-authors provide a combination of depth and breadth in their cases and their application of their e-commerce adoption model that does full justice to the very different contexts and different outcomes. They thus report the rich variety of business context and outcomes. But what comes through so clearly is that while the drivers, inhibitors, consumer factors, market factors and above all organizational and operational factors vary widely in their details and timing, it's literally the same the whole world over.

On the surface, consumer-focused e-commerce has appeared very different in its rollouts and impacts across the world and even within countries. If that were indeed the case, then the subtitle of this book, *Strategies and Models*, would be meaningless. Instead, we would continue to talk about visions and stories. Each major innovator has indeed been a story in itself, a story where it is often still unclear whether there will be a happy or sad ending and one with many twists in the plot. The US has provided most of the epics and melodramas – Amazon, Yahoo, Webvan, Expedia, Pets.com, eToys, eBay and others. Outside the United States, Boo.com stands out as a disaster story and Tesco's online supermarket as a so-far success, with thousands of mini-novellas. This kaleidoscope has been bewildering, a dazzling glitter — a surface.

Electronic Commerce shows what's beneath the surface: the creative tension between market and management. I often semi-jokingly reply to the frequent question as to what we can learn from the now-past dot.com era that there are two lessons (1) Brains and capital can transform any industry, and (2) Brains and capital plus adult supervision can turn that transformation into success. This book is about adult supervision: a management discipline that is adept in handling the newness of e-commerce — its innovation side — and in implementation of the core of strategy, organization and operations that the dot.com phase too easily ignored. Many of the early entrepreneurs and visionaries thought that innovation in itself would create and sustain the business. It didn't. Management matters. There are no easy wins. That lesson was an expensive one and it has become a cliché that a dot.com website is not a business. The problem has been to go beyond that truism. *How* exactly should managers manage e-commerce?

Electronic Commerce provides very sound answers. There's a richness of analysis and holism of interpretation that I have not seen in any book on the topic (including my own half dozen). The very pace of Internet-based e-commerce meant that no one had the time or perspective to step back from the dramatic and new to tease out what might be termed the ordinary. E-commerce is now part of business as usual — everyday, commonplace, and core to managerial routines. 'Strategy' has to be brought down from the grand vision to management as usual. It has to model the whole dynamic of environment, market, organization and operations. *Electronic Commerce* provides that focus. It is fundamentally a research study but for me it goes well beyond that. The research provides the grounding and evidence that gives weight and credibility to the conclusions and testing of the core adoption model. That makes the research of immediate value to managers; the book in many ways defines the profile of the e-commerce manager. It also provides students with a rich mapping of the terrain.

I hope and believe *Electronic Commerce* will reach a wide audience. I know it will have a long shelf-life by the very fact that it is about the core of e-commerce, not the situational. It's about real companies, not statistics and surveys. Above all, it's about the core structures of e-commerce management that are, almost literally, becoming universal. Every business revolution is in reality a management revolution; otherwise it's just a flash in the pan. E-commerce really is a revolution — an incomplete one. This global comparative study will help us move from the business stage to the management one. I recommend it highly and thank the authors for the impact their work is having on my own thinking and practice.

Peter Keen, Chairman, Keen Innovations

Virginia, USA

February, 2002

Contributors

Niels Bjørn-Andersen
Centre for Electronic Commerce, Copenhagen Business School, DK 2000 Frederiksberg, Denmark

Don Lloyd Cook
Department of Computer Information Systems, J. Mack Robinson College of Business, Georgia State University, University Plaza, Atlanta GA 30303-3087, USA

Georgios Doukidis
Athens University of Economics and Business, 76 Patission Street, Athens GR104 34, Greece

Steve Elliot
Central Coast School of eBusiness and Management, University of Newcastle, Australia

Bob Galliers
London School of Economics and Political Science, Houghton Street, London WC2A 2AE, UK

Jan Pries-Heje
Department of Computer Information Systems, J. Mack Robinson College of Business, Georgia State University, University Plaza, Atlanta GA 30303-3087, USA

Benz Jacob
Department of Computer Information Systems, J. Mack Robinson College of Business, Georgia State University, University Plaza, Atlanta GA 30303-3087, USA

Mathew Lee
School of Information Systems, City University of Hong Kong, 83 Tat Chee Avenue, Kowloon, Hong Kong

Nikos Mylonopoulos
Athens University of Economics and Business, 76 Patission Street, Athens GR104 34, Greece

K. Pramatari
Athens University of Economics and Business, 76 Patission Street, Athens GR104 34, Greece

Sandeep Purao
Department of Computer Information Systems, J. Mack Robinson College of Business, Georgia State University, University Plaza, Atlanta GA 30303-3087, USA

Jonathan Wareham
Department of Computer Information Systems, J. Mack Robinson College of Business, Georgia State University, University Plaza, Atlanta GA 30303-3087, USA

Anne Wiggins
London School of Economics and Political Science, Houghton Street, London WC2A 2AE, UK

Series Preface

The information systems community has grown considerably since 1984, when we began publishing the Wiley Series in Information Systems. We are pleased to be a part of the growth of the field, and believe that this series of books is playing an important role in the intellectual development of the discipline. The primary objective of the series is to publish scholarly works that reflect the best of the research in the information systems community. These works should help guide the IS practitioner community regarding what strategies it ought to adopt to be successful in the future.

To this end, the current volume—*Electronic Commerce: B2C Strategies and Models*, edited by Steve Elliot—provides a key addition. A major impediment to the success of electronic commerce has been the lack of comparative examples. Organizations simply do not know if there are any 'best practices' in the business-to-consumer arena, and if so, what they are. This book should help them greatly.

Based on research in six countries—the United Kingdom, the United States, Denmark, Greece, Hong Kong (China) and Australia—this book addresses the uncertainties of Internet retailing by presenting the experiences of leading examples of business-to-consumer electronic commerce in each of six economies.

The countries represent a broad range of environments to identify issues that may be specific to a particular market. The firms have been selected as significant examples of Internet retailing in industry sectors recognized as leaders in the use of the Internet, including travel, books, music CDs, technology sales, gifts, groceries, and general merchandise.

Rudy Hirschheim

1
Introduction to B2C Strategies and Models

STEVE ELLIOT

OBJECTIVES

This book focuses on business strategies and models in business-to-consumer (B2C) Internet electronic commerce. It analyses the elements of success through intensive study of examples of successful Internet retailing. Major components of each Internet innovation, the organization, customers, website and environment, are examined holistically to identify characteristics that lead to success. Recognizing that the basis of success may differ in different countries, this is an international study. Five success stories are examined in each of six countries on four continents: Asia, Australia, Europe and North America. Through holistic analysis of each implementation of Internet retailing, the questions to be answered by this study are the following.

- Which organizational factors influenced the Internet innovation and how?
- What characteristics of their websites influenced consumer acceptance of that innovation?
- What encourages and discourages their consumers from purchasing over the Internet?
- Did environmental factors influence the innovation and, if so, how?
- What international/cultural differences arise from the study, and can generalizations be made from these?

The book sets out to investigate these questions and to identify how successful business strategies and models can be created from interaction of these varied factors. The intention is not to specify a series of golden rules that would, inevitably, lead to success. This is certainly not achievable in an area developing as dynamically as electronic commerce, if at all. The investigation aims to address the great uncertainty that exists about Internet electronic commerce by examining examples of success. Insights arising from the study as it develops answers to the questions listed above may assist entrepreneurs, chief executives and executive management in their strategic planning and implementation for Internet-based electronic commerce.

THE INTERNATIONAL RESEARCH PROJECT

This book is based on an international research project that aimed to assist organizations seeking to apply business-to-consumer electronic commerce through a comparative international study of successful implementations. The study also sought to make a significant theoretical contribution through testing of proposed extensions to current theory on how organizations successfully adopt innovations (see also Chapter 9: Research Model and Theoretical Implications).

The study is significant owing to its intense investigation of a broad range of examples of Internet electronic commerce across different countries. The richness and completeness of the data collected help develop a holistic view of Internet innovations that, previously, has not been available. The firms investigated sell across a spectrum of the most popular Internet products, including books, gifts, groceries, music, technology, tickets and travel but also extend into less likely areas such as building products, home maintenance services, a factory outlet for name-brand fashion and fine wines.

Examination of the interaction between firm, consumer, website and the environment in a single consistent study of Internet innovation acknowledges that at this early stage in our understanding of electronic commerce a narrowly focused investigation of any area in isolation may lead to incomplete and inaccurate conclusions. A major strength of this project is its detailed analysis and direct comparison between consistent research studies conducted in a range of national markets at a comparable period in time.

A summary of the countries, firms, products and researchers is given later in this chapter.

ELECTRONIC COMMERCE DEFINITION AND SCOPE

There are numerous terms and definitions relating to electronic commerce. A simple view has been adopted that reflects its likely level of impact on business, namely as the source of fundamental change to business practice initiated by the substitution of existing arrangements by computer-aided processes. Terms such as electronic business, e-business, Internet business, e-commerce, Internet commerce and new economy are all treated as synonyms for electronic commerce.

A broad scope has been applied to include an extended transaction cycle and all parties critical to a transaction. The transaction cycle extends from a consumer's initial investigation about products and services through payment and receipt of goods to a firm's back-office processing of the transaction including inter-organizational settlement, posting of ledgers and reporting. An e-commerce order fulfilment chain from retailer to customer includes all participants that have a critical role in the transaction, potentially including specialist providers such as telecommunication companies, Internet Service Providers (ISPs), website hosting firms, website mall providers, warehousing and logistics specialists, payment processors and customer service providers. When a customer purchases over the Internet, any firm providing a service that could beneficially or adversely affect the customer's willingness or capability to purchase from an online retailer is considered as critical to the transaction.

BOOK STRUCTURE

This introductory chapter sets the scene for the book, explaining the focus and implementation of the international study and providing background details on strategies and models of electronic commerce. The researchers in each country and authors of the country chapters are introduced.

Chapters 2–7 focus on Internet retailing in a single country: Australia, Denmark, Greece, Hong Kong (China), the United Kingdom and the United States. These chapters provide an overview of the environmental factors in the countries and the firms examined. The five case studies in each country include descriptions of the background, business models and strategies, implementation, critical success factors, innovation factors and processes, website developments and consumer issues. The chapters conclude with a summary of the most important innovation issues in each country.

Chapter 8 looks at the research tools developed specifically for this project to support analysis of website characteristics and consumer experiences. To identify factors leading to success it is necessary to be able to distinguish between firms and to analyse how they implemented the Internet innovation. The Centre for Electronic Commerce (CEC) website evaluation framework was developed for this purpose. A view of consumers' experiences with particular websites helps clarify the most important issues for Internet retailers to address. An Internet-based customer survey was developed for this purpose. Full details of the CEC website evaluation framework and the customer surveys are provided to enable executives to compare their own Internet innovations and customer experiences with those of the firms included in this study.

A secondary aim of this research study was to consider theoretical implications of the examples of Internet electronic commerce. Chapter 9 explains the research model applied by the project teams in each country and, based on the research findings and analysis, proposes an integrated research model for electronic commerce.

Chapter 10, the conclusion, brings together the research findings and analysis and looks at lessons for firms. Details of the key factors and processes leading to successful adoption of Internet retailing are described, business models and strategies developed from these factors explained and a conceptual model illustrating the integration required between innovation elements and processes proposed. A comparison of how two products, books and technology, are sold over the Internet by firms in different countries demonstrates similarities and differences in implementations of electronic business.

Finally, a reference list and index complete the book.

TARGET AUDIENCES

This book is intended for several discrete audiences. The primary audience is practitioners—executives and entrepreneurs who see business opportunities from the Internet but who are uncertain how best to proceed to realize those opportunities. The examination of how 30 examples of successful Internet commerce in six countries came to be successful captures the experiences, both good and bad, of those who have led the way. For executives commencing their engagement with e-business, the minicase examples also identify lessons learned and contain advice from the successful companies for other firms. Analysis of the cases reveals further lessons and suggestions for good practice.

Executives can also benefit from the description of the tools developed for this international project. Full details of the CEC website evaluation framework and the Internet consumer survey are shown in Chapter 8. These tools can be used by firms with websites to analyse their current situation and to compare their web features and functions with those of the firms examined.

The second audience segment is comprised of e-business researchers. In parallel with the uncertainty of business leaders about e-commerce is uncertainty within the ranks of researchers. Current theory in many areas of business research is unable to explain the phenomenon of e-commerce and is unable to assist industry to anticipate the directions and outcomes of the transforming impact of the Internet. Researchers may benefit from the intensive, holistic details and analysis of successful Internet firms across different countries and cultures. The research tools for website evaluation and surveying customers provided for executives may be equally important for researchers. An important outcome of this project is the proposal of an integrated, multi-disciplinary research model for e-business that may help a wide range of researchers to place their investigations into context.

The third audience group is students of e-business. The variety of examples and the range of experiences of Internet retailers in different countries will assist students to better understand the transforming impact of e-business, the opportunities for firms and the ways that firms can address these challenges. In many respects the current students of e-business are the most important audience since this group, as graduate employees, will be the people open to new ideas who work to transform firms from 'old economy' organizations into dynamic e-businesses.

SELECTION OF COUNTRIES, SECTORS AND FIRMS

As mentioned above, the objective of this research project was to assist organizations seeking to successfully exploit business-to-consumer electronic commerce through an international, comparative study of successful implementations. The experiences of both firms and their customers were examined in a single, consistent and integrated study in six economies: the United States, the United Kingdom, Denmark, Greece, Hong Kong (China) and Australia. A reasonable question arises: Why these countries?

Any international study of leading examples of electronic commerce or electronic business must examine United States firms. In effect, United States firms such as Amazon, eBay and Yahoo initiated and defined Internet business. In less than seven years, these companies have become household names not only in the United States but internationally. While United States firms are generally considered to lead the world in e-business, some international evaluations (e.g. LSE/Novell 1999, 2000) have ranked European firms as at least equal to the best United States examples. Despite the efforts of the European Union, Europe cannot be viewed currently as a single coherent market. Wide variations in national economies, interests and lifestyles are apparent. Similarly, Internet activity varies markedly in different countries. Scandinavia has had high levels of Internet use for several years while Southern Europe in general has appreciably lower levels of e-business use and experience.

Studies such as the one by NetValue (2000) show Denmark has the highest level of Internet penetration in Europe with over 50% of households connected, the United Kingdom is in second position, with nearly 30%, Germany is in third place with 25.7%, followed by France (17.5%) and Spain (12.7%). Other studies place Italy, Spain and Portugal at the lowest levels of Internet use. Greece is of particular interest since it has been ignored in studies of European Internet activity. Researchers appear to presume that Greek Internet activity is so low as to be of little significance. While acknowledging that Greek firms have been slow to establish themselves in this area, the research team in Athens found significant examples of Internet retailing that add a valuable perspective to the study.

Consequently, countries from north (Denmark) and south (Greece) were examined to capture the range of European experiences and to support analysis of the diversity of success factors. With the largest volume of e-business activity in Europe and several of the top rated Internet sites internationally, the United Kingdom was also included in the study.

Hong Kong's contribution is as a major international business centre, a source of cultural diversity for the international study and a market with a low level of

Internet adoption. Australia provides diversity as a developed country with a very high level of Internet adoption that has a small domestic market and is remote from the major markets of Europe and North America.

To help identify the best firms to study, surveys of industry sectors that were most used for Internet purchases were consulted. In the United States these included (in order of significance) travel, books, music CDs, technology sales, gifts, groceries and general merchandise. These sectors were similarly popular in other countries, although the order varied (GVA 1999, Forrester Research 2000a) and www.consult research series). Financial service providers were not examined since they were not identified in surveys at the time as being leaders in Internet use. Lessons from firms in sectors most experienced with Internet retailing were seen to be most significant in clearing the fog of uncertainty. In addition, firms that were identified by the research teams in each country as making a significant contribution to Internet retailing from other sectors were identified to ensure a broad base for analysis.

In selecting the firms in each sector, efforts were made to include startups and traditional 'bricks and clicks'. The question of which of the thousands of e-tailers to examine was a challenge. The influence of major United States pioneers such as Amazon and eBay extends across the breadth of the Internet. Startups and traditional businesses alike sought to emulate the business models first developed and implemented by these firms. This project did not, however, examine these well-known companies. Details on these firms have already been exhaustively reported to the point of reader fatigue. This project sought to contribute through expanding the level of knowledge in an area of uncertainty rather than rehashing old news. Therefore, the United States, authors selected other examples of lesser known but successful e-tailers.

Firms were selected for investigation based on their success and their likely significance to other firms. Although there is a valid argument that much can be learned from failure, no failed Internet ventures were studied in detail. Reasons for failure are clearer after the event when the implications of actions taken become apparent. Reasons for success are often more complex and reliant on the interaction of many elements that change over time. Consequently, this book has focused on the more complex and dynamic aspects of successful innovation to address the documented uncertainties of business and consumers with Internet retailing.

STRUCTURE OF EACH INVESTIGATION

Each firm's Internet innovation was examined holistically to identify the most important factors determining success. As shown in Chapter 9 in the development of the research model, the factors were grouped into four categories: environmental, organizational, innovation and consumer. Most of the theory of innovation focuses on organizational issues and the characteristics of the actual innovation. Environmental issues are frequently assumed to be constant and consumer issues have received too little attention in innovations research. The international research project reported in this book attests to the importance of all categories of factors. This anecdote illustrates why.

Ian Shiels, a senior KPMG executive, returned to Australia after several years in the New York practice. While in New York he had been a keen purchaser of products and services over the Internet, not just books, tickets and CDs but also electronic equipment, food and clothes. Six months after his return to Sydney he had not purchased a single item over the Internet. Why? Because in New York he had a doorman who reliably received each item and securely stored the purchases even if Ian was away on business at the time. Australians typically live in houses rather than apartments and even secured apartments maintain their safety through electronic access control rather than a doorman. This sole reason for a reluctance to purchase was totally unrelated to the retailer, products or services available, cost of purchase, customer demographic or concerns over data privacy or credit card security. This vignette emphasizes the fragility of the Internet retailing transaction cycle. If even a single element is not perfectly aligned, then the transaction will not take place. It also emphasizes the critical importance for executives and researchers alike to consider Internet retailing holistically and not to become fixated on just one particular aspect.

Investigation of the innovation focused on websites, which are subject to ongoing change. Many of the websites examined were also revised as a direct result of this research project as firms reviewed the feedback from their customers and the formal assessment of their website using the CEC website evaluation framework. As a result, the website details described in this book are unlikely to reflect the current websites for the firms. The aim of this book was not to present the current website status of a range of leading Internet retailers in six countries. Given the dynamic nature of the Internet, the relentless drive for improvement in websites and the inevitable time delay between preparation of a book and its publishing, such an aim would be impossible to support. Instead, our aim is to capture the initial experiences of a diverse group of successful Internet retailers so as to better understand the complexities and to address the uncertainties of this new medium.

BUSINESS MODELS

Introduction

Business models specify the relationships between different participants in a commercial venture, the benefits and costs to each and the flows of revenue. Business strategies specify how a business model can be applied to the market to differentiate the firm from its competitors, e.g. by addressing a particular segment of the market, by competing on cost and/or levels of service. Firms may combine strategies, e.g. a bookstore may target the education segment of the market (a niche) and have the widest range of books available (service) or, alternatively, may advertise it has 'the cheapest technology books in town'. Irrespective of the model or its level of complexity, all business models seek to address a simple equation:

$$\text{profits} = \text{revenue} - \text{costs}$$

Internet startups fail when they lack sufficient focus on this equation, where assumptions and predictions made about revenue have not been realized, or when costs have exceeded estimates or anticipated cost reductions have not been achieved.

A classic example of changing business models illustrates this formula. In its simplest form, a supermarket has relationships with consumers and suppliers with revenue flows from customers to the store and on to suppliers. Customers are mainly attracted by lower prices and larger ranges of products. Suppliers seek to sell larger volumes of products to these larger stores. Supermarket business strategies are predominantly as low-cost, high-volume operations with lower margins on each product. Supermarkets have lower costs than smaller stores because they can purchase products in bulk from their suppliers and so receive lower prices. They can further reduce costs by displaying products on shelves with consumers selecting what they want to purchase, carrying the selections to the cashier, packing their shopping into bags and taking them home. The key success factor for supermarkets is attracting consumers to the store, so they need to be in a location with easy customer access (e.g. a main street or a mall) and they may deliberately sell some products at a loss (loss-leaders).

When this supermarket develops an Internet operation it actually changes its business model—from shop to e-shop—but is often unaware of the implications. Many supermarkets set up a website to attract orders but fulfil the orders by having staff walk around the supermarket selecting the products for individual orders from the shelves, packing and then delivering. Consequently, the supermarket costs have increased substantially due to staff involvement. The low-cost, low-margin, high-volume strategy is endangered. The loss-leader concept is applied to all products purchased online but the supermarket cannot recover its full costs for Internet sales since consumers expect (unrealistically) that all Internet operations will have lower costs than traditional retailing. Any firm that charges more then its normal shelf prices must be exploiting its customers. At this stage, losing money with its core business threatened by alienated customers, the supermarket declares it is throwing out the Internet operation since it cannot make a profit and because it always knew that the Internet wouldn't work for this type of business anyway!

One of the main cost advantages of e-shops is that firms do not need to locate themselves on expensive main streets or in shopping malls to attract customers. They can be located in low-cost warehouses since customers are attracted through the Internet site. So, a supermarket that incurs the additional order fulfilment costs of an e-shop (picking, packing, delivery) without exploiting the low-cost options available (lower rent, larger range, larger volume, lower margins—see next section below) is creating the conditions for its own failure. Note that the business strategy of low cost, low margin and high volume may remain the same when moving a supermarket online. It is the elements of the business model, i.e. the relationship between the major players and their cost:benefit:revenue components, that change.

Types of Business Models

A comprehensive review of B2B and B2C Internet business models is examined by Paul Timmers in his book, *Electronic Commerce: Strategies and Models for Business-to-Business Trading*. Based on analysis of Porter's Value Chain, Timmers proposes a range of 11 models appropriate for B2C operations including: e-shops, e-malls, virtual communities, third-party market-places and value-chain integrators. Figure 1.1 shows these models categorized by the degree of innovation and the level of functional integration.

Describing these business models in more detail, e-shops are single firms selling their products and services over the Internet. Increased revenues are sought from access to a larger market due to factors including broader geographical reach, the attraction of a larger range of products or longer opening hours (24×7). Many Internet ventures relied on anticipated additional revenue streams from Internet advertising, but this benefit has proven to be largely illusory. Lower costs may result from store location (the firm does not have to be in a premium location since customers are attracted and business conducted through the Internet), volume discounts on purchases and improved inventory management.

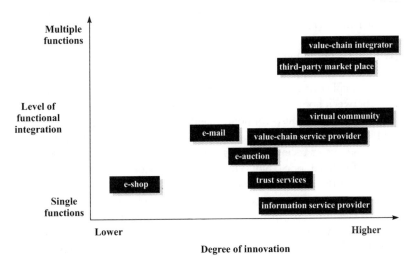

Figure 1.1 *Classification of Internet business models.* Reproduced from *Electronic Commerce: Strategies and Models for Business-to-Business Trading,* Paul Timmers, © copyright 1999 by John Wiley & Sons, Ltd, Chichester, with permission.

In its classic form, as originally implemented by Amazon, the e-shop business model relies on the abolition of inventory costs and risks by the firm purchasing only what it has already sold to customers and holding no inventory—deliveries are made to customers directly from a supplier's warehouse. This initial approach also enabled Amazon to pare its fixed costs to a minimum (no overhead warehouse lease or staffing costs) so that the costs of running the business were more directly related to sales. Note that this classic Internet implementation may not be scalable and that Amazon has subsequently committed to the establishment of its own warehouses, inventory and order fulfilment operations. Most commercial websites are electronic shops that sell, for example, technology, tickets, books, music CDs, groceries, gifts and flowers. Most of the minicases investigated utilized this business model. E-malls are amalgamations of e-shops where individual businesses share a common website and common transaction processes. E-malls are the electronic equivalent of department stores where the individual departments may be independently operated businesses but all function under a single name and have common transaction processes.

Virtual communities have a focus on adding value through communications between and contributions by members. A firm provides the environment within which members have unedited communications, feedback and information exchange. The firm seeks membership fees, advertising revenue and opportunities to cross-sell products and services. Firms included in this book typically implemented this model in conjunction with the e-store model.

The third-party market place business model is useful where companies see advantages in having a third-party firm provide Internet marketing and transaction services for them. The third-party firm may also provide aggregation of consumers' demands. Most often this is applicable when established companies seek an entry level Internet exposure without major cost or time commitments. Third-party revenues may be generated by membership fees for companies, fees on each transaction or a percentage of transaction value. Provider companies pursue reductions in their marketing and other costs of attracting new business.

As an example of a third-party market-place, HomeToDo saw a role in creating a market between homeowners requiring maintenance and home repairers seeking work. Aggregating requests for home maintenance and matching those with fixed price bids from pre-qualified service providers appeared to be a business opportunity. Homeowners received a free service, maintainers paid a small fee based on the successful fixed price bid. This model was not ultimately successful for HomeToDo in the market and was subsequently revised.

Value-chain service providers specialize in a particular function within the value chain, e.g. electronic payments, inventory management or logistics. Providers accrue fee income or a percentage of services provided. UPS is an example of this model. The range of Internet ventures examined in this book have been categorized by their apparent business models; see Figure 1.2. As will be seen in Chapter 10, the actual business models implemented were much broader than anticipated.

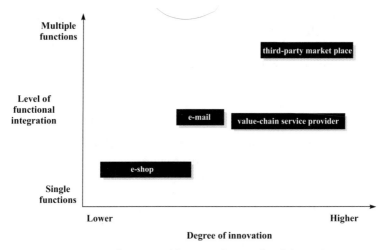

Figure 1.2 *Primary Internet business models examined.* Reproduced from *Electronic Commerce: Strategies and Models for Business-to-Business Trading,* Paul Timmers, © copyright 1999 by John Wiley & Sons, Ltd, Chichester, with permission.

Tech-wreck, the Death of the Internet and Business Models

Any examination of e-commerce business models after the NASDAQ crash in April 2000 and the widespread stock market upheavals in 2000 and 2001 should address some of the sweeping criticisms directed at Internet business in general and B2C in particular. In a complete reversal of their previously unreserved adoration of all Internet-related business ventures, since April 2000 critics have slammed the same ventures with all the savagery of rejected suitors. Neither position is sustainable. Uncritical support for business ventures that relied on activity, novelty and enthusiasm instead of more traditional business success factors such as customer service, revenue streams and cost containment is as unhelpful as the rejection of all Internet ventures irrespective of their business fundamentals that followed.

Much of the criticism was simply uninformed. Contention that the Internet is not suitable for any consumer-focused business model ignores the diversity of successful business models applied by traditional firms. These range from fashion boutiques to supermarkets and convenience stores and from hair or beauty salons to motor repairers and roadside vehicle assistance. All are viable with different target markets, cost factors, revenue streams and competitive threats. Each of the Internet business models shown in Figure 1.1 has similarly different business factors. Every venture implementing a business model must be considered on its merits.

Online retailing was further criticized due to the type of products sold over the Internet. The proposition was that 'old economy' (i.e. physical) products were unsuitable for 'new economy' firms. Consumers expect lower prices over the

Internet but these firms have high costs due to marketing and delivery. As seen above, cost models for Internet firms can realize savings due to lower fixed costs and by linking operating costs to increased sales. Marketing and fulfilment costs are certainly substantial but each firm must analyse its business factors to determine how the firm can best compete with traditional and online firms.

Phases in Application of Business Models

Ill-informed criticism aside, many Internet startups failed because their business models and strategies were flawed. In their purest form, the initial (pioneering) phase in the application of business models and strategies for an Internet startup is the perceived opportunity to transform an industry. New Internet-based firms would challenge the established firms in an industry or sector and drive change based on the innovative use of technology to deliver lower pricing and radical improvements in service levels. Most startups obtained equity-based funding through initial placement offers (IPOs) or venture capital support and ran at an operating loss as they spent massive amounts of money on advertising to attract customers. The principle was to grow rapidly to control the market through this first-mover advantage. Profits would flow once market control had been established.

In the second (startup proliferation) phase other startups entered the market in recognition of the potential advantages from industry transformation to compete with the pioneers for ultimate control. These fast followers mirrored the pioneers' business models and fine-tuned their business strategies. Traditional firms, losing market share to the startups, responded to these new competitors with limited Internet operations.

The third (consolidation) phase was initiated by the technology crash in April 2000 when funding sources dried up, but was inevitable. This phase was characterized by failures, mergers and acquisitions. Many startups lost their focus with unconstrained cash-burn in pursuit of new customers. This led to the spectacle of small startups advertising at the US Super Bowl—amongst the highest advertising costs in the world for any event or medium. Some pioneers reliant on self-funding or with limited funding were unable to grow rapidly enough to control the market and so had to focus on developing operating profits. Expectations of profitability were not always well founded. In many cases, anticipated profitability was based on assumptions about future revenues from advertising to Internet consumers visiting the website rather than from margins on actual business operations.

Online advertisers became more sceptical about returns from their banner ads on websites and consumer concerns about security, privacy and timely fulfilment of their orders reduced the growth rates of Internet purchases. Rather than driving rapid transformation of industry sectors through new types of products and services, the startups found themselves in a war of attrition with established, traditional firms. The winners in this phase were always going to be those having the largest capital reserves. Profitable and successful startups were equally at risk. The drastic fall in share prices for Internet firms provided traditional firms with an opportunity for entry into Internet retailing through low-cost acquisition.

A fourth (organizational transformation) phase is under way with traditional firms applying the lessons learned by startups to their own organizations. The objective is for the traditional firms to become more nimble in a dynamic and uncertain retail market. The focus is in applying the Internet to improve market responsiveness and to achieve economies by more tightly integrating the supply chain and the transaction cycle. These actions will inevitably alter relationships with suppliers and customers and will, therefore, result in the necessity for a revised business model.

CONTRIBUTIONS

This book is the collective effort of a large number of people in six countries. Details of the primary authors of each chapter are shown below. Additional acknowledgements are made within the chapters, as appropriate.

Chapter 1 Introduction, Chapter 2 Australia, Chapter 8 Evaluating websites (jointly with Niels Bjørn-Andersen) and Surveying customers, Chapter 9 Research model and theoretical implications, and Chapter 10 Conclusions.

Steve Elliot (selliot@mail.newcastle.edu.au) commenced his career in the computer industry in 1972 and has worked in Australia, Europe and Asia in business, government, education and with the United Nations. He is Professor and Head of the School of eBusiness at the University of Newcastle, Australia. He was previously Director of the Information Technology Research Centre at the University of New South Wales in Sydney. Steve has degrees in economics and information systems from the University of Sydney and the University of Technology, Sydney, and a PhD in strategic information systems planning from Warwick Business School at the University of Warwick, UK. His enduring research interest is the strategic management of technology-enabled innovation by organizations, particularly the management of innovation in electronic business. Steve initiated and managed the international study of successful implementations of business-to-consumer electronic commerce on which this book is based. He is currently exploring the impact of e-business on the banking industry.

Chapter 3 Denmark and Chapter 8 Evaluating websites (jointly with Steve Elliot)

Niels Bjørn-Andersen (nba.inf@cbs.dk) is full professor in informatics at Copenhagen Business School, where he is director of the Center for Electronic Commerce (CEC) and the director of the part-time executive MBA program: global e-management. He has published 15 books and more than 50 refereed articles. He was the president of AIS in 1996 and has been key-note speaker at over ten international conferences. His main interests include 'organizational issues of IT', 'e-business/e-management' and 'management of IT'. He is on the editorial board of several international journals including *Information Systems Research, Information Systems Journal* and *Journal of Strategic Information Systems*. Currently he is directing a million euro large research program on transformation of traditional companies to the digital economy.

Chapter 4 (Greece)

Nikolaos Mylonopoulos is assistant professor of information systems at ALBA (Athens Laboratory of Business Administration), Greece. He has teaching and research interests in the areas of information systems management, electronic commerce and applications of economic theory in these areas. He has taught at Loughborough University Business School, Warwick Business School, Birkbeck College (University of London) and the Athens University of Economics and Business. His work has been published in international refereed journals and conferences, including the *International Transactions in OR*, the *Journal of Logistics and Information Management*, The European Conference on IS and the UK Academy for IS conference. He has acted as referee for journals and conferences such as the *Journal of Strategic Information Systems* and the European Conference of Information Systems. Dr Mylonopoulos has been actively involved in over seven national and European funded research projects in the areas of telematics, electronic commerce and recently mobile commerce.

Katherine Pramataris is PhD student at Athens University of Economics and Business (AUEB), Greece, and research officer at eLTRUN (Electronic Trading Research Unit), working on marketing information systems in the electronic retail environment. She has worked as a systems analyst for Procter & Gamble European Headquarters for two years, on the development of global category management applications, and another year in the Marketing Department of Procter & Gamble Greece. During her studies she has been granted eight state and school scholarships and has published more than twenty journal and conference articles. During the 5th European ECR Conference in Turin she received the Silver Academic Award by ECR Europe for her work in the field of electronic retailing.

Chapter 5 (Hong Kong, China)

Matthew K.O. Lee is professor and Head of the Information Systems Department at the City University of Hong Kong. Prior to joining the City University, Dr Lee was a lecturer at the University of London and a research scientist at British Petroleum Research International in the United Kingdom. Dr Lee holds a first class honours bachelor's degree in electronic engineering, a doctorate in computer science, an MBA, and two law degrees from London University. He is qualified as a barrister-at-law (Lincoln's Inn), a chartered engineer and is a professional member of both the Hong Kong Computer Society and the British Computer Society.

Dr Lee has a research and professional interest in electronic commerce, information technology adoption and diffusion (focusing on systems implementation management issues) and legal informatics, which encompasses both the legal, ethical and policy aspects of information technology. He is a member of the IT Projects Vetting Committee of the Innovation and Technology Fund, Innovation and Technology Commission of the HKSAR Government. He is also a member of the IT Training Committee of the Vocational Training Council. Dr Lee is a founding vice-chairperson of the HK Computer Society's Special Interest Group on e-buisness. His publications in the information systems area include a book as well as over 60 articles in international journals (e.g. *Communications of the ACM* and the *International Journal of Electronic Commerce*) and conference proceedings (e.g. HICSS and ICIS). He is also on the editorial board of *Information Systems Journal*. Dr Lee is a non-executive director of Computer and Technologies Holding Limited, which is a major systems integration and e-business company listed on the main board of the Hong Kong Stock Exchange.

Chapter 6 (United Kingdom)

Bob Galliers (r.d.galliers@lse.ac.uk) is professor of information systems at the London School of Economics and former Dean of Warwick Business School, UK. He was previously foundation professor and head of the School of Information Systems at Curtin University, Perth, Western Australia. He has a BA degree in economics from Harvard University, a master's degree in management systems from Lancaster University and a PhD in information systems strategy from the London School of Economics. In 1995 he was awarded an Honorary Doctor of Science degree by Tuka School of Economics and Business Administration, Finland. He is Program Co-Chair of ICIS 2002, Barcelona, Spain, and is editor-in-chief of the *Journal of Strategic Information Systems*. His research centres on the strategic, managerial and organizational issues associated with IT.

Anne Wiggins (a.wiggins@lse.ac.uk) is currently researching her PhD at the Department of Information Systems of the London School of Economics. The main focus of her research has been the strategic implications of e-business on small and medium sized enterprises. She also holds an undergraduate degree from the University of Sydney and a masters degree from the University of London's Birkbeck College. As a consultant in the fields of IT and the Internet she has worked at public and commercial cultural organizations and corporations in the United States, Australia and the United Kingdom.

Chapter 7 (United States)

Don Lloyd Cook is an assistant professor of marketing at Georgia State University. He was previously an assistant professor at Louisiana Tech University for one year prior to joining the Georgia State faculty. He has a PhD in marketing from Virginia Tech where his research focus was on electronic commerce, and BSBA, MBA and JD degrees from the University of Arkansas.

Prior to entering his PhD program he practised law with a particular emphasis on appellate practice. He is admitted to the bar in state courts in Arkansas, Federal District Courts in Arkansas and the Northern District of Oklahoma, the Eighth Circuit Court of Appeals, and the United States Supreme Court. While in his doctoral program he became the first Virginia Tech Congressional Fellow and served on the staff of Congressman Rick Boucher, a founder of the Internet caucus, as a Legislative Assistant. He was also Virginia Tech's, American Marketing Association Doctoral Consortium Fellow in 1999. At Georgia State University he is actively working on electronic commerce and legal issues within the marketing department and the Centre for Digital Commerce. His work (including work with co-authors) has been published in both marketing journals and law reviews including the *Journal of Public Policy and Marketing, Journal of Business Research, Journal of Consumer Marketing* and the *Journal of Law and Commerce.*

Benz Jacob is an independent software consultant. He has previously worked for Webvan and Oracle Corporation. He lives in Atlanta with his wife Alice and their three children.

Jan Pries-Heje is a visiting professor at the Department of Computer Information Systems, Georgia State University. His research interests include information systems development, software engineering, and software process improvement. He has published in these areas in journals like *Journal of Accounting Management and Information Technology, The Data Base for Advances in Information Systems, European Journal of Information Systems, ACM Computer Personnel and the Scandinavian Journal of Information Systems.* Dr Pries-Heje's thesis on methods and tools for developing IT systems won the Tietgen Gold Medal in 1993. He is certified ISO 9000 auditor and BOOTSTRAP assessor. He is the Danish national representative to IFIP Technical Committee 8 (TC8) on Information Systems, and Secretary for TC8 since 1999. He was Conference Chair for the European Conference on Information Systems (ECIS) in Copenhagen, June 1999.

Sandeep Purao is an assistant professor of computer information systems at Georgia State University in Atlanta. He holds a PhD in MIS from the University of Wisconsin—Milwaukee. His work has appeared in several journals including *Communications of the ACM, Journal of Management Information Systems, Decision Support Systems, Information & Management*, and *DataBase.* His current research interests include reuse in design, theories of design and coordination practices.

Jonathan Wareham holds an AB in economics and an AB in comparative literature from the University of California at Berkeley, an MSc in accounting and finance and a PhD in information systems from Copenhagen Business School. He is currently an Assistant Professor with the department of Computer Information Systems and the eCommerce Institute at Georgia State University in Atlanta. Prior to pursuing graduate studies, he held management positions with Unilever and within the high-tech sector. His research focuses on the intersection of information technology and economics. Specifically, he is interested in the way that IT changes business models and the transaction patterns between consumers, firms and markets. Dr Wareham's research has been published in such journals and proceedings as the *Information Systems Journal, the European Management Journal* and the *International Conference on Information Systems.*

SPONSORSHIP

The international research project that led to this book has received sponsorship from several sources, all of which are gratefully acknowledged. The general support of Steve Elliot's research program in Electronic Commerce by the KnowledgeLab, UK, warrants particular mention. This funding initiated the whole project. Additional funding from the University of NSW enabled the Australian project. Individual project teams sought sources of research funding within each country, e.g. from the Danish Social Science Research Council and the Centre for Electronic Commerce at Copenhagen Business School.

EXCHANGE RATES

The approximate exchange rates at the time of publication were:

	US$	EURO 1
A$	2	1.72
DK Kroner	8.3	7.5
G. Drachma	381	341
HK$	7.8	7
UK pound	0.69	0.61
US$	1	0.89

2
Internet Retailing in Australia

STEVE ELLIOT

INTRODUCTION

Australians have readily accepted electronic commerce (e-commerce) with one of the highest rates (47%) of Internet use world-wide. Acceptance of new technology-based products and services is a characteristic of the country with similarly high rates for adoption of automatic telling machines (ATMs), electronic funds transfer at point of sale (EFTPOS) and mobile phones. As in most countries, the e-business market in Australia is growing very rapidly. While business-to-business (B2B) is larger, business-to-consumer (B2C) represents a significant segment. IDC (2000) estimates the overall e-commerce market in Australia in 2000 as A$5.6 billion with B2C being A$2 billion and forecasts the market to be about A$70.5 billion by 2004 with B2C some A$19.5 billion.

The Australian market is comparatively small and isolated, which has advantages and disadvantages. It is a major step for well-established international competitors to extend their operations to the smaller Australian market but less of a jump to do the reverse. E-commerce has provided international opportunities for new Australian firms with competitive products and services, e.g. ERG and LookSmart.

The smaller population and correspondingly smaller pool of expertise has resulted in the development of multi-skilling that is particularly critical for website design and development. The smaller market has also forced Internet startups not to rely on novelty or specialized business models. Complex interactions of business models are tried, revised and rolled out in a manner not necessary in larger markets.

The lack of a well-developed venture capital market may have reduced the number of Internet startups but may also have helped those that did receive funding by the rigor of their approval processes. The crash in US technology shares in April 2000 had a flow on to the Australian market which shook out some of the less well-performing firms and may have given the newly established startups some breathing space from further pure-player competition. Conversely, the down turn in Internet stocks has created an opportunity for traditional firms to venture into the Internet market-space by taking over well-established pure-players. Owing to expansion into Internet channels and strategic acquisitions since the tech-crash, the online operations of traditional retailers now dominate Australia's e-tail market.

Products and services most frequently purchased in Australia in 2000 (in order from highest) were books, computers and related products, CDs and other recorded music, tickets and reservations, clothing, videos/film, financial services and consumer electronics. Mass surveys indicate the profile of a 'typical' Australian Internet user to be young (20–29 years is the largest category with 32% although users over 30 years represent 62% of the total) and male (55%). Online shoppers are very satisfied (43%) or fairly satisfied (38%) and when using the Internet their major concerns, in order, are computer viruses, poor Internet response times, junk email/intrusive marketing and then security and privacy (www.consult, 2000).

The legislative regime, if not generally supportive of e-commerce to date, has not been overtly restrictive except in the areas of Internet censorship and online gambling. The federal Electronic Transactions Act 1999 aims to give electronic transactions the same legal status as offline transactions. Corresponding state-based legislation is not available in all jurisdictions. Copyright issues for materials transmitted over the Internet have been clarified by the federal Copyright (Digital Agenda) Act 2000 (applicable from March 2001). Interestingly, although privacy is not rated as the highest consumer concern, personal privacy protection in e-commerce is poor. A Privacy Amendment (Private Sector) Bill 2000 comes into effect in December 2001. This will extend privacy protection obligations to private sector organizations as well as the government departments previously covered. The new Bill has been criticized by consumer groups because it exempts non-departmental government agencies, small businesses, media and political organizations from having to conform to its standards. Small business (a turnover of less than A\$3 million) describes about 94% of Australian firms. All of the businesses examined will need to comply with the legislation.

Overview of Cases

Four of the five retailers selected come from retail industry sectors most widely using the Internet—books, computer products, groceries and music CDs. The fifth, a wine retailer, has received national awards for best Internet site. All but one of the firms are Internet startups. The exception is a traditional bookseller established for over 120 years.

Chaos Music Market was set up so that bands could provide their music directly to fans and bypass the major recording firms that controlled the market. Chaosmusic has developed into one of Australia's largest Internet music retailers and is an international pioneer in direct digital distribution of music.

In response to the potential threat of `amazon.com`, traditional bookseller **Dymocks** has developed Australia's most successful book-selling site. Channel conflict arose between the corporate-run Internet operation and the major source of the firm's growth, its franchisees.

E-store started out selling computer products. Once it had established its operations it rapidly expanded to the current range of 120 000 products including TVs, videos, freezers, sporting equipment, mobile phones and lawn-care chemicals. Initiated and funded privately by colleagues in a publishing firm, e-Store generated operating surpluses within six months of opening.

GreenGrocer was launched by a founder with perfect qualifications applying a classic Internet value proposition: buy only what has already been sold and have no fixed costs. Often painful experience has led to a very different implementation.

WINEPLANET's founders had a vision that the Internet could deliver 'the ultimate wine experience'. The site has won national awards but rapidly outgrew the local B2C wine market. The firm extended its products, its focus in B2B and its international reach with a launch of operations in the United Kingdom.

CHAOSMUSIC—'TALKING ABOUT A REVOLUTION!'
(`chaosmusic.com`)

Introduction

As a law student in 1995, Rob Appel became interested in the impact of the Internet on the music industry. At that time the major recording firms (Labels) controlled access by bands to the local market. His revolutionary idea was to use the Internet as an uncontrolled vehicle for new bands to make their music publicly available. Today's multi-faceted firm has developed a long way from that initial concept, but founders Rob Appel and Victoria Doidge retain their commitment to the bands and to driving change in the industry.

Since December 1999, Chaosmusic has been publicly listed. Equity funding has enabled the firm to invest substantially in marketing and brand-building. There are 60 full-time staff evenly divided between the head office in Sydney and a physical store located in Melbourne. Gross revenue for the year to June 2000 was A$5.4 million. Growth rates have been at 100% each quarter since late 1998.

Business models

The Chaos group operates multiple business models; retailer (online and offline), publisher of digital music and provider of content for online firms. Additional revenue streams are generated from web advertising, bulk sales to firms, schools and libraries, commission sales and syndication of content.

Retail

Chaosmusic purchased the Gaslight Music store in Melbourne in December 1999 to create a wholly owned local supply solution. The physical store was necessary since the record companies in Australia decline to supply products to purely online retailers. Around 80% of orders are supplied by Gaslight. Physical products are delivered locally by post at no additional charge with an option for delivery by courier at extra cost. The remaining 20% of purchases are shipped by Valley Media (now I-fill, the world's largest Internet fulfilment firm). Using an outsourced distributor in the United States has advantages and disadvantages. Chaos does not need to hold stock but does not have direct leverage to negotiate discounts for volume purchases with specific suppliers. About 5% of Chaos's sales are to international customers, mainly in the United States and United Kingdom.

The Chaos Music Market website initially contained information on one band and its music. This moved rapidly into a site for different bands and with more functions. By 1997, the website listed approximately 10 000 titles for sale from independent labels. Phantom Records provided the dispatch.

The retail business focuses on developing volume sales and building the brand while creatively constraining costs. In response to a major online competitor's rapid expansion of physical stores Chaos has arranged for a chain of 80 stores selling radios and hi-fi equipment to sell Top40 CDs on commission. Online affiliates are paid commission for sales originating from their sites. Provision of content (in the form of a newsletter) and backup services further encourage affiliates. Chaos is moving its emphasis from retail operations into more of a community business model that also accepts customer-generated content. Rather than waiting for this to develop naturally the firm offers a A$10 purchase rebate as an incentive for customers to provide product reviews.

Publishing

The traditional music supply chain is for bands to create music that is published by Labels that sell to distributors who sell to retailers who sell to consumers. With the Internet and publishers like Chaos the bands can sell directly to consumers. Chaos charges consumers A$2 for these albums and takes 25% from each sale. The remaining A$1.50 is more than bands receive from a traditional supply of an album. This strategy relies on volume to generate sufficient return. Chaos has 600 artists signed up with non-exclusive rights to publish their music on the Internet. While most of the artists are unknown, some are well established and internationally recognized who support direct distribution of their works. The old and new ways of doing business are running head to head at present and it is unclear how the structure of the industry may change as a result.

Content Provision

Portals are currently charging content providers to present their wares but with new delivery mechanisms such as through mobile phones and with telecommunication service providers desperate for content it is likely that at some stage content providers will be paid. Other revenue possibilities include using content to promote a product (e.g. listen to a track over the Internet and then buy the complete CD), through content packaging or through syndication. With syndication, Chaos works with a Label to create a virtual on-demand video clip channel. This is then distributed through the Internet, by pay-TV and perhaps free-to-air TV. Revenue is generated from consumer access fees and/or advertising sponsorship.

Industry, Competitor and Environmental Analysis

Chaos is part of the online music industry. Music has a different character to other industries since it is a high profile entertainment medium. Issues of copyright and piracy are politically very sensitive. Possible uses of information technology (IT) for strategic advantage in the music industry are still developing but will require changes in other areas, e.g. legislation for better copyright protection. IT supports radical change in the value chain that may lead to industry transformation.

Chaos is one of the largest Australian retailers of online music. The local online music market had revenues of about A\$40 million in 2000 (A\$15 million in 1999). The offline market is about A\$600 million. While the online market is growing very rapidly the traditional market has flat growth. Online sales are moving toward 10% of traditional sales but are expected to become bigger than offline in music publishing.

Industry analysis indicates significant motivation for innovation. The rate at which products/services become obsolete in this industry is extremely high. Software has the shortest time frame to obsolescence. Music itself is long term but product storage technologies are medium term. Competitors' actions are very predictable in retail but less so in publishing/entertaining, e.g. Sanity is predictable as a retailer but mp3.com.au as a publisher is unpredictable.

Chaos's Chief Executive Officer (CEO) claimed little difference between Chaos's retail products/services and those of competitors. However, Chaos sees itself as representing a new generation of music distributor—retailer, publisher, distributor and supporter of the music community. Price competition was rated by the CEO as a moderately important factor. To secure supply, online music stores in Australia also need an offline presence. An online price war against offline stores would, therefore, result in firms 'cutting their own throats'. Notwithstanding these comments by the CEO, customer survey responses identified price as being the most important factor in purchasing from Chaos. A price check showed Chaos's prices for some popular music CDs to be lower than online and offline competitors by between 16% and 24%, respectively. This may, however, be no more than a short-term or targeted sales campaign that coincided with the customer survey period.

Differentiation is based on presentation of the products and of the firm as a rebel brand and Australian music specialist. The CEO rates the risk of declining demand if no business model emerges for digital distribution of music as being moderate. Supply is not so much a competitive threat as a complex part of the business since there are barriers to entry for online firms with distributors refusing to provide products for purely online stores. Competition from local online stores may have been reduced by the downturn in the stock market as it will be harder to raise capital now. International competitors such as Amazon are seen by the CEO to be a huge threat, especially once they develop the capability for local fulfilment of orders.

Customer demands and tastes are generally predictable. The traditional retailers' approach has been to develop demand through advertising and marketing and through the use of periodic retail targets, e.g. Christmas, Mothers' and Fathers' Days, Easter, sales, etc. This approach applies equally to online music retailing. Technology has a high rate of change. Sound systems are constantly being modified, e.g. records, cassettes, CDs, DVDs, etc. with different incremental developments. Software for online delivery of music is also constantly developing.

Key Business Drivers and Threats

Key business success factors are complex and inter-related. There have been significant first-mover advantages. Chaos has been around since the beginning of the Internet, having started at the same time as CDNow but not grown as quickly since the Australian market is so small. Recognition of Chaos as a pioneer in the development of digital distribution and a rebel against the control of the Labels has established the firm as a key part of the music community. Other drivers include marketing to present the brand, product range, pricing, order fulfilment and service.

The greatest threat seen by the firm would be a downturn in the stock market and 'a lower share price that means the firm is vulnerable to takeover'.[1] There is also a threat that the Labels will go direct to customers and provide better service than online retailers. The biggest threat for the industry lies in the digital distribution of music. There was considerable publicity in mid-2000 on music piracy featuring the band Metallica and Napster. The Napster saga continued into 2001. Rob Appel sees much of this tension as being between Labels and the community over control of the music industry.

Production of content was and is going to be the key issue (CEO).

---

[1] This concern had substance. In July 2000 CDNow was taken over by German publisher Bertlesmann.

Innovation Factors and Processes

Chaosmusic as a concept developed over time from the original Chaos Music Market, a space for information on and distribution of music that lacked formal governance or corporate control. For the first two years there was no revenue. Then they loaded up the catalogue for a music store, Phantom Records. During the day Rob was developing his skills as website designer, developer, online content producer (in legal matters) and then as a manager of business content for the Internet Service Provider (ISP) Ozemail. At night he worked to develop Chaosmusic, which became Ozemail's music channel.

Chaosmusic became a company in 1997 when it was necessary to raise capital. With a policy not to go into debt, the necessity to attract capital forced the development of a formal business plan, which was 'traumatic at the time' but ultimately proved to be very useful. The firm did not need to advertise; customers came through the Ozemail link. The requirements of the IPO in December 1999 necessitated further formal strategic planning. The most important factors that led to this company were:

- Label companies' control of music distribution restrained access by new bands to the market;
- the opportunity to use technology to bypass the Labels' control; and
- the decision to become a full retail/music publishing operation developed incrementally.

Major obstacles that needed to be overcome for the project to be a success were:

- technical and design issues (how to do it, what worked!);
- developing expertise—the types and levels of skills kept changing; and
- finance.

Website Development and Operational Issues

The original Chaos website was designed and developed by Rob with help from some friends. In 1995 the www was seen to be a fad. Rob worked to develop his skills and experience by setting up the youth website 'Recovery' for the national public radio and TV broadcaster. He had absolute editorial freedom and could explore different options to see what worked well. That site was a great success, receiving one million page impressions a month in 1997. The Chaosmusic logo appeared on the site. This experience was a great opportunity to learn, but:

> Genuinely starting from scratch, including having to learn the technologies and web design issues with little assistance, was very hard. (CEO).

Today, the market is more saturated, sites have developed experience and there is no longer the necessity to experiment and learn as you go. Once the company was formed, full-time technical staff were appointed. Having internal technical staff was seen to be essential to avoid communication problems that could lead to problems with the site development.

The initial retail operation based on Phantom Record's catalogue required filling out an online form that was e-mailed to Rob who initiated the order. Real-time retail operations commenced in 1997. Since then there has been constant, on-going incremental development—'perpetual beta mode'. Operationally there were lots of problems but then expectations were low, e.g. the Recovery site introduced image mapping, a great advance at the time, but there were always problems with getting the technologies to operate reliably.

Website Features

Evaluation of the Chaos website (see Table 2.1) shows that, as with many e-tailing sites, product information and transaction-related functions are well developed but more details on the company and its operations could be presented. Improvements in usability and in innovation to enhance the customer experience are also desir-able. One of the distinguishing factors of the online retailing industry is its responsiveness to customer feedback. Feedback forms have been on the website from the beginning. Chaos's customers are very vocal and forceful about what they do and do not like on the site. Surveys of customers, general surveys of non-customers (e.g. by market research firms) and analysis of customer paths through the site are all conducted. Where problems are identified, e.g. where customers are being lost before completing their purchases, then changes are made to the website very quickly.

Customers responded to the survey that they were less satisfied with the site than they were with the Internet as a whole (see below). Customer survey sugges-tions for site improvements were predominantly seeking additional functions or features; e.g. song titles for each CD. One customer lamented there were, 'no track listings for any of the 65 Waylon items on search!'.

With hundreds of thousands of CDs in their catalogues and track details that may vary for a single CD released in different countries a simple request such as this will pose a challenge for e-tailers. The online systems are fully integrated—one of the requirements for opening an account with Valley Media was to have fully integrated transaction-processing systems. The business systems are mostly integrated. Finance reports are produced from the online database. The accounting system was fully integrated with online systems by end 2000. The CEO considers the current site to be satisfactory in terms of traffic analysis, as shown by page impressions and membership growth rates. The conversion ratio of visits to sales and gross revenue are other key measures.

Customer Perspectives

For a rebel music retailer Chaos's customer profile contains some surprises. The largest age grouping was 21–30 years (46%) which could be expected but the next largest groups were not youth aged 20 years or less but aged 31–45 years (26%) and 46–60 years (16%). Customers were male (72%) and the largest occupational groups professional (41%), office worker and student. About half were university graduates. Most were living in a major city (55%) with incomes reported as average (14%), above average (34%) or lower (36%) than the national average salary. Customers access the Internet daily (64%), from home (62%) and are experienced web shoppers with 56% having purchased more than five times. Apart from music, Chaos's customers use the Internet for buying books (45%), tickets, banking services, computer products and toys/gifts for personal use (76%).

Reflecting the standardized nature of music, 45% of customers visited the site to purchase a specific product and mostly visited two or three times before purchase. The site is successfully appealing to new customers (39% not having purchased from the site before) but is retaining existing customers. Customers came to the site due to a wide range of factors including prior knowledge of the firm (27%), a link from another site, personal reference, an online advertisement and via a search engine.

A broad grouping of financial, personal and product-related factors led customers to buy from this site; price (21%), convenience, range of products, availability of products and the total cost of purchase. Being an Australian firm was a factor positively identified by customers, partly as a source for Australian music but largely since the local price was not affected by exchange-rate fluctuations. The greatest barriers to deciding to purchase were concerns about security (23%), usability of site (e.g. speed of loading and completing purchasing processes) and uncertainty about products/services.

The purchasing process was considered very easy (41%) or easy (26%). Customers were very satisfied (38%) or satisfied (50%) with the Internet as a whole and very satisfied (38%) or satisfied (34%) with this site. Some 53% would definitely purchase again from the site and 35% would purchase again from other sites. More than 58% of customers would recommend the site to others even though they sought improvements in the site in more details on products and services (42%), prices, speed of loading, delivery details and the range/availability of products.

The Future

Chaos sees the biggest challenges in the future for small, non-traditional, Internet start-ups to be:

1. Learning how to make a profitable business model.
2. Moving quickly enough to get sufficient market share. Over time, the current plethora of Internet firms is expected to consolidate into a few large and some small specialist firms. Firms need to avoid being caught in the mid-range of sizes where costs will be high.
3. Finding the right balance between operational costs and revenues.

4. Finding your market niche and attacking it globally (i.e. not being con-
    strained geographically).

Faced with the opportunity to start again there is not much that Rob could have
done differently. They would still have to learn the business, so roughly the same
path would be followed although they may have had different partners. The
fundamentals would be unchanged, however, namely never go into debt, align
the business with music creators and encourage a more open business model for
music distribution.

For the future Chaos sees more publishing and generating more revenue from
content, e.g. being an entertainment provider first then a retailer. Also there are
opportunities to expand geographically, e.g. by entering other markets (like
Singapore) and by translating the site into different languages. Chaos has
announced plans to outsource order fulfilment to the international specialist
YCH Group to obtain best practice and to establish a platform for international
expansion.

Rob Appel's advice for other firms seeking to start up is to ensure they establish
the right alliances and adopt business models that do not rely on a big marketing
spend. Franchising may be a model, however, if you are using other's products you
need to be careful about paying too much. Also, founders should not be too
precious about owning everything as equity is a major source of capital. Strong
IT skills in-house are a must. Intellectual property rights for your own software are
critical, especially if outsourcing development.

Conclusion

In 1995, Chaosmusic was one of the first Internet startups in the retail music
industry. The firm had a rebel orientation from inception with the stated intention
of breaking the Label companies' control over the market. The Internet presented
an opportunity to use technology to bypass the Labels, letting new bands access
the market directly. Subsequently, the firm developed into today's full retail/music
publishing operation.

Since Chaos was such an early entrant its major obstacles included pioneering
issues, Internet technical and design issues (what worked, how to do it), developing expertise when the types and levels of skills kept changing and the perennial
problem, finance. In response to Australian record companies' refusal to supply
products to purely online retailers, in 1999 Chaos purchased a physical music
store. An alliance with a chain of 80 hi-fi stores provided a nation-wide physical
sales channel. In 2000, local and international fulfilment of online sales was outsourced to specialist firm YCH and Chaos entered a joint venture with a Singapore
firm to set up a Singapore operation.

Postscript. Rob Appel's concern that lower share prices would expose the firm to
a takeover bid was justified. In early 2001, a rival online/offline chain of music

stores made an offer for all shares at the then current price. The bid was not successful.

DYMOCKS—'IT'S IN THE NAME!' (dymocks.com.au)

Introduction

Initiated as a business imperative for an established bookseller in response to the potential threat of amazon.com and developed in a seemingly *ad hoc* manner, Dymocks has defied all odds by producing Australia's most successful book-selling site. The tensions and channel conflict that arise between corporate-run Internet retailing and franchisees are also illustrated.

Established in Sydney in 1879, Dymocks is a privately owned traditional book-store that has expanded throughout Australia and to New Zealand, Hong Kong and Singapore. In 1988 the firm had eight stores. Expansion to the nearly 100 stores today has been as a result of franchising. Annual revenue was about A$150 million in 2000. In recent years annual growth has been around 5% although this is dependent on the opening of new stores. In the last year fewer stores were opened due to a decline in the retail market. In early 1990s 10–15 new stores were opened each year. With a predominantly franchised operation, the firm has a small core of only 50 staff.

Business Model

Dymocks' Internet venture was in direct response to the potential competitive threat posed by amazon.com. In 1996, an Internet presence was seen by the bookseller to be a business imperative. Little consideration was given to business models or to the possible longer-term implications of an Internet service competing directly with the firm's franchisees.

Initial implementation of the Internet service in February 1997 was 'complex and clunky' but it worked. Website development was outsourced. The website developer (who also hosted the service) received the orders. That firm e-mailed the order details to the flagship store along with credit card details. The franchisee of the flagship store employed staff to process the orders and received reimbursement from the corporate office. These staff received orders and checked the store's database. If the book was in stock, they went into store. If found, it was wrapped and dispatched. If not found, it was added to the store's orders. Staff tried to identify it as an Internet order, although this was not a simple process without making changes to the order system. When the store orders came in, then the Internet staff were advised. They would collect the book, wrap and dispatch. Delivery at a range of service levels (e.g. by courier or post) was a separate charge for customers.

Today, apart from secure payment processing and some streamlining of procedures to update the website database of books (which remains separate from the store's database), the order fulfilment processes essentially remain the same.

This type of implementation is common as a business model for traditional retailers venturing onto the Internet. It is rarely profitable. The additional costs of website development, website operation and use of employees to locate, wrap and dispatch orders cannot be recovered when Internet sales are at usual store prices. The potential cost savings from Internet operations (i.e. lower fixed costs and no inventory costs) are not available. An additional cost complication for Dymocks is the necessity to negotiate the level of reimbursement by the corporate office to the franchisee providing order fulfilment.

None the less, from Dymocks' corporate perspective the operation that has evolved could be viewed as implementation of a pure Internet business model. All activities from web development and website hosting to ordering, payment (by credit card), fulfilment (by franchisee) and delivery are being outsourced. Apart from development of the website and supporting software there are no capital costs. Nor are there inventory or operational staff. However, Dymocks' corporate and franchise operations cannot be viewed separately.

The two major problems with these types of implementation are that they are neither profitable nor scaleable. As orders increase in volume and customer service levels become increasingly less competitive a dedicated, integrated and streamlined fulfilment operation will be required. In the meantime, firms specializing in Internet order fulfilment and distribution are emerging that may enable Dymocks to maintain its outsourcing approach.

Industry, Competitor and Environmental Analysis

Dymocks is a key part of two industries: franchising, with its unique characteristics and legislation, and retailing, where the focus is on the customer and not the franchise owner. Dymocks does not see itself as being part of the book industry, i.e. publishing. Retailers sell the publisher's products. Major differences between these and other industries are the high level of customer contact and customer focus in the retail industry and its susceptibility to economic cycles (e.g. increases in interest and inflation rates reduce disposable incomes and so reduce book sales). The franchise industry is very dependent on the types of products and services sold.

The retail industry is heavily dependent on IT, particularly point of sale terminals. Big retailers have a higher IT cost as a percentage of revenue than other industries, although this is masked in Dymocks by franchise operations. However, the level of technology integration is low. There is no network linking the point of sale systems in one store with other stores.

The Australian book retailing market is very fragmented. With about 10% of the overall market Dymocks is the second largest retailer but the biggest Internet player. Dymocks also sell software, which is the third largest source of sales after books and stationery.

Dymocks' environmental analysis reveals an industry with standard products that become obsolete slowly, where local competitors are very predictable and where the bases for differentiation are price and the quality of service provided. Customer demands are less predictable:

> If we knew what people would buy we'd only stock that book. Who would have predicted the success of *Angela's Ashes*? (MD).

The threat of international competition raised by the Internet in 1996 remains today. The industry also has an evolving tension between the franchise model and the trend towards superstores selling books and a range of other merchandise with a coffee shop. The level of capital investment required for a franchisee needs to be within the limits of personal borrowing, but the cost of a superstore is much higher. The rate of change of IT in the industry is variable. The Internet is changing fast but retail technology is changing very slowly. IT systems that were developed in the mid 1980s are still being used in stores.

Key Business Drivers and Threats

For the business to succeed Dymocks needs to supply price-competitive products and provide services that customers want while enabling franchise owners to make a profit. Dymocks' role is to support and encourage franchisees. Innovative marketing is less important than supplying store systems and minimizing store costs through negotiation of bulk discounts, lower rentals and more cost-effective telecommunications.

Channel conflict is a serious issue. Two of the business strategies critical to Dymocks' future, namely customer relationship management and growth through franchising, are essentially incompatible. Customer details are held only at a franchise level while the Internet operation is run by the corporate office. The challenge is to find ways for the Internet service and franchisees to work together. The ground rules for resolution of this issue are still being defined. In 2000, a court case between Dymocks corporate and several franchisees upheld the corporate right to operate an Internet service separately from the franchisees.

Innovation Factors and Processes

Dymocks' major motivation was the emergence of amazon.com in 1996. The franchisee of the flagship store first raised this as a potential competitive threat. Verbal presentations were made to the Dymocks' Board by the General Manager Retail (an early adoption enthusiast who developed the Internet proposal) and the franchisee of the flagship store. The MD at that time supported the proposal. The outcome was a Board minute to proceed. No funding limit was documented. No ball park budget was documented. The original concept was simply to replicate Amazon's operations.

The need for a defensive reaction to the potential threat of Amazon and the subsequent necessity for the business to learn about Internet technology were the twin drivers of this project. The venture was not consistent with any part of the strategic business plan; there was no formal business proposal and no anticipation of making money.

'This approach had all the hallmarks of a disaster but it actually worked (MD).

Major obstacles or barriers to be overcome for the project to be a success were a lack of understanding of the issues at board level, unease in franchise owners about the venture and uncertainty as to its implications for franchisees. These feelings of unease tended to simmer.

Illustrating the necessity for firms to think carefully before implementing an Internet activity, the approach adopted by Dymocks further complicated the problem. Franchise owners contribute to an 'advertising fund'. The original idea was to use this fund to set up the Internet site since it was the only vehicle existing for collecting funds from franchisees. The idea was for any surpluses to be returned to the advertising fund to help pay for future advertising. This approach proved to be a mistake because it lacked clear aims, objectives, responsibility and direction. From the franchisee's perspective, it also had them funding a competitive channel. The corporate office subsequently took responsibility for the Internet operation.

Website Development and Operational Issues

Dymocks has outsourced all website development and operations. The first developer was technically rather than business oriented so Dymocks had to suggest website features. The initial site was intentionally basic with development progressing in small incremental steps. The first implementation took four months to develop, going live in February 1997. Sales were made from day one. Owing to the limited alternatives at that time the website developer also hosted the site. This arrangement was not successful. 'We had to ring to tell them the server was down.'

Within 12 months the site was re-developed by a large and experienced systems firm. Their project was tightly briefed and delivered as requested. To include more creativity, Dymocks insisted that the developer partner with an advertising firm although this arrangement actually was not used as much as anticipated. The new website had secure payment facilities and was hosted by a facilities management firm. There have been no major operational problems.

Website Features

Evaluation of the website (see Table 2.1) shows product information and transaction-related functions to be well developed but suggests that more details on the company and its operations would be well regarded by customers. A high percentage of customers were satisfied with the site (see below). Customer recommendations for improvement of the site highlight the information intensity of books with more details on products and services requested as well as lower prices/costs. Since Dymocks recognizes the critical importance of service and customer relationship management it is anticipated that innovations in support of these areas will be introduced. Innovation (or lack of it) is a significant area of exposure to future competition.

Currently there is no integration of business systems and Internet operations. Franchisee systems are not linked with each other. At a corporate level there are sales reporting and accounting systems that are separate from the store systems and from the Internet systems. There is no real reason for the lack of integration except the costs outweighed the perceived benefits. This lack of systems integration emphasizes the lack of scalability of Dymocks' Internet operation.

The MD considers the Internet operation to have been a success based on increasing sales, traffic visiting the site and constant requests from Internet companies wanting to form strategic alliances; e.g. Ozemail, Yahoo, Sydney Futures Exchange, Westfield, and startups.

Customer Surveys

Dymocks' customer profile is more broadly based than other firms (male 50%; female 50%), age 31–45 years (42%), professional (62%), university graduate (54%) living in a major city (55%) with average (26%), above average (33%) or more than twice the national average (23%) salary. Customers access the Internet daily (71%), from home (63%) and have disparate levels of experience with web shopping (28% having purchased more than 11 times, 28% 2–5 times and 19% no prior purchases).

Other than books, Dymocks' customers use the Internet for buying computer products (39%), banking services, music CDs and tickets for personal (55%) or a mixture of personal and work use. Reflecting the standardized nature of books, 82% of customers visited the site to purchase a specific book and mostly purchased on their first visit. The site is very successful at attracting new customers with 61% not having purchased from the site before and 20% having purchased once. Most customers came to the site due to prior knowledge of the firm (62%).

The most important factors in deciding to buy from this book site were convenience (43%), availability of products and the trusted name of the firm. Being a local firm was another factor positively identified by customers, for reasons of patriotism and speed to customer. Greatest barriers to deciding to purchase were concerns about delivery (22%), security and uncertainty about products/services.

The purchasing process was considered very easy (53%) or easy (31%). Customers were very satisfied (45%) or satisfied (46%) with the Internet as a whole and very satisfied (44%) or satisfied (44%) with this site. Some 56% would definitely purchase again from the site and 42% would purchase again from other sites. More than 62% of customers would recommend the site to others even though they sought improvements in the site in more details on products and services (40%), the total cost of purchase, price, delivery details and the availability of products. Customer suggestions for improvement of the website reflected ambivalence about international competition. One wanted 'customer reviews like Amazon' while another suggested 'leave it like it is—we don't want another Amazon!'.

The Future

Dymocks sees the biggest challenges to firms in future use of the Internet as:

1. Establishing a brand name since it is a very powerful competitive advantage.
2. Determining a viable business model for the whole organization. What is the value driver for customers from your Internet site, e.g. mass customization, personalized welcome, customer recommendations, community building? How to become cost-effective? What is the source of competitive advantage?
3. Keeping the website fresh and different. Personalizing it for each customer. How to do it better. This all takes time and money.
4. Being prepared to continually invest in innovation.
5. Managing the pace of change. The cycle of change–benefit–change is easy and quick. The problem is everyone can do this.
6. Back-office order fulfilment.

If Dymocks was facing the same decision (to develop an Internet presence) today, they would do it by the book. They would determine what to do to drive value better than competitors, how to jointly leverage electronic business and franchisers and would establish resources at the appropriate level with a proper business plan.

Their advice for other firms seeking to develop an Internet service is: to know what you are doing, why you are doing it and define it carefully. It is a matter of getting the strategy right. Key performance indicators were an area of concern. Firms will know if they are doing it right from traffic and feedback not just performance indicators. Firms need to recognize that there is little basis for setting targets such as first year revenues. The product mix for a traditional retailer between Internet and stores is different so you cannot set targets for one based on the other. Ultimately, orders are what count for retailers. Other issues are: what percentage of visits lead to orders and the percentage of cancellation of back orders. Since marketing on the Internet is an entirely new area, new key performance indicators for marketing will be required.

Conclusion

Dymocks is an established and traditional firm in a stable industry that relies on franchise operations for growth. The case illustrates the critical importance of the threat of external competition as an incentive to establish an Internet operation. The firm had no Internet-based business model or plan apart from mounting a defensive response to Amazon. The venture caused serious concerns among franchisees that ultimately led to a court case. The traditional implementation using in-store staff for order fulfilment reduces profitability and precludes scalability. A more dedicated approach will be required to maintain competitive levels of service as orders increase.

Irrespective of the lack of strategic planning and inefficient implementation, Dymocks has been successful in overcoming its lack of knowledge of how to use the Internet effectively, a lack of understanding of the strategic implications of Internet retailing and channel conflict that resulted in litigation to become the most successful Internet bookseller in Australia.

E-STORE—'THE PUREST PLAYER' (estore.com.au)

Introduction

E-Store was established in November 1998 by three senior executives from the publishing and advertising industries who saw in the Internet a 'once in a generation' opportunity to establish a new type of business. Their vision was to develop an Internet superstore. Their primary target market was technology buyers since this was a large and rapidly growing group, web-proficient, ready to purchase computers and then perhaps other appliances, and likely to influence other potential customers. The store would focus on technology products at first and expand the product range once the operations were working properly. The three founders were determined to retain control of the venture and funded the A$1 million startup costs from their own resources. One of the founders resigned to become the full-time CEO, the other two maintained their previous positions. The first website was designed by the CEO, Steven Spilly, and implemented on 1 March 1999.

Initially, E-Store focused on sales of computer products in its Sydney market but quickly expanded to Melbourne. After 12 months of operation, on 1 March 2000, multiple product types were offered. E-Store currently sells a huge number of products in an eclectic range of major categories: computer hardware and software, electronic equipment, kitchen, laundry, health and fitness, climate control, music, games, home lawn care and mobile phones. The firm claims lowest-price leadership and offers home delivery anywhere in Australia.

The 2000 technology crash has not had a negative impact since the founders retain control of the firm and there is no necessity to seek external funding. Within six months of operation, E-Store began generating operating profits. The annual revenue for the year January–December 2000 was around A$16 million and projections for 2001 are A$19–20 million. Monthly revenues have grown from A$40 000 in March 1999 to over A$1 million a month by mid 2000. Staff numbers fluctuate according to business activities but remain fewer than 30 staff full-time. The determination to be self-reliant for funding meant that growth may have been slower but this was seen by the founders to be preferable to loss of control of the venture. Equally important was the sense that the firm did not have 'cash to burn' and needed to adopt a frugal approach in running the business. This focus on reduction of costs and generation of revenues has prepared E-Store well for survival in the post technology crash Internet retail market.

Business Models

E-Store's mission is to provide wide choice amongst high-quality brands in a convenient, secure shopping environment open all day, every day. They guarantee the lowest prices nationally, without exception. Encouraging price comparisons, their motto is: Shop around, buy from us. The firm currently sells 120 000 products, the only limit being the willingness of suppliers to enter into partnerships to deliver their wares to customers.

From conception, E-Store's business models have sought the purest implementation of the new Internet-based business opportunities. E-Store has no stock, no stores, national reach, direct fulfilment and home delivery. Product offerings are not limited by the market dictating specific products (i.e. the firm is not required to push something in stock). In principle, an unrestricted range of products could go to up to 10 million products. E-Store could sell any product brands but only takes products with post-sales support direct to the customer. Only first tier brands are sold. Post-sales service is seamless and seen to be by E-Store whereas service actually comes direct from the supplier.

This 'pure' Internet business model means that E-Store does not incur product selling costs until after they receive the order and its payment, by credit card. The business is strongly cash positive since partners are paid on 30-day terms. The cash flow is used to fund the firm's growth. Steven Spilly argues that it is more cost-effective for e-tailers to use 'best of breed' for fulfilment. The disadvantages of having your own warehousing include: the warehouse is useless if empty, possible stock losses, wastage, fire and theft—these are all fixed-cost overheads that do not have to be there. E-tailers like Amazon have huge revenues and could turn their losses into profits very easily by minor adjustments in their business approach, e.g. a reduction in marketing costs. For e-tailers without the large revenues of an Amazon, a high level of fixed costs can kill a business. This is especially a problem for a typical e-tailer that relies on massive marketing spend. They cannot stop advertising otherwise they will die, and so a small drop in revenues can cause a cash flow crisis. Subsequent failures of well-known e-tailers from cash burnout have confirmed Spilly's analysis.

A price check was made to examine implementation of the low-cost leadership business strategy. On a range of large whitegoods (refrigerators, washing machines) E-Store's prices were about 8% lower than traditional stores for the same product. For music CDs the prices were up to 20% less expensive; however, the charge for delivery was much higher than for similar products from other e-tailers. Customer surveys show price as the most important reason to purchase from E-Store.

However, the essence of E-Store's success is shown by its integrated computer systems that enable the firm to effortlessly analyse competitors and rapidly respond through the addition, deletion and modification of products and prices. The systems present a low-price, uniform and seamless retail operation to customers across multiple suppliers and allow detailed monitoring of performance at each stage of the operation. The focus on cost reduction, revenue generation and growth through internal funding has positioned E-Store well as the economy becomes less buoyant. This business model is applicable equally for B2C or B2B.

Industry, Competitor and Environmental Analysis

E-Store sees itself belonging to the Internet retailing industry. Most Internet retailers are large, established firms who have ventured onto the Internet but who still apply their traditional bricks and mortar business practices. As seen above, E-Store has a different business approach, namely few overheads and a huge range of products. The use of IT is different to other industries in that IT is the means of customer contact. With B2B, firms buy through the Internet the same as usual (i.e. face-to-face contact is not essential); however, B2C is different since IT is interposed between the customer and the retailer.

Compared with local competitors, E-Store's product range is 'largest', its sales 'massive' and its operating costs 'smallest'. The firm's costs are comparatively low because, currently, all of E-Store's major competitors have in-house order fulfilment.

The company sees the rate at which some products become obsolescent as being extremely high. About 25%–30% of IT products could change in a month compared with 10% of non-IT products. The actions of competitors are rated as being very predictable since their business models are well established, recognized and unlikely to change. E-Store uses its search engine to determine competitors' business models (typically on their launch) and then rely on customers advising price comparisons unless competitors run a special campaign. There were few identified imperatives for E-Store's innovation except as a business opportunity.

Key Business Drivers and Threats

'Firstly,' says Steven Spilly, 'the website has to work.' The website and fulfilment software is critical to the success of E-Store. It needs to be compatible with every browser. Navigation must be clear. Functionality must be simple—it is too complex in many sites. The site needs to be secure and robust. Technology-based features such as flash or Java-based facilities are avoided, using only html and basic technologies. The site has to be quick. Secondly, content is key, particularly the range of products. The site needs to provide standard products from known high-quality manufacturers. Thirdly, customers' needs must be met. Easy placing of orders, secure payment processing, and prompt delivery of products all lead to customer satisfaction enhanced by money-back guarantees. Fourthly, there must be a focus on generating operating profits through minimization of fixed costs by outsourcing as many functions as possible.

As could be expected from a firm with a business strategy of low-cost leader-ship, price is a major competitive threat. Product quality is not an issue since products are the same for all retailers. Declining demand, scarce supply and local/international competition are all seen to have little impact as competitive threats. The greatest threat facing the firm and the industry is Internet companies failing and thus lowering confidence in Internet-based retailing.

Customers' demands and tastes are rated as unpredictable because there are too many products and product categories available to manage properly. Technology in the industry, particularly Internet technology, is volatile and changes frequently.

Innovation Factors and Processes

The most important factors that led to E-Store were, firstly, the perceived business opportunity. The web appealed since it was immediate, real time and presented a rare chance to establish an entirely new type of business. Two of the partners had senior executive positions with the (traditional and online) publisher Ziff-Davis. The third partner came from advertising/marketing. The project was driven 100% by business issues. No partner had any IT development experience. Since the project was totally self-funded there was no necessity to prepare formal plans. An informal business plan was prepared. Secondly, a two-month evaluation of the business opportunity showed it to be viable. The final factor was timing. There was a perceived benefit for the first to market in a new type of business. Such business opportunities do not come up often, about every 20–30 years. If the worst case occurred and the venture failed then it would have been very good experience even though it was considered high risk.

The firm was launched with a view to have an expanded set of product cate-gories. Once the website was working with IT products then all that was needed to expand the product categories was partnerships with other suppliers. The new products in the expanded range of product categories were those that were logical from a retailer's perspective, not necessarily those with high margins. There has not been a revision of the original vision of the business model or the plans, just how the website would work. Major obstacles were:

1. Supplier acceptance of the differences between Internet and traditional busi-ness models. Suppliers were not used to working with resellers who wanted to make deliveries directly and promptly from supplier to customer. This remains as a key obstacle. Suppliers need to understand that this is a differ-ent way to sell and distribute and that it may become the 'norm'.

2. Lack of knowledge about effective use of the technology. What makes for a successful website and how to build it? There were some US examples but the firm finally decided to build from scratch.

The processes were:

1. Identification of Internet retailing as a business opportunity (based on several years of experience with the Internet and websites)
2. Preparation of an informal business case
3. Evaluation of the potential for an Internet-based computer store
4. Obtaining finances required (self-financed)
5. Proceeding to implement the business plan
6. Development of a website
7. Securing partnerships with suppliers

Major business concerns were:

1. Risk—lack of experience and a shortage of successful models to examine.
2. Uncertainty about the business viability of the plan. It was speculative to say that consumers would purchase online.
3. Some potential business partners suggested that the business plan was premature and could not happen for a few years: 'Initial reactions to an innovation are generally negative simply because it is new'.

Internet Development and Operations

The first website took four months to develop. Steven Spilly designed the structure of the site and the code was outsourced. There were two attempts at the first version, 'after three weeks we decided to bin it and start again'. From the first version they learnt a lot:

> You only find out what you need on your website once you start trading and start to analyse customer requirements and interactions. Until then you just speculate and your processes are built on guesswork (CEO).

Feedback from customers showed that version 1 of the website was unsatisfactory. The developer used Java and dynamic html for special effects that did not work with all browsers. There were problems with navigation and the firm could not make any changes to the site without developer intervention. The second version was developed with a different developer. This version was robust, it worked and feedback from customers was satisfactory but there were some problems, e.g. relatively few pictures with each product. If a retailer operates only through the Internet, then the site needs to offer more.

> A successful site must do the complete job for the firm so it is not necessary for customers to make phone calls. The site needs to do the job for us (CEO).

All development was outsourced. Apart from the fixed costs of internal staff, a business risk in having website developers in-house was recognized. E-Store took a business decision to outsource website development to a company that would have a team to support their firm. The business risk was rated as being lower when services are contracted. Ownership of the website code could be maintained and breach of contract was seen to be a stronger remedy than rights over a former employee.

Version 2 took three to four months to develop. This version was built to enable the easy addition of stores (i.e. new product groups) and categories. New stores and categories could be added in about 10 minutes by administration staff. New products were just added to the stores and categories. Prices are changed as easily. This version also loaded and operated much more quickly. Apart from the inconsistency problems with different browsers in version 1 of the website there had been no particular operational problems.

Website Features

All IT systems and business processes are built around the website and an account-keeping database (MYOB). The sales, prices, profits and purchase orders for E-Store's orders are all downloaded into the database. The website and fulfilment software is considered critical to the success of E-Store.

> Competitors can reverse engineer your website but they are only copying the visible front-end, that may represent 5% of the site. The back end is the competitive tool, i.e. the capability to add content and manipulate it and do it all in real time with little administrative or operational overhead. It enables E-Store to be agile and responsive to the market at little cost (CEO).

This emphasis on low prices to attract customers and a focus on the back-end systems are reflected in both the website evaluation and customer responses. The website (see Table 2.1) has full transaction capability but other areas, including information, ease of use and customer service rate lower than other sites. Innovation in service delivery is completely ignored. Customer survey responses indicated they were less satisfied with this site than with the Internet as a whole. Although nearly three-quarters would purchase again, fewer than half would recommend the site to others. Customers sought improvements in the range of products, purchase procedures and details on products and services.

System success is determined by a combination of measures, including industry average sale price, conversion rate (the rate at which Internet visitors actually proceed to a purchase), the average length of time a customer spends on the site, cost-efficiency for processing orders and paying suppliers and order fulfilment capability. Other relevant measures include traffic, and the number of user sessions. However, it is important that Internet firms do not focus on trying to attract traffic—just buyers.

Consumer Perspectives

Probably as a result of their extremely large product range (120 000 products), E-Store's customer profile is unusually diverse. Customers are distributed right across the spectrum of major age categories: 31–45 years (26%), 21–30 years (21%), more than 61 years (18%) and 46–60 (15%). Customers are predominantly male (77%), professional (54%), living in a major city (41%) or city (31%) with above average (62%) income. Customers access the Internet daily (74%) mostly from home (56%) and are moderately experienced web shoppers (36% having purchased 2–5 times and 31% 6–10 times).

Apart from computer products, E-Store's customers use the Internet to buy books (46%), for banking, tickets and music for personal (44%) or a mixture of personal and work use. E-Store is very successful at attracting new customers with 64% not having purchased from the site previously. New customers found the site from search engines and from links or advertisements on other websites.

As may be expected from the firm's strategy of price-based competition, the most important factors in deciding to buy from this site were price (59%) con- venience and availability of products. Greatest barriers to deciding to purchase were completing purchase procedures (28%), uncertainty about products/services and concerns about security.

The purchasing process was considered very easy (31%) or easy (26%). Customers were very satisfied (31%) or satisfied (44%) with the Internet as a whole but were less very satisfied (18%) or satisfied (41%) with this site. Perhaps reflecting the difficulties in developing customer loyalty with a low- price policy, some 74% would purchase again from the site and 80% would purchase again from other sites. Only 46% of customers would recommend the site to others. Improvements were sought in the range of products (39%), purchase procedures and more details on products and services.

The Future

The biggest challenges for e-tailers in the future are seen to be:

1. Generating revenue, becoming profitable and growing. A related challenge is to build the market. Part of the challenge in generating revenue is to have the right focus, i.e. a focus not solely on customer acquisition and marketing but looking more at customer fulfilment—actually providing the size and range of products.

2. Moving more into B2B. One option would be to house E-Store on a company's intranet for their in-house purchasing. This capability is expected to be used increasingly in the future.
3. Supply is a constant challenge. Distribution channels are not reliable. For example, one of E-Store's suppliers (Dataflow) failed during 2000. At that time, E-Store sourced about 20 000 products from them and then had to find an alternative supplier willing and able to work in partnership.

E-Store plans to offer more products and more services. Expansion will be in both B2B and B2C markets. New services may be technology-enabled, e.g. wireless application protocol (WAP). Another possibility is an exploration of broadband possibilities and content development targeted at that.

If the firm were facing the same decision (to develop an Internet presence) today, little would be done differently. Their current implementation is very flexible and successful and there is little incentive to modify it. Advice for firms seeking to develop an Internet service is to concentrate on building business with substance rather than generating funding. 'If you provide something for customers the market will reward you, eventually.'

Conclusion

E-Store demonstrates the importance of relevant experience. The three founders, senior executives in business with knowledge of the Internet, proposed a simple Internet-based business model for a specific target market and successfully implemented the proposal. E-Store is characterized by its differences from many other e-tailers. Spurning external funds so they could retain control of the venture, the firm adopted a frugal approach characterized by word of mouth marketing and a focus on profitability. A pure Internet model was implemented with all major functions in order fulfilment outsourced. The primary target market, technology buyers, has been successfully serviced and operations became profitable within its first six months of operation. It is difficult to conclude that the three founders were able to get so much so right simply by accident.

The most significant driver for the creation of E-Store was the perceived once-in-a-generation opportunity to establish an entirely new type of business. The higher risk due to a lack of precedents was seen to be balanced by a potential first-to-market advantage. Major obstacles overcome were resistance by suppliers to making deliveries directly and promptly to consumers and an uncertainty about how the Internet could best be used. Both barriers persist today for Internet-based retailers.

E-Store has successfully implemented the simple Internet business model of minimizing fixed costs and purchasing only those products already sold. E-Store has managed to reduce the number of links and costs of an extended supply chain and to by-pass the business overheads in maintaining and managing inventory.

Table 2.1 *Evaluation of selected Australian websites*

Firms	Company information/5	Product/ services information/5	Transactions/5	Customer service/5	Ease of use/5	Innovations/5	Total/30	CEC scale © (%)
ChaosMusic	3	5	5	5	4	2	24	80
Dymocks	2	5	5	5	5	0	22	73
E-Store	3	4	5	2	3	0	17	57
GreenGrocer	2	5	5	4	4	0	20	67
WINEPLANET	5	5	4	4	5	3	26	87

GREENGROCER—'THIS IS FOR ME!' (greengrocer.com.au)

Introduction

In late 1996 Douglas Carlson decided to set up an Internet-based company. His background as a systems analyst applying leading-edge computer technologies in business and an MBA provided a solid foundation. However, it was an article on Jeff Bezos of amazon.com that inspired him to act on his long held desire to run a firm of his own. He quit his job and started planning an application of the Internet to the courier industry.

While he was working at home on this plan, a local buyers cooperative delivered a box of greengroceries. These cooperatives originated as informal associations of friends and neighbours who pooled their orders for groceries and purchased in bulk from the wholesale fruit and vegetable markets. Benefits were lower prices from bulk purchases, lower overheads than grocery shops (many operate from home out of the garage) and fresher produce.

Supermarket companies purchase produce from wholesale markets, send it to distribution centres and then forward it to stores where it may be kept for several days before being offered for sale. The produce is handled during distribution and by customers. Each night unsold produce is taken from the shelves and stored in cool rooms, to prolong the shelf life. Supermarket buyers recognize the need to purchase produce that will withstand handling and will not spoil too quickly. Some producers artificially ripen their fruit so it appears attractive and ready to eat although it is still hard and able to endure handling. Wastage and spoiling is estimated to represent between 5% and 10% of the costs of a greengrocer.

In October 1997, GreenGrocer commenced selling fresh fruit and vegetables and now supplies more than 600 products including bread, dairy products, fresh meats, seafood, prepared foods such as salads and, in December, Christmas trees. The firm is privately owned. Revenue for the calendar year 2000 was an estimated A$20 million. Monthly growth rates have been between 10% and 50%, with an average of 20% since startup. Growth could have been faster with greater expenditure on marketing through a public float but Douglas preferred to rely on private funding. There are currently 135 full-time staff, mostly packers and drivers.

Business Model

GreenGrocer initially sought to apply a simple Internet retailing business model of holding no inventory and receiving payments for customer orders before the firm purchased the products (as originally implemented by Amazon). Douglas considered that the specific industry for his venture was of less importance. The real challenge came in analysing how well fresh produce fitted with Internet-based processes and how the Internet could be leveraged to improve the products and services to support a successful business model. The plan was to use the Internet to provide an integrated solution and to automate as many of the business processes as possible. Buying the products only after they had been sold meant no risk in decision-making about what to buy or what might sell. Wastage and spoilage could be reduced to a minimum.

The simple e-tailing business model extended beyond decision-making and cash flow to include reductions in operating costs resulting from shortening the supply chain, i.e. by by-passing the grocery store. Douglas finessed this model by focusing on premium level produce and by providing high levels of service. He recognized an opportunity to facilitate the flow of information from growers to consumers that had been lost with supermarkets. Most stores make little attempt to educate customers about products, e.g. a supermarket would not place a sign above a bin of apples saying that they are not a good buy at present. GreenGrocer can do so, explaining when is the best time to purchase seasonal varieties.

Implementing the Business Model

The business model has remained the same from the beginning—but the implementation has changed substantially. The original plan was to keep fixed costs down by outsourcing core functions. They did not want to hire people for IT, buying, packing groceries or making deliveries. However, outsourcing these functions proved to be a disaster.

Development of the first website was done externally between March and October 1997. This met the initial requirements for functionality, however the cost of making changes was greater than the cost of hiring an experienced programmer. The lack of responsiveness by the developer in making the changes was also a major issue.

Discovering that premium quality produce is often not available in the markets to the general public, Douglas pursued acquisitions and partnerships in Sydney and Melbourne with firms that supply leading restaurants. These firms buy produce for GreenGrocer. Bulk purchases are carried to a rented warehouse where packers wrap each piece of produce in tissue paper and place each order in a sturdy box or refrigerated container.

The distribution function was a catastrophe. Perishable products are time and location sensitive. They cannot just be left around anywhere. Experience with three different courier firms led to the conclusion that the best courier firms available simply did not understand the concept of customer service. Drivers did not follow delivery instructions (e.g. place the box around the back of the house or put it in the shade), they threw boxes around so the produce was damaged. One driver even insisted to a customer: 'You should go to a store to purchase your groceries!'

As GreenGrocer's product range expanded, few courier firms had capacity for refrigerated products (dairy foods and seafood). Analysis showed that the volume was sufficient for economies of scale to be available if the firm did its own deliveries. Delivery costs (ranging between A$3.50 and A$6) are absorbed by the firm in their minimum charge of A$25 per order.

Now all core functions are in-house. There were few business concerns about the project. The business model for perishable foods worked. Numbers were on a low scale—100 orders each day was profitable. However, the subsequent necessity to grow the company more rapidly than self-financing would support has led to some dilution of equity.

Industry, Competitor and Environmental Analysis

GreenGrocer operates in the grocery retailing industry. The major difference between this and other industries is size—food and grocery is the largest retail industry with more than A\$50 billion annual sales in Australia. The retail industry as a whole is characterized by low margins, high turnover, small orders and regular purchases. Food is one of the largest periodic household purchases.

Among pure Internet retailers, with 500–600 orders daily GreenGrocer is one of the largest. The major national grocery chains, Woolworths and Coles, are now implementing Internet operations and must also be seen as competitors.

The traditional mindset of grocers—increased profitability comes from paying lower prices to their producers and suppliers through bulk purchases—is, perhaps, not conducive to increased expenditure on IT. Douglas's analysis suggested that established grocery firms were comparatively poor at using IT effectively and efficiently to reduce costs and to provide better services for their customers. The question of whether the major retailers in Australia can utilize the Internet more effectively remains unanswered at this stage.

Environmental issues were analysed to identify potential drivers of innovation, e.g. levels of competition, uncertainty, etc. The most severe competitive threats for GreenGrocer are issues of price and quality. Differentiation is based on product quality and levels of service. Competitor actions and customer demands are relatively predictable. Therefore, there were no identified imperatives for innovation. The major drivers for establishment of the firm were not related to issues within the grocery retailing industry.

Key Business Drivers and Threats

So what has to go right for the business to succeed? Douglas says, 'Seriously, everything!' Market positioning (to find the site) has to work well and be easy to use. Payment, order processing, logistics and order fulfilment and delivery must all work perfectly. If any part fails, then they stand to lose the customer unless the customer service staff can make a positive out of the negative.

Internet startups are seen to have an advantage. A major difficulty for traditional business is that they are not set up to be cross-functional.

'Internet retailing is brutally cross-functional with marketing, IT, distribution, logistics all needing to be absolutely synchronized' (CEO.)

If customers' expectations are not met, then it is so easy just to click onto a competitor's site. Success factors are the best marketing, perfect product and very good service.

The greatest threats facing the firm and industry would be an international competitor entering the local market or local competitors getting it right. It generally takes about two years for a firm to develop its site and functionality to the level of being serious competition. The quality component of the firm's products and services give some protection. There are few apparent threats at an industry level, although if the security of Internet transactions became an impediment or if online payment methods came under suspicion, then these could be problems for the industry.

Innovation Factors and Processes

The most important factors that led to this project were:

1. The principal's long-standing determination to set up and run his own company.
2. The principal's professional interest in the Internet from technical and business perspectives.
3. The principal was inspired by an article on Jeff Bezos of amazon.com and thought 'this is for me'!
4. The principal's background. He has an MBA and experience as an IT professional in business. His father's experience as a venture capitalist helped identify key business questions and facilitated private funding. The preparation of full strategic and business plans indicated that the concept was viable.
5. The identification of fruit and vegetables as the vehicle. and low barriers to entry. Anyone can go to the wholesale markets and buy produce. It was originally thought that experience, warehouses or industry expertise were not needed. Even without these the firm has grown at an average of 20% monthly.
6. Having carefully analysed international success stories in Internet retailing, Douglas's final reason for selecting the greengroceries sector was that perishable products require local operations and so were protected from global competitors.

Only one major barrier to success was identified: technological capability. The principal wanted to use a Microsoft platform but at that time no service provider would host this software. He ended up with the original web developer running the server from a bedroom in his house. This may appear a modest barrier compared with other issues involved in setting up a firm with an untested business model in a dynamic environment. However, it must be remembered that the principal had both qualifications and experience in technology and business and had a venture capitalist father. Therefore, all steps in the project were formally identified, rigorously assessed and carefully planned. The wild-card factor—technology capability—was the only issue not able to be prepared for and so was considered the greatest barrier.

The innovation processes were:

1. Inspiration from amazon.com
2. Resigned career as a business analyst
3. Commenced looking at Internet-based business opportunities
4. Prepared business and strategic plans
5. Identified fruit and vegetables as the vehicle
6. Specified, designed and had website developed. Arranged for hosting
7. Hired a buyer, rented warehouse space, employed a courier company
8. Commenced business

Website Development and Operational Issues

The Microsoft package used required modifications since, initially, off-the-shelf software for processing Internet orders had a separate page for ordering each product. This is because it originated from an information-rich sector (e.g. books) that benefited from detailed information on each product (e.g. author, title, synopsis, reviews). This level of detail was unnecessary for an information-poor commodity sector dealing with potatoes and tomatoes. The software needed to be modified to produce a shopping list for each order. This highlights the lesson that different websites need different functionality reflecting the requirements of different products. All the IT work is now done in-house.

Website Features

Evaluation of the website (see Table 2.1) shows that transaction-related functions are well developed but suggests that more details on the company and its operations would be well regarded by customers. A high percentage of customers were satisfied with the site (see below). Customer recommendations for improvement of the site relate to products and services. Since GreenGrocer's business model emphasizes service and customer relationship management it is anticipated that innovations in support of these areas will be introduced. Innovation (or lack of it) is a significant area of exposure to future competition.

Currently there is close to 100% integration for all business systems and operations. GreenGrocer uses standard software packages but all are integrated. The accounting system will be integrated within three months. Real time inventory is generated by computer (also packing slips, routing, etc.) and all operations are fully linked, e.g. can monitor in real time what is happening in Melbourne. It is easy to say that competitors could duplicate these standard systems, but nothing in business is easy. The challenges involved to get it all right should not be underestimated.

The system is considered by the CEO to be a success. The system is the business. Success measures are sales growth and customer satisfaction (determined by the number of complaints received by e-mail compared with the number of orders).

Customer Surveys

GreenGrocer's customer profile represents a specific niche, predominantly aged 31–45 years (63%), female (78%), professional (59%), university graduate (63%), living in a major city (83%) with above average (40%) or more than twice the national average (34%) salary. Customers access the Internet daily (69%), from home (67%) and are experienced web shoppers (60% having purchased more than 11 times).

Apart from groceries, customers use the Internet for banking (54%) and to buy books, flowers and tickets for personal (63%) or a mixture of personal and work use. As may be expected with a food retailer, a high percentage of customers are repeat shoppers with 29% purchasing between 2–5 times, 22% 6–10 times and 24% having bought from this site more than 11 times.

The most important factors in deciding to buy from this grocery site were convenience (72%) and the quality of the produce (7%), although one customer responded simply 'broken leg—hunger'. Greatest barriers to deciding to purchase were concerns about security (26%), uncertainty about products/ services and concerns about delivery of the food produce.

The purchasing process was considered very easy (66%) or easy (20%). Customers were very satisfied (63%) or satisfied (32%) with the Internet as a whole and very satisfied (76%) or satisfied (20%) with this site. An extremely high percentage of customers (86%) would purchase again from the site and 43% would purchase again from other sites. More than 89% of customers would recommend the site to others even though they sought improvements in the site in the range of products (50%), price, speed of loading and more details on products and services.

The Future

GreenGrocer sees the biggest challenges to firms in future use of the Internet retailing as:

1. Managing integration. Managing a holistic, integrated solution to business. There is the need to 'rip the guts' out of an existing business to achieve the level of real time integration required.
2. If you get it right, then needing to manage the growth. Having a scalable solution.
3. Needing to have a full service solution on your website. This means you need to jump into e-commerce with both feet. Companies that do a test and

a pilot are doomed to failure since a pilot cannot be both fully functional and fully integrated. Therefore a pilot is rarely successful. Companies often cancel the pilot, comfortable with the knowledge that the Internet is not a success and are happy to get out of it.

Advice for other firms seeking to develop an Internet service is: not to underestimate what it takes, and the perception is that it is easy. An integrated approach is very difficult and very expensive. There is a need to focus on making the business more efficient in logistics, supply chain, and information flow. More important than having good ideas is how those ideas are implemented.

Conclusion

The GreenGrocer experience emphasizes the importance of relevant experience in the principal(s), careful business planning and flexibility in implementation. A clear vision of the potential competitive advantage for the firm, the capability to implement a profitable business model and the ability to experiment with and to revise the means of implementing that model as the company develops expertise were all seen to be critical to success.

Postscript. In December 2000 the nation's second largest supermarket chain purchased 38% of GreenGrocer. The company expanded its range of supermarket products. In October 2001 the remaining equity was acquired for A$7 million.

WINEPLANET—'FIRST TO GLOBAL MARKET?'
(wineplanet.com.au)

Introduction

Lawyer Mark Mezrani (CEO) and wine writer/consultant Rob Walters founded WINEPLANET in June 1998. Mark's first foray into wine retailing began with his purchase of a Sydney retail chain, Camperdown Cellars, out of receivership in 1993. He managed expansion of the group to seven retail outlets. Retaining just one of the stores and the corporate business, the rest of the group was sold to establish WINEPLANET.

Rob's concept of a content-rich online wine shop provided the vision for WINEPLANET. He had Internet experience as a wine specialist for NINEMSN (Australia's most visited website). Rob recognized that retail outlets were generally not meeting customers' expectations for advice and expert knowledge on wine. Adding information to the transaction cycle would enhance the B2C purchase experience and provide strong product and brand differentiation. The website's content would be authoritative, up to date, flexible and responsive. The site would not be restricted to text but could include video and audio materials. This vision has been well implemented. In 1999 the website won several national awards.

From its Sydney head office, the firm delivers to all states of Australia, mostly to the state capitals. WINEPLANET has been publicly listed since September 1998. The firm has substantial reserves from its listing and its financial stability was further enhanced in February 1999 when the Fosters group purchased 25%. The firm has more than 110 staff. Reported revenues for 2000 were A$14.6 million of which an increasing percentage (currently about 75% of total monthly revenue) is from online sales and advertising. Since its September 2000 launch in the United Kingdom the firm claims to be the world's largest online wine distributor.

Business Models

WINEPLANET has implemented an intricate web of business models designed to establish itself as the first global wine brand in the Internet sector. These include retail (online and offline) with market segmentation (wine lover and mass market), community development, commission marketing to the community, on-site advertising, affiliate sales (paying 2%–5% of sales to customers coming from other websites), and media commerce (purchasing/commissioning text, audio and video and, potentially, packaging for sale).

Bottled wines may be standard products but WINEPLANET is not a standard retailer. The firm sells more than 6000 wines, a very large stock. Apart from range, the main differentiation is in the provision of services. WINEPLANET provides logistics, delivery and customer services in a call centre. Two main types of B2C services are generally available in the wine market, catalogue and content, and the company does both in an integrated way.

The WINEPLANET brand is important and being first to market in April 1999 has helped to establish the brand. The firm has developed a 30 000-member community that is strategically important. Apart from providing information and special wine offers (sometimes for commission), WINEPLANET encourages members' reviews of wines, comments and discussion and allows members to store details of their own cellars (including tasting notes) on the firm's systems. There is an additional customer base of more than 80 000 regular purchasers, defined as customers who store their credit card details with the site and who have purchased more than three times in the past 12 months.

Chasing revenue and growth, in November 1999 the firm diversified into beer and spirits. The local wine market has annual revenues of A$3 billion, spirits A$1.6 billion and beverages A$13 billion. The company's focus was similarly broadened and at that time sought to become the ultimate food and liquor portal in Australia. Six months later, with the UK launch well advanced, the corporate aims were refocused to offering the ultimate wine and related products site and to being the pre-eminent source of discussion and information on wine and related products.

The firm views the inseparable core issues in e-commerce to be logistics and customer service. Its initial concept of a firm holding core stock only and ordering additional products from distributors after sale to customers was not well received by distributors. This was not considered a major problem since the firm has come to realize that online companies need to control the whole customer service cycle.

WINEPLANET has introduced an express delivery service with a core range of products (200 wines, spirits, beer, and soft drinks). Costs of deliveries can easily become a problem for an online retailer. The firm offers free delivery for orders over A$120 (A$9 for orders under A$120) to major cities and nearby areas. A small handling fee of A$9 applies to orders of two bottles or less. The corporate business has always been delivered with orders being received by phone and fax. Business-to-business sales and customer service are supported by a telephone call centre.

Industry, Competitor and Environmental Analysis

WINEPLANET sees itself as being in three industries—Internet retailing, wine and media. There are different challenges in each industry. However, the focus is on wine, a very established and very traditional industry. WINEPLANET was first to market as an online wine retailer. The firm's successful on-line services are helping to introduce change, but the industry has been slow to understand and adopt e-commerce. Some major wine retailers are reported to have responded adversely to the Fosters Group purchasing a strategic share holding (25%) in the firm by boycotting products from Fosters' wine producers.

The use of IT in the wine industry has been very limited until recently, except for stock management. When WINEPLANET sought to provide a content-rich site the firm requested additional details from wine suppliers. Many suppliers initially hand-wrote the product details and faxed them. The potential of e-commerce, particularly for B2B, and the introduction of the new goods and services tax provided the impetus for suppliers to utilize IT more extensively. The Internet has led to the firm having relationships with many competitors and all are learning together and working to increase the size of the online market.

The company rates price as being only a moderately important factor but states none the less that 'Our policy is to offer the best wine prices in Australia.' Quality is seen to be very important, but there is a segmented market for consumers with price, convenience, quality and service all being rated highly. Other factors, e.g. declining demand or scarce supply, are considered of little significance.

The United States is the most likely source of international competition but has complicated regulations governing alcohol sales. Liquor laws are determined at a state and county level. Some US states do not allow home delivery. Other states require customers to be 21 years of age and to present two forms of ID to receive delivery. Therefore, the legal environment is seen to be a constraint on the development of a successful national wine retailer in the United States.

Key Business Drivers and Threats

The key business drivers are: to be clear in priorities (you cannot do everything), to do the right things well, to learn from customers and their needs (gain feedback and provide timely response), to learn from competitors, and to secure adequate funds for expansion. The greatest perceived threat at present is a limitation on the firm's growth by the current size of the online wine market. There is a need to grow the online wine market faster so the firm can grow more quickly. This requires increased customer and supplier awareness of e-commerce. A major threat to the industry could be if the perceived quality of Australian wine was to fall.

Customers' demands and tastes are relatively unpredictable since customer demographics are constantly changing. Initial online sales had high bottle price, high order value and virtually all customers were male. Now, the average customer's purchase price and order size are dropping and sales to females are rising. Online sales are different to store sales. Cask wine is still the largest wine category by volume sold in Australia but its online sales are negligible. WINEPLANET's newly introduced express delivery service for wine, beer, spirits and soft drinks is likely to change the demographics again.

Innovation Factors and Processes

The most important factor that led to WINEPLANET was the perceived business opportunity. Rob recognized the potential for B2C e-commerce in the wine industry. He convinced Mark and both developed a business case that received financial backing for setup. The founders recognized that they could not 'just put a toe in the water' but had to establish a business with a fully functional website and order fulfilment process.

Formal strategic business plans were prepared. Strategic planning is undertaken quarterly with value being added monthly since the market is dynamic and there is a need to be able to react quickly. Major obstacles that had to be overcome were:

1. The viability of the concept. Initially, it seemed like 'a hare-brained idea'. The lack of wine-related role models in Australia and internationally raised questions about its viability.
2. Lack of assistance. Technology companies were still learning at the same time so were of limited assistance in determining the best ways to proceed.
3. Current business practice. The firm proposed some very different and challenging business practices for the wine industry, e.g. delivery of small orders from distributors directly to customers rather than delivering to WINEPLANET.
4. Order fulfilment. The necessity to have its own trucks and drivers (and eventually to set up its own warehousing in each capital city) in order to provide full levels of service.

The decision-making processes were:

1. Determining the business case.
2. Obtaining private funding for setup.

3. Obtaining public funding for the longer term. The firm was listed publicly 'through the backdoor', i.e. through a mining company in July 1998 as Mogul wines. The IPO was in September 1998. In February 1999, the Fosters Group purchased 25%.
4. From October 1998 to April 1999 a beta site was made available to the wine industry to test customer and industry acceptance of the concept. The 1999 Wine Australia event (B2B and B2C) provided exposure to 30 000 people and showcased the site. The site went live on 15 April 1999.

The major business concern about the project was the high level of risk. The only way to test the vision was to do everything necessary. This required total commitment and full business implementation.

Internet Development Activities

Initially the firm used external IT resources. The web designer was in Sydney and a company in Melbourne developed the database management system (DBMS). Today, program design and basic coding are undertaken in-house with a staff of four programmers. In-house IT is cheaper and has greater flexibility. The ERP Oracle Financials is the platform for all systems.

The first development took two months. During this time of testing in industry (October 1998–April 1999) version 2 was developed. A lot was learned during the test period. Version 2 was launched in April 1999 with very sophisticated functionality and a catalogue of 3000 wines. This version had full transaction capability plus information on products, images, and navigation by purchases and information. Consumers could review each wine, the first facilities for the community were established and customers could provide feedback. The website was sophisticated because of Rob's vision and because they found ways to do what they wanted. One expressed advantage of being first to market was in not knowing what 'could not' be done.

Version 3 was released in April 2000. This had an enhanced look and feel and there were more shops (not just wine). By then the firm had learnt how to better direct customer traffic and sales and how to better combine content and commerce. Video material provides information but is essentially a sales and marketing tool. Under each product there are suggested purchases (if you like this you might like these wines at a range of prices). Future developments include: food, gifts, books and other wine-related services.

The level of capability to implement the business plan determines the level of internal satisfaction with the site. Rob's philosophy is: If you're going to do anything then you must do it well. The site also needed to offer tools to help customers make more informed decisions and to enable them to interact with other wine lovers.

Website Implementation and Operation

Many difficulties arose with implementation but mostly these came from a lack of experience. Neither Rob nor Mark had directed technical teams. Extensive testing was undertaken but often errors did not arise until launch. The version 2 site was very complex and there were many routes through the site. Part of the planning was the decision to use a relational database as a platform for all developments. This was an important decision because it enabled on-going integration of all business functions.

Operationally there are many potential problems, but WINEPLANET has managed to anticipate and to cope with them.

Website Features

Evaluation of the website (see Table 2.1) shows a very high rating for this national award-winning site. Details on the company and its operations are presented at the highest level. Transaction and customer services are also well established. Further innovation in support of additional customer services would be well regarded by customers. Innovation (or lack of it) is a significant area of exposure to future competition.

Initially, the firm used a liquor industry standard package that provided less than 50% integration of the business systems. The Oracle Financials ERP, implemented in July 2000 for the new national goods and services tax, provides 100% integration of the website with the company's back-end system and streamlining of all business processes (including stock control, order entry management, customer fulfilment and financial reporting). The system also provides the capability for the company to more easily access a range of marketing information relating to its customer database and, as a result, market more effectively to its online community. Increasingly, data mining is being conducted to determine when and where people shop, e.g. many purchase from work so that sales at the weekends are slow.

The system is considered to be a success as determined by growth in traffic, members, sales and customer satisfaction. Brand recognition and recognition of WINEPLANET by other industries, e.g. as a case study on how to progress with e-commerce, customer retention and repeat purchases (building loyalty) are all-important indicators of success.

Consumer Perspectives

WINEPLANET's customer profile is changing as it adds different product lines and an express delivery service. However, currently it is: aged 31–45 years (41%) with 21–30 years (33%), male (66%), professional (70%), university graduate (65%) living in a major city (79%) and affluent, with above average (36%) or more than twice the national average (45%) salary. Customers access the Internet daily (80%), from home (52%) or work and are experienced with web shoppers (50% having purchased more than 11 times, 27% 6–10 times and 15% 2–5 times).

Apart from wine, the firm's customers use the Internet for buying books (57%), banking services, music CDs, tickets and computer products for personal (63%) use. Only 30% of customers visited the site to purchase a specific product (26% were comparing prices) and 45% purchased on their first visit. The site is successfully attracting new (37% not having purchased from the site before) and retaining existing customers. Most customers came to the site due to prior knowledge of the firm (47%) and personal referral.

The most important factors in deciding to buy from this wine site were convenience (36%), availability of products, the product range and price. Being a nation-wide firm was an advantage. The greatest barriers to deciding to purchase were concerns about delivery (17%), completing the purchase procedures and security.

The purchasing process was considered very easy (47%) or easy (30%). Customers were very satisfied (53%) or satisfied (38%) with the Internet as a whole and very satisfied (53%) or satisfied (36%) with this site. A very high 70% would definitely purchase again from the site and 46% would purchase again from other sites. More than 67% of customers would recommend the site to others even though they sought improvements in the site in price, more products, speed of loading and ease of use.

The Future

The biggest challenges for the future are:

1. Logistics
2. Customer service
3. The high level of competition; leaders are expected to emerge
4. Small market size; online sales are still only a small part of the total national and international wine market and will take time to become mainstream
5. The downturn in the technology stock market inhibits new competitors and may result in some online firms failing but may also increase customer concerns about online retailing
6. Fulfilling promises
7. Making sales

The firm acknowledges that many of these challenges are generic rather than being specific to online retailing. Future changes in Internet services are anticipated. The core business is wine but services will not be limited to wine. The ultimate wine experience includes food, glassware, food and wine-books, wine-related travel, etc. Extending the geographical reach is another avenue for future development.

If facing the same decision (to develop an Internet presence) today, the firm would be better informed about many things. Data mining has helped to identify when and where people shop. Now there are clear leaders in technology areas (e.g. object forms) but then these were not well known. The firm has tried to balance keeping up with the Internet and doing things properly, and that will not change.

Advice for firms seeking to develop an Internet service is not to go into e-commerce just because everyone else is. Firms need to have a clear vision, ideas and a means to implement their plans. E-commerce may not be appropriate for every type of business. Being on the Internet by itself is not enough; you need a business proposition to attract and to keep customers. The key business principles remain unchanged whether online or offline—these are logistics and customer service.

Conclusion

WINEPLANET demonstrates the importance for an Internet startup of properly understanding the role of the Internet. The founders saw a business opportunity to use information delivered by the Internet as a potential source of strategic advantage. However, success would come not from the Internet but from the capability of the business to cost-effectively provide products for customers attracted by value-added, Internet-enabled services. As the first to market in a traditional industry, WINEPLANET experienced scepticism, lack of knowledge and supplier resistance. In overcoming these restraints, the firm rapidly outgrew its original target market. Future growth is based on broadening the range of products and services and extending the firm's reach internationally.

Postscript. In May 2001, WINEPLANET was acquired by its minority shareholder Fosters Group. At the time of purchase the firm had cash reserves equivalent to the purchase price. Fosters stated its action was in response to boycotts of its wines by Australian retailers who did not appreciate competition from the online retailer. WINEPLANET's fulfilment capabilities were to be applied to Fosters' international wine club sales.

CHAPTER CONCLUSION

The firms profiled illustrate a variety of successful implementations of Internet retailing that have been developed from a diverse set of motivations.

Drivers

The most important motivating factors that led to these successful Internet initiatives were:

- The experiences of amazon.com were both a threat that directly influenced a book seller to establish an Internet operation and an inspiration resulting in a grocery startup (Dymocks and GreenGrocer).

- The perceived business opportunity to use information delivered by the Internet as a potential source of strategic advantage (GreenGrocer and WINEPLANET).
- The perceived business opportunity to use the Internet to provide a low-cost superstore with a very large product range (E-Store).
- The perceived once-in-a-generation opportunity to establish an entirely new type of business (E-Store) or an opportunity to establish own business with a very specific business model and implementation (GreenGrocer).
- The perceived opportunity to use technology to drive a restructuring of the industry, not initially a business opportunity (Chaos). Label companies' control of music distribution was seen to restrain access by new bands to the market.
- The preservation of business. Dymocks' major motivation was a defensive reaction to the potential threat of Amazon and the subsequent necessity for the business to learn about Internet technology. The venture was not consistent with any part of the strategic business plan; there was no formal business proposal and no anticipation of making money.
- The founders had experience and understanding of a business role for the Internet beyond novelty (Chaos, Dymocks, E-Store, GreenGrocer and WINEPLANET).

Inhibitors

The most important barriers to be overcome were:

- Uncertainty about the Internet. The greatest obstacle to be overcome for the project to be a success was a lack of understanding at board level and with major business partners of the Internet's strategic implications (Dymocks).
- A lack of knowledge, initially about how the Internet could best be used, then technical, design and skill issues (how to do it, what worked, acquiring the skills required!) (Chaos, Dymocks, E-Store, GreenGrocer, WINEPLANET).
- Finance/funding (Chaos, Dymocks, WINEPLANET).
- Supplier resistance at various levels was experienced. This ranged from declining to provide products to purely online operations (Chaos) to supplier scepticism and reluctance to deliver directly to customers (E-Store, WINEPLANET). GreenGrocer had to enter into partnerships to obtain access to premium produce.

Inhibitors arising after operations commenced include:

- The necessity to revise and expand the initial business models, strategies, products and markets in response to early experiences (Chaos, E-Store, GreenGrocer, WINEPLANET).
- The firm rapidly outgrowing its original target market (WINEPLANET).
- The necessity to bring core functions in-house due to unsatisfactory experiences (GreenGrocer).

- Outsourcing core functions to obtain best practice levels of performance (Chaos).
- Channel conflicts. These arose directly between Dymocks and its franchisees and indirectly with WINEPLANET where traditional retailers reduced their stocks of a major wine producer's products after it had purchased 25% of the online firm.

Overcoming scepticism, lack of knowledge, lack of funding, supplier resistance, fulfilment catastrophes, channel conflict and outgrown markets, these firms have persisted and refined their business models and operations. A determination to find a way to success is an observable characteristic common to all of the firms.

While these motivating and inhibiting innovation factors were identified by the firms as being most important, they need to be considered within the broader context. Perceived business opportunities arise due to favourable environmental, organizational and consumer contexts, not through ignorance of these areas. A more detailed examination of Internet innovation may be found in Chapter 9.

3
Internet Retailing in Denmark

NIELS BJØRN-ANDERSEN

INTRODUCTION

Denmark is a small, relatively homogeneous, urbanized, Scandinavian country with a population of 5.3 million and a tradition of adopting new IT-based services. Electronic bank transfer of payments, salaries transferred from employer to banks, direct debit cards for shopping and check-less electronic clearing between banks were available and used for the majority of transactions from the mid 1970s.

From the late 1990s Danes and Danish companies have adopted the Internet to a high degree. Denmark's Internet user profile is mature with 52.5% of users more than 35 years old (the largest category is 33% aged 35–49) and largely male. Only 37.7% of users are women (NetValue 2000). Denmark is among the leading countries for use of home PCs, access to the Internet and mobile communications (ITU 2000) although behind the United States in the uptake of business-to-consumer (B2C) sales. Online turnover in Denmark was around 1% of the total retail trade in 2000 and is 2% in 2001 in spite of the setback for dotcoms.

Official government policy is very strongly in favor of supporting IT in general and Internet-based commerce in particular. In the speech to the nation on 31 December 2000, the Danish Prime Minister, Poul Nyrup Rasmussen, said:

> I envision a Danish society that is the world leading IT nation in 2003. This is not an impossible dream. All Danish citizens need to have access to the Internet and the possibility of having an e-mail account. The public sector needs to be at the cutting edge with regards to exploiting IT.

This is more than an 'empty' vision statement. It is followed by a large number of initiatives from liberalizing the telecom market, pushing legislation (e.g. electronic signature), increasing IT education and supporting innovators/ entrepreneurs to enforce procurement portals for the total public sector. Every year the Minister of Research and Information Technology reports to parliament about Denmark's progress as an information society. Political initiatives often use the public sector as an engine to push Internet and IT adoption.

Overview of Firms

The selection of the five cases for this study was not easy. The two most highly profiled Danish B2C websites, toycity.com (toys marketed at discounted prices in all European countries) and gubi.com (high profile branded apparel sold at recommended retail prices in all European markets from a so-called 'life-style' site), were initially selected. Both had received e-commerce prizes in Denmark and had a lot of public support. However, they lacked the management and business skills and funding to cope with the technology turndown and in the spring of 2000 both companies went into receivership and have subsequently closed.

The Danish companies examined come from five very different sectors: clothing (haburi.com), software (ravenholm.dk), travel (rejsefeber.dk), books (saxo.dk) and building materials (velux). Three were startups (Haburi, Rejsefeber and Saxo) and two were online innovations from traditional firms (Ravenholm and Velux).

Haburi was a new venture that managed to obtain funding in the spring of 2000 in spite of the bleak business prospects at that time. They created a virtual factory outlet mall for fashion clothing and accessories on the Internet. The firm had a presence in most European countries with Denmark and United Kingdom being the largest markets. They received the Danish e-commerce prize in 2001.

Ravenholm was the first firm in Denmark to sell shrink-wrapped software to their business-to-business (B2B) and B2C customers. Their advantage from being first to market vanished when they failed to maintain the momentum of innovation and lost customers to competitors who had introduced a new generation of web solutions.

Rejsefeber was a leading site selling third-party travel tickets online. Originally part of one of the largest portals; Scandinavia Online, it is now independent. Rejsefeber received the Danish e-commerce prize in 1999.

Saxo was originally established as a joint initiative by the two largest Danish book publishers. It was intended as a virtual bookstore selling books at the recommended retail price plus packaging and postage. Saxo was to be the focus of a community of intellectuals writing, reviewing, buying and reading books. The collapse of this dream led to Saxo's absorption by a company owning a freely distributed Sunday newspaper and a new, rigorous business approach.

The last case, Velux, is a global company producing skylights and roof windows in 13 countries, selling these in 43 countries and employing 5700 staff. Traditionally they have been in the B2B market only selling their products through architects, retailers and building contractors. However, Velux felt at a competitive disadvantage because they were too far removed from their ultimate customer, the consumer. Velux has also won an award from a national newspaper for its website.

HABURI—THE VIRTUAL FACTORY OUTLET[1] (haburi.dk)

Introduction

This case focuses on an organization that introduced a new market concept to the Internet. Haburi profiled itself as the first virtual factory outlet mall for fashion clothing and accessories on the Internet. As a result of the stock market crisis during 2000, many Internet companies experienced difficulties in obtaining investment capital after April 2000. However, Haburi was able to secure significant investment capital, due to its well-designed business model and experienced management staff. The firm was founded in Denmark in April 2000. At the end of 2000 the company was present in 15 European countries and employed around 30 people at the time of the launch. Haburi's major business sites were located in Denmark, Sweden, Germany, the Netherlands, and the United Kingdom.

The first rough draft of Haburi's business and IT strategy was first developed at the end of 1999, and the company was launched online in less than 180 days following the decision to proceed with the project. The three founders of Haburi; Michael Vad, Ulla Brokenhuus-Schack and Michael Aagaard, insisted on keeping the stated launch date, although most Internet startup organizations frequently postpone the launch more than once to perfect the website technologies. Michael Vad, Chief Executive Officer, believed that the main reason for most organizations to postpone the launch was that they were trying to develop immaculate technologies. Instead, they lost sight of what was really important throughout this process—meeting the public's expectations.

Haburi launched with much work yet to be completed even though Michael Vad stressed the importance of a well-designed and functional website. Owing to devastating experiences by other Internet startup organizations (e.g. boo.com and toycity.com), Haburi decided to create a website without any complex user-intrusive technologies. Before the Haburi startup the three founders investigated the possibility of creating a physical outlet mall. However, throughout the research process they realized that it would be more advantageous to pursue the more flexible Internet market-place instead of the static features of the physical outlet mall. Extensive research showed that the average factory outlet shopper would have to drive for 90 minutes both ways to reach the physical outlet mall. Another contributing factor in the pursuit of the virtual factory outlet project

---

[1] The case write-up was conducted by Ann M. Olsson, CBS research assistant.

was the increase in the growth of factory outlets across Europe, and particularly in the United Kingdom. The final contributing factor to the launch of the Haburi project was their finding that brand suppliers cleared at least 15% of their stock through factory outlets during the year 2000.

It was very difficult to secure the financial support for an Internet startup company[2] during the year 2000. None the less, due to Haburi's professional preparations, operations and well-stated business plan, the company managed to acquire sufficient investment capital. In June 2000, Haburi closed its second round of investment capital and obtained a total capital investment of 13.8 million euros.[3] The following organizations were part of the investment group that provided the second round of capital injection into the firm: Venture IT, Magasin, Tryg Baltica, Uniinvest, Venture Partners, and 2M Invest.

> It is our objective to offer our customers high quality fashion brands at the lowest possible prices—Haburi Mission Statement.

Haburi made an effort to place the customer in focus from day one, which was apparent when viewing the firm's mission statement. Haburi's ability to focus on the customer provided it with a turnover of 2.7 million euros for the first seven months. Michael Vad estimated that Haburi would obtain an approximate turnover of 13.4 million euros in 2001.

Environmental Issues

Haburi was part of the retail industry and, more specifically, the clothing and accessories segment of the industry. This segment could be divided into three major sections: offline, online and mixed (these are organizations who are present both online and offline). Haburi was classified as a pure online clothing and accessories organization, in view of the fact that the vast majority of its business was conducted online. However, Haburi did not define itself as a regular online clothing and accessories organization, because there was one aspect differentiating it from traditional online retailing. The firm benefited greatly when other retail organizations failed to predict the demand for the period. On the other hand, it attained a poor result when its suppliers estimated their product sales correctly, since Haburi then experienced difficulties building a critical mass of products. Consequently, Haburi viewed itself as being highly affected by the threat of scarce supply, though only moderately affected by other external threats.

---

[2] NASDAQ, primarily consisting of technology-heavy organizations, plunged 40% during the year 2000. This made the American venture capitalists more reluctant to invest in promising Internet companies, and made it more difficult to obtain investment capital in the Danish market.
[3] The conversion rate (746.69 euros) from Danish Kroner (DKr) to euros was obtained from Unibank's website on 22 January 2001.

It was difficult to define the specific competitors that Haburi encountered within the retailing industry. If one considered all retail organizations (on and offline) offering similar products (fashion clothing and accessories), the competition was fierce. The main reasons for the highly competitive business environment was the high turnover rate of products in the industry and the high similarity among the products offered in the clothing and accessory industry (i.e. the organizations in the industry were competing for the same customers).

Conversely, if one only considered the competition within the virtual factory outlet segment, there was essentially no competition worth mentioning. Although Haburi was first to market as a virtual factory outlet mall, there were many traditional gigantic organizations holding a large portion of the clothing and accessories market share, which Haburi was aspiring to acquire.

Business Model

Haburi constructed its organization and business model with the focus on both the upstream and the downstream relationships within the value chain. The most crucial task during the initial pre-launch phase was to establish a reliable relationship with the brand suppliers. This was not an easy challenge, since the organizations were very protective of the image of their brand names. Yet, Haburi succeeded in convincing some of the most exquisite brands in the market to clear their stock through its website. DKNY, Calvin Klein, Cerrutti, Valentino and Marlboro Classic were just a few organizations supplying products to Haburi's website. Michael Vad was confident that Haburi would obtain more than 50 brand suppliers within 12 months of operations.

Haburi's approach of clearing its suppliers' stock had two major advantages. First, Haburi provided a virtual marketplace where suppliers could control the clearing of their stock. To enable suppliers to observe this process, Haburi created an *Extranet* feature that allowed the companies to view which products were moving well. Secondly, Haburi provided a 'safe' market-place for these exquisite brand names to clear their stock. The brand suppliers traditionally cleared their stock in countries such as Poland, however, sometimes this backfired and the merchandise had a tendency to return to its initial market.

Downstream, Haburi has realized the great importance of a strong relationship with the customer and has therefore allowed the visitors to customize its website. As a result, visitors could tailor their shopping environment by registering their profiles—by size, style and price range—so that next time they visited Haburi the site would display only products meeting their profile characteristics. Furthermore, the company committed itself to meet the customers' expectations through offering the products at prices 25%–70% below the leading retail stores and via an uncomplicated website for visitors at any user level. Additionally, the company's pricing model met customers' expectations and compared favorably with other prices of similar products found on the Internet. Haburi was confident that it could continue to provide significant savings to its customers while clearing the brand suppliers' stock. In addition to all the other value-adding services, Haburi also pay freight fees if the total purchase of products exceeds 100 euros, and customers obtain their products within the stated time frame (five working days) because Haburi had positioned its distribution centers strategically throughout Europe.

Although the founders had a strong business background and significant experience in the Internet environment, they realized that it was crucial to obtain the knowledge of experts in the areas where the management crew felt they were lacking competency. In particular, four organizations contributed to Haburi's successful business: McKinsey & Company, IBM Denmark and ProActive A/S, Proffice Communication Center A/S, and SAS Institute.

McKinsey & Company contributed with knowledge in the pre-launch phase, and its role was to give its input on the development of the business plan. IBM Denmark and ProActive A/S were contacted to deliver the technical platform to the website. They devised a solution for Haburi in less than three and a half months, which was set in a flexible manner to enable the firm to easily expand into new markets. The technical solution provided by the two companies included IBM RS/6000, IBM WebSphere Commerce Suite, IBM Global Merchant, IBM e-business Hosting, and IBM Global Financing.

Another important key organization in the realization of Haburi's business model was Proffice Communication Center A/S. Proffice's role was to compose the site as customized as possible in order to increase the customer service level. Moreover, Proffice provided Haburi with all the traditional call center functions such as e-mail and telephone services, but it also supplied Haburi with an extensive customer care program. Any Haburi customer could get in contact with a Haburi consultant with just one click on the website. In addition, Proffice was responsible for supplying all Haburi's customers with correct information regardless of question or situation. Finally, Proffice also assisted in the process of providing the needed language capacity to all the European countries in which Haburi was present.

SAS Institute is the last organization to be discussed in terms of its contribution to Haburi's business model. As a result of Haburi's endeavor to eliminate or limit as many obstacles as possible, the company decided to apply a business intelligence approach, entitled SAS Institute's *Balanced Scorecard*, which was implemented in order to assist the decision-makers in establishing strategic decisions. The business intelligence solution provided by SAS Institute was holistic and involved the majority of activities that occurred in the organization. Moreover, Haburi was using the Balanced Scorecard method to prepare distribution, logistics, customer contact, and to create greater opportunities for the brand suppliers.

During 2000, it was difficult to direct an Internet organization due to the volatile nature of the market. However, Haburi strove to decrease the effects of macroeconomic changes by continuously updating its strategic plan, constantly assessing itself to ensure that the stated model was closely followed, and by outsourcing crucial activities to organizations who had the expertise in these areas.

Key Business Drivers and Threats

The initial key business drivers for the firm were its clear vision of being first to market as a virtual factory outlet mall, establishing solid relationships with brand suppliers, and obtaining sufficient investment capital. The first main obstacle that Haburi encountered during the pre-launch phase was the difficulty, even for the best IT system implementers, to deliver a satisfactory solution within the projected development time. The second obstacles were to conquer the difficulty of obtaining investment capital due to the market crash that occurred just a few months earlier and gaining the trust of suppliers.

One year following the launch, there were three key drivers related to the organization's success. The first was the suppliers' willingness to clear stock through Haburi. Accordingly, Michael Vad stressed the importance of a healthy relationship with suppliers. Haburi continued to be highly dependent on the suppliers' performance and trust in Haburi. The second key driver was customer acceptance leading to purchases.

The third was the firm's capabiliity to meet customer and supplier expectations, i.e. its ability to build critical mass (both product volume and number of customers) at a high rate. Haburi rapidly needed to prove to all stakeholders that it was able to accomplish the stated objectives, thereby ensuring future investments in the organization. In addition, it was also important for Haburi to create critical mass to stimulate an upward success spiral—i.e. if suppliers provided Haburi with a large selection of products to offer to its customers, the customers would be satisfied. Satisfied customers would return to the website and purchase more products, and as a result the suppliers would clear stock faster. Haburi's final obstacle was its susceptibility to the media's opinions. Poor media evaluations would have a detrimental impact on Haburi's profitability.

Innovation Factors and Processes

Haburi's existence was based on the founders' ability to implement a highly innovative project. Their specific innovation factors were the growth in consumer purchases from factory outlets across Europe, the discovery that brand suppliers cleared about 15% of their stock through factory outlets and the potential business opportunity presented by an online option that could be accessed by customers across Europe rather than a traditional operation limited to customers in a particular market. The major barriers were acceptance of this new approach by suppliers and investors (leading to funding) and the capability to implement an innovative website on time and within budget. The founders of Haburi did not just create a unique business, they founded an entirely new online retailing segment: the virtual factory outlet. Since Haburi took 'a road less traveled' it was motivated to implement a relatively formal innovation process. The following eight steps describe, in broad terms, the innovation process that transpired during the first 12 months of operation:

- The three co-founders conducted market research and discovered that it would be beneficial to create a virtual factory outlet.
- The formal business plan was created with the assistance of a team from McKinsey & Company.
- First capital investors agreed to fund the Haburi project.
- An IT team was selected, and IBM Denmark and ProActive A/S began their implementation.
- Proffice Communication Center A/S and SAS Institute began their implementation.
- The launch of the website took place 175 days later.
- A second round of capital investment was secured.
- Haburi expanded the website into new geographical areas and new product categories.

Website Development and Operational Issues

Haburi operated under a highly centralized organizational structure. Although the organization had websites in approximately 15 different countries, the decisions regarding its activities were made at the Danish headquarters. The logic behind this high degree of centralized decision-making was the founders' belief that there should be few innovation decisions being made outside central management. If not the result could be an organization that was impossible to manage.

To ensure quality, control, and cost efficiency, Haburi outsourced the creation of the IT platform and other technical functions. Yet, central management was the sole creator of the conceptual framework and controlled its implementation process in-house. Michael Vad stressed the importance of disallowing the IT function to gain even slight control of any decision-making functions. This could cause the management team to lose control of some of the most essential functions of the organization, such as website layout, marketing, back office integration, etc.

Website Features

Michael Vad was generally satisfied with the development of the website but emphasized that there was still room for improvements. Both pros and cons existed in terms of the outsourcing concerning IT development and other major functions. Haburi experienced some problems with the technical integration, yet these were obstacles that Internet organizations had to be prepared to meet when launching a website. Michael Vad believed that many of the problems that occurred could have been avoided if the contract organizations had not underestimated the challenge.

Furthermore, Haburi realized the importance of visitors being able to navigate quickly and easily around the website, so the company deliberately kept the first site version simple and free from heavy graphics. As the customer became more familiar with the website, Haburi would increase its complexity by adding new features to the site. This strategy was synchronized with the company's mission statement, which concentrates on customers' needs and wants.

Evaluation of the Haburi website rated it highest among Danish firms (see Table 3.1). Product information and transactional capability were at the highest levels and ease of use close behind. Surprisingly for a firm differentiating itself by price, product range and customer service, the online services rated only moderately. The innovative approach of supporting customization of websites by customers was well regarded but more innovation could be made.

Customer Perspectives

Haburi's customer profile was: the largest age groupings 21–30 years (48%) then 31–45 years (27%); females were 57%; the largest occupational groups were students, then professionals and office workers (equal). About 45% were university graduates. About 46% were living in a major city with incomes reported on or either side of the national average salary. A very high percent of customers access the Internet daily (89%) from home and are very experienced web shoppers with 48% having purchased more than 11 times. Apart from clothes, Haburi's customers use the Internet for buying books (66%), music and banking services for personal use (70%).

Reflecting the variable product range of a factory outlet, 46% of customers visited the site to browse. Repeat sales are an important factor with 41% having previously purchased 2–5 times. Customers came to the site due to a range of factors including a link from another site (34%), personal reference or an online advertisement.

Customer benefits sought from this site were price (59%), convenience and the range of products. The greatest barriers to deciding to purchase were uncertainty about products/services (25%), delivery and security. The purchasing process was considered very easy (48%) or easy (36%). Customers were very satisfied (43%) or satisfied (50%) with the Internet as a whole and very satisfied (43%) or satisfied (46%) with this site. Some 52% would definitely purchase again from the site. More than 64% of customers would recommend the site to others even though they sought improvements in the range of products (66%), more details on products and the availability of products.

The Future

In 2001, Haburi was a young organization and there will be many potential challenges in the years to come, most of which could be very difficult to foresee. Nevertheless, based on past experience, Michael Vad identified three major challenges that Haburi should focus on in the future.

1. The firm needed to become profitable faster than would generally be expected of it.

2. It would be necessary for Haburi to continue building strong brand relations.
3. Haburi needed to continue expanding into potentially profitable geographical regions and to penetrate the existing markets better.

One could anticipate quite a few changes to Haburi in the future. One of these changes could be adding new product categories (i.e. sports equipment, consumer electronics, textiles, etc.). Moreover, Haburi was preparing to initiate its next expansion phase into Eastern Europe and Asia. Lastly, the company was confident that it would be able to obtain a large group of brand supplier during 2001.

If Haburi could change any decisions made during its first year of operations, what would it change? Not much, according to CEO Michael Vad, who was content with the overall performance. However, he would have attempted to implement stronger executions and make sure that all staff members focused more on their tasks instead of being innovative.

Michael Vad's final advice to organizations planning to launch a new concept on the Internet was: 'Have realistic expectations, emphasize the importance of good management of all the sub-contractors, and implement vigorously.'

Conclusion

Although Haburi has experienced some turbulence during its first year of operations, the outcome has been satisfactory in terms of turnover, technical functionalities, capital investments, public response, and establishment of critical mass (i.e. product volume and website traffic). The specific factors that led to this innovative firm were the growth in consumer purchases from factory outlets across Europe, the discovery that brand suppliers cleared about 15% of their stock through factory outlets and the potential business opportunity presented by an online option rather than a traditional operation in a particular market. The greatest barrier was gaining the acceptance of suppliers.

The most crucial success factor in the case of Haburi was its strong and knowledgeable management team consisting of Michael Vad, Ulla Brokenhuus-Schack, and Michael Aagaard, who have succeeded in creating and implementing an innovative business model. The management recognized its lack of knowledge in key areas (e.g. strategic planning for Internet retailers, website development and operation and customer service) and sought professional assistance from firms including McKinsey, IBM, Proffice and SAS.

RAVENHOLM—'WHEN THE FIRST MOVER LOSES ITS PACE'
(ravenholm.dk)

Introduction

Selling software on the Internet should be simple. Customers are prepared to search, order and pay for products on the net. As the largest independent player in the Danish market for shrink-wrapped software, Ravenholm was well placed to become a first mover in utilizing the new sales channel.

Accordingly, Ravenholm established its first e-commerce solution in 1996, and after a number of less successful attempts it launched its fourth version in August 1998. There were plans to further develop the fifth generation, but serious efforts were not mounted until one of their biggest B2B customers from one day to the next announced that they had decided to move all their business. 'Imagine, we lost to a competitor having a more fully-fledged e-shop.'[4]

Ravenholm was established in 1985, and was the first company in the Falconholm International Corporation. It is represented with a group of wholly owned subsidiary companies operating local sales companies in Denmark, Sweden, Norway, Finland, Switzerland and the United States. In 2000 Ravenholm was the largest software specialist retailer in Denmark with 10%–12% of the total market. Ravenholm is targeting B2B as well as B2C. About 10%–15% of the turnover is B2C, especially what is termed the 'professional' market. This should be borne in mind when evaluating the conclusions. However, in what follows we shall only refer to B2C as is done in the rest of the cases. The holding company providing administrative and IT services to all of the companies in the corporation is located in Copenhagen.

The Falconholm Group has grown steadily since the first Ravenholm Computing was established in 1985. The growth was primarily attained through 'organic' growth in each company in the group. It has also expanded geographically by starting new business areas. As of year 2000, the Falconholm Group had acquired several other companies and merged them into the group.

Ravenholm was originally established as a catalogue sales firm specializing in software. It had a broad as well as a deep range of products, which could be divided into two groups: shrink-wrapped products from major software developers, e.g. Microsoft, Adobe and Borland, and license agreements for organizations to use these standard software products. During 1998 the entire production process was automated, and Ravenholm had, in 2000, one of the largest specialized software catalogues in Denmark.

Furthermore, Ravenholm offered training to its customers in most of the standard products, e.g. Microsoft Office, Corel, WordPerfect, Lotus SmartSuite, and Seagate Crystal Report, as well as more specialized products. Ravenholm specialized in educating/training programmers, but offered a large variety of educational programs to its customers.

Revenue has grown steadily from 1995 to 2000. While the revenue was not revealed for competitive reasons, the profit was disclosed to be around US$1.2 million for 1999 and 2000 which could be considered quite good for a company with only 38 full-time staff.

---

[4] Statement in interview on 14 March 2001 by incoming CEO Klaus Hansson taking office in April 2000.

Since 1996, Ravenholm has worked with concept of the Learning Organization seeing it as a kind of umbrella covering the company's way of working externally both with customers and partners, and internally in their own organization. An open environment in all respects, encouragement of knowledge-sharing, and focus on improvements were the key factors in accomplishing this objective. Ravenholm had defined a set of common defined values.[5] These were creative thinking, flexibility, proactive behavior, involvement, goal-orientation, and team spirit.

The mission and vision of Ravenholm both served as guiding principles to the organization as a whole.

- *Mission.* It is our goal, through sales and training in standard software, to make our customers more effective in the implementation of their business processes.
- *Vision.* We intend to be the preferred software and training partner both for our customers and our vendors.

On a day-to-day practical level the mission and vision were attained through implementation of The Circle. The Circle consisted of three inter-linked elements:

- We must create loyal customers.
- We must attain excellent earnings in order to ensure a future in which we can fulfill our mission and our vision.
- We must attract and keep competent employees and fill them with enthusiasm.

According to MD, Klaus Hansson,[6] 'each and every employee in Ravenholm Computing A/S must always make sure that all three elements of The Circle are considered. This is done through our common values, and this will lead to a realization of our mission and our vision.'

Environmental Issues

Ravenholm belongs to the IT retail industry. The company's main business area was purchasing software products from manufacturers and reselling it to end-user companies or distributors. End-users could be classified into large-scale accounts (500 largest companies in Denmark), small to medium enterprises (SMEs), and private customers/home offices. The IT retail industry has, unlike many other industries, an intensive use of IT for managing sales and distribution of a large product range. In the industry, the level of IT was very similar since they all operate within various areas in the same field. Managing Director Klaus Hansson considered Ravenholm's products and services as being very similar to those of competing companies. Ravenholm's largest competitors in 2000 were VM-Data, eterra, Connection, and Computer Store. Ravenholm evaluated and monitored

---

[5] Ravenholm Annual Report, 1998.
[6] CEO of Ravenholm until April 2000.

them at least annually and strengths, weaknesses, opportunities, threats (SWOT) analyses of the competitors were an integrated part of the annual strategic planning.

The IT retail industry was not seriously threatened by environmental factors in general. Quality assurance, declining demand, scarce supply as well as local and international competitors' services were not considered to be crucial factors. While Ravenholm was downloading software from vendors using the net it should be noted that electronic software download (ESD) was accounting for only 1% of the turnover for Ravenholm early in 2001.

Price competition was the only actual threat considered by Ravenholm. This was mainly due to the fact that its products did not differ from its competitors, since most products and services were not unique and thereby easy to substitute. Ravenholm earlier made its full assortment available to a search engine 'Edb-priser', but since price was the only sales parameter used, Ravenholm subsequently withdrew its participation with the engine.

In general it was felt that the demands and tastes of the company's customers were highly predictable, since the majority purchased products for standard platforms. However, customers were getting smarter and better technically at the same time as the numbers of products were increasing rapidly. The rate of technological changes in the IT retail industry is very high, which forced Ravenholm to consider its marketing focus at least once every year.

Business Model

Since 1998 it has been possible at the Ravenholm Computing's e-shop to order software 24 hours a day. The 7000 sales items are classified into more than 20 categories with detailed product descriptions developed by Ravenholm in Danish. The Internet shop was intended to be an additional sales channel in parallel with the catalogue sales where orders were often obtained, typically via fax.

For the largest 500 potential customers special interfaces are being established typically using electronic data interchange (EDI)/EDIFACT and/or direct communication between the enterprise resource plan (ERP)[7] systems of Ravenholm and that of the buyer.[8] For SMEs and for professional/private customers it is the intention to move customers to the website as quickly as possible.

The function of the website includes ordering, checking stock availability, tracking and tracing deliveries, historic overview of orders by a particular

---

[7] Ravenholm is using Navision, a Danish developed ERP system, which has more than 30% of the Danish market and is marketed worldwide. Originally Ravenholm had modifications done in the very kernel of the Navision ERP system. This has, however, turned out to be far too cumbersome and costly in programmer time. Accordingly, Ravenholm decided in 2000 to implement the standard Navision system in order to be more flexible in integration with ERP systems and the procurement systems of buyers.

[8] The first integrated B2B solution between the sales part of the Ravenholm ERP system and the procurement system of a buyer was established early in 2001 with Novo Nordic, one of the largest and certainly one of the most IT advanced manufacturing companies.

customer, and expected delivery time. There is also a lot of information available on the net about the different software packages.

In 1998, the first year, after the e-shop became a reality, the total turnover of the e-shop accounted for 2% of the total turnover obtained by Ravenholm. The percentage went up to 3.5% in 1999, to 10% in 2000 and is expected to reach 15%–20% in 2001.

The relative great success that the e-shop enjoyed right from the start had two important consequences: the investment in the necessary technology paid for itself in only three months, and Ravenholm could maintain its position as the preferred supplier of software on the Danish market. In 2000, Ravenholm initiated the establishment of SoftWareOnline, which provided the customers with the possibility of ordering and receiving software directly via download (ESD). However, so far this is only used for less than 1% of sales.

With the relative success of the e-shop and Ravenholm themselves being in the IT business, one would expect a high level of sophistication regarding the internal integration of IT in the business processes associated with the e-shop. Not quite so. In the spring of 2001 it was still the case that when customers order SW on the web, the orders were printed out at Ravenholm, and then manually re-entered into the ordering systems, which is part of the ERP solution.

Innovation Factors and Processes

The factors driving and inhibiting the original Internet venture were relatively simple.

- An Internet presence was seen as a business imperative. A software retailer needed to be there, for its image and for its customers.
- The Internet was a suitable medium to present product information.
- It was thought that it would be possible to save money on catalogue printing costs.
- The corporate environment was sympathetic to technological innovation.
- There was a clear willingness to experiment and further build up knowledge and experience with the Internet based on feedback from customers and on own experiences.

The most significant inhibitors were:

- Uncertainty about how the Internet could most appropriately be used for the business and a lack of Internet skills to implement its plans. No one in the firm knew what was possible or how to do it. A trial-and-error approach was adopted.
- Technical difficulties arising from the trial-and-error approach in website development and operation.
- Subsequent failure to maintain an ongoing program of website and system innovation.

As of the spring of 2001 the Ravenholm retail Internet project was into its sixth generation. It was started in November 1996. It was a 100% business driven project and was considered a natural element of Ravenholm's business strategy of using all sales channels. It was seen as a business imperative, i.e. a software retailer needed to be on the Internet to preserve its image and service its customers. The Internet was seen as a suitable medium to present product information, and it was thought to be a realistic possibility of saving money on catalogue printing costs. The company used a mix of web development agency consultancy and in-house programming to launch the various generations of the website.

The fifth generation website was delayed until late 2000, which caused Ravenholm to lose momentum and competitive advantage to one of its competitors. One day in the second half of 2000 one of the largest B2B clients decided, totally out of the blue, to stop buying. When interviewed by the incoming CEO, Klaus Hansson, a customer answered by showing the new e-shop of one of the competitors. This was clearly superior to that of Ravenholm. Ravenholm had lost out to a competitor because its website was not state-of-the-art. This was a sudden wake-up call, and the signal was given to develop its sixth generation website.

Key Business Drivers and Obstacles

The critical elements of success are responsiveness to customer requirements; capability to deliver; reliability of service; availability of products; and product knowledge. The key drivers of the e-business developments of Ravenholm were a committed top management (both the old and the new CEO), plus a general strategy to be creative, flexible, proactive, and goal-oriented. This was achieved with a lot of involvement of staff and team spirit. In general this enabled Ravenholm to:

- obtain a first-mover advantage rather than be a fast second (or even laggard);
- utilize the Internet (important since they are an IT provider);
- increase its responsiveness to customer requirements and enhance its capability to deliver;
- improve reliability of services and/or availability of products;
- enhance product knowledge of staff (knowledge was an important differentiator for Ravenholm which enabled them to compete with other software retailers offering similar products).

The major obstacles for Ravenholm could be summarized in the following points:

- Too little understanding of what could be done with the technology compared with the wishes of the company.
- No prior experience with the Internet within Ravenholm. When it first started, employees had to approach the project in a trial-and-error way (or rather the incremental development approach, which later turned out to be quite valuable if they had not missed the step).

- Nobody took responsibility in the beginning for the website and twice the site had to be closed down.
- Too little attention to what customers wanted, until rather late.
- Lack of innovation once the first generations were working.
- Lack of innovative capability.
- Lack of competence regarding web-based software solutions—a need for outside consultants.

There is no question that if one wants to survive in the software distribution industry or for that matter any other branch of industry, one really needs to be extremely alert and constantly push the limits of what technology can do and what the organization can cope with (Klaus Hansson).

Website Development and Operation

Ravenholm was not able to develop the different generations of the website/web solution on its own. They had some in-house capability, but they needed outside support for the larger innovations.

Another key factor was the need to re-engineer virtually all key business processes to achieve integration with the web-based softward solution. As of early 2001, four years after the introduction of the first website, orders received on the web were still printed and then re-entered into the internal ordering system. Clearly, this is not state-of-the art, but so far still cheaper than establishing the cumbersome integration with their current ERP system. During 2001, however, this crucial missing link will be established due to the compelling need to achieve efficiency objectives.

Website Features

When assessing the Ravenholm website (see Table 3.1) it should be borne in mind that we are looking at a website which is oriented towards professional customers (B2B or B2C) and not the occasional buyer surfing 'for fun'. Accordingly, it is not a particularly flashy site, but a site aimed at improving efficiency and giving the impression of a high level of professionalism. On this basis, the overall website rating of 57% is reasonable. Notable shortcomings are 'Customer services' and 'Innovations' where the CEC score is 0 and 1, respectively, out of five possible points.

First dimension 'Company information' is well stated. Pricing is clear, and there is an excellent way of showing promotions as well as a clear display of new and future products. This is also reflected on the dimension 'Product/service information', where it is noteworthy that the shopping trolley is large, there is accurate information about transaction costs, and there is just a two-click purchasing process. 'Ease of use' gets a top score for consistent layout and design as well as easy identification from all search engines.

On the less successful side, it is noteworthy that the site gets no points for 'Customer services', and that 'Innovation in services' only gets one point for the track and trace service, which no doubt is valued by the customer. All considered, the website could benefit from improvements in the areas receiving few points, especially the five elements within the customer service dimension.

The Future

As of early 2001 the future looks bright for Ravenholm, according to the new CEO Klaus Hansson. Ravenholm has decided to develop what could be called the sixth generation of their website in order to be at the forefront regarding Internet use. The new version will remove superfluous features, will improve the coding of the kernel to make it faster, will improve search facilities, will support better interaction, will be more customer directed, and will especially cater for 'inter-organizational collaboration'. Furthermore, Ravenholm is going to team up with the most popular 'information/content' website in Denmark called 'ITSVAR'. Here one would find >1500 articles about IT, a service called 'IT-doctor', where users and staff provide advice, test of new HW/SW and information about all articles published in the most popular trade magazines. Anyone wishing to buy software from the 'ITSVAR' website are automatically transferred to the Ravenholm website.

Conclusion

Ravenholm was the first mover in the Danish market, but as the case study has shown, Ravenholm was not able to maintain its position and missed a step. The first important lesson is that even though one might have an excellent state-of-the-art website, there is no time to rest. The next release should be in the pipeline. A second lesson is that the incremental strategy has demonstrated its value. A third lesson is that separating B2B from B2C (especially since Ravenholm focuses on professional users) might not be the most relevant distinction. A customer is a customer, and all accounts outside the top 500 list should preferably serve themselves via the website with a minimum of intervention from staff at Ravenholm. Fourthly, the most important lesson concerns the need for drivers like a committed top management, and a person or group responsible for the management/maintenance/development of the website, which more and more is becoming a key store-front for customers.

REJSEFEBER—'YOUR TICKET TO THE WORLD' (rejsefeber.dk)

Introduction

In August 1997 the parent company Scandinavian Online started a Danish division of its Internet based portal (www.sol.dk). In May 1998 Scandinavian

Online launched a travel agency, Rejsefeber (translated as 'travel fever'), as part of its portal.

Scandinavian Online's idea was only to provide information in order to attract customers to the portal. Prospective customers would telephone Rejsefeber in order to purchase their tickets. This approach did not generate sufficient revenue for the portal to be financially viable. Within the first quarter of 1998, Scandinavia Online in Denmark had a loss of US$1.45 million (11.6 million DKr), and due to this deficit the company was forced to change strategy to keep up with the competition in the market. The change in strategy resulted in the sale of different business areas. Rejsefeber was sold in February 1999.

The board members of Rejsefeber decided to continue Rejsefeber as an independent company, but with a changed strategy. Rejsefeber therefore became Rejsefeber A/S[9] and a new website was launched in June 1999. Today Rejsefeber is an Internet-based travel agency in the category of business-to-consumer. Scandinavia Online still owns 40% of Rejsefeber and the Norwegian venture partner Multimedia owns 55%. Rejsefeber itself owns the last 5%.

Rejsefeber has divisions located in three Scandinavian countries and these divisions employ a total of 26 persons, where the Danish division accounts for 8. The hierarchical structure within the company is very simple. In all three divisions there is a sales manager who handles the distribution of the different assignments and he is the person that the other employees report to. The other employees are webmasters. Their assignments depend on what needs to be done technically, commercially or editorially within the business, and their qualifications are in direct relation to those assignments.

Rejsefeber is, if seen physically, a very small agency, but if measured on growth and other indicators can be considered as one of the largest within its business area—traffic has grown 100%, employees 30% and sales 2000%. Currently Rejsefeber's largest market is Scandinavia. Within the next year or two Northern Europe is expected to be the largest and in five years hopefully the Baltic Countries and Russia will follow.

Rejsefeber's product range can be divided into three main groups: airfares, charter holidays and package holidays. Airfares go across all the products, but is also seen in isolation as one product. Charter holidays are airfares and hotels. These products are handled through partner agreement, where the partner company is responsible for the airfare and the hotel, and Rejsefeber only acts as a sales agent that sells the holidays that the partner companies provide to the customers.

Package holidays are Rejsefeber's main focus and these involve greater effort than the two others because more partners are involved. Package holidays contain the airfare, which can be several stops during the trip and not just a one-stop or a round trip ticket, hotels, car rental and, in some cases, passes to different experi-

---

[9] A/S is the Danish abbreviation for Ltd, and is meant when it says Rejsefeber in the rest of the case.

ences like museums and adventure parks. The uniqueness of these package holidays is that customers can tailor the trips to match their preferences.

Environment

Rejsefeber operates in the travel industry, which is a very complex industry. There exist many players on different levels and the industry depends on certain conditions that are unique to this industry.

The players in the market can be divided into two groups—those who only offer airfares and those who offer everything (airfares, hotels, car rental and access passes at all destinations). Rejsefeber operates in the second category—it offers everything but does not own anything. Instead it deals with partner agreements. A partner in this case could be a flight company, a hotel owner, a car rental company or a travel agency that carries charter holidays. Since the partners provide the products, the company is essentially dependent on the offerings of its partners for any competitive advantage. Selection of partners and monitoring of the competitiveness of their products are essential.

Competition in this industry is very tough, because it demands a lot of start up capital just to enter, but also to be ahead with offers and partner agreements. Fredrik Kinnunen, the sales manager at the Danish division of Rejsefeber, spends about 10 minutes on each competitor's website each week, looking for changes or upcoming initiatives, so that Rejsefeber can respond according to changes. Potential competitors (national and international) are also under consideration when monitoring the market situation.

Besides competition the travel industry also depends a lot on certain environmental conditions. The weather is the most important factor that can have a significant impact on the industry. If the summer is predicted rainy, the sale of charter holidays will often boom and vice versa. Package holidays do not depend to the same degree on the weather but more on current trends and underlying experiences, but according to Fredrik Kinnunen these are also hard to predict. Too large fluctuations in preferences result in products becoming obsolete very fast. Tax changes and new political initiatives are factors that are hard to predict the implications of. These can have just the same effect as the weather.

Rejsefeber is not concerned about the quality aspect, because they inform their customers thoroughly in case of low-quality offers. On the other hand, price competition on package holidays and scarce supply play a significant role. Since Rejsefeber offers common products, it makes it difficult to keep the customers loyal.

Business Model

When Rejsefeber became an independent company the business model changed from an information-based to a more Internet retailing model.

In May 1998 most of the airlines began establishing a common digital ticket sale system. Rejsefeber was among the first travel companies to purchase this system, which was launched in November 1999. It was now possible for customers to make their reservation directly via the Internet without having Rejsefeber involved. Rejsefeber offers different kinds of payments and when the transaction is completed the customer receives a reference number and a time schedule, either electronically or physically, depending on their wishes. Rejsefeber now appears to have implemented multiple business models. The primary model is as a fully functional electronic mall where the company provides access to products and full transaction processing for sale of the products.

In one respect, the company is implementing a pure Internet retailing business model where it is not committed to the capital costs of establishing and providing products. Nor is it exposed to risk in decision-making as to what products are likely to be in demand. The partners carry the costs and the risk of the products while Rejsefeber carries the costs of establishing and maintaining the website. Everything besides a single sub website was made in-house.

Details of the division of revenues between the partners and Rejsefeber were not available. However, the company's experiences of not being able to cover its costs with the initial business model illustrate the importance of equity of revenue distribution to the on-going success of the mall.

To differentiate the products and to establish an additional source of competitive advantage not depending on partners, Rejsefeber implemented an additional business model. They added value to their customers through the provision of community services. Their website community allows users to share experiences, put questions to experts, post pictures from their vacations and, as a bonus, members of the community receive special offers either via the website or via a weekly newsletter. The community has at the moment 53 000 mail addresses on its weekly mailing list, where 13 000 of these are categorized as users. Furthermore, Rejsefeber adds value by offering a telephone support service for customers having problems with any action.

Key Business Drivers and Barriers

As mentioned above, Rejsefeber has implemented several multiple business models. The fully functional electronic mall requires the firm to arrange partnerships with suitable third parties able to provide products and services on demand. To be successful, Rejsefeber's partners must have appropriate products for its customers at competitive prices. The website offering full transaction processing for sale of these products needs to be efficient and accessible as well as scalable in peak periods. For the additional community services business model, the key success factors are for the site to be usable, responsive to questions and provide the capacity for consumers to post their pictures.

Major barriers include acceptance of the Internet-based service by travel product providers and customers alike. The downturn in the world economy may be a threat to more expensive holidays. Competitors offering more appropriate packages for customer' needs will be a constant threat. The website needs to meet the business needs of consumers quickly and reliably. Adequate levels of funding are always a concern.

Innovation Factors and Processes

Some of Rejsefeber's major concerns in the startup process were that it was very important for the company to earn money right away, which required traffic on the site. These concerns convinced Rejsefeber to undertake a formal strategic business planning, and with this change its original business model to become Internet based.

To get traffic on the website meant that Rejsefeber had to enter partner agreements due to the initial strategy of not owning anything themselves. During the process of getting these agreements, Rejsefeber experienced startup problems. It was an unknown company and therefore nobody was willing to enter agreements in the light of an estimated budget. After an intense struggle the process of getting additional agreements went smoothly. Without the partner agreements Rejsefeber would be nothing today.

How to keep customers loyal was yet another crucial area, which Rejsefeber to a certain degree dealt with by establishing the community.

The most important factors that led to this Internet initiative were:

- an opportunity for an Internet-based channel for the parent company;
- financial difficulties with the information-only website;
- the decision to give it one more try after Scandinavia Online's deficit;
- determination among the employees to make a success of the venture.

The initial development process began right after an acceptance from the top management, even though the overall decision was made in plenum internally in the company's three divisions. Major inhibitors were technical difficulties in implementing and operating the website/systems and the levels of acceptance by providers and customers.

Website Development and Operational Issues

Rejsefeber decided to develop the entire project in-house and only outsource sub sites where they would not be responsible for the content.

The process from the beginning of the development to the first draft was finished and implemented in about six months. Rejsefeber did experience a major obstacle during the implementation process, namely the network provider postponed the setup for three months, which meant that the whole project was delayed for that period of time. The software in-house was not fully integrated from the beginning, due to restrictions on the technology. Since the startup most of the systems have been changed and currently almost 80% are fully integrated. Rejsefeber is expecting to have full integration by 2002,

The website evaluation rated Rejsefeber at a reasonably high level of 70%. For a firm differentiating itself by price and customer service the ratings for product information, transaction capabilities and ease of use at the highest level were appropriate. The site suffers from limited company information, its online customer services and a lack of innovative customer services, which appear to be inconsistent with the firm's objectives.

Fredrik Kinnunen considers the project to be a success, which is proven by the award of IT-Brancheforeningen's Danish e-commerce prize in the spring of 2000. The e-commerce prize evaluates the Internet companies on how user-friendly their websites are, their design, integration of the e-solution and the other systems within the companies, and the security within these sites. Besides this success measure, the traffic, sales and employee growth also indicates that so far Rejsefeber has gone in the right direction.

Customer Survey

Rejsefeber's customer profile was: the largest age grouping 21–30 years (33%) but 62% were aged more than 30; 54% were males; the largest occupational groups were professionals then office workers. Education was split evenly between university graduates, trade qualifications and high school graduates. Some 44% were living in a major city with incomes reported above the national average (46%). Customers access the Internet daily (70%) from work and home and are moderately experienced web shoppers with half having purchased up to 5 times previously. Apart from travel, Rejsefeber's customers use the Internet for tickets (52%), buying books and banking services for personal use (59%).

Some 46% of customers visited the site to purchase a specific product. The site appeals to new customers with 66% not having purchased previously from the site. Customers came to the site due to a search engine (34%), a link from another site or an online advertisement.

Customer benefits sought from this site were price (31%), convenience and the availability of products. The greatest barriers in deciding to purchase were uncertainty about services (30%), delivery and security. The purchasing process was considered very easy (43%) or easy (33%). Customers were very satisfied (32%) or satisfied (44%) with the Internet as a whole and very satisfied (36%) or satisfied (41%) with this site. Some 44% would definitely purchase again from the site. More than 46% of customers would recommend the site to others even though they sought improvements in the details on products and services, more details on deliveries, the range of products and services and the ease of use.

The Future

The largest challenge in the future for Rejsefeber is to maintain its leading position and also to keep its customers loyal. So far the company has had mixed experiences during its time in the travel industry—the company has had good times, which is illustrated by the e-commerce prize and the growth in traffic and sales. But Rejsefeber has also had bad times, but it has fought its way through these and survived in spite of the intensely competitive travel industry.

Fredrik Kinnunen admits that if they had to do it again they would eliminate areas that do not create value for customers and they would have focused more on the 'What's in it for me' approach. What now? What will the future bring? Rejsefeber predicts its future in the following sentence:

> Our future will probably be that we are the best in offering weekend tours with the airfares as well. And that we will go beyond Scandinavia as a customer market.

The advice Fredrik Kinnunen gives to other companies who want to develop an Internet-based service is to know exactly what they want and then find a niche where they can practise this. Most importantly they should not do it just for the money.

Conclusion

The Rejsefeber experience shows that it is not always possible to be a success. At Scandinavia Online the project resulted in a not so pleasant experience, but since its rebirth as an independent company has had better times and is looking at a brighter future because it is well established in the market at the moment. This establishment was one of Rejsefeber's largest barriers—it did not possess products and was therefore dependant on partner agreements. But the whole idea of entering this market after a failure was a challenge that was worth trying out. If a company is planning to do business this way—by entering partner agreements—then it must be aware of the problems that follow. Because the company is not known in the market it is therefore necessary to establish its brand as fast as possible.

SAXO—'SALES ARE EVERYTHING' (saxo.dk)

Introduction

The privately owned Søndagsavisen Group[10] is the largest publisher of free newspapers in Scandinavia with a weekly circulation of 4.2 million newspapers from 53

---

[10] The Søndagsavisen Group consists of a number of subsidiaries in Denmark, Sweden and Norway, besides the Danish parent company, Søndagsavisen.

Table 3.1 Evaluation of selected Danish websites

Firms	Company information/5	Product/ services information/5	Transaction/5	Customer service/5	Ease of use/5	Innovations/5	Total/30	CEC scale © (%)
Haburi	3	5	5	3	4	2	22	73
Ravenholm	4	4	3	0	5	1	17	57
Rejsefeber	1	5	5	3	5	2	21	70
Saxo	3	5	3	3	5	0	19	63
Velux	2	2	3	1	1	1	10	33

different publications. The head office is situated in Søborg, just outside Copenhagen. The overall strategy for the Søndagsavisen Group is, in order, to be the largest, the best, and the richest.

The Søndagsavisen Group has three main areas of business activities:

- The distribution of unaddressed consignments to households.
- The publication of newspapers to be distributed to households free of charge.
- Internet services for professional and private users.

Revenue for the group in Denmark increased even in a market generally characterized by stagnation. The overall revenue increased by 20% to a total amount of DKr 944.3 million or US$118 million. The Søndagsavisen Group's result was better than the industry as a whole, mainly due to an increase in job and education advertisements.

Søndagsavisen Online is part of the Søndagsavisen Group. Its main field of business is to mediate bargains and provide information for consumers. It operates the second largest Internet portal in Denmark, ShoppingForum. The online company is to be separated from Søndagsavisen in order to expand internationally and to be introduced on the Stock Exchange. The mission of Søndagsavisen Online is to be the leading content provider of advertising information and selected online services in selected countries. This is achieved by operating as an Application Service Provider (ASP) for professional users on the Internet.

Business Model

Saxo was the first Internet bookstore in Denmark. It was originally founded in Copenhagen in the spring of 1999 by the two Danish publishing houses, Gyldendal and Munksgaard, who saw an opportunity to unite the entire book industry on the Internet by developing a community for their target market (e.g. with reviews of books and other items of interest). Today, Saxo is owned 100% by the Søndagsavisen Group, but the company is no longer run according to the same strategy as before. It has been changed to match the challenges facing any company operating on the Internet, since Saxo was not suited for e-commerce before the acquisition. According to Jan Lundsgaard (the new manager for Denmark):

> It was an intellectually sophisticated meeting place. And that is not what we want with Saxo. We want to change it into a place where everybody comes naturally with no specific preferences to any literary élite using it as their place.

Saxo had four employees working closely together with the staff at Søndagsavisen Online. Its organizational structure has a product manager responsible for the various areas/markets who are reporting to Jan Lundsgaard, the country manager. Typically the product manager is responsible for a number of salespersons and sales assistants and aside from that the product manager draws on a development environment that he himself is not directly responsible for. There is no record of an annual revenue at this stage. According to Jan Lundsgaard, the disadvantage of Saxo is that most of the book sales throughout the year are concentrated in the fourth quarter of the year for Christmas. This is the time when people buy books. So Søndagsavisen is still waiting with anticipation to see whether acquiring Saxo has been a success.

Saxo operates two separate business models, distinguishing between professional buyers (the largest source of income) and private consumers. Professional buyers are universities, schools, libraries, etc. buying multiple books at one time. Therefore, they are more sensitive to price, range and delivery than the private consumer. The Søndagsavisen Group is still not sure how to approach this segment successfully, so the first obstacle is to close some deals with business customers to make sure that they will continue to use Saxo. A tension exists between the exclusively B2C orientation of the parent group and the B2B activities of Saxo's largest target market. Jan Lundsgaard expresses a sense of confusion in this connection:

> Sales are everything! That was exactly Saxo's problem before the acquisition. Having a fancy website is not enough, however. We know that the focus should be on sales, but we do not quite know how to obtain this.

The private consumer is easier to approach. The buying pattern and behavior of the customer is fairly transparent. According to Jan Lundsgaard it is mostly about giving them an enjoyable, safe experience while they shop. There is a natural synergy with the groups's other activities with advertisements being printed in the group's newspapers to promote Saxo. Even though it is possible to measure consumers' behavior 100% through the Internet, the demands and tastes of the customers are still very unpredictable to the Søndagsavisen Group. It requires a thorough analysis to understand where and why there might be a lack of communication with the customers. The Søndagsavisen Group has not reached that deep into Saxo yet in order to determine what can be changed to attract and keep the customers.

Industry, Competitive and Environmental Issues

Saxo belongs in the book retailing industry, with multiple suppliers in various categories. There is keen competition from traditional bookstores that have the advantage of letting customers touch and feel the books, which is very important for some people. The disadvantage for the bookshop around the corner is that they, in principle, have very few books. The advantage of Saxo is therefore that they can offer the customer 100 000 titles.

One important environmental issue is that sales of Danish language books are restricted by law to Danish bookstores. This certainly operates as a constraint on international competition for Saxo. Faithful to its origins, Saxo has specialized in selling only Danish titles. They guarantee their customers delivery within 3 days, which would not be possible if foreign titles were sold as well. Fast delivery is one of the parameters for Saxo, differentiating Saxo's products compared with some of the company's competitors. Having a large range of products makes Saxo a large player on the market, but at the same time the overall revenue suggests something else. Saxo is still a minor player on the Internet as a whole, but it functions as a market leader within this specific niche. However, with a population of only 4.5 million people, a market niche catering for the literary élite in Denmark was too small to sustain the cost of development and operation of a fully functional Internet-based retailer. The Søndagsavisen Group's focus on an Internet retail operation for a broad market appears more able to cover these costs.

Key Business Drivers and Threats

The key success factor for new Saxo is to generate sales and produce profits. This requires a focus on the separate professional and consumer markets and needs to reconcile these two diverse but overlapping markets that have different requirements. Saxo considers competition on price and quality as severe threats to its business. Breadth of product range is seen as a necessity to attract and keep customers. The greatest threat for Saxo, though, is the existence of competing bookshops on the Internet—local as well as international competitors for non-Danish titles.

Innovation Factor and Processes

Even though the Søndagsavisen Group undertakes formal strategic business planning, it remains a very flexible organization. The acquisition of Saxo was not a strategic consideration, but rather an opportunity that appeared. According to Jan Lundsgaard that is exactly how this market works. It is characterized by fast decisions and intensive analytical work. The planning is therefore continuously adjusted but still there exists a fixed framework for employees to work to. It is a matter of balance to stick to the overall business plan at the same time as taking on new challenges and opportunities.

The e-commerce project within the Søndagsavisen Group can be divided into three phases—the acquisition, the 'in business', and the future. On 1 November 1999 the Søndagsavisen Group made the decision to acquire Saxo. It started as an informal discussion between the Søndagsavisen Group and the previous owners, Gyldendal and Munksgaard, of the possibility for the Søndagsavisen Group to take over Saxo. Jan Lundsgaard explains the considerations behind the acquisition:

> We saw the bad exploitation of a so far unused potential. There existed bad strategic considerations about the objective of Saxo. We felt we could turn that objective in a right direction that would be economically rewarding. It was primarily a matter of strengthening the forms of payment on the Internet and make it easy to shop on the Internet through Saxo. We already had a know-how concerning payment on the

Internet through ShoppingForum. That's the reason we felt we were better at running such a business than Gyldendal and Munksgaard, even though it actually does not fit quite into our overall strategy, where we would rather handle more regular advertising information. But we still felt there were potential synergies and that we had the know-how required to continue the deal.

The project was 100% business oriented. The Søndagsavisen Group saw an opportunity to obtain a long-term profit and at that moment Saxo was the best solution for the Søndagsavisen Group. The negotiation was not a difficult process. Both parties were quite unanimous on the price of Saxo. The only problems, or rather considerations, for the Søndagsavisen Group were

• the need to make money, and
• the dilemma of whether Saxo would fit into an existing portal.

Because—apart from making money—the Søndagsavisen Group wanted to have a large group of users using their range of services on the Forum portal. Would Saxo be able to attract traffic? If so, the Søndagsavisen Group knew that the users most likely will use some of the other services on the portal as well. In that case, Saxo would function as a traffic generator. It has therefore not been an obstacle that the Søndagsavisen Group had no earlier experience within the field of books.

Website Issues

Gyldendal and Munksgaard had various contacts with publishing houses, etc. and that is what the Søndagsavisen Group paid the money for. Saxo had some acceptable software, so it has been a matter of continuous development to make Saxo's website work effectively.

Part of the software development is outsourced (depending on the expertise available) although Jan Lundsgaard would rather have all activities in-house. The physical removal of IT equipment after the acquisition was very difficult, since it was located in multiple places.

There are still aspects missing to complete the integration of the acquired equipment/resources with the Søndagsavisen Group's existing IT systems and business processes. These are everything concerning order systems, logistics, communication with the warehouses, etc.

Evaluation of the website returns a reasonable rating of 63% (see Table 3.1). Product details and ease of use are rated at the highest levels, but company information, transaction capabilities and customer services are only moderately well implemented. There has been no innovative use of the Internet for customer services. This current state of the website is, perhaps, indicative of the level of ambivalence about Saxo's major target markets. The larger, price conscious professional market may be more interested in offline sales and the consumer market may be satisfied at present with the product details and ease of use. However, a firm facing strong domestic and international competition in the market for Danish customers cannot allow its website to become uncompetitive.

Customer Surveys

Saxo's customer profile was: the largest age grouping 21–30 years (36%) but 56% were aged more than 30; females were 59%; the largest occupational groups were office workers, students then professionals. About 39% were university graduates. Some 47% were living in a major city with reported incomes slightly above the national average salary. Customers access the Internet daily (74%) from work and home and are experienced web shoppers with 44% having purchased previously up to 5 times. Apart from books, Saxo's customers use the Internet for banking services, tickets and buying music for personal use (54%).

Some 41% of customers visited the site to purchase a specific product. The site appeals to new customers with 48% not having purchased previously from the site. Customers came to the site due to a link from another site (38%), prior knowledge of the firm or personal reference.

Customer benefits sought from this site were convenience and the availability of products, price and the range of products. The greatest barriers in deciding to purchase were concerns about security (23%), delivery and completing purchasing procedures. The purchasing process was considered very easy (31%) or easy (26%). Customers were as satisfied with the site as with the Internet as a whole. Some 31% would definitely purchase again from this site and 36% from other sites. More than 44% of customers would recommend the site to others even though they sought improvements in prices (42%), details on products and services and the range/availability of products.

The Future

The main challenge for Saxo as part of the Søndagsavisen Group is to match the group's overall strategy with its business models. That is, to be the largest, the best and the richest within its niche. If Saxo succeeds in the Danish market, the Søndagsavisen Group will consider expanding its services internationally. A further consideration for the future is to focus attention not only on attracting new customers, but also to keep existing customers loyal in order to increase the customer base. Until these issues are resolved and the firm has gained more experience with its online operations, it doesn't consider itself in a position to offer advice to other firms.

Conclusion

Saxo is a complex case that illustrates how dynamic life can be for an Internet startup. Originally conceived by two publishers to develop a community of book-lovers rather than to be a retailer, the firm failed to cover its costs and was acquired as a business opportunity by a commercially-oriented group. The acquisition provided energy, focus, funding and some synergy within the group but also posed some major difficulties.

Drivers include:

1. Initially, a bright idea to promote books and a book purchasing culture.
2. A bright business idea to expand the product range of the group's Internet portal, even though it was not aligned with the group's business plans or strategies at the time.
3. The determination to go on and reformulate strategy after initial failure to cover costs.
4. The determination to succeed being a strong driver behind the process with commitment from the top of the organization.
5. The existence of an innovative environment and funding.

Operational drivers included:

1. Incremental development with a clear willingness to experiment and modify business strategy based on feedback from customers and on own experiences.

The most significant inhibitors were:

1. Risk of channel conflicts in the initial implementation with publishers as parent firms.
2. Difficulty in obtaining financing (initially).
3. Lack of Internet knowledge and skills (initially).
4. Technical difficulties in implementing and operating the website and systems (initially).
5. Lack of appropriate book retailing management skills and uncertainty about how to successfully address the largest market (after acquisition).

Operational inhibitors included:

1. Failure to maintain an ongoing program of website and system innovation (initially).
2. Difficulty in getting a critical mass of customers (ongoing).

Many of these issues are equally applicable to firms outside the book retailing industry.

VELUX—'ONE EXPERIMENT IS WORTH A THOUSAND EXPERT OPINIONS!' (velux.dk)

Introduction

The building products industry may not seem to be a 'natural' for the Internet. Products are physical rather than digital and the installers appear to be more familiar with hammers than computers. A very large, traditional, privately owned company may also seem unlikely as an Internet leader.

In 1941 the company Vilum Kann Rasmussen & Co. was founded in Copenhagen, Denmark, and the year after renamed Velux. Today the company is known as the Velux Group. The initial idea behind Velux arose when the founder saw the potential of transforming the attic into living space to meet demand for additional housing. Velux facilitated a new way of living—life in the attic. Today Velux is the market leader of skylights and roof windows, and the so-called Velux Systems (sun-screens, roller blinds, remote control devices). The firm has developed, patented and produces 19 different types of windows in 20 different sizes. Most windows require modification to meet the regulations specific to each country. The broad product range creates value for customers at many levels in the supply chain—architect, retailer, builder or end-consumer.

Velux manufactures in 13 countries, sells in 43 countries and employs 5,700 people. The major sites are located in Sweden, Germany, the United States, Canada and Hungary and the company has an annual revenue of approximately $US 8.5 million (6.8 billion DKr). Europe, North America and Japan will be targeted as major markets within the next five years.

Environmental Issues

Velux is part of the building materials, loft conversions and home improvements industries. These industries are characterized by extreme conservativism (change happens slowly), large numbers of small players (at all levels in the supply chain) and long product life spans so that the rate of new product development is infrequent. There is a very low level of IT penetration in these industries.

Competitive threats and environmental issues are very difficult to generalize over 43 countries. The building industries in these countries are complex with regulations and requirements being specific to each country. Different products are sought after in different countries, i.e. heat resistance blinds may be essential in Southern Europe but are unnecessary in Scandinavia. The firm markets its products to customers at different stages in its supply chain (architects, distributors, retailers and end con-sumers). Competitors are mostly focused in particular markets and regions and may be manufacturers or retailers with their own 'house' brand of windows.

The company is not faced with any of the common incentives to innovate such as declining demand, scarce supply, competitive threats or changing customer tastes and preferences. The main reasons for product innovation are the potential as a means of reaching different market segments and the culture of experimentation. Consequently, Velux had few external drivers to innovate with the Internet.

Business Model

The firm prides itself in providing the best quality at a moderate price which provides a competitive edge since quality normally attracts a price premium. In

1995 Velux applied an Internet information provision model. Through the website it was possible for customers to find information about the company, and Velux requested feedback on the site. If customers then wanted to place an order, they had to call Velux over the phone, whereby Velux then forwarded the order via e-mail to the distributor, who confirmed the order by sending an e-mail to the customer with the order number, customer information and delivery date.

Velux did not adopt a specific strategy to achieve this model. Instead it operated with a pull strategy to gain experience. The company followed the learning-by-doing approach for a couple of years and after that it used the experience obtained to work out a plan for the best way to use the Internet. The result was the launch of a new Internet-based activity, namely the e-shop that was an extension to the initial business model. The e-shop made it possible for customers to browse through an online store of products, place an order and pay by credit card, without even involving Velux in their ordering process.

Key Business Drivers and Barriers

The opportunity to gain experience on the Internet was one of the most important drivers for the decision behind the project in Velux. One thing was to be present on the Internet—another thing was the experience of being on the Internet.

Initially Velux expected only a single site, `velux.com`, as a global medium. That was easier said than done. Velux did not have any knowledge about the Internet or how it could be used, and that was the reason why the first version of the website requested feedback from its customers. The initial analysis showed that the Internet was ubiquitous, which meant that one single website would enable Velux to provide information on products that could be accessed from anywhere in the world. Their experience subsequently showed the flaw in this reasoning and led to the recognition that the Internet instead could be used to target customers at different stages of the value chain, in countries with different regulations and requirements. The result is that Velux has designed websites for each country where they do business.

The greatest threat that Velux faces is lack of innovation, because part of Velux's success is based on ongoing development. Another significant threat is the possibility of shifts in building traditions. Both these threats are in the physical world—the Internet part of Velux would not be affected in the short run, only in the long run.

What has to go right for the business to succeed? The firm's key business drivers are product quality, distribution, after-sales services and confidence in the product—confidence that if you make a hole in a roof and install a skylight it will not leak in six months or six years time. If a problem arises, then there is someone to help.

Innovation Factors and Processes

The founder's fundamental belief was that one experiment is better than a thousand expert opinions. Velux had this belief in mind when, as a player from the building industry, it decided to experiment on the Internet.

The main innovating factor for the experiment was the potential of reaching different market segments and the culture of experimenting. Velux's intention of reaching end-customers was in order to fully meet the demands for the products and to provide more up-to-date, accurate, technical details and the requirements and regulations in each country.

The innovation processes were:

1. An informal meeting held at head office.
2. The feasibility of the project was established.
3. Experiment in small steps—the first website targeted end-consumers requesting feedback on their requirements through e-mail.
4. The web page received an award from a Danish newspaper within three months of launching the website.
5. Customer feedback received from the e-mail facility provided on the website. Most feedback e-mails came from US and Danish customers.
6. Within two years had established five sites—Denmark, Switzerland, Italy, Canada and the United States.

Website Development and Operational Issues

The Internet site is managed by Marketing—since it was seen as a customer issue rather than a technical issue. Michael Kragh Rasmussen is responsible for Internet and marketing communications. The Velux brand is coordinated centrally. Internet activities are arranged similar to a newspaper editing activity—the central office is responsible for structure and the local office is responsible for content—controlled by specific function and location.

The IT platform is controlled centrally. The ISP function manages the platform with IT professionals who could also be external consultants. In some countries an external ISP is used. In Copenhagen the multi-media department manages the ISP function with seven professionals. Velux divided the responsibilities for the e-commerce project into three areas:

- Structure—supported centrally
- IT platforms—supported centrally
- Content—supported locally and regionally

The first version of the website (the single velux.com site) was developed in-house with assistance from an external agency, though their role was primarily to set up the platforms and the networking facilities. The website was launched in November 1995, but was later revised.

The development of the information-based website took approximately four months—Velux had only budgeted two months. The implementation process took eight months longer than expected, due to political issues (the amount of information available on the website).

Cultural conflicts arose because the management in different country divisions did not want to reveal company information, even though customers requested it. The company then had to resolve how to have a uniform corporate approach to the Internet to support international clients, but at the same time support local requirements (allow local offices to tailor their content for the local market).

The decision to have an e-shop service running first for a year only in Denmark also caused some disquiet in other countries. The problems were most of all because Velux had allowed the countries to develop their own Internet expertise and with the e-shop the company limited their activities. The real problem though was not the cost but exposing the company to a lack of control over the costs in changing from static to dynamic mental perceptions.

Website Features

Evalaution of Velux's website produces a disappointing rating with only 33% of the information and functions of an ideal site (see Table 3.1). This is partly due to the original objective in establishing the website, namely to experiment with ways of reaching customers along the supply chain rather than to undertake business transactions. Five years after initial implementation the website is only starting to support transactions. Customer service, ease of use and innovation all rate poorly. In contrast to the objective of reaching out to customers, the provision of information on the company and its products are also poorly implemented. Velux could and should obtain much more support from its website but the lack of competitive pressure in this industry provides little incentive to do so.

Overall, Velux is satisfied with the project. The learning-by-doing approach has given the company a better understanding of the Internet and greater cost control of the project. This approach is recommended by Velux to keep competitive edge. The external services were and still are costly; however, it was essential to set up the first website.

If Velux were facing the same decision today, it would not have done it significantly differently—it would still have tried to build internal competence within the company. Velux admits that it is still learning and it considers the rate of learning as satisfactory. The problem with the in-house development is that the learning curve takes longer than outsourcing parts of it; however, the outcome is consistent and stable. Self-reliance is very important to Velux. If external consultants fail, then the in-house group can take over. In 13 national sites and at the head office the Internet has become an integral part of business strategy, hence the need for internal know-how.

Customer Surveys

Velux's customers extend along the supply chain from architects to builders, retailers to installers and, finally, to householders and other property owners. The challenges and complexities confronting Velux in dealing with all customer types through the website were not able to be adequately catered for by the standardized customer questionnaire used throughout this project.

The Future

The greatest challenges that Velux is facing in its future are:

- E-business—seamless value chain from customer to suppliers
- Organizing to do business as above
- Overcoming traditional way of doing business.

The advice Velux gives to other companies that are facing the same question about entering the Internet or not, is that they have to think differently and be completely open to new ideas. They have to continuously question everything they currently do and ask themselves why and how they do this. The whole company has to be a part of the project, and the Internet activities should be arranged similar to a newspaper editing activity—the central office responsible for structure and the local office responsible for content—controlled by specific function and regional experts. The IT platform should be controlled centrally. Velux states that: 'Our experiences indicate that the best way to manage the Internet activities is as outlined above—a three-way split in responsibility.'

Do not forget information becomes knowledge when you use it.

Conclusion

Most companies innovate and expand by entering the Internet because they are facing a competitive threat or declining demand/supply. This was not the case with Velux, because there was an absence of environmental drivers to innovate. This conclusion is reinforced by the mini case that shows the main reasons for innovation were the potential as a means of reaching different market segments and the culture of experimentation.

The approach that Velux followed by getting the project to work properly before disseminating it worldwide is the right approach, but it does cause tension when allowing the local companies to develop their own expertise and limiting their activities. Even though Velux has a strong corporate culture it could not have avoided this tension. The question is rather: How could they have handled it differently?

CHAPTER CONCLUSION

The five B2C companies discussed in this chapter illustrate the diversity in foundation as well as in motivation and in execution of the Internet ventures. Haburi have what they and many observers acknowledge as a unique business idea of moving the traditional factory outlet to the net thus creating a much wider customer base. However, implementation was less than easy. Difficulties in getting supplies have been higher, and the frequency of customers buying lower, than expected. But they pin their highest hopes on two new customer reationship management (CRM) systems potentially unlocking the secrets behind what makes customers buy. The successful second round of financing in the spring of 2001 increased the level of optimism.

Ravenholm took a first-mover advantage by launching a site to sell packaged software on the Internet. They lost their momentum by neglecting to up-date their website in order to remain competitive. Rejsefeber was first part of the large portal Scandinavia Online (SOL), but due to financial problems for SOL Rejsefeber was sold off. Management and staff were committed to making it a viable business venture and several improvements were made to the business model and its website. A strong determination to survive with a keen eye on the competition was the key to success here.

Saxo also had to go through what could almost be called a metamorphosis when the initial attempts to establish a 'book-lovers' site turned out to be too costly to maintain and further develop. A willingness to write off the initial investments and sell off the site to a 'more business driven' company proved to be the crucial determinant of survival. Velux created a website to target different customers in 'all' the different stages in the value chain following the route of incremental implementation—'following the book'. It avoided the channel conflict with existing wholesale/retail trade by allowing them to retain the right to invoice (and make their traditional profit). It received an award for the best web page by a newspaper.

In summary, the most important drivers and inhibitors in the five cases are mentioned below. A more complete examination of all innovation factors may be seen in Chapter 9. Drivers include:

1. The existence of incubator/innovative environments assisted establishment and funding (Haburi, even after the market crash, Ravenholm, Velux, Rejsefeber, Saxo).
2. A vision for the future—the bright business idea (Haburi, Rejsefeber, Velux, Saxo).
3. A perceived business opportunity to use the Internet to provide a low-cost operation (factory outlet Haburi), to extend geographic reach (Haburi), to establish an entirely new type of business (Haburi).
4. A perceived business necessity to use the Internet (Ravenholm).
5. The determination to succeed being a strong driver behind the process with commitment from the top of the organization (Haburi, Rejsefeber, Saxo, Velux).
6. The determination to go on and reformulate strategy in spite of receiving a severe blow (Rejsefeber, Saxo).

7. The willingness to explore the potential of the Internet for possible strategic advantage (all firms).

Operational drivers included:

1. Incremental development with a clear willingness to experiment and modify the business strategy based on feedback from customers and on own experiences (Haburi, Ravenholm, Rejsefeber, Saxo, Velux).
2. Acceptance by suppliers and customers (Haburi).
3. The ability to secure or generate ongoing funding (all).

The most significant inhibitors were:

1. Lack of Internet knowledge and skills (Velux, Ravenholm, Saxo).
2. Lack of appropriate management skills (Ravenholm, Saxo).
3. Uncertainty about supplier and customer acceptance (Haburi).
4. Technical difficulties in implementing and operating the website and systems (Haburi, Rejsefeber, Velux, Ravenholm, Saxo).

Operational inhibitors included:

1. Failure to maintain an ongoing program of website and system innovation at some stage in the process (Ravenholm, Saxo).
2. Difficulty in obtaining a second round of financing (Gubi and Toycity are prime examples) but also some of the companies in the current sample (Haburi, Saxo).
3. Risk of channel conflicts (Velux, Saxo).
4. Difficulty in getting critical mass in the form of enough customers (Gubi and Toycity are prime examples) but this also holds true for companies in the survey (Haburi, Saxo).
5. Difficulty in obtaining customer loyalty (Haburi, Rejsefeber).
6. Too much focus on marketing and not being aware of the broad range of other business skills necessary to run an Internet business. (This was especially the case for the two companies originally included in the study, (i.e. Gubi and Toycity), that both failed.

While these motivating and inhibiting innovation factors were identified by the firms as being most important, they should be considered within the broader context.

4
Internet Retailing in Greece

NIKOLAOS MYLONOPOULOS AND KATHERINE PRAMATARIS

INTRODUCTION

The Internet and electronic commerce adoption statistics in Greece are not very positive but they show fast and steady growth. Specifically, according to European Union (EU) there were 7 Internet users per 100 inhabitants by the end of 1999 (EU average: 19), which shows an increase of 55% since the end of 1998 (EU average: 51%). Additionally, 32% of all companies had Internet access by the end of 1999 (EU average: 63%), which represents an increase of 28% since the end of 1998 (EU average: 27%). According to OECD there were 69 secure servers per 6 million inhabitants in March 2000 and 70 000 Internet hosts per 7000 inhabitants in September 1999. However, recent figures (early 2001) show that almost 10% of the population has access to the Internet.

Internet shopping is not very popular at the moment, since only 12% of Internet users bought something in 2000 and we can term 'online consumers' only 3.5% of the Internet population. The total value of goods that were bought online in 2000 (business to consumer—B2C) was 20 billion euros and only 10%–12% was from Greek sites. However, a considerable cluster of Internet users has or is willing to undertake on line shopping activities in the next year and we expect that by the end of 2001, 20% of Internet users will buy something online. Market research has indicated that consumers rank extended product information, quick access, comparative shopping and additional product images as the most important features of an electronic store. Greek Internet users are already using the Internet in order to collect information regarding multiple topics including product and market content (30%). Additionally, 50% of the adult population own a mobile phone and the fact that these users are quite advanced in using added value services for remote information retrieval of the cellular networks is a positive indication for the increased use of information and communication technologies (ICTs) in the future.

Overall, there are more than 7500 corporate sites currently operating in the Greek web market (end of 2000). The majority of them are hosted and operated by Internet Service Providers (ISPs) or technology providers and mainly promote the company profile (static pages). Among them, there is a significant number of companies (mainly medium to large corporations) that have invested in establishing infrastructure for their web presence and provide periodically updated content and services. Almost 20 000 companies are considered to have access to the Internet.

The first scientific survey on the adoption of electronic commerce from large companies took place in February–April 2000 at the Athens University of Economics and Business (ELTRUN). Top managers from 240 Greek companies that belong to the top 2000 companies in the country participated in the survey. Some of the findings of the research are the following: 38% of the participant companies use electronic commerce practices, 12.5% integrated to their business and the rest 25.5% are opportunistic. Some 47% of the companies are planning to adopt electronic commerce, with 33% of those planning to do so within the next year.

A positive indication is also the emergence in the last 6 months of business-to-business (B2B) marketplaces in vertical markets. For example, yassas.com operates in the hotel sector and is expected to facilitate by the end of 2001 procurement transactions worth 20 billion Greek drachmas (GrDr) or 60 million euros (three times the total B2C e-commerce market in 2000).

Finally, as far as business-to-public administration electronic commerce is concerned, the ministry of finance has taken an interesting initiative. Specifically, the TAXISnet system has been established, giving Greek taxpayers the possibility to submit their VAT statements and their debts electronically to the Ministry of Finance using phone or Internet banking. This system is the result of cooperation between the ministry and the Hellenic bank association. Citizens who participate in the programme are not obliged to pay any additional fees for its use. At the beginning of 2001 more than 50 000 people had expressed their intention to use it.

The importance in the exploitation of information technology for the economic growth of the country has been recognized by the Greek government. According to the policy document *Greece in the Information Society* basic principles include innovation and entrepreneurship (including the digital economy), education and culture, services to citizens, an improved quality of life, and communication. The total cost of the program is 2.8 m euros for the period 2001–2002.

A concentrated effort in the e-commerce direction was started in 1996 with the participation of agents such as the General Secretariat for Research and Technology of the Ministry of Development. In this framework a number of e-commerce projects included in the business industrial programme of the ministry of development (sectoral electronic data interchange (EDI) projects, exemplary e-commerce projects and e-commerce centres) have taken place since 1996. This initiative has had a big impact with 4 million GrDr invested for the funding of 1000 Greek companies.

The result of those activities has been a continuous growth in the Greek market of e-commerce. Some relevant indicators include the high percentage of mobile phone users (over 60% of the population), and the expression of interest from companies to use the Internet as a tool for gaining competitive advantage or even setting up new virtual organizations according to international standards.

Finally, the cooperation of the government with professional associations and other key players in the market such as universities and telecommunication authorities has proved to be very effective. For example, the Greek ministry of development with the cooperation of the Hellenic Organization of Small and Medium Size Enterprises and Handicraft (EOMMEX) has started an initiative called 'go digital' within the framework of the 'Information society' program of the EU. The objective of 'go digital' is the financial support of small enterprises in order to familiarize them with the Internet and the digital economy in general. Participating companies can get partial funding for equipment and professional training on the exploitation of the Internet. The programme has a budget of 31.5 billion GrDr (92.4 million euro) and will run for three years. Currently 11 000 companies from all over Greece have shown an interest in participating in the programme.

In the last few years the e-commerce market has grown continuously. Although the number of enterprises that use traditional e-commerce technologies, mainly for B2B communications (i.e. traditional EDI) has stabilized at relatively low levels and mainly in the grocery sector, there is a continuously growing interest in B2C applications and online transactions for products and services.

The continuous changes in the IT industry have positively affected the e-commerce market. Acquisitions and strategic alliances that are frequently announced drive the transformation of the market, proving its dynamic nature. At the same time, more and more IT companies have announced their intentions to develop and offer e-commerce services. Thus they create an image of exceeding supply in relation to the number of companies using IT technologies in Greece. Additionally, a growing number of companies participate and take advantage of the government's subsidies for new technologies and use e-government systems for their communication with the public authorities. These indicators show that the Greek business community has realized the strategic opportunity for economic growth that e-commerce can offer to the country. What is needed is coordinated action between the government and the business community for the design and implementation of a long-term national e-commerce strategy.

Overview of Cases

Three of the five retailers selected sell products most widely sold on the Internet— books, technology and music CDs. The other two provide beauty products and e-commerce solutions. Only one of the firms was an Internet startup. The other four examples are Internet ventures from well-established traditional stores.

Beauty Shop is the largest and most modern chain of cosmetic stores in Greece. It offers its clientele modern shopping areas, a hospitable atmosphere and a wide selection of products and quality service. Beauty Shop's online and traditional stores provide a complete selection of cosmetics from all the well-known beauty brands, as well as everyday use and private label products.

Best-e specializes in e-commerce applications, providing dedicated solutions to businesses that wish to promote their products or services through the Internet (B2B) and to final consumers through the creation of commerce sites in Greece's first e-mall. Best-e is a subsidiary of the Germanos Group and was founded in February 2000. The group operates two retail chain stores in electronics, computers and mobile phones and is a leader in the respective markets.

E-shop is the first Greek online store. Having only an electronic presence in the Greek market, e-shop managed quickly to win many loyal customers, even from large competitors who dominate the market with their bricks-and-mortar shops. E-shop offers approximately 80 000 products including entertainment (books, DVDs, games), office products and supplies (computer components, accessories and consumables), and accessories.

Papasotiriou bookstores have always aimed at being leaders in their field. Ever since this family-owned company shifted its business focus from publishing to book retailing, management has made a series of successful strategic choices that established Papasotiriou as the leader in technical and scientific books and one of the top players in the Greek book market overall.

Plaisio is the first Greek online store for consumers' electronics, PC systems, mobile phones and office supplies. It operates as a complementary channel to the bricks-and-mortar parent company, which is the market leader.

BEAUTY SHOP—'MAKE-UP YOUR MIND; MAKE-UP YOUR STYLE'
(www.beautyshop.gr)

Introduction

Beautyshop.gr, the first cosmetics online retail store in Greece, became a reality thanks to the drive and inspiration of the company's IT and e-commerce manager. The site, in line with the bricks-and-mortar company's modern image and focus on customer value and service, offers its online customers a broad range of products paired with a number of advantages not available to offline customers. The focus is clearly placed on building relationships with customers by understanding their preferences, needs and habits, with the ultimate goal to increase their loyalty to the brand, both online and offline. The company is prepared to invest in doing so, while the objective of gaining profit through online sales is placed at a second stage.

Beauty Shop is the biggest in terms of the number of outlets and the most modern chain of cosmetics stores in Greece. Owing to its long and successful presence in the market, it has established an image marked by a high level of aesthetic concept, offering its clientele modern shopping areas, a hospitable atmosphere, a wide selection of products and quality service. Beauty Shop mainly provides the female public with a complete selection of choice cosmetics from all the well-known beauty brands, as well as everyday use and private label products, while at the same time allocates operating space for men's beauty. The chain operates in all major Greek cities, as well as in the largest tourist resorts, either independently or through franchising, and aims at further domestic, as well as overseas growth. The philosophy and the daily effort of all the Beauty Shop associates are embodied in the concepts of value and customer satisfaction.

Today there are more than 50 Beauty Shop stores in the country, and this impressive development is not confined within the Greek borders. This has been proven by the recent inauguration of the first Beauty Shop store to open abroad, in Romania, which is the largest cosmetic store to have opened there to date.

The online business of the firm, `beautyshop.gr`, is a separate business unit, formed in September 1999. The website went live in April 2000, while online sales capabilities were offered as of June 2000. This movement made the company the first to offer a broad range of cosmetics and relevant products to online Greek customers and one of the first online retail stores in Greece.

Business Model

Beauty Shop builds on the synergies provided by the bricks-and-mortar business of the company, adopting off-the-shelf product picking and delivery from the store. More specifically, all the online orders are sent to a central Beauty Shop store with its own stock. Dedicated personnel, belonging to the online business unit, gather the orders and do the picking of the products off the shelf, either for each order individually or for all of them at once. The distribution process is outsourced to a courier service which picks the orders from the store and delivers them throughout the country within one or two days, depending on the distance. This model can satisfy up to 100–120 orders per day and per employee. In case the customer demand increases and cannot be fulfilled by one central store, the model will expand to include more stores that have their own stock and can meet the requirements of this operation.

On the customer side, there is no lower limit per order and no charge for delivery. Upon registration, consumers get a free gift-pack with products, even if they do not buy anything, while additional gifts and samples may accompany their orders. In addition, prices online are more attractive, with a standard 10% discount offered to the first online order and a 5% discount offered to all subsequent orders per customer. Regarding payment, there are two options offered: either credit-card online or cash on delivery.

Although the whole package constitutes a very attractive offering for the online customer, this offering is rather costly for the company when we look at the profitability of the online operation. The reason behind this investment on the Beauty Shop's side is clear: the objective is not to gain short-term profit but to build long-term customer relations, which will eventually drive loyalty and long-term sales in this rather high-margin retail market.

Implementing the Business Model

The owner of the idea and leader of the project since its start has been the company's IT and e-commerce manager. The decision process was rather informal, requiring that the management board be convinced first, in order to allocate the required budget and resources. The management board perceived the project more as a marketing rather than as a new sales channel initiative, not directly linked to the company's strategy, an opportunity to build the company's image and a test-bed for future activity. These facts further guided decisions on the implementation and setup of the new business case.

The decision on the business model to be adopted was simple and straight-forward: the existing infrastructure should be utilized to the greatest degree possible and so that the current operations were not disrupted. Thus, a big store with its own stock was selected as the central point for fulfilment of all the orders. One person was hired as dedicated personnel to fulfil the orders. The rest of the main operations of the online store, i.e. website development and hosting and distribution, were outsourced to third parties. Website development and hosting was handed over to an IT company that undertakes similar tasks, with whom the company maintains close links. The distribution process was outsourced to a courier service that could also handle payments, for a fixed-per-delivery fee and predefined delivery times.

Initially this project was added as a new duty on top of employees' existing responsibilities, which in many cases resulted in a scarcity of resources for the tasks that had to be performed. Finally, a separate business unit was created, a year after the initial decision had been made, with the clear mandate to develop and run the online operations of Beauty Shop.

Industry, Competitor and Environmental Analysis

Beauty Shop operates in the retail cosmetics industry. The company, together with its main competitor, Hondos Center, are by far the leaders in the sector organized as big retail chains, with all other competitors working as small independent cosmetics stores. Beauty Shop is bigger in terms of the number of stores, while Hondos Center has a greater market share in terms of turnover, covering a broader product range.

The main areas of differentiation between the two companies are product range and quality. While Hondos Center places more emphasis on variety and on the breadth of product assortment, extending it to many other categories beyond cosmetics, Beauty Shop has a clear direction towards a choice of the best cosmetics brands, in addition to offering its private label brand. A second differentiation factor is the emphasis that Beauty Shop places on the modern image of its stores and its life-style proposition.

The market as such is characterized by rather high product turnaround, especially in the make-up segment, with product types and colours replaced or extended every season. The main product segment is that of choice cosmetics, with leading brands maintaining their own booths and personnel offering expert advice in the store.

In the online market, Beauty Shop is the only Internet retail store in the cosmetics sector. Its product assortment is different online in that it does not include the leader brands of choice cosmetics. The reason for this is that choice cosmetics supplier companies object to their products appearing in a list next to all other products in a category or segment and contrary to the booth concept applied in physical stores. This fact, paired with the different profile of online consumers, makes the make-up segment an online leader by far, accounting for 50% of online sales, while its offline share is just around 4%.

Key Business Drivers and Threats

Within the company, the main driver that led to the implementation of this new business idea has been the vision and personal leadership of the company's IT and e-commerce manager. On the other end, the major obstacle has been the different perception and objectives that people and departments had for this same project. Perceptions ranged from seeing the website as a mere mass marketing tool to a relationship-building tool supporting one-to-one marketing strategies and online sales. Finally, the latter approach prevailed, which is also considered as the major challenge and at the same time threat facing the companies in the whole industry today.

In the external business environment, `beautyshop.gr` had to face all those obstacles standing in the way of the first-mover, mainly the communication and exchange of information with product suppliers. Even today, not all suppliers have responded to the company's request to send detailed product information, usage instructions and marketing information, including images. On the other hand, the first-mover advantage can give the company a greater market share in the online sales channel, or rather exclusivity, as long as the key competitor does not open online operations. However, this benefit can only be short term and the only way to maintain a long-term advantage is through exceptional customer service and a unique online shopping experience. This is why the company's main concern is currently on building personalization features on the site and linking it to a Customer Relationship Management software in order to meet this challenge.

At the back office, the company has not solved the problem of integrating the online operations with the rest of the processes. Separate processes have been established in order to support the fulfilment of online orders, while IT systems are standing totally apart. The website is hosted on an external server and orders received through it have to be re-entered to the company's proprietary enterprise resource plan (ERP) system. This is currently one of the major bottlenecks of the operation.

On the delivery side, the level of service currently offered by the third-party courier company—with items delivered to the home within one or two days and a half-day delivery window—is acceptable to customers, especially since this is free and no competitor has a better offering to make. Moreover, this is a market where delivery times are not critical; seldom is there a need for express deliveries and orders are comparatively small and easily transported.

Innovation Factors and Processes

As already mentioned, the most important factors that led to the accomplishment of this project were:

1. The personal drive of the e-commerce leader in the company.
2. The identified opportunity to build the company's modern image through online sales.
3. The opportunity to test a new market channel and see its potential.
4. The possibility to build a customer data base with detailed information regarding their preferences and online shopping behaviour.
5. The long-term potential of online sales in a comparatively high-margin market.
6. The synergies identified with the offline operations, in supporting the new business model and driving customer loyalty and sales.

The major obstacles and barriers that beautyshop.gr had to face, especially as a first mover in the sector, include:

1. Different objectives and vision per department; for example, the marketing department was oriented towards mass marketing and had a different idea of what the web could offer.
2. Informal processes and procedures in order to make a decision and allocate budget and resources to the project.
3. The need to outsource key operations, such as IT and logistics, and the selection of the appropriate partner.
4. Scarcity of resources, as no additional people were hired for this project but it had to run with existing personnel, especially at management level.
5. Major problems in building the product assortment online (e.g. collection of images, information, etc.), which required extended communication and cooperation on the side of product suppliers.

Website Development and Operational Issues

The development and hosting of the `beautyshop.gr` site has been outsourced to a third-party IT company, as this was recognized to be an expensive and difficult to implement task based only on inhouse expertise. The Beauty Shop online business unit defined the functional requirements and the website design, including the creative part of it. The rest of the development was then performed by the third-party IT company, starting development in September 1999. The site was launched on 14 April 2000, two months behind schedule. This initial version did not offer online sales capabilities and could only accept registrations from customers. The online sales functionality went live in June 2000 and since then only minor improvements have been made to the site.

According to the company's IT manager and head of the `beautyshop.gr` unit,

> the main problem in our cooperation with the third-party IT company has been their slow response to our requirements and new needs and the lack on their side of idea generation ... they expect us to define every small detail of work; this would take ages; for us these are self-explanatory things that correspond to a minimum standard of quality. ... If we were to make the same decision now, we would probably use different criteria for selecting our IT partner.

Table 4.1 shows that the `beautyshop.gr` website supports the firm's focus on creating customer value and service. The product details, transaction capability, ease of use and customer services are well developed. With a chain of 50 stores the firm clearly considers it unnecessary to provide additional details on the company as a whole. Since Beauty Shop is the sole online store in the cosmetic industry there is little incentive to innovate further.

The Future

What the company sees as its immediate next steps are extending both the content and functionality of the website. The first refers to extending the breadth of the product assortment to include hair colouring products and, at a later stage, all the choice cosmetics brands. The second includes building personalization features into the site, linking it to an integrated customer relationship management (CRM) software, providing customers with the possibility of tracking order status via SMS messages, updating customers on new products and discounts via e-mail, short message service (SMS), or telephone.

These plans further reinforce the company's deeply held belief that the end result is mainly dependent on the degree of customer loyalty. Companies operating either offline or online still cannot appreciate the great potential and benefits behind it.

Conclusion

The major drivers and inhibitors for the firm were:

1. The IT manager championing e-commerce in the company.
2. The identified opportunity for building the company's modern image through online sales.
3. The opportunity to test a new market channel and see its potential.
4. The possibility to build a customer database with detailed information regarding their preferences and online shopping behaviour.
5. The long-term potential of online sales in a comparatively high-margin market.
6. The synergies identified with the offline operations in supporting the new business model and driving customer loyalty and sales.

The major obstacles and barriers that beautyshop.gr had to face, especially as a first mover in the sector, include:

1. The different objectives and vision per department; for example, the marketing department was oriented towards mass marketing and had a different idea of what the web could offer than the IT department.
2. The informal processes and procedures required in order to make a decision and allocate budget and resources to the project.
3. The need to outsource key operations, such as IT and logistics, and the selection of the appropriate partner.
4. The scarcity of resources, as no additional people were hired for this project but it had to run with existing personnel, especially at management level.
5. The major problems in building the product assortment online (e.g. collection of images, information, etc.), which required extended communication with and cooperation from product suppliers.

BEST-E—'THE GREEK ELECTRONIC MALL' (www.oops.gr)

Introduction

At the beginning of 2000 the Germanos Group of companies founded Best-e, a company intended to focus on e-commerce. The starting step of this company was to open one of the first online retail stores in Greece, the e-mall named oops.gr. The project resulted from the Group's strategic need to penetrate the Greek e-commerce market. The site focuses on customer value and service, offering its online customers a wide and continuously increasing range of products. The management's ultimate goal is to increase customer loyalty and establish the OOPS brand name as the first choice in the sector for Greek online customers. Best-e also considers the operation of OOPS as its first step towards establishing a leading presence in the new economy. Future plans include expansion into other areas of e-commerce, such as offering B2B applications, e-business consulting and creating a portal. The company is prepared to invest in doing so, but the objective of gaining profit through online sales is not the first priority at the moment since the Greek electronic retail market is not considered mature enough yet.

Best-e is a company specializing in e-commerce applications, providing dedicated solutions both to businesses that wish to promote their products or services through the Internet (B2B) and to final consumers through the creation of commerce sites. Best-e is a subsidiary of the Germanos Group and was founded in February 2000. The Group primarily operates two retail chain stores in electronics, computers and mobile phones and is a leader in the respective markets.

In the first stage of its activity in the electronic environment, Best-e started by investing in B2C applications, its first move being the creation of OOPS, the biggest e-mall in Greece. At the electronic address www.oops.gr some of the most well-known shops in Greece are hosted, serving the 'shop-in-a-shop' concept, according to which consumers are able to make online purchases in the most simple and convenient manner, every day, 24 hours a day, selecting from a large variety of products.

The site went live on 26 November 2000, becoming one of the first online retail stores in Greece. OOPS is the building block for Germanos's dynamic entry in the e-commerce area. The electronic mall currently offers more than 200 000 different items through its strategic alliance with 16 specialty retail shops in Greece. Best-e aims to form approximately 40 such alliances by the end 2001 in order to offer its customers a very wide range of products as well as high quality. In order to facilitate its growth, OOPS aims to keep high standards of customer service (customer care and after-sales service) and to continue investing in resources and technology.

Throughout 2001 Best-e plans to announce new activities in the field of e-commerce, such as B2B applications, e-business consulting services and the creation of a portal, aiming to establish a leading presence in the new economy.

Business Model

The target customers of OOPS are the group of Greek Internet users, experienced or not, either men or women, who mainly belong in the age group of 18–44 and are positioned in the middle or upper economic and educational classes. Nevertheless, the product mix of OOPS covers all the needs of its customers, independent of age or sex. In addition, during 2001 OOPS plans to systematically approach the Greek international community in order to attract all Internet users of Greek origin throughout the world.

By investing in know-how and technological infrastructure, developing strategic alliances, creating competitive advantages, providing reliable and quality services to its customers and utilizing the power of the Germanos Group as well as the experience from other countries, Best-e aims to establish a leading presence in e-commerce in Greece. Moreover, OOPS addresses the needs of Greek online customers providing them with the widest available range of products, differentiated services, special offers, confidentiality, transaction security and high-quality customer service. In this way the company aims to become a synonym for electronic purchases in the minds of Greek Internet users and to become their number one choice.

The Germanos Group provides Best-e with very important synergies, enhancing its competitive advantages with

- support from a very powerful group of companies, able to make large investments and showing intensive activity in the information economy;
- customer trust in the brand name and in the new activities of the group;
- utilization of the bargaining power of the group (purchasing, media);
- logistics know-how;
- retail know-how, taking advantage of the experience gained from the world of traditional retailing;
- economies of scale in organizational and human resources;
- know-how in quality of service; and
- product offerings from other companies that belong to the group.

At the same time, the know-how that Best-e is obtaining from its own experience and the infrastructure it develops empowers the Germanos Group in its quest to establish a leading presence in the new economy and supports its expansion to international markets through the Internet in cooperation with other Greek and foreign companies.

As far as the functional part of OOPS's operations is concerned, all the online orders are handled at the e-mall's headquarters. No inventory is kept by OOPS. Dedicated personnel, belonging to the online business unit, gather the orders and then products are picked up from the stores of participating companies. OOPS boasts of being the only e-mall in Europe that offers all the shopping in one basket without involving different accounts, deliveries and payment policies for different participating stores, as is common elsewhere.

The distribution process is outsourced to one of four affiliated courier services which picks the order from the store and delivers it throughout the country within four to six days (guaranteed), while orders usually reach the customer in one or two days, especially in Athens. This operation can satisfy more than 500 orders per day.

On the customer side, there is no lower limit per order, while at the present stage there is no charge for delivery. Different promotion schemes are operating, offering free gifts, special offers and more attractive online prices to customers. Regarding payment, there are two options offered: either online payment with a credit card or by cash on delivery.

Despite the fact that the whole range of offerings is very attractive for the online customer, the whole operation is not profitable. However, the objective is not to gain short-term profit but to build long-term customer relations. OOPS expects to build loyalty and long-term sales in the future when the market will grow and become more mature in Greece. The source of revenue for the e-mall at the moment is the transaction fee charged to suppliers. They anticipate to shift to a subscription-based model, paid by participating shops, once conditions mature.

Implementing the Business Model

The decision to develop `oops.gr` was made in the spring of 2000 and was the result of strategic intent of the Germanos Group. A separate business unit was created employing 15 people, with a clear focus to develop and run the online operations of OOPS. The initial business development budget amounted 500 million GrDr (approximately 1.47 million euros). Another 500 million GrDr are planned for investment throughout 2001.

Best-e invested dynamically in e-commerce infrastructure, website management, fault-tolerant operation and in transferring experience and know-how into the area of e-commerce. The technological infrastructure that it uses facilitates the automatic modification and transmission of data for use in many different electronic environments [PCs, interactive television, personal digital assistants (PDAs) and mobile phones]. Although the company does not exploit any electronic channel other than the fixed Internet, its intention is to make a strong presence in any channel when the business opportunity arises.

Aiming to achieve the high standards set out by the management for the operation and functionality of OOPS, state-of-the-art technology was used both in planning the site and in terms of infrastructure. Significant investments in hardware and in software applications were made as well. Special attention was also paid in the inhouse development of fully automated logistics mechanisms, adequate to facilitate many transactions on a daily basis.

The rest of the main operations of the online store, i.e. website development, distribution process, security issues and call centre, were outsourced to third parties. IBM and Opticom undertook web-site development and hosting, while the distribution process was outsourced to four of the largest courier services in Greece. Furthermore, the more established and up-to-date policies for transaction security and privacy were used in collaboration with Winbank, the electronic bank of the Bank of Piraeus. Finally, the operation of a call centre, which operates 7 days a week from 9 am to 10 pm, was undertaken by eValue. All in all, the development of OOPS essentially creates the foundation for the extended support of all the e-commerce applications that Best-e plans to offer to the Greek online community in the near future.

Industry, Competitor and Environmental Analysis

OOPS operates in the online retail industry. More specifically, it operates as an e-mall and has obtained first-mover advantage by becoming the front-runner in its field in the Greek online market. The company monitors its competitors closely.

However, in an environment that is still quite young and in its formative stage in Greece, it is not surprising that the company constantly has to reconsider who might be its main competitor. In March 2001, the main competitors were considered to be shop21.gr (although it offers only very specific products), prom.gr, e-shop.gr and enable.gr.

Although any quantitative measures are not yet available in the Greek online market concerning market share and profitability data, the general feeling is that OOPS is currently the leader in its sector. The main source of differentiation between OOPS and its competitors is that it has formed alliances only with well-known brands offering products of the highest quality and that it offers by far the largest variety of products to the final consumer. The online market is characterized by rather high product movement, while the technology changes at a high rate. As a result, frequent changes are demanded in the marketing practices of OOPS in response to competition.

By the first quarter of 2001, OOPS secured the advantage of being a first mover in the Greek online e-mall market. Traditional Greek malls do not seem very willing to enter the online market because: it is still very small; demands special skills; it is a culture that is not widespread in Greece; it requires different positioning; and it is difficult to find the right personnel. The management of OOPS considers as its biggest competitive threat the possibility of giant international online retailers creating Greek sites, thus exploiting all the competitive advantages they have obtained from their long presence in the field.

Key Business Drivers and Threats

Within the company, the main drivers that led to the implementation of this new business idea were:

- The fact that the market was an area of strategic importance for the Germanos Group.
- The opportunity to develop a new sales channel.
- The desire to strengthen the company's technological innovation.
- The desire to be ahead of competition and achieve first-mover advantage.

On the other end, the major barriers that the firm has had to overcome for the project to become a sustainable success have been:

- The small target audience
- The lack of Internet culture which led to difficulties in understanding the business model by partners and customers
- The need to develop alternative marketing techniques
- The large budget needed for the site to evolve

In the external business environment, OOPS had to face the problem of limited Internet penetration in Greek society. However, Internet penetration has increased and the situation looks to be slowly but steadily improving. In addition, market growth is hampered by the absence of a regulatory framework for e-commerce, the lack of familiarity with Internet transactions and the delayed establishment of an electronic settlement system. At the same time, suppliers themselves are characterized by a lack of awareness and this also created some initial problems.

The first-mover advantage can only be maintained in the long term through the provision of exceptional customer service and a unique online shopping experience. This is why the company plans to offer personalization features soon, as well as to link the operations of the site to both a Customer Relationship Management software and an Enterprise Resource Planning system in order to meet the challenges that are expected to arise.

On the delivery side, the level of service currently offered by third-party courier companies is satisfactory. So far deliveries are free of charge and no competitor has a better offering to make. Besides, in this product market delivery times are not usually critical.

Another source of concern for OOPS was the recruitment process, since the lack of experience and understanding forced the company to draw its human resources mainly from companies outside the Germanos Group and from abroad.

Despite all these problems, OOPS has managed to evolve and grow stronger. Its strength can be identified mainly in the following points:

- It is the only e-mall in Europe offering a unified order execution service (a unified order means packaging, delivery and payment).
- It specializes and has know-how in e-commerce.
- It has reliable technological infrastructure in hardware and software applications.
- It attracts the biggest and most well-known brands at one electronic address.
- It offers exclusive deals with cooperating retailers.
- It offers a wide range of products (more than 200 000) which cover almost all the needs of Greek e-customers.
- It is a site that is functional and user friendly.
- It offers competitive prices, bonus schemes and special offers.
- There is a high level of customer service (before and after sales).
- Its infrastructure guarantees security of transactions and protection of private information of customers.
- It has the support of a very big group (Germanos).

Website Development and Operation

The development and hosting of the oops.gr site has been outsourced to IBM and Opticom. The reason behind this decision was that the project was considered to be expensive and difficult to implement based only on inhouse expertise. The OOPS online business unit defined the functional requirements and the website design, including the creative part of it. Development took six months and the site went live on 26 November 2000, exactly according to schedule. There were no major problems in building the product assortment online (e.g. collection of images, information, etc.), despite the extensive communication and cooperation on the side of product suppliers that was needed. The initial site layout has been improved three times since then. The first improvement had more to do with the installation of new hardware and software applications, while the second aimed to improve the content of the site. The final improvement aimed at improving the aesthetics (look and feel) of the site. All three improvements were considered successful by management. However, according to management itself, the decision to outsource some activities has not produced the desired levels of effectiveness since it has led to a limited degree of flexibility.

Table 4.1 shows that OOPS's website supports the firm's focus on service moderately well. The company details, transaction capability and customer services are well developed but have room for further improvement. Three areas of critical importance for an e-mall (product and service information, ease of use and innovations in customer service) need attention, particularly as the firm has expressed concerns about the potential threat of international competitors.

The Future

The online presence of OOPS at the time of this analysis has reached a lifespan of 4 months. In this period OOPS managed to overcome most of the initial obstacles and is now starting to steadily increase its sales. The management's next aim is to improve the content and functionality of the website. Content refers to renewing the product line and making the product range wider through forming around 20 new alliances within 2001. Functionality involves building personalization features in the site, linking it to an integrated CRM software and investing in an ERP system. In addition, Best-e aims to make the site more appealing to Greek customers who live abroad. Finally, the company will try to take advantage of its experience from OOPS and the infrastructure that lies behind it when it starts the other e-commerce related activities it has planned, namely B2B applications, e-business consulting and a portal. The management has a clear vision of the direction in which it wants to drive the company and is aware that establishing the site and securing customer loyalty in the long term are its primary objectives. The questions that lie ahead are whether the Greek online market will grow fast enough, how OOPS will increase its sources of revenue, and finally how it will respond to potential competition from one of the global Internet players.

Conclusion

The main drivers that led to the creation of Best-e and its implementation as an e-mall were:

- The market was an area of strategic importance for the Germanos Group.
- There was an opportunity to develop a new sales channel.

Table 4.1 Results of Greek application of the CEC framework

Firms	Company information/5	Product/ services information/5	Transactions/5	Customer service/5	Ease of use/5	Innovation/5	Total/30	CEC scale © (%)
Beauty Shop	2	5	5	4	4	0	20	67
Best-e (oops.gr)	4	3	4	4	3	2	20	67
E-shop	2	4	5	3	3	2	19	63
Papasotiriou	2	3	5	3	4	1	18	60
Plaisio	5	4	5	3	4	0	21	70

- There was a need to strengthen the company's technological innovation.
- There was a desire to be ahead of the competition and achieve first-mover advantage.

The major barriers that the firm has had to overcome have been:

- the small target audience;
- a lack of Internet culture which led to difficulties in understanding the business model by partners and customers;
- the need to develop alternative marketing techniques; and
- the large budget needed for the site to evolve.

E-SHOP—'A WINDOW TO THE MARKET'—(www.eshop.gr)

Introduction

E-shop, Greece's first online store, was the result of an experiment by three young entrepreneurs in their free time. One of the most successful electronic shops in Greece started 'as a hobby', just to see whether they could do it or not. Not only did they succeed, they also managed to get customers from major competitors who are also engaged in the bricks-and-mortar business. 'It is all a matter of liking what you do, not being afraid to realize your ideas and trying out new things' (Costas Mavroeidis, co-founder and CEO).

Founded in December 1998, e-shop is the first Greek online store. Having only an electronic presence in the Greek market, e-shop managed quickly to establish a good reputation and earn many loyal customers, even from large competitors who dominate the market with their bricks-and-mortar shops. E-shop offers approximately 80 000 product codes, under three major categories, i.e. entertainment (books, DVDs, games), office products and supplies (computer components, accessories and consumables), and accessories.

In order to cope with competition, e-shop places great importance on issues such as *security*, *quality* of customer service and *innovation* in the services and products offered. The shop expands its catalogue with new products very often, and is also offering web page hosting services.

Although e-shop still operates without profits, its revenues increased from 6 million GrDr in 1999 to 67 million in 2000. The shop receives approximately 15 online orders per day; however, orders are also being placed via fax or phone.

Business Model

E-shop plays the role of a channel retail business, building a just-in-time operation based on good relationships with suppliers and stock keeping of the most frequently purchased products. Most of the products being ordered are purchased from the suppliers after the orders have been placed. E-shop maintains low prices by building long-term relationships with suppliers. Prices and discounts are agreed with suppliers on a monthly basis, depending on the total of the products purchased by e-shop.

Distribution is handled by either post or courier services, and in some cases by the company itself. The company has managed to ship 10% of the products within hours of order placement. From the rest, 80% is available the next day. A small percentage of products (5%), which might appear to be in short supply, is being replaced in consultation with customers by alternative, comparable products, so as not to delay shipment. The rest of the orders are usually shipped within two days from placement. E-shop has a number of customers among the Greek communities outside Greece. It is one of a very few sources of Greek books online. Distribution abroad is usually fulfilled by international post.

As far as the customer is concerned, there is no lower limit per order. The customer can choose from a variety of 80 000 stock keeping units (SKUs), either by using the store's search engine, or by picking products on 'virtual displays' (updated twice a week). It is also possible to search for a product by company, or by product category. Delivery charges vary according to the order size; the larger the order, the lower the delivery cost per unit. Orders can be placed online, through fax or phone. Payments can be made either with a credit card, or cash on delivery.

Implementing the Business Model

The idea of building e-shop belongs to three young entrepreneurs who wanted to try their abilities in an 'internet experiment'. Their initial goal was not to make a profit, but to 'have fun' in starting their own business. The company was established in December 1998. The first year of operation went by with many mistakes and oversights. The three entrepreneurs admit being occupied with other things as well. Traffic in the shop started in September 1999. In the months that followed they saw e-shop more seriously, placed greater effort in it, and started to enlarge the company developing the product catalogue and improving the services offered.

There were not so many options on the business model to be adopted, since the company wanted to achieve the best results with the lowest possible costs. Therefore, the goal was to establish agreements with suppliers in order to achieve relatively low prices without keeping a large inventory. Most of the products are purchased after being ordered, while fast moving goods (such as DVDs) are kept in inventory, mainly because of the suppliers' inability to deliver at short notice.

The website development and hosting was originally outsourced to an IT company. However, as the company grew in experience, it took over site development and maintenance and moved the server to its premises, now being able to provide a better quality of service, store availability and response. The company currently employs 12 persons, in three main departments: fulfilment (including accounting and warehouse keeping, and service provision), catalogue and database maintenance and update, and internet infrastructure maintenance.

Industry, Competitor and Environmental Analysis

E-shop operates in the retail industry, without focus on a certain product category. One of its major strengths, according to the CEO, is that it offers customers the option to collect several different products in the same basket, without having to visit specialized electronic shops, and thus having to pay for multiple deliveries. Moreover, the company offers web hosting services, mainly as an alternative means of increasing revenue.

Although the company is relatively small, it may be considered medium-sized in terms of revenue and customers acquired, in relation to the competition. E-shop's main competitors are store chains such as Germanos and Plaisio, which focus on computer components, accessories, books, games, etc. Although such chains are the leaders in the traditional economy, e-shop has managed to attract many of their customers by innovating faster, achieving better prices and better quality of service, especially after-sales.

The main area of differentiation among e-shop and its competitors is after-sales service. E-shop provides customers with the ability to track their order, and places great emphasis on product guarantees. This is important especially for distant customers, and builds customer loyalty. Indeed, many of e-shop's customers are regular shoppers.

The market that e-shop operates in is characterized by a wide variety of products and a rather high product movement, especially in the computer segment. The competition in general is not perceived as difficult to predict. What e-shop's CEO sees as the main threat is the ability of leaders in the bricks-and-mortar market to make a massive investment online. E-shop would be easily dwarfed in such a scenario. However, so far the competition is either limited to one of e-shop's segments or is still making little progress online. For this reason, e-shop is constantly seeking to extend its product assortment.

Key Business Drivers and Threats

The main driver that made the e-shop project a success was the eagerness of the original entrepreneurial team to work and try new concepts and ideas. The Internet as such made it quite easy for them. On the other hand, for a small company such as e-shop, the major obstacle is the marketing budget available to other companies of the sector. E-shop cannot cope with the budgets of the traditional retailers, and the CEO considers himself lucky that currently most shops put effort into advertising their traditional instead of their virtual stores.

E-shop's most common ways of advertising themselves is by using their logo on packaging, receipts and invoices, and by placing banners on other web pages, especially on major Greek portals. They also use their mailing list to inform customers about offers, new products and services, and partner with other web-sites for reciprocal promotion. In general, their effort is on maximizing advertise-ment effectiveness within their very limited budget. Their big advantages, namely low prices and high quality of service, are also advertised by word of mouth, resulting in new but loyal customers every day. Word of mouth has proven to be a powerful mechanism for drawing new customers and their loyalty turns out to be a significant asset, even if the company does not quantify it.

The CEO's primary concern is on quality of operations. Correct order fulfilment is one of e-shop's key business drivers. Importance is placed on correct orders, on-time delivery, product variety, good prices, good organization and, above all, a steady level of quality, in order to build customer loyalty and a good reputation.

Issues such as price and quality competition, and services offered by competi-tors are considered as a threat to the company, which copes with relatively low profit margins, but are also viewed as opportunities for the company to differ-entiate itself and provide a better overall proposition to its customers. The possibility of a declining demand or scarce supply is handled by the company by keeping inventory only of frequently selling products, or products that are difficult to acquire within a few hours. By operating just-in-time for most of the products, e-shop can handle fluctuations in demand without suffering big losses.

During the early stages, e-shop faced difficulties in building agreements with suppliers. The whole concept of an online store operating just-in-time was foreign to most suppliers, who did not see any profit in selling few items at a time at wholesale prices. Moreover, many suppliers were engaged in building their own electronic shop, thus presenting a conflict of interest. Since then, e-shop has managed to establish strong long-term relationships with key suppliers.

At the back office, the online operations are not integrated with the rest of the processes. The CEO considers an ERP system too expensive and not needed at the present time. The various system applications are not interconnected, and the transfer of data is being done manually. Although the company has substantial data on customer preferences, page visits and most wanted products, the CEO is not satisfied with the way that they are used. The company is still developing data mining and analysis tools for the extraction of patterns and conclusions regarding online consumer behaviour.

Innovation Factors and Processes

The most important factors that have led to e-shop's success so far are:

1. The eagerness and effort placed by the entrepreneurs.
2. Good relationships with banks and financial institutions.
3. The fact that they were the first to implement an online shop in Greece.
4. The scarce presence of major competitors online.
5. E-shop's emphasis on total quality.

The major obstacles and barriers that e-shop had to face, include:

1. Outsourcing website implementation. The process was characterized by unsuccessful partnerships.
2. Infrastructure problems (the first Christmas that e-shop operated, the system was down, resulting in many lost sales).
3. The difficulty in creating relationships with suppliers.
4. The initial product selection.
5. The immaturity of the Greek market towards electronic shops.

Website Development and Operational Issues

E-shop outsourced the initial development and hosting of the website to an IT company, since e-shop's management team did not have neither the required know-how, nor the infrastructure to implement the project themselves. Development took approximately four months, but the result was far from satisfactory. The system was vulnerable, and unreliable. The company lost sales when the ISP let the system down during the peak season of Christmas 1999, when e-shop was the only live online shop in Greece.

The CEO admits to having made many managerial and technical mistakes during the first months of e-shop's operation. He believes the company should have made a wiser, more selective choice of products, and should have been more careful in choosing a web-developing partner. It criticizes the company that took over the website implementation as lacking know-how on several aspects, not being able to solve several problems, being indifferent and delaying the project. This is indicative of the immaturity of the web services market at the time. The CEO attributes most of those problems to their inexperience and small budget.

During 2000, e-shop acquired the infrastructure to host the system in its own premises. Building on their know-how and experience, they now create and update their web pages themselves, keeping the website services on a high, satisfactory level. Table 4.1 shows that the website is moderately well developed in support of the firm's objectives but further work is required on company information, customer services, ease of use and innovation.

The Future

E-shop's management is aware of the fact that dot.coms need a long period of time to produce a return on their investment. Although e-shop is not making any profit yet, its management stays focused on the goal of total quality and innovative products and services. At the beginning of 2001 e-shop managed to break even on its operating budget after a cost-cutting exercise. However, it is not involved in long-range planning, but sets goals within the range of four months. These plans are informal and adapt frequently as new needs and issues arise.

Future challenges include the offering of smart, innovative products and services, ideally renewed every three months, that track closely the needs of customers, and are being fulfilled without mistakes and delays. It hopes it can increase revenues and margins through extending the web hosting services. Its target is to lower its cost per order to less than 3000 GrDr (approx. 9 euros), and increase its profit margin, which currently ranges from 7% to 30% depending on the product.

Considering e-shop's short presence in the Greek market, it is quite an achievement that it managed to break even. The CEO bases success on profits, functional, friendly web pages and an effective promotional effort. Remembering the three young entrepreneurs' original goal, however, namely to try their abilities, www.eshop.gr is definitely a success.

Conclusion

The most important factors that have led to e-shop's success so far are:

1. The entrepreneurs' eagerness and efforts.
2. Good relationships with banks and financial institutions.
3. The fact that they were the first to implement an online shop in Greece.
4. The scarce presence of major competitors online.
5. E-shop's emphasis on total quality.

E-shop's major obstacles and barriers include:

1. Outsourcing website implementation. The process was characterized by unsuccessful partnerships.
2. Infrastructure problems (the first Christmas that e-shop operated, the system was down, resulting in many lost sales).
3. The difficulty in creating relationships with suppliers.
4. The initial product selection.
5. The immaturity of the Greek market towards electronic shops.

PAPASOTIRIOU—THE FIRST GREEK ON-LINE BOOKSTORE
(www.papasotiriou.gr)

Introduction

Papasotiriou bookstores have always aimed at being leaders in their field. Ever since this family-owned company shifted its business focus from publishing to book retailing, management has made a series of successful strategic choices that established Papasotiriou as the unarguable leader in technical and scientific books and one of the top players in the Greek book market overall. The drive always to be ahead of the competition and predict new market trends and business opportunities also inspired the online store venture, which was launched at a time when the Internet in Greece was still at its infancy (1998). Despite the immaturity of the market and the uncertainty regarding future trends, management endorsed the effort. The rationale was to establish a presence on the new 'medium' and to gain valuable experience in the process. Sales and profit were not primary goals at that stage. A few things have changed since then. Papasotiriou entered book retailing in 1981, introducing the first 'Technical Bookstore Papasotiriou' in Athens. The effort to target specific customer segments and offer them the best possible service was obvious: the bookstore was strategically located next to the National Technical University of Athens (the largest engineering university in Greece), in a region where a large number of technical and scientific businesses also reside. Nowadays Papasotiriou operates 20 bookstores in every major Greek city and is established as a leader in the markets for software, multimedia CDs and scientific books. It is also one of the top bookstore chains in Greece, in terms of number of stores, annual sales and turnover (with an average turnover growth rate of about 20% for the past four years).

Rather than trying to fulfil the needs of every book buyer and cover the enormous range of book categories available, Papasotiriou chose to concentrate on specific areas of interest and provide a depth of selection that no competitor could match. In that scope, the first specialized 'Art Bookstore' was introduced in 1991 and a year later a new branch provided exclusively scientific and academic books. A major turning point was the 'Multimedia Store', launched in 1996, which provided the largest CD-ROM collection in Greece. Since then, IT books and software products started gaining increasing importance within the company's product mix. The management had once again foreseen the 'boom' in computers and information technologies that was soon to follow early enough to gain a competitive advantage and dominate this new and promising market.

The online store still remains a proportionally small part of Papasotiriou's business, yet management believes that the internal, as well as the external environment are now mature enough to justify an organized and well-planned effort to enhance it and potentially establish it as a major business asset in the years to come.

The Business Model

Despite the fact that Papasotiriou's site was introduced as early as 1998 and provided e-commerce capability from the very beginning, relatively few modifications and enhancements have been introduced since then. The main reason was that the Greek net market did not have the critical mass to justify a larger investment that would bring the site to a higher quality level. This also applies to the business model, which is more or less the same as the one that the online store was introduced with. Papasotiriou had decided not to invest further in creating the market through extensive promotion of and innovation on their website. Instead, they established their presence and waited for market conditions to mature.

One of the main drivers of the early Internet venture was the importance of IT-related products for Papasotiriou's business. It was only natural that the top 'IT-oriented' bookstore would be the first to step into the Internet. The main issue for management was to establish an early presence and gain experience in a field that could prove of strategic significance later on. Furthermore, the site could facilitate users in finding exactly what they wanted by making available rich product information and 'news updates'. The size and maturity of the target market did not allow any expectations of high sales and profits; yet the opportunity of providing customers with an easier way to access Papasotiriou's comprehensive product range and highly competitive prices together with additional services could not be overlooked. In any case, books and software are, by nature, products very popular to Internet shoppers and have provided the foundation for Internet giants such as amazon.com.

Better integration with the rest of the company's business modules is an issue that has to be faced in order for an online store to grow. Management's recent decision to replace its legacy information system with an ERP provided by SAP, indicates its intend to rely on new technologies as a competitive advantage in a constantly evolving market, where keeping up to date means staying competitive. Together with database integration, a redesigned logistics process that would reduce cycle time while raising the level of customer service and satisfaction should be considered.

The Greek Internet market still remains small in size, but the growth rate is faster than ever, with enhanced security technologies and publicity efforts attracting more and more Internet 'believers'. In addition to this, the inherent advantages of online shopping create an environment mature enough for Papasotiriou to invest in a new online store that will provide functionality, personalized services and information-rich content, close to what the global leaders are already offering.

Implementation of the Business Model

The original website development was outsourced. The planning stage took about four months and another four were required for implementation. The introduction process did not face any problems, but managing and supporting the site turned out, predictably, to be much more costly and complex than they had originally anticipated. At present, a two-member team manages the online store (one for technical issues, one for order processing). They are sufficient to handle the 30–35 sales that occur each day (with an average of 1.5 books or 35 000 GrDr (103 euros) per sale out of 2500–3000 daily visits). More staff will be needed if the online store is to be upgraded.

The online store's catalogue is based on data transferred from the company's main database, with the disadvantage of slow updating, especially about product availability, given the vast size and constant updating of the product range. Only registered customers (about 3500 at present) can place orders and payment can be arranged either by credit card (which is manually processed) or by cash on delivery. The person in charge of order processing transfers the orders to the company's inventory management and distribution channels, which are the same as those of the physical stores. There is no special logistics planning or other arrangement dedicated to the e-store, since the volume of business is not large enough to justify this.

The site facilitates a variety of search methods and substantial book information. Apart from placing orders from the catalogue, customers can ask for books that are not in stock through a special ordering process available on and offline. There is also a customizable service that notifies registered customers about new editions or other developments in their areas of interest, which is very useful considering the vast range and constant renewal of available titles. In that sense, the site serves customers as a means of keeping up to date with subjects of their interest (especially important for scientific books). The site also offers promotions or lower prices for online purchases, but they are not considered as a major attraction. What the company wishes to achieve by upgrading its online store module is enhanced site functionality and superior customer service.

Industry, Competitor and Environmental Analysis

Papasotiriou operates in the book retail industry, and although it specializes in specific categories, its product range covers almost all types of books. Its main competitor is Eleftheroudakis. There also exist other more or less specialized book stores but none in the fields where Papasotiriou concentrates, at least not big enough to pose a serious competitive threat.

With respect to scientific and especially IT-related books, Papasotiriou is the market leader and the most established brand name. The decision to focus on the IT/scientific niche proved to be successful and has resulted in an estimated current share of 45% in this market. We should not disregard the software market as well, which is of critical importance for the company. Here Papasotiriou has to compete off and online with many major computer-store chains (Plaisio, Multirama, E-motion, etc.), yet has managed to outperform many of them by offering good product variety at competitive prices.

For the online store in particular, competition originates primarily from established Internet giants, with Amazon prevailing among them. Despite the fact that Papasotiriou is only targeting the Greek market, the years of experience, advanced logistics, brand awareness, unmatched product range and global scope make Amazon a feared rival. As it turns out, Papasotiriou can offer a better final price for small orders (up to about four books). For bigger orders Amazon's final prices are superior, as higher total shipment cost becomes negligible per book in comparison with base price savings. In addition, the website cannot achieve the same product range as Amazon. Considering that Papasotiriou accounts for a mere 1% of the company's annual turnover and targets a market limited in size, creating a system similar to Amazon's does not make financial sense for the time being.

The key success factors for Papasotiriou are product availability, order cycle time, inventory management and flexibility to fulfil special customer orders. The company is not formally measuring these parameters. They consider themselves doing well but they also see the need for further investment and performance improvement.

Key Business Drivers and Threats

The idea for the site originated from the IT personnel in the company and quickly gained support from top management, which has proven very open to innovative decisions through the years. The introduction of computer-related literature and software as the most important elements of the product mix, provided the background for entering the Internet market. The physical proximity to the scientific world and the fact that Internet penetration among Papasotiriou's customers is much higher than the average for Greece, strengthened the case. Despite the support for the online store from inside the company, the main obstacle that has kept Papasotiriou almost unchanged for the last three and a half years is the small size of its target market. There were just not enough customers to justify any further investment.

Currently the site promises delivery within a day, for major cities, with no extra charges and uses third-party couriers and mail. This is quite satisfactory for now, but there is much room for improvement. The small size of Papasotiriou makes these promises relatively easily attainable for the time being. Future growth will require fundamental rethinking and formalization of business processes. The main issues that have to be faced are:

- better integration with the company's ERP system, in order to keep the catalogue up to date and to streamline order processing; and
- enhanced logistics systems and processes in order to deliver the response promised by Internet shopping.

Innovation Factors and Processes

It seems that the main factors that led Papasotiriou to this project are:

1. The management's desire to stay ahead of the competition, discover new business opportunities and invest in new ideas. The rationale was to establish a presence on the new 'medium' and to gain valuable experience in the process. Sales and profit were not primary goals at that stage.
2. The nature of the product: books and software, together with music CDs are the most typical e-commerce goods.
3. The technological character of the product mix (computer-related books and software) and the proximity of Papasotiriou to the scientific world at large.

4. The increased penetration of Internet among the company's target customers, calculated roughly as five times that of the average population.
5. The potential of the Internet market. Papasotiriou wanted a presence in a medium that is expected to attain great importance in the future.
6. The example of global giants like Amazon, shows that this is a growing industry, despite short-term obstacles and global competition.

On the other hand, many obstacles have hindered the online store's growth up until now:

1. The low Internet penetration in Greece.
2. The unfamiliarity of the Greek market with new technologies in general and lack of trust in this new means of commercial transaction.
3. Despite the fact that Papasotiriou's customers are much more familiar with the Internet and e-commerce, their number is still rather limited.
4. The cost of upgrading the site's functionality and services to world-class standards is considered too high given current market conditions.
5. Papasotiriou has been operating at break-even.
6. The Amazon case: if the world's most well-known online bookstore cannot return in a profit, how could we?
7. Lack of systems integration and streamlined fulfilment processes.

Website Development and Operational Issues

Papasotiriou started out as an experiment in innovation and was originally developed in collaboration with a research and development (R&D) group at the national technical University of Athens. Since then, site maintenance and updates have been handled internally. Although it immediately became clear that a commercial Internet presence requires intensive and continuous support for service enhancement, the company did not face any compelling reason to engage in major updates. Therefore the site itself is characterized by a 'spartan' interface, which has met only incremental improvement over the years.

Table 4.1 shows that Papasotiriou is a web bookstore that delivers value to its customers. With over 20 000 Greek and 60 000 non-Greek titles, it is a respectable source of books for its market segments. The 'spartan' character of the site means that it is primarily utilitarian, geared towards making consumer transactions (purchases) as efficient as possible. For this purpose, the site offers comprehensive support for the whole range of ordering, payment and invoicing methods that are applicable to the Greek market. The straightforward structure and layout makes navigation and product search very easy. We might argue that Papasotiriou is addressed to the knowledgeable and determined book buyer and not so much to the casual bookstore browser. In other words, the site provides little more than the basic data and functionality needed by someone who knows what he or she is looking for. In contrast, curiosity shoppers are not sufficiently catered for and impulse buying or cross selling are not pursued.

Over the past year the company's IT resources have been overwhelmed by the ERP project. As expected, this has been a tremendous technological and organizational exercise and an invaluable learning experience. Now that the ERP system has stabilized, Papasotirious is revisiting its e-commerce strategy by exploring a variety of exciting new ideas that may, potentially, be implemented. Meanwhile, the natural next step is to install and exploit SAP's e-commerce modules. This is considered to be a relatively straightforward project (since the basic SAP modules are already in place) that will, however, become a quantum leap in terms of online functionality and customer service as a result of the capability offered by the system.

The Future

It is a common belief among the company's IT personnel and management that the time has come to raise Papasotiriou to a new level. The market is mature enough and the number of potential customers has risen sufficiently to justify the investment that will be required. Furthermore, the company has gained valuable experience during the three and a half years of the project and the technology is mature and offers a large variety of e-commerce platforms, tools and security mechanisms that can ensure easy and safe transactions. A major issue that is being discussed is the provision of personalized services to customers, a feature that most modern e-commerce or non-commercial sites have already incorporated. Another key in the upgrade effort is the enhancement of front-end functionality for customers, as well as that of back-office processes. Given the compatibility of the target market with the Internet as a means of commerce, the company believes that it will be ready to compete in equal terms with local and global players for a substantial share in the emerging Internet market.

Conclusion

The main factors that led Papasotiriou to this project are:

1. The management's desire to stay ahead of the competition, discover new business opportunities and invest in new ideas. The rationale was to establish a presence in the new 'medium' and to gain valuable experience in the process. Sales and profit were not primary goals at that stage.
2. The nature of the product: Papasotiriou sells books, and books, software and music CDs are the most typical e-commerce goods.
3. The technological character of the product mix (computer-related books and software) and the proximity of Papasotiriou to the scientific world at large.
4. The increased penetration of the Internet among the company's target customers, calculated roughly as five times that of the average population.

5. The potential of the Internet market. Papasotiriou wanted a presence in a medium that is expected to attain great importance in the future.
6. The example of global giants like Amazon shows that this is a growing industry, despite short-term obstacles and global competition.

On the other hand, many obstacles have hindered the online store's growth up until now:

1. The low Internet penetration in Greece.
2. The unfamiliarity of the Greek market with new technologies in general and lack of trust in this new means of commercial transaction.
3. Despite the fact that Papasotiriou's customers are much more familiar with the Internet and e-commerce, their number is still rather limited.
4. The cost of upgrading the site's functionality and services to world-class standards is considered too high given current market conditions.
5. Papasotiriou has been operating at break-even.
5. The Amazon case: if the world's most well known online bookstore cannot return in a profit, how could we?
7. Lack of systems integration and streamlined fulfilment processes.

PLAISIO—'EVERYTHING YOU WANT TO BUY!' (www.plaisio.gr)

Introduction

Plaisio.gr is the first Greek online store for consumer electronics, PC systems, mobile phones and office supplies. It operates as complementary to the bricks-and-mortar parent company, which is the market leader. The online store is seen as another distribution and communication channel. Therefore, it shares the very same image as the parent company, and offers the majority of the products one can find in the traditional stores and the company's catalogues. The top management of the company took the initiative to develop the online store, which means that they fully support it. The primary focus is on synergies that the online store can create with the other channels of the company, while profitability of the online store in itself is less of a priority. The company will keep investing in the online store.

Plaisio Computers SA was founded in 1969. At the time the company had one retail outlet in Athens where it was selling office supplies. In 1986 Plaisio opened a new specialized store where it assembled its own line of PCs, branded as TURBO-X. In 1996 Plaisio began selling its products through catalogues. Orders could be placed by phone, fax, and mail. The main target group for the catalogues was—and still is—business customers. In 1999 Plaisio entered the Stock Market. The same year the company created its first online store providing its customers an alternative way to place orders. This was the first attempt by the company to join the e-commerce bandwagon and it was mainly addressed to consumers. In 2001 two new electronic stores were presented. The first one is `plaisio2b.gr`, which targets business customers. The other one is `plaisiowap.gr`, which enables customers to place their orders through their mobile phone.

Currently, the company specializes in assembling and selling PC systems, software, computer peripherals accessories, office supplies, mobile phones, and special products like drawing equipment. It has 380 full-time employees and 12 physical stores, 9 of which are in Athens. Plaisio owns all 12 stores and has no plans for franchising because of the very low profit margins in the industry. Additionally the company owns two logistics centres and the headquarters. Sales for 1999 were up to 18 370 billion GrDr (U$49 333 978) with profits reaching 1388 billion GrDr (US$3 728 064). The company is financially secure and in a position to undertake almost any kind of project, which will support its future growth.

The company has an informal structure, which enables rapid decision-making. The corporate culture is team oriented and this is physically apparent at its open-plan office headquarters where department signs do not correspond to any spatial segregation. Customer service is the main concern of the company as well as its core competence, which is seen to provide competitive advantage. The CEO of the company is also its founder. He makes most of the decisions in collaboration with his executives. Plaisio has received a number of awards, including joining Europe's 500 fastest growing companies in 1999.

The company's main strategy is to have few large stores in key areas. Additionally, they wish to be present in every new channel (e-commerce, m-commerce, interactive TV, etc.) and to provide their customers with as many possibilities to transact as possible—to become the place where one can find 'everything one wants to buy!'.

Business Model

`Plaisio.gr` is strongly connected to Plaisio Computers SA. In fact, it can be seen as the sequence or supplement of the company's catalogues. It builds heavily on the bricks-and-mortar company. It shares the same brand name and everything that derives from that: image, loyal customers, credibility. That means that all basic operations (marketing, logistics, production, procurement, etc.) are common. This provides Plaisio with a great advantage, namely experience and knowledge of the particular industry.

All orders are initially sent to a central database. A specific employee collects them every 30 minutes and enters them in the ERP. Apparently, there is no integration between the two systems yet. Every order is verified by a phone call. An employee calls the customer and verifies that all information in the order is correct. This is necessary because many of the orders that the company receives have mistakes and/or omissions. Later, the whole process works identically to the catalogues. The order is prepared (for example, a computer with certain parts is assembled) in the central warehouse–logistics centre and is ready for the customer to receive it. As far as the shipment of the order is concerned, there are three alternatives.

1. The customer collects the order him/herself from any of the company's physical retail outlets.
2. Plaisio delivers the order wherever the customers wishes (within 24 hours in Athens and Thessaloniki and within two to three days in the rest of Greece). This is possible only during normal working hours and days.
3. Third-party parcel delivery.

The first two alternatives apply only to orders that are to be delivered in Athens or Thessaloniki. For all other areas in Greece only the third alternative is offered.

As far as payment is concerned, one can pay either by credit card (Visa or MasterCard) online or by cash on delivery. These are the two options when the customer chooses to either collect the order him/herself from the physical store or Plaisio delivers itself the order. When a third transportation company does the delivery, the payment is done either by credit card (Visa or MasterCard) or by a bank deposit.

Should the product prove to be defective or there are problems with the order, the customer can get in touch with the customer service department and return the product.

In general the online shop receives around 100 orders per day, which represents 1% of Plaisio total sales. So, it is not profitable. However, management believes the online store has a positive effect on the other channels and on the company as a whole. This effect may not be quantifiable but it estimates it to be of significance and totally justifying the respective investment.

Implementing the Business Model

The owner and CEO of Plaisio Computers SA conceived the idea of the online shop and personally oversaw the initiative. Along with the company's marketing manager, they decided to target primarily the consumer market. The decision process was quite informal and very quick. After a few discussions and taking into consideration that the company was in a good position financially, the decision was easily made. This movement was totally aligned with the company's strategy, which is to be the leader in the market, providing every new technology that becomes available. It is indicative that the company launched a wireless application protocol (WAP) site, even though they knew all along that this technology is not mature, that the whole market is very limited and that there is a chance that this technology will not become mainstream.

As far as the choice of the business model is concerned, there was not really any other option. The company simply needed a way to sell its products on the Internet by taking advantage of the entire infrastructure that was developed to support its other operations. Therefore, the classic e-shop was the indicated solution. It is interesting that Plaisio Computers SA decided to launch a commerce site from the very beginning, instead of starting with an information site (brochures, company info, product list, advertising, etc.) first.

Clearly, `plaisio.gr` is designed in a way very similar to `dell.com`, even if not as sophisticated. Plaisio Computers SA already had almost a decade's experience in assembling PCs to order through its stores or catalogue. One noticeable difference from Dell is that Plaisio addresses the more computer-literate segment, as online buyers have to specify detailed technical specifications (e.g. CPU fan) on the form. This is another reason why telephone confirmation, even modification, of orders is often necessary.

A new team was established in the company to support the online store. Additionally, several other employees and executives in the company undertook their part of the new project. For example, people working at the company's call centre are now handling requests from online customers and make the call to verify online orders. The existing logistics operation is also used for fulfilling online orders.

It is important to mention that the online store does not offer all the products that the company sells in its physical stores. The same of course applies to the catalogues as well. The products that a visitor can purchase online are the most popular and new additions. This is justified by the fact that products in this particular industry (computers) become obsolete very quickly. Therefore, it is not considered of value and/or significance for 'old' products to be available online. In this way, the online store becomes the fastest moving of Plaisio's channels.

Industry, Competition and Environmental Analysis

Plaisio Computers operates in the Greek market for office supplies, computers and peripherals and mobile phones. Competition is intense and margins are compressed. According to the ICAP Greek Financial Directory there are around 150 major competitors in the office supplies business, around 367 major competitors in the computers and peripherals business, and around 120 major competitors in the retail mobile phones business. Taking into consideration that many more, smaller competitors exist in all three business sectors, we clearly see that Plaisio has to deal with intense competition, especially in the B2C market. As far as the national online market is concerned, there are four main competitors: Multirama, e-motion, Microland, and Grammi. These are of course competitors in the offline market as well. It is of interest that all four competitors entered the online market a long time (from a few months to a year) after Plaisio Computers did.

The B2B market is a different case since small suppliers cannot compete. This is the sector where Plaisio makes the majority of its sales and profits. According to the company its competitive advantage lies in customer service and after-sales support. They want their customers to trust them and view them as their partners rather than their suppliers. According to the marketing manager's own words 'We keep our Promises.' Furthermore, Plaisio Computers tries to offer the greatest product variety at the best prices (it wants its prices to be at least as low as its competitors') with the best customer service and the best service quality. Plaisio Computers sees itself as indeed keeping its promises and being far ahead of the competition. Having secured a leading position in this market, it does little in terms of quantifying the quality of its services or its competitive differentiation. By no means does this mean that it does not make new efforts in order to keep its position as leader in the market.

Computers and related products have a very short life cycle. They are often replaced within months. Furthermore, this is an industry where prices change usually on a daily basis, sometimes more than once a day. Additionally, profit margins are low. In this context, Plaisio Computers is proud of its sophisticated purchasing process. Plaisio manages a portfolio of relationships with hundreds of suppliers worldwide and continuously monitors prices, availability and market trends. Adjustments in the supply chain worldwide are almost immediately reflected on the retail side.

Key Business Drivers and Threats

The primary business driver is the company's philosophy and strategy, which suggests continuous improvement and innovation in the services offered to customers in order to retain market leadership. The decision to launch plaisio.gr was based on the successful projection of the company's top management about the role that the Internet and e-commerce would play. It is important to note that at the time when plaisio.gr was launched, the Internet was at a much earlier stage of adoption in Greece. Today's Internet users are estimated to be less than 10% of the population but growing rapidly.

The company did not face any serious obstacles. Top management provided full support, resources were no object, and no competition existed. The only problem that Plaisio faced in the beginning had to do with the poor state of the public telecommunications infrastructure. Since then, significant investments by the public telecoms operator have improved the situation dramatically. One could possibly consider a threat the lack of experience along with the lack of previous cases in Greece at the time. However, Plaisio had already great experience from its catalogues business and a well-established call centre and a distribution system. Of course, it is still 'educating' the market into using the Internet for commercial transactions.

Innovation Factors and Processes

The innovation factors as already identified and presented were:

1. The personal vision of the founder and CEO.
2. Consistency with the company's strategy as being the market leader and offering the best customer service.

3. Enhancement of the company's image as state-of-the-art innovator.
4. The opportunity for another sales channel and synergies with the other offline channels.
5. The acquisition of first-mover advantage.

The innovation process can be characterized as one of serendipity and informality. The company's top management came up with the idea after watching foreign markets and decided to implement a similar model in Greece. Indeed, this is characteristic of its overall management style. The major barrier was the poor state of the public telecommunications infrastructure that resulted in unreliable connections to the Internet. This problem has since improved dramatically.

Website Development and Operational Issues

The development and hosting of the `plaisio.gr` website was undertaken by the company itself. It acquired all the necessary equipment, and hired the necessary human resources. Some external help from consultants was also sought. All systems were built and are managed in-house. Development lasted about six months and the site was launched in July 1999. The company decided to present a simple layout without complex graphics in order to emphasize a utilitarian environment targeted at knowledgeable users who knew what they were looking for. According to the company's marketing manager, 'If we did it again, we wouldn't do anything differently.'

Table 4.1 shows that Plaisio has implemented a website that generally supports its business objectives, although a service-based firm cannot afford to have its lowest rated element as customer service. The transactional elements are at a high level. Innovation, rated zero, would ordinarily be viewed as a concern but it reflects the limited size of the market and the restricted levels of competition.

The Future

The next steps of the company involve launching two new websites, namely `plaisio2b.gr` and `plaisiowap.gr`. Both have already been presented but are not fully operational yet. `Plaisio2b.gr` is the company's B2B service, targeted at corporate customers. It believes that once again it will have to 'educate' its customers—its business customers this time—into using this new channel. As for the WAP site, the company has low expectations. It is simply developed because the respective technology is available. The mobile commerce horizon is still hazy and there are few, if any, success stories, at least in Europe. However, if it is going to grow, Plaisio wants to be among the first to exploit it. Plaisio invests and operates under the strategic assumption that Internet pure-plays cannot survive in the long run. Thus, its overall business model involves multi-channel commerce and its strategic posture is that of an early adopter/first mover.

Conclusion

The primary business driver was Plaisio's philosophy and strategy: continuous improvement and innovation in the services offered to customers in order to retain market leadership. The decision to launch `plaisio.gr` was based on the successful projection of the company's top management about the role that the Internet and e-commerce would play. It is important to note that at the time when `plaisio.gr` was launched, the Internet was at a much earlier stage of adoption in Greece. The company did not face any serious obstacles. Top management provided full support, resources were no object, and no competition existed. The only problem that `plaisio.gr` faced in the beginning had to do with the poor state of the public telecommunications infrastructure.

CHAPTER CONCLUSION

The firms profiled above illustrate a variety of successful implementations of Internet retailing that have been developed from a diverse set of motivations. A more complete examination of all innovation factors may be seen in Chapter 9.

Drivers

The major drivers and inhibitors for the Greek firms were:

1. The IT manager championing e-commerce (Beauty Shop). The entrepreneurs' eagerness and efforts. (e-shop).
2. The market was an area of strategic importance for traditional firms (Best-e, Papasotiriou). Plaisio's philosophy and strategy: continuous improvement and innovation in the services offered to customers in order to retain market leadership.
3. The identified opportunity for building the company's modern image through online sales (Beauty Shop).
4. The opportunity to test a new market channel and see its potential (Beauty Shop, Best-e, Papasotiriou, Plaisio). Sales and profit were not primary goals at that stage (Papasotiriou).
5. The possibility to build a customer database with detailed information regarding their preferences and online shopping behaviour (Beauty Shop).
6. The long-term potential of online sales in a comparatively high-margin market (Beauty Shop).
7. The synergies identified with offline operations in supporting the new business model and driving customer loyalty and sales (Beauty Shop, Papasotiriou).
8. The drive to strengthen the company's technological innovation (Best-e).
9. The desire to be ahead of the competition and achieve first-mover advantage (Best-e, E-shop, Papasotiriou).

10. Good relationships with banks and financial institutions for funding (E-shop).
11. The nature of the product: Papasotiriou sells books—books, software and music CDs are the most typical e-commerce goods.

Inhibitors

The major obstacles and barriers included:

1.   Different objectives and vision per department; for example, the marketing department was oriented towards mass marketing and had a different idea of what the web could offer than the IT department (Beauty Shop). Difficulties in understanding the business model by partners and customers (Best-e). The need to develop alternative marketing techniques (Best-e).
2.   Informal processes and procedures in order to make a decision and allocate budget and resources to the project (Beauty Shop).
3.   The need to outsource key operations, such as IT and logistics, and the selection of the appropriate partner (Beauty Shop).
4.   Scarcity of resources, as no additional people were hired for this project but it had to run with existing personnel, especially at management level (Beauty Shop).
5.   Major problems in building the product assortment online (e.g. collection of images, information, etc.), which required extended communication with and cooperation from product suppliers (Beauty Shop).
6.   Low Internet penetration in Greece. The small target audience and their limited levels of Internet sophistication. Lack of trust of the Internet (Best-e, E-shop, Papasotiriou).
7.   Funding needed for the site to evolve (E-shop, Papasotiriou).
8.   The Amazon case: if the world's most well-known online bookstore cannot return a profit, how could we? (Papasotiriou).
9.   Lack of systems integration and streamlined fulfilment processes (Papasotiriou).
10. The poor state of the public telecommunications infrastructure (Plaisio).

Acknowledgements. The authors gratefully acknowledge the assistance of graduate students Elena Avatangelou, Yiannis Baseas, George Daskalakis, Dimitris Drossos, Chris Lazaris, Marina Psiloutsikou, Antonis Sideris and Nancy Spiliopoulou.

5
Internet Retailing in Hong Kong, China

MATTHEW LEE

INTRODUCTION

Internet retailing in Hong Kong cannot be understood without understanding the economic context within which Internet retailing operates. Hong Kong as a cosmopolitan city having one of the highest GDP *per capita* in the world, and is a relatively affluent society with a well-entrenched and sophisticated consumer spending culture. Consumers are always tuned in to the latest shopping trends. According to a recent study released by the Yankee Group, Hong Kong is a regional leader in Internet usage, with an estimated 2.67 million (39%) of its population connected to the Internet as of November 2000. The same study has also found that 17% of Internet users in Hong Kong have tried online shopping, although there are still many concerns about online product quality and transaction security.

A recent report released by the Hong Kong Productivity Council has estimated that business-to-consumer (B2C) revenues in the Greater China region (i.e. Hong Kong, China, Taiwan) will grow from US$130 million in 2000 to US$3.6 billion in 2005. Internet shopping in the region therefore presents interesting new opportunities to the retail sector. Internet retailing cases in Hong Kong are interesting because they are indicative of what is to come in the Greater China region.

The economic transformation in the last two decades has created a new generation of well-educated, middle-class consumers in the region, who are becoming impatient about certain products that they want but cannot purchase conveniently locally because local retail stores (because of their size and conservatism) tend to move slower than this group of dynamic and aspiring consumers. Although the strength of local retailers lies in the trust that they inspire in local customers, their cost structure is high. Cities in the Greater China region (Hong Kong in particular) tend to be densely populated with high land prices and rents. Local retailers simply cannot rely on huge sales volumes and big stores operating in rural areas to lower their cost structure and compete on prices alone, as is the case in North America and some other parts of the world. There is therefore unique room for Internet retailers to operate in this region to satisfy unmet and growing demands and yet they do not have to compete head on with the local retailers on prices.

The five cases included in this chapter represent successful examples of online stores in Hong Kong. Out of the five cases, four belong to the small to medium sized enterprises (SMEs) category, with each employing fewer than 50 employees. They were chosen because the 300 000 SMEs in Hong Kong constitute over 98% of business organizations in Hong Kong, employing over 60% of the total work-force. Another reason for choosing the four SME cases was that their online stores are all experiencing rapid growth and operating profitably. The research assistance of Miss Christy Cheung in preparing this chapter is acknowledged.

Overview of Cases

Two of the five retailers selected sell products widely sold on the Internet—department store items and flowers. The other three provide an interesting extension to the cases in other countries: DVD videos, baby carriages/furniture and an online games site. The department store, flower shop and baby-ware shop were operating prior to the Internet venture. The other two examples were Internet startups.

Ambassador was operating as a small floral shop until 1997 when the owner decided to experiment with a website as a marketing channel. Jody Yan soon realized that the online store would be capable of turning in significant revenues. Now `ambassador.com` is a well-established online florist and gift store with an international client base (half of its revenue comes from overseas orders). Coupled with direct marketing and catalogue sales, the online operation has been so successful that the physical store has been closed.

DVDshelf is probably the largest Internet shop in the world for Chinese DVD, VCD, and CD titles. It was launched in July 1999 and started to break-even after three months, returning a significant profit after only six months. The shop now has 32 000 customers worldwide, offers over 55 000 titles online, and sells over 25 000 items each month. Yet the shop manages to run its sizable operations with only a small number of staff engaged mainly in purchasing, inventory and logistic support.

Ebabyasia shows how a traditional retail shop manages to leverage the opportunities of the Internet. Seeing the Internet as an opportunity to expand sales into the neighboring regions Cameron Homarvar launched `ebabyasia.com` in

February 2000. Even while other Internet ventures were failing, ebabyasia.com proved to be a success with the firm doubling its sales revenues in just a few months. The success of ebabyasia soon attracted the attention of a venture capital firm, Techpacific, which paid US$2 million in June 2000 for a 25% stake.

Net Fun is an online entertainment website founded in 1994. In 1996 the firm launched its flagship product, Cyber City. Membership shot up quickly, reaching 180 000 within two years. However, the firm was making a substantial loss. In 1998 the new owner of the firm, Peggy Chan, changed its revenue model from advertising based to subscription based. Membership suffered a severe blow in the beginning but recovered gradually. Now netfun.com is a profitable firm with a digital product delivered online.

The Wing On Department Stores Group (**Wing On**) was established in 1907. Since then it has established itself as a local household name with seven outlets in Hong Kong. Wing On is probably the first major department store in Hong Kong to set up an online store, in August 1998. The online store has been experiencing double-digit annual growth in sales revenue; the number of products has increased to 2000. Despite its sales volume, the online store has a full-time staff of only one! Channel conflicts have been carefully managed.

AMBASSADOR—'CUSTOMER SERVICE AND VALUE FOR MONEY'
(ambassador.com.hk)

Introduction

Jody Yan, a creative designer working in the marketing field, started up Ambassador in 1987 as a small floral shop. In 1997, an online auction site asked Jody to sponsor gifts to the auction site, and she agreed. Intrigued by the business potential of the Internet, she decided to set up an online store herself. A few months of preparation led to the opening of ambassador.com in 1998. The online store began as an experiment and Jody was expecting it to be an additional marketing channel more than a source of real revenue. When real orders started to flow in, Jody was pleasantly surprised. She quickly realized the potential of the online store as a revenue channel and decided to put in additional investments to upgrade the store and enhance the transaction infrastructure, adding online payment, for example. In the first year of operation the online store accounted for about 10% of the total revenue of the firm. Online sales have since doubled every year, accounting for 30% of the firm's total revenue of around HK$5 million (US$640 000) in 2000.

Ambassador is an up-market florist selling designer flower baskets, flower bouquets, cakes, and fruit and gourmet gift baskets, all attractively packaged. Products are sold at an average of US$100 each. Colorful pictures of all products are displayed on the online storefront. In addition to the office in Wanchai, the firm runs a warehouse in Aberdeen on the south side of Hong Kong island. Fresh flowers are sourced from local wholesalers or air-shipped from Holland and New Zealand to be processed and packaged in the firm's Aberdeen warehouse. The firm no longer operates a physical retail shop. Mail order catalogs, direct marketing, and the online store are the main means through which the firm sells its products. The firm is privately owned. There are currently 12 full-time staff and 8 part-time staff. Additional temporary workers are hired during peak seasons such as Christmas and Valentine's Day.

Business Model

Ambassador initially sought to use the Internet mainly as a marketing channel to supplement its existing sales channels. Encouraged by the initial success of its online store, the firm switched to a multi-channel retailer model with the online store playing an increasingly important revenue generation role. Jody considered floral products to be very suitable for sale on the Internet. Most of her customers purchased floral products as gifts. There would be no need to physically feel and touch the products before making a purchase decision. Even if customers were to visit a physical floral gift shop, they would go there merely to place the order and make payment. The shop would deliver the product some time later. Since floral products were highly perishable, even in a physical floral shop the customer would be unlikely to see a real sample of the product. In most cases customers visiting a physical floral shop had to resort to ordering from catalogs displayed in the shop. Jody therefore reckoned that an online floral shop would be able to offer customers added convenience since it can be reached by anyone, anywhere, anytime with Internet access.

Since Jody had been running a floral business for some years before she started the online store, and so had all the back-end operations from supply through packaging to delivery logistics well in place to support the online store. The online store was simply an additional storefront for reaching customers and taking in purchase orders. There was little change to the operational model of the firm except that the firm had to cope with a more erratic sales pattern from the online channel. However, Jody did use the Internet to leverage customer services and save operational costs. Customers would receive through e-mail a detailed picture of the actual product to be delivered at the time of delivery, for example.

Implementing the Business Model

Since the back end (e.g. supply and logistics) of the business model was already fully operational, initial implementation of the business model required merely the setting up of the new website. The first version of the online store with catalog and shopping cart facilities took only two weeks to complete. However, it took three more months to put in the additional functions (e.g. payment and customer services), integrate the online store with back-end operations, and make the website reliable.

The firm initially licensed a general purpose online shopping implementation software package from a US-based company, hoping that it could be easily configured for the online store's use. It turned out to be very difficult to configure the software to suit the specific requirements of the online store, e.g. the need to display highly detailed color photographs for all the products sold by the store. The firm eventually hired an IT consulting firm to develop the online store from scratch. Satisfied with the system that the consulting firm had delivered, Jody decided to outsource the entire maintenance, hosting, and operational support functions to the same consulting firm. Flexibility and reliability on the part of the developer are crucial to Jody's satisfaction.

> The developer was reliable and accommodating to changes in the specifications of the online store, which is critical to us as we wanted to implement new ideas all along the way, (Jody Yan).

Although it actually costs the firm a lot more money to outsource the development than to hire programmers to develop the system in-house, Jody firmly believes that the outsourcing decision is right for her.

> I am not an IT person. I don't want to manage an IT function. I would rather like to focus on our core competence, which is floral product design and marketing. There is absolutely no need to build an in-house IT function when you can outsource it to reliable experts, (Jody Yan).

Both an in-house team and an outsourced company were used to support local deliveries. The outsourced delivery company helped the firm to cope with seasonal fluctuations in the delivery workload. Courier companies were used to carry out international deliveries. There were few business concerns about the project. The multi-channel business model for floral gift products worked. The profits from additional sales generated by the online channel soon covered the investments put in. One reason was that the firm had already established the back-end infrastructure of the business at the time the online store opened. Adding the online channel involved only marginal costs.

Industry, Competitor and Environmental Analysis

The main differences between the floral gift products industry and other consumer industries are its highly seasonal nature, the emphasis on personal customer services including product delivery, and the fact that customers do not need to physically see and examine the products before making a purchase decision. In Hong Kong, the floral gift products industry is specialized and highly fragmented. There are many small traditional players but no clear market leader. Although a number of traditional shops are starting to establish an online presence, and a small number of pure online floral gift shops are starting to appear, the use of the Internet as a significant sales channel is still relatively rare. Many online floral gift shops are still not accepting online credit card payment, for example. Players in this market tend to be SMEs. As with most SMEs in Hong Kong, the use of IT tends to be very limited. Jody reckoned that most of her competitors had no clue about how to use IT effectively to leverage their business. The exception would be wickerexpress.com, which is also operating a substantial online floral gift shop.

Environmental issues were analyzed to identify potential drivers of innovation, e.g. levels of competition, uncertainty, etc. Although there are many competitors in this market, price competition is not a threat as most of the competitors tend to price products along similar ranges. In addition, the gift market is not particularly price-sensitive. Customers tend to be in a relatively generous mood when they choose floral gift products as many of them purchase these products for their loved ones. Demand is growing as the local economy improves. The most severe competitive threats for Ambassador are issues of product quality and service. Differentiation is mainly based on product quality, design, and levels of service. Competitor actions and customer demands are relatively predictable. Therefore, there were no identified imperatives for innovation. The major drivers for establishment of the online store were not related to issues within the floral gift products industry.

Key Business Drivers and Threats

> Customer service is critical to the success of the firm. You have to make your customers feel good and satisfied. They need to feel that they are getting excellent value for money, (Jody Yan).

As most of the routine business processes are automated, the staff of the firm spent their time mostly on customer services, e.g. answering e-mails. Most of the employees have been with the firm for over six years. The firm's customer-oriented culture has taken root within the staff: 'The quality, self-discipline and loyalty of the employees are a key to our success'.

The competitive pressure is not high in the local industry, as many competitors are still far behind in the effective use of the Internet as a sales channel. Overseas competitors are not a serious threat as none of them focuses on Hong Kong and they do not know the specific tastes and preferences of local customers. The greatest threat facing the firm would be local competitors getting it right. However, the firm reckons that it is a couple of years ahead of its competitors in terms of getting the online store right, and their product design team is far superior. In addition, the firm reckons that they have established a good online brand. It would be difficult for competitors to catch up quickly. There are no apparent threats at an industry level.

Innovation Factors and Processes

The most important factors that led to this project were:

1. The principal was inspired by an Internet auction site and thought that she too could sell products through the Internet.
2. The principal's analysis that floral gift products are suitable for selling through the Internet.
3. The principal's extensive experience in the floral gift products business.
4. Back-end operations for the online floral gift shop were already in place, and so additional costs were marginal.
5. The identification of the online store as part of a multi-channel retailing strategy.
6. Initial pilot implementation resulted in sales orders.

A few obstacles were identified. First, the firm did not have a significant IT capability. How could the firm deal with the technical problems involved in the implementation and operation of an online store? Outsourcing provided the answer. After a couple of trial-and-error encounters with consulting companies, a suitable company was identified which implemented the project successfully. The second obstacle was the need to re-educate the employees on how to operate an Internet business and to re-train them so that they can use the necessary Internet and computer tools to do their new jobs effectively. Business re-education was spearheaded by Jody while IT re-training was provided by the same consulting firm. The remaining obstacle was to convince customers to shop on the Internet. As Internet shopping was quite close to mail catalog shopping, this obstacle did not turn out to overly onerous for the firm, but the general lack of trust towards Internet transactions remains an important inhibitor. Contrary to popular belief, the convenience of physical shopping in a highly populated city such as Hong Kong is not thought by the firm as an inhibitor of online shopping, especially in the floral gift products industry.

   The innovation processes were:

1. Inspiration from the Internet auction site
2. Analyzed the suitability of floral gift products for Internet sale
3. Prepared plans and budgets for experimentation
4. Identified the software for implementing the online store and started implementation
5. Realized that the software was not good enough for this particular online store
6. Outsourced the implementation from scratch to a consulting firm
7. Outsourced hosting, maintenance and training to the same firm
8. Commenced online business
9. Enhanced online store functions and integrated with other business and IT systems

Website Development and Operational Issues

Initially, the firm bought a license from a US-based company to configure a generic online shopping system for the firm's use. A programmer working in a local subsidiary of the US-based company carried out implementation and maintenance. It soon became clear that the generic system was not flexible enough to meet the firm's specific needs. The firm later engaged an IT consulting firm to develop the online store from scratch. From the very beginning, flexibility in the design was emphasized. Flexibility was important, as this was the firm's first online store. As more experience was gained, it was inevitable that the design of the online store would be changed to reflect lessons learnt. This highlights the lesson that different websites need different functionality reflecting the requirements of different products, and that flexibility in the software is of paramount importance. All the IT work is now outsourced, including training, maintenance and hosting.

Website Features

The firm's website has obtained a modest score of 57% on the CEC scale (see Table 5.1). Evaluation of the website shows that although product/service information is sufficient and the site is quite easy to use, it would benefit from including more details on the company and its operations, and providing more alternative payment options and enhanced customer services such as the inclusion of a frequently asked questions (FAQs) page and links to relevant sites. While there is little current competition, the lack of innovation is a significant area of exposure to future competition.

There is 100% integration for all business systems and operations. Order processing is automatic, saving the firm a lot of time and effort. In fact, the online store accepts only credit card payment from private customers to ensure efficient automatic order processing although cash on delivery arrangements can also be made. A secured credit card payment gateway with 128-bit secure sockets layer (SSL) encryption and secure electronic transaction (SET) protocol has been established with a major local bank. The inventory management and order processing systems are integrated. Customers are able to verify whether an item is in stock before ordering. The most time-consuming task turned out to be answering customer e-mails since the firm has a policy of replying within 24 hours. Same-day delivery is promised for orders made before 1 pm, except Sundays, public holidays and peak seasons.

The online store is considered by the owner to be a success. Success measures are sales volume and revenue growth generated by the store and customer satisfaction (determined by the number of complaints received by e-mail compared with the number of orders), in the context of the limited investment being put into the project.

Customer Details

Ambassador's customers are mainly in the 25–40 age group. About half of their customers are from outside Hong Kong. Local customers are mainly composed of IT professionals and employees of large corporations. Overseas orders tend to come from students (mainly Hong Kong students studying abroad). Overseas customers tend to be proficient Internet users. Some local customers do not know how to use the Internet well and they would phone in to ask the firm to teach them how to use the website to make an order.

The firm believes that product variety, attractive display pictures, special product design, convenience, and a good level of customer service are the main factors driving customers to shop with Ambassador. The firm also reckons that maintaining a long-term customer relationship and continuously creating new value-added services is key to attracting and keeping its customers. However, the firm believes that the slow rate of e-commerce adoption in Hong Kong and the general lack of trust towards Internet transactions are important inhibitors. Jody does not consider that the convenience of physical shopping in a densely populated city such as Hong Kong is an inhibitor of online shopping, particularly for floral gift products.

The firm believes most customers are satisfied with its online store, judging from e-mail feedback, customer rating, and the amount of repeat purchases. The firm has a presence on Yahoo's local shopping mall with Yahoo providing a customer rating service to the firm.

The Future

Ambassador sees the biggest challenges to firms in future use of the Internet retailing as:

- maintaining a pioneering position in your own industry; only the leaders and the first movers will be able to maximize returns;
- perfecting order fulfilment in a highly dynamic and unpredictable environment; and
- dealing with global competition from large and resourceful companies.

In the near future the firm will expand its product range, find more marketing partners (e.g. bookshops), and create more high value-added services. For example, the firm is exploring the use of mobile services to enable customers to shop and track product delivery through mobile phones.

Advice for other firms (not familiar with e-commerce) seeking to develop an online store is to do it gradually as learning and adjusting will take time. It is very important to integrate the online store with all the offline operations and systems to improve efficiency and customer service. Traditional stores would have a customer base and the shops need to educate their customers on the use of the Internet for shopping. There is no point spending a large amount of money on advertising, as the effects are uncertain. It would be more cost effective to partner with other companies (e.g. credit card companies) in customer referral programs and group marketing efforts. 'Do not believe in page views; they have no relationship to revenue or profit!' (Jody Yan).

Conclusion

The ambassador.com experience emphasizes the importance of relevant business experience in the principal, choosing the right products for an online store, and flexibility in implementation. The need for an integrated business and IT system is of paramount importance, although how it is provided (i.e. in-house or outsourced) seems to be of less significance. Website implementation needs to be carefully tailored to meet the specific requirements of each online store. Online stores are particularly valuable for firms having established back-end operations, supplier chain, delivery logistics and order processing capabilities (e.g. a traditional store). If implemented right, an online store can be a very useful part of a multi-channel retail strategy.

DVDSHELF:—'MAXIMIZE CUSTOMER VALUE, MINIMIZE COSTS'
(DVDshelf.com)

Introduction

DVDshelf.com is probably the largest Internet shop in the world for Chinese DVD, VCD, and CD titles. It was launched in July 1999, after six months of planning and preparation. It started to break even after three months and returned a significant profit after only six months. Revenue has been growing rapidly at an average rate of 31% each month with an estimated revenue exceeding HK$20 million in 2001. The shop now has 32 000 customers worldwide, offers over 55 000 titles online, and sells over 25 000 items each month. Yet the shop manages to run its sizable operations with only a small number of staff engaged mainly in purchasing, inventory and logistic support. The value proposition is clear: to offer customers anywhere in the world a convenient, easy-to-use, and secure shopping environment for the most comprehensive range of Chinese DVD, VCD and CD titles at guaranteed lowest prices. With a strong IT and business background, the founders of the firm believe that a fully integrated business and IT system is key to the successful implementation of the shop and delivery of the value proposition.

Ricky Leung and David Ho have known each other since early school days. Building on early friendship, qualifications in IT and a common interest in the IT industry, they founded ITOK Technologies Ltd in 1994, focusing on the business of VCD production systems, MPEG and Video CD 2.0 coding services. Film distribution companies and production houses were the major clientele of the company. Feeling the enormous potential of the Internet and facing increasingly intensive competition from the traditional VCD production business, in 1997 the company decided to wind up its VCD production business and start to embrace e-commerce fully. In 1998 a new company called ITOK Media Ltd was formed to launch its first e-commerce initiative, jobeasy.com, which is an online job agency still operating today. Encouraged by the initial success of JobEasy, the company quickly expanded to the e-tailing sector, establishing its first Internet shop, DVDshelf.com, in July 1999. DVDshelf employs around 20 people, over half of them (especially IT and administrative support staff) also work for other projects (e.g. JobEasy).

The customers of DVDshelf are mainly local and overseas Chinese interested in Hong Kong movies and music titles. Overseas customers come from the United States, Canada, England, Holland, Taiwan, Singapore and Australia. Although the number of local and overseas Chinese customers are similar, overseas Chinese customers account for over 70% of the sales revenue as they tend to buy more titles in a single transaction to reduce shipment cost. The revenue from the sales of DVD titles accounts for about half of the total revenue.

Business Model

The DVD, VCD and audio CD retail industry is characterized by the need to carry a large range of titles for a geographically diverse range of customers. The industry is dominated by a small number of large chain stores. Small retail shops have found it almost impossible to compete because of their inability to provide access convenience and stock a large range of titles. Ricky and David saw the Internet as providing an opportunity to change this situation and they chose the worldwide Chinese community as their target customers. Their value proposition is to offer customers worldwide a convenient, easy-to-use, and secure shopping environment for the most comprehensive range of Chinese DVD, VCD and CD titles at prices guaranteed to be the lowest in the market. The firm offers a written price guarantee to all customers, promising a refund if the same title is sold at a lower price at any online store.

To deliver the value proposition, DVDshelf had to devise a very effective business model to enable the firm to cater for a large title range at the lowest cost. This required the use of a simplified and automated business process integrated with effective IT support at every stage. Product searching, ordering, inventory management, payment, logistics, fulfilment, and customer relationship management processes all needed to be integrated and automated as much as possible. Since wholesale suppliers were reluctant to ship to individual consumers, the firm had to carry an inventory. To increase customers' trust in the certain and timely delivery of its products, the firm would not take an order for a title (except a 'pre-release' title) unless it was actually in stock, and the customers were able to verify stock availability online. To estimate the optimal level of inventory for each title and to keep the estimates updated turned out to be an important challenge.

Implementing the Business Model

The business model was implemented from scratch in less than six months. Capitalizing on the good network and relationships established with the suppliers when Ricky and David were in the VCD production business, the relevant supply chains were put in place quickly. Core IT functions were provided in-house, as both founders were IT professionals themselves with an established IT staff in-house. Online cataloging, title searching and ordering functions were developed in-house using C++ and Visual Basic on a standard e-commerce development platform (IBM's Net.Commerce). Delivery logistics were outsourced to courier companies and the post office, although packaging was done in-house. Since Hong Kong is a small geographic region, the firm also provided a pick-up counter for local customers to collect ordered titles from its office if needed to avoid postal costs. However, the firm ran its own warehouse to keep its inventories.

Customers were able to search for desired titles, check stock status, order and pay (using both online and offline means) on the same website. Depending on the projected popularity of a title, a stock buffer ranging from 2 to 50 was kept at the firm's warehouse. When the stock level for a title dropped to a certain level, the system would generate an ordering request to replenish the depleting stock, and the order would be faxed to the relevant suppliers. Orders had to be faxed since none of the suppliers was connected to the firm electronically. Their inventory systems were simply not accessible to anyone outside the companies. Any title with a stock level over a certain amount for an extended period would be flagged for inclusion in the numerous regular sales promotions organized by the firm. To increase consumers' trust, the site has employed SSL encryption and obtained VeriSign security certification, and this fact is displayed prominently on the front page of the website.

The business model has remained more or less the same from the beginning— but the implementation has become more sophisticated. Taking credit card payment, for example, the firm initially had to process credit card payments offline. Each credit card payment had to be checked manually and a phone call had to be made to the relevant card center in order to obtain authorization. This process would take at least 30 seconds, introducing a transaction bottleneck. This bottleneck was particularly serious in high shopping seasons (e.g. around Christmas) and a lot of temporary staff had to be employed to handle this task. In late 2000, the firm started to link up with the payment gateway of a major bank, thereby fully automating the credit card payment process. Customer service and workflow automating functions have also improved, allowing customers to ship to different addresses from a personal address book in a single order, and track ordering and delivery status online through integrating with the relevant logistic systems of the outsourced courier companies. The marketing focus of the business model has also shifted from conventional advertising to membership referral programs and cross-marketing partnerships with a wide range of businesses such as banks, universities, and Internet Service Providers (ISPs). Through a bonus-points system, referral customers will get immediate bonus points (equivalent to HK$10), which can be redeemed at future purchases. Existing customers successfully introducing new customers will also get bonus points. Members of marketing partners who make purchases from the store will get additional discounts and bonus points.

There were few business concerns about the project. The most critical decision was to find the right category of products for the Internet shop. Chinese DVD, VCD and music CD titles turned out to be very suitable for Internet sales as they are standard items that customers do not need to physically examine before they buy, are small in size and easy to ship, and the firm could capitalize on the Internet to offer a wide range of titles to a very diverse group of customers geographically without the need to maintain a large physical retail network. The business model worked and the project started to make operating profits very soon after the launch.

Industry, Competitor and Environmental Analysis

DVDshelf.com operates in the DVD, VCD and music CD retail industry. The major difference between this and other industries is product standardization. VCDs and music CDs carrying the same titles have exactly the same contents and product quality standard no matter which outlets they are sold from. Although DVD titles are restricted by a zoning system defining the geographical regions within which DVDs can be played, Chinese DVD titles are invariably 'all-zones' allowing the disks to be played on machines anywhere in the world. As new titles are introduced very quickly and frequently, the rate at which products become out of date (and hence the price of which has to drop) is fast.

As a specialist Internet DVD, VCD and CD retailer targeting the Chinese community, with over 25 000 disks sold per month DVDshelf is one of the largest in the world. The major chain stores (such as HMV) have also established online operations but are not focused on customers from the Chinese community and hence carry far fewer Chinese titles. Closer competition comes from large Internet stores focusing on the Asian entertainment products market (such as yesasia.com). However, these stores sell many other entertainment products (e.g. books and electronics) in addition to DVD, VCD and music CD titles.

The DVD, VCD and music CD retail industry is still a very traditional one dominated by a small number of large chain stores with fairly uniform product pricing practices. DVDshelf reckoned that existing mainstream players in the market were not particularly keen or effective in the use of IT to reduce cost and to provide better customer services. An Internet shop with highly integrated and automated business processes would enable the firm to compete strongly both on price, product range and the quality of customer service. The question was how to attract enough buying customers in a short time without burning a lot of cash on advertising so that the project could start to make money in six months. Ricky and David both reckoned that in a place like Hong Kong a privately funded venture would only have six months to prove that the business model would work (i.e. make a profit), unlike in the United State where Internet shops could afford to lose money for a couple of years.

Environmental issues were analyzed to identify potential drivers of innovation (e.g. levels of competition, uncertainty). Differentiation is mainly based on product range, pricing and levels of service. Competitor actions and customer demands are relatively predictable. Therefore, there were no identified imperatives for innovation. The major drivers for establishing the firm were not related directly to issues within the film and music retailing industry. The demand for Chinese film and music titles from the Chinese community worldwide has existed for a long time. The Internet just happens to provide a much more convenient and cost-effective means to fulfill this demand.

Key Business Drivers and Threats

For the business to succeed, it is critical to offer a large range of up-to-date titles at discounted prices, to have highly effective and integrated system support and back-end logistics arrangement in place, to implement the right strategy, and to have a global market perspective (Ricky Leung).

The most important element of the strategy was cost management and customer service. Ricky says,

We would rather spend money on customer services rather than on expensive advertising. A lot of Internet shops spend huge sums on advertising and decorating their outfits instead of focusing on getting profitable customers and retaining them. Many Internet shops have failed as a result!

DVDshelf actually did advertise on TV once. It was expensive but the effect was not obvious. Now the marketing strategy of the firm has shifted towards relationship marketing with a focus on customer referrals from existing customers and marketing partners. These sources turned out more new customers than any other sources. Security was also emphasized in the firm's marketing strategy.

Online shopping still entails a certain amount of risks. Once a customer is happy with the security, reliability and customer service of a certain online shop, he is more reluctant to switch to a new unknown store because of the inherent risks involved (Ricky Leung).

The greatest threats facing the firm and industry would be the emergence of broadband infrastructure and products, allowing titles to be downloaded directly without the need to purchase and ship physical disks. This would enable new business models (e.g. online rental rather than purchase) that existing stores (both online and offline ones) would find it difficult to support. As regards competition from other online stores, Ricky did not think they would become serious competitors. 'Our technology skills are far ahead and our supplier and customer networks and relationships are very well established', says Ricky. It would be hard for new competitors to catch up.

Innovation Factors and Processes

The most important factors that led to this project were:

1. The principals' early experience with the Internet. They were early users and felt the enormous potential of the Internet personally.
2. The identification of Chinese DVD, VCD and music CD titles as suitable products for an Internet shop. Demand for these titles from the Chinese community worldwide has existed for a long time. The Internet provides an effective channel to fulfill that demand.
3. The principals were engaged in the VCD production business and had built up good relationships with film distributors and production houses, thereby providing them with good supplies of DVD, VCD and music CD titles.
4. The principals had a strong IT background and were comfortable with the technology involved.
5. Successfully setting up `jobeasy.com` encouraged the principals to expand into the Internet retailing market.

A few barriers the firm had to overcome for the project to be a success were identified. First of all was the payment system. Initially the firm had to rely on offline payment processing methods, resulting in processing bottlenecks and a relatively high level of commission payments to credit card companies. This problem was resolved when the firm integrated its payment processes with the payment gateway of a major bank. Another obstacle was that many potential customers were not used to Internet shopping. This problem has lessened as Internet and e-commerce penetrations have accelerated globally in the last year. Lack of trust was another barrier. It was not easy to engender sufficient trust in potential customers to enable them to shop with DVDshelf online. The firm had to offer extensive guarantees on price, information security, product return, and quality of customer service to help build the necessary trust. However, once a customer has built up a sufficient level of trust and is happy with his or her initial shopping experience, a strong sense of customer loyalty tends to emerge. Many of the firm's customers are repeat customers.

The innovation processes were:

1. Increasing competition and falling profits from the VCD production business
2. Commenced looking at alternative business opportunities
3. Identified Internet-based business opportunities
4. Identified Chinese DVDs, VCDs and music CDs as the vehicle
5. Prepared business model, worked out business and strategic plans
6. Specified, designed, developed and hosted website using IBM's `net.commerce` platform.

7. Hired operational staff, rented warehouse space, partnered with courier companies
8. Commenced business

Website Development and Operational Issues

The firm wanted to capitalize on its existing IT expertise and have a speedy and scalable implementation. After evaluating several alternative solutions, they adopted a well-established e-business system capable of integrating both off-the-shelf applications and self-developed applications that were scalable on a range of technology platforms (IBM's Webspere Commerce Suite (Net.Commerce) with DB2 Universal database). The firm developed its own data and product entry applications. Contents management and personalization applications were handled in-house. Visitor relationship management and web traffic analysis (WebTrends) provided statistics and analysis on visitors, page views, revenue generation, banner advertising effectiveness, etc. A separate customer relationship management (CRM) system was utilized (Siebel). The firm implemented its own bonus point marketing system, payment application, supply chain management and e-logistics applications, including order fulfilment, e-procurement, inventory management, bar code management, packing and delivery system. C++ and Visual Basic application were the main tools employed for development and systems integration.

Systems implementation took four months to complete with a team of three to four programmers composed of mainly young graduates. Although the chosen IBM platform was comprehensive and flexible (allowing the addition of many user functions), it was very complex and demanded a lot of on-the-job learning. Data entry for several thousand titles also turned out to be a substantial task, taking a couple of months. Like books, movie titles are information rich and each entry had additional information.

A multiple addressing function was added soon after launch as many customers bought disks from the site as gift items. Numerous functions have been added to the system since then. There were five major releases (versions) in the 21 months since launch. This highlights the need for flexibility and the capacity for rapid system development as the requirements of an Internet shop tend to be extremely fluid and dynamic.

Website Features

Evaluation of the website (see Table 5.1) shows a relatively high score (83%) on the CEC scale. Transaction and customer-related functions are all well developed but suggest that more details on the company and its operations would be well regarded by customers. Innovations in services and technology (e.g. delivery tracking and the use of multi-media) are noted but more could be done. For example, more support for customer feedback relating to storefront contents and functions as well as customer reviews of titles bought would be useful enhancements.

Currently there is 100% integration for all business systems and operations from visitor relationship management through accounting and inventory management to payment and delivery. System integration was a design priority from the very beginning. Both the front end and the back end of the system are Internet based. Data entry and contents management personnel, for example, can do their work with a standard browser anywhere, anytime there is Internet access. This flexibility turns out to be very advantageous as data input and content management are very human resource intensive.

The system is considered by the firm to be a success. Ricky says, It is reliable, flexible, effective, and highly integrated, allowing us to shorten order cycle-time and to minimize inventory level. Success measures are sales growth, customer satisfaction (as determined by the number of complaints received by e-mail compared with the number of orders), and the fact that the system enables the firm to handle a large volume of business with only a small handful of operating staff.

Customer Details

DVDshelf has 32 000 registered customers in Asia, Europe, North America, and Australia. Around 90% are ethnic Chinese. Nearly three-quarters are under 35 and many have received a degree-level education. There is no significant male/female domination. Most of the customers are frequent Internet users and many are repeat customers. Existing customer referrals and referrals from marketing partners are the main sources of new customers. Customers from Hong Kong tend to buy more old movies as they are difficult to source from conventional stores. Overseas customers tend to buy more brand new titles as they can get them cheaper and quicker through DVDshelf. Customers are mainly interested in Hong Kong movies and music titles. Although the numbers of local and overseas Chinese customers are similar, overseas Chinese customers account for over 70% of the sales revenue as they tend to buy more titles in a single transaction to reduce shipment cost. The revenue from the sales of DVD titles accounts for about half of the total revenue.

The firm believes that its extensive product range, excellent customer services, ease of website navigation and transaction, cheaper prices and quick delivery are the main factors driving customers to shop with DVDshelf. However, the firm also reckons that a general lack of trust towards online stores is an important inhibitor. The relatively low Internet penetration rate among Chinese communities in some countries remains a problem. Also, online shopping requires customers to change their shopping habits, which can only occur slowly.

The firm believes that its customers are very satisfied in general. Although no formal satisfaction survey has been carried out, the high rate of repeat purchases and customer referrals implies a level of customer satisfaction. Some customers have proactively provided feedback to the firm through e-mail, suggesting enhancements in the interface and search functions.

The Future

DVDshelf sees the biggest challenges to firms in the future use of the Internet retailing as:

- finding the right products to sell that can benefit uniquely from the characteristics of the Internet channel;
- integrating all the backend systems from supply chain management to delivery logistics; and
- coming up with profitable business models (plans) that are not easily imitated by competitors.

In the near future, the firm will expand to the B2B wholesale market for DVD, VCD and music CD titles through the provision of a global e-market place. For this purpose, a new website (aveasy.com) was launched in February 2001. In the longer run, the firm wants to be the premier e-market place for all Chinese DVD, VCD and music titles in the world for both individual and business customers.

Advice for other firms seeking to develop an Internet shop is that they must first work out a profitable business model and learn how to control cost effectively. E-business is like any other business—it has to return a profit! The best way to achieve this is to figure out how to deliver maximum customer value while keeping costs well under control.

Conclusion

The DVDshelf.com experience shows that even small Internet shops can reach a global market effectively. The importance of the relevant experience of the principals, a good network with suppliers, careful business planning, and flexibility in implementation are emphasized. Finding a market niche in which the firm has an inherent competitive advantage is critical. It is very important to have a clear vision of the potential competitive advantage for the firm, the capability to implement a profitable business model, and the ability to experiment with and to revise the means of implementing that model using a scalable and flexible IT infrastructure. In addition, the importance of a fully integrated business and IT support system is paramount in improving customer services (e.g. shorter order cycle time) and reducing costs (e.g. through automation).

EBABYASIA: 'SYNERGIES BETWEEN ONLINE AND OFFLINE CHANNELS' (ebabyasia.com)

Introduction

Cameron Honarvar has been living in Hong Kong for the past 10 years. After graduating from New York University he worked in finance for several years. It was in 1995 when Cameron decided to quit his job and start his own baby products specialty retail store called Karin's Korner, focusing on the concept of safety, service and selection, with safety-certified baby products imported directly from the United States and Europe. The business has grown steadily since then. While opening the third retail store in Hong Kong in 1999, Cameron decided that it was time to expand his store concept to other markets in the region. Inspired by successful cases in the United States, he reckoned that the Internet was the best vehicle to realize his expansion plan. After teaming up with Clifford Tse, his technology partner, ebabyasia.com became operational in just a few months. Clifford was no stranger to technology and the Hong Kong market. Being a Hong Kong native and having graduated from MIT with Silicon Valley entrepreneurial experience, Clifford was the ideal person for the job of Chief Technical officer (CTO) in ebabyasia.

Ebabyasia soon proved to be a success, enabling the firm to double its sales revenues in just a few months. Prior to the launch of the online store, the retail firm was growing at an annual rate of only around 10%. The success of ebabyasia soon attracted the attention of a venture capital firm, Techpacific, which paid HK$2 million in June 2000 for a 25% stake in ebabyasia. The firm now has a staff of close to 30, operates 7 retail shops in Hong Kong, Singapore and Taiwan and expects sales revenue to grow from HK$1.4 million in 2000 to HK$4 million in 2001, with the online store contributing roughly half of the total revenue. The online store is displayed in five languages (English, Traditional Chinese, Simplified Chinese, Japanese, Korean), carries over 800 products, operates an online parents community, and is supported by a multi-lingual customer service team through hotline, fax and e-mail.

The 60 000 or so registered customers of ebabyasia are mainly middle-income expatriate professionals working in Asia, of whom about 75% are women and about 40% are based in Hong Kong. Most of the firm's customers are frequent Internet users but for many of them shopping with ebabyasia has been their first ever Internet shopping experience. With a complementary 'click-and-mortar' strategy, the firm expects to expand further into larger regional markets such as Japan and Korea, from where substantial further contributions to revenue are anticipated.

I have no idea which channel is supporting the other as both channels are seeing rapid growth in revenue; but what is clear is that together they have enabled our dramatic growth since early 2000 (Cameron Honarvar).

Business Model

With over 55 million new babies born each year in Asia, this increasingly affluent continent represents a huge market for baby products. In Hong Kong, the market is dominated by large chain stores such as Mothercare and Jusco. While large chain stores tend to cover a comprehensive range of baby products from baby clothing to milk bottles, ebabyasia focuses on imported wooden furniture, strollers, cots, car seats, and specialty educational toys, all with a high degree of safety and quality standards. The emphasis on safety is particularly noteworthy as there is a lack of legislated safety standards for baby equipment in many parts of Asia.

> We concentrate on items where we can make a difference—hence we do not sell diapers and baby clothing (Cameron Honarvar).

The value proposition is clear: to offer the largest range of safe and quality baby products for shipping to destinations in Asia at the best possible prices. Apparently, all products sold by ebabyasia comply with national safety standards such as ASTM (US), BSI (UK), or EN (European Union).

To deliver the value proposition, ebabyasia devised a business model that cut out the middlemen and worked in strategic partnership with logistics companies to lower costs. The model also integrated the online channel with the offline channel, with one complementing the other. The physical outlets helped to establish brand image and increase customers' trust. The online channel extended the reach of the physical channel and provided customers with added convenience together with extended product information and advice. In addition, the online channel provided parental community support for both online and offline customers of the firm. The firm was not particularly concerned about channel conflicts as the channels were complementary in nature and, in any case, the firm did not have a large number of physical outlets.

Implementing the Business Model

The online business model was implemented in just a few months. To increase customers' trust, the firm provided a multi-lingual customer enquiry service and a guaranteed product return policy. In addition, online buyers would get a 5% price break over prices in the physical outlets. The firm negotiated its supplies directly with manufacturers in North America, Europe and Australia, often resulting in huge discounts (as much as 65%). The firm also managed to hammer out a 40% discount with United Parcel Service, thereby ensuring effective delivery logistics are in place without draining the firm of huge capitals or high operating costs. Hong Kong was used as the transshipment point where all packaging was done in the firm's special purpose warehouse/packaging center.

Ebabyasia was treated operationally as just another retail outlet sharing all the back-office support systems (e.g. payment processing, order fulfillment) with the other physical retail stores of the firm. In fact, the operational staff of its physical outlets provided the multi-lingual customer service support for ebabyasia. Hotline enquiries were routed directly to the relevant physical stores. Internet kiosks were made available in the retail stores so that customers visiting physical outlets could access the entire catalog and order online to get the price discount, if they didn't mind waiting for delivery, which could take a maximum of one week. In a way, the physical store outlets were also treated as some kind of showroom for the firm's products.

To draw more customers to the site and keep them interested, ebabyasia also hosted an online parental community to enable its customers (including both would-be parents and actual parents) to communicate with each other and share views and experiences (through moderated chat rooms), and get access to a host of useful information (such as pregnancy advice and child development advice). In addition, experienced pediatricians were available to provide advice and answer questions from customers through e-mail. These questions and answers would then be posted on the site for other customers to refer to.

The business model has remained more or less the same from the beginning, although the implementation has become more sophisticated. With payment, for example, customers can now pay by faxing their credit card information to the firm or through the secure online payment gateway of a major bank. The design of the website has also become more sophisticated, with more functionalities and contents added periodically. The website has already gone through six major revisions, for example.

There were a few business concerns about the project. One was the need for capital to cover the start up and running costs of the online operation. Another concern was the need to provide real-time customer support services to online customers, as their expectations from an online store were high. The capital issue was resolved when the venture capital firm, Techpacific, invested in the firm only four months after ebabyasia went online. The real-time customer support issue was resolved when Cameron decided to use the existing sales staff from physical retail outlets to provide the service. There had been some reluctance in the beginning, as the physical retail staff did not quite see the point of them providing support to customers of the firm's online channel. However, they soon realized that the firm's online customers might also be its physical retail customers at the same time. In addition, the performance of the sales staff was evaluated not on individual store sale performance, but on the aggregated sales from both channels. As a result, the prevailing retailing culture shifted and the sales staff was motivated to support the firm's online customers.

Industry, Competitor and Environmental Analysis

Ebabyasia operates mainly in the Asian baby products retail industry. With 55 million new babies born every year in the region, this industry is booming. The major difference between this and other consumer product industries is the strong emphasis customers put on product safety. Stringent safety standards exist and are legally enforced in many developed regions such as North America, Europe, and Australia. However, in Asia there is a shortage of safety-certified baby products. Exploring this market niche, ebabyasia has chosen to focus on imported top-line American and European safety-certified baby products.

The baby products retail industry is still a fairly traditional one with a lot of manual sales staff and only a modest level of IT usage. In Hong Kong, baby products are sold mainly by Japanese department stores (e.g. Jusco, UNY) and multinational chain stores (e.g. Mothercare and Toys 'R' Us). The Japanese department stores offer a wide selection of products for customers with a liking for Japanese designs. The British-based chain store, Mothercare, has several outlets in Hong Kong covering both maternity and baby products, with a focus on quality and safety. The US-based toy store chain, Toys 'R' Us has expanded into the baby products market in addition to selling toys in their stores in Hong Kong. However, most of these traditional shops have only a weak Internet presence in the Asia region. In addition, none of them provides multi-lingual support. Although there are a few Chinese language online stores for baby products based in Taiwan and Mainland China, they tend to focus locally and hardly sell outside their home base. For ebabyasia, there seems to be little direct competition and Cameron reckons that the actions of his traditional competitors are very predictable. Supply was also plentiful and it was also not difficult to negotiate good deals with European and North American suppliers many of whom are keen to break into the growing Asian market.

Environmental issues were analyzed to identify potential drivers of innovation (e.g. levels of competition, uncertainty). Differentiation is mainly based on product range, pricing and levels of service. Competitor actions and customer demands are relatively predictable. Therefore, there were no identified imperatives for innovation. The major driver for establishing ebabyasia was to use it as a means quickly to expand the store network beyond Hong Kong. The demand for quality and safe baby products in Asia has been growing steadily for some time. The Internet happens to provide the firm with a convenient and cost-effective means to tap into this growing market.

Key Business Drivers and Threats

'For the business to succeed, it is critical to get inventory and logistic management right', says Cameron. As Hong Kong is used as the transshipment center for all products, ebabyasia had to establish its own warehouse in Hong Kong with specialist packaging capability. Since most of the items (e.g. baby beds) sold were sizable and prone to damage on long journeys, skilful packaging took on an important role. 'Sales and marketing management has to be done right too as the sales staff also have to provide critical online customer support', says Cameron. In addition, a clear dual-channel strategy was instrumental in the success of the firm. 'The existence of synergies between the online and offline channels is critical for the success of the firm', says Cameron.

The greatest threat facing the firm in its effort for regional expansion is the increasingly cumbersome import regulations starting to be imposed by some countries in the region. Cameron reckons that some of these regulations are really trade barriers in disguise and the real intention is to protect the local baby product industry. Cameron explains:

> Some regulations and standards are virtually impossible for any manufacturer in the world to comply with except one or two local manufacturers for various local and situational reasons are able to comply. For example, one Asia country insists on adopting an obsolete European standard to which no manufacturers in the world is producing products except two local manufacturers.

Innovation Factors and Processes

The most important factors that led to this project were:

1. The principals' drive to use the Internet to expand the business beyond Hong Kong.
2. The principals' awareness of successful e-retailing cases in the United States.
3. The principals' belief that the online channel would offer a competitive advantage.
4. The principals' belief that the online channel would be compatible with the existing offline channel.
5. The principals' complementary skills in finance, retailing and IT.

A few barriers the firm had to overcome for the project to be a success were identified. First of all was the need to source quality imported products at a good price discount. Traveling the world, Cameron managed to negotiate huge price discounts (as high as 65% in some cases) with his suppliers, many of whom were eager to break into the Asian market. Another obstacle was the need to meet the delivery challenge without draining capital. The firm managed to hammer out a 40% discount with UPS, who at the time was eager to get a foothold in Asia. Establishing the payment gateway also turned out to be tough as there were few choices available and the banks charged a high commissioning rate. Getting the operational staff to understand the vision of the senior management also took much time and effort to achieve. Last but not least was the challenge to position the online and offline channels in such a way they would be complementary and synergistic instead of conflicting with each other. It took some trial and error to fine-tune the positioning strategy and its implementation.

The innovation processes were:

1. The initial success of the baby product store concept
2. Identified market opportunities to expand the store concept abroad
3. Identified the Internet as the main vehicle for expansion
4. Worked out business plan
5. Recruited the right senior management team with both IT and operations expertise

6. Specified, designed, developed and hosted website
7. Firmed up the supply chain and delivery logistic arrangements
8. Commenced online business

Website Development and Operational Issues

With Clifford Tse as the CTO, the firm undertook most of the website development in-house. Industry standard development tools and platform were employed. The development of the website went smoothly and according to schedule, taking only two months to complete. The website was a standalone system not integrated with the other IT systems in the firm. The website was regarded as simply an additional store displaying products and taking in orders. The orders were then processed through the normal systems (e.g. order fulfilment and inventory management) used by the firm's physical retail outlets. The parental community features were added later. There have been six major revisions since the site was launched. Minor feature updates occur almost once every two weeks. An in-house team provided operational support. The difficulty was not in the technology implementation, but in the need to provide for a highly interactive website with a rich and consistently updating content in five different languages! Both Cameron and Clifford were totally satisfied with the in-house development of the website. 'It was on-time, within budget, and met our expectations' (Clifford Tse).

Website Features

Evaluation of the website (see Table 5.1) shows a very high score (87%) on the CEC scale. The website appears to be very well designed. The site scores well on every category, with transaction and ease of use functions achieving maximum scores. Many innovations in customer services and technology are noted. For example, an order-tracking function is provided. Channels for product reviews and customer experience-sharing are provided. The website can be customized individually. The only weaknesses are in the use of animation, the provision of company financial and ownership information, information on new products, and lack of links to related websites.

The system is considered by the firm to be a success. It based its satisfaction on good feedback from users (both customers and employees) and the fact that the website did generate a large volume of business, thereby achieving its business objectives. The firm's revenue increased almost 100% in the 12-month period after the launch of the online channel, with the online channel accounting for almost half the total revenue.

Customer Details

The customers of ebabyasia.com are mainly in the 27–35 age group. Most of them are frequent Internet users in the middle or upper middle-income groups.

About one-quarter of the customers are male. The firm has a registered customer base of some 60 000 and with many of them their first online shopping experience is with ebabyasia. Over 30% of all purchases are repeat purchases. The customers of ebabyasia tend to communicate with the firm through e-mail. About 40% of the firm's customers are based in Hong Kong, with the rest coming from Singapore (20%), Taiwan (20%), Japan (10%) and other Asian regions (10%). The average value of each online order is around HK$200. All payments are done using credit cards. About half of the payments are completed online using the payment gateway provided by a major bank. The remaining half is done through customers faxing over their credit card details.

The firm believes that its emphasis on safe products, wide selection and reasonable prices are the main factors driving customers to shop with ebabyasia. Moreover, the firm also believes that the existence of their physical outlets gives their online customers an added degree of confidence. The firm reckons that general security and privacy concerns towards online shopping act as an important inhibitor. Also, online shopping requires a certain degree of technology acceptance from customers and some change to their shopping habits, which can only occur slowly.

The firm believes its customers are very satisfied in general. Although no formal satisfaction survey has been carried out, there are many repeat purchases, implying a certain level of customer satisfaction. Customer feedback is encouraged and facilitated through the firm's website. The firm cannot recall having received any complaint, again implying a certain degree of customer satisfaction.

The Future

Ebabyasia sees the biggest challenges to firms in the future use of the Internet for retailing in Asia as:

1. Getting full support from banks. Asian banks are generally not keen to invest in or facilitate the business of online shops (e.g. getting banks to establish a payment gateway turned out to be an onerous task).
2. Getting customers to change their shopping behavior. Unlike consumers in the United States, Asian consumers are generally not used to online shopping.
3. Getting customers to feel safe and secure in an online shopping environment. Despite various technology solutions and legislative measures, Asian consumers are still very concerned about the security and privacy of online transactions.

In the near future, the firm will expand its product range and enrich its online parental community. The firm also plans to better integrate its supply chain and to enhance customer relationship management on its website. The online store will

Table 5.1 *Evaluation of selected Hong Kong websites*

Firms	Company information/5	Product/ services information/5	Transactions/5	Customer service/5	Ease of use/5	Innovation/5	Total/30	CEC scale © (%)
Ambassador	3	4	3	3	4	0	17	57
DVDshelf	4	4	5	5	5	2	25	83
Ebabyasia	4	4	5	4	5	4	26	87
Net Fun	4	4	2	4	3	2	19	63
WingOn	3	4	5	5	5	2	24	80

be integrated with the IT and business systems of its physical stores to reduce costs. 'Bungled operations should not be held up as a reason why Internet retailing should not work' (Cameron Honarvar).

Advice for other firms seeking to develop an Internet shop is that they must first get the business basics right: sourcing, purchasing, warehousing, delivery, customer services, languages, local regulations and tariffs. Cost management is critical and fixed costs must be minimized since demand fluctuations are often extreme for online stores. Never compete with the large physical chain stores on price alone. The ability to provide a clearly attractive alternative to local retail stores is essential to succeed. Websites can start up in a simple way and expand/ evolve over time, but a good Internet presence must be established as soon as possible.

Conclusion

The `ebabyasia.com` experience shows how an Internet retail channel can synergistically complement a physical store channel in achieving a firm's regional expansion plan. The importance of relevant business experience of the principals, good relationships with suppliers, careful business planning, delivery logistics, and good website implementation are all emphasized. Finding a market niche in which an online firm has an inherent competitive advantage is critical. For example, the market for high-end baby products is information intensive (as knowledgeable and well-educated parents want to know the details of what they are buying for their precious young ones), and the Internet can be leveraged to satisfy the information needs of the customers.

NET FUN—'PRODUCT DIFFERENTIATION AND VALUE PROPOSITIONS' (`netfun.com`)

Introduction

A group of creative designers and technologists founded Net Fun Limited in 1994 out of personal interest. In the beginning the firm engaged in the development of online games and also offered its technical development expertise to other firms. The firm launched its key product, *Cyber City*, in July 1996, hoping that the product would spearhead the firm's development as a major player in the multi-player online games (MPOG) industry, focusing on indigenous Chinese games. Despite rapid customer growth, in 1997 the firm was in financial difficulty, losing over HK$20 million (US$2.56 million) annually. Peggy Chan, who was the founder and CEO of an IT consulting firm (Excel Technology) at the time, saw the potential of Net Fun in the growing Chinese MPOG market and decided to acquire 90% of Net Fun's equity herself with Excel Technology acquiring the remaining 10%.

Peggy soon implemented drastic changes to the firm, changing its business model fundamentally, reducing its staff size by half and transferring some technical staff to Excel Technology. With Catherine Szeto in place as General Manager, the firm soon made the much-needed turn-around. Losses were reduced quickly and profitability returned a couple of years later. In September 2000, despite increasing global concerns about the viability of B2C operations, Cheung Kong (Holdings) Limited, a leading global conglomerate based in Hong Kong with a total market capitalization of over HK$600 billion (US$84.3 billion), acquired 42.88% of Net Fun's equity, becoming a strategic investor of the firm. At the same time, a UK-based fund management company, Enterprise Asia, also acquired 8% of the firm. However, these acquisitions have not affected the management of the firm, which is still largely led by Peggy and Catherine.

Net Fun now offers some 15 online Chinese indigenous games, with a new game rolling out every two months. The firm has a paid customer base of some 34 000 with an annual turnover of over HK$13.3 million (US$1.7 million). It employs a staff of 15, composed mostly of creative designers and programmers. The firm is privately owned, with Peggy Chan and Cheung Kong (Holdings) Limited as its major shareholders.

Business Model

The global Chinese online game player community is the target of Net Fun. The firm initially sought to apply a simple Internet business model consisting of two parts. One part was to use free indigenous online games to attract players from the Chinese community and to build up a large community of habitual visitors and players quickly. The other part was to leverage on the large online community to attract advertising dollars and to cross sell other products. This simple business model was quite commonly practiced in the early days of e-commerce (i.e. 1996–1998). While most other competitors would use information portals to build customer base and get page views, Net Fun used Chinese-based online games instead. Chinese-based online games were chosen because although the user market was huge, there was very little competition from local or international competitors, and the interactive multi-player nature of most online games would be conducive to the building up of an interactive online community.

Implementing the Business Model

The first part of the model was implemented using a software platform called *Cyber City*, which the users could download from the firm's website. Installing *Cyber City* on the user's PC would enable the user to access the variety of online games available from the website. *Cyber City* would also enable other functions such as chat-rooms, score boards, searching for online game playing partners, etc. and act as a three-dimensional (3-D) virtual reality interface between the user and the games and other facilities available on the website. *Cyber City* and all the other games offered by the firm were developed in-house. Promotion was done mainly through road shows and exhibitions in major shopping malls. Very little money was spent on traditional advertising. This part of the model worked and a large community of repeat local users built up quickly, reaching 180 000 in just 21 months. At that time the total Internet user population was only around one million. However, the second part of the model did not work and advertising dollars were only trickling into the firm in small amounts. By 1997 losses had mounted up to over HK$20 million (US$2.56 million) and the firm changed ownership. The incoming Director, Peggy Chan, reviewed the business model of the firm and decided to make a drastic change. A monthly subscription charge of HK$180 (US$23) was imposed. Membership dropped rapidly by almost 95% to a low of 10 000 but then gradually picked up again to 25 000 in 1999 and to 34 000 in May 2001, despite a doubling of subscription fee to HK$360 (US$46) in the same period. Currently, membership is composed of individual paid subscriptions and bulk subscriptions from other companies (such as ISPs and portals) for the benefit of their members.

Unlike other online shops, Net Fun's products did not need any physical delivery. Delivery logistics, which was a major implementation challenge for most online stores, was irrelevant to the firm. Supply chain management issues were not a problem either as all the products were indigenous and developed in-house by a team of devoted games developers/enthusiasts. In the beginning, the firm did not even charge a membership subscription fee, therefore payment arrangements were irrelevant too. When the firm started charging a membership subscription fee, it had to be paid through depositing cash or making a bank transfer payment to the firm's banking account. An online payment option was added only in late 2000.

Industry, Competitor and Environmental Analysis

Net Fun operates in the Chinese multi-player online games (MPOG) industry. Although there are numerous players operating in the MPOG industry (e.g. see the MPOG directory at http://www.mpogd.com) and many of them offer free online games, surprisingly there are almost none focusing exclusively on indigenous Chinese games. Moreover, Net Fun not only provides games; it is also a virtual community in which game players can interact with each other through game competitions, chat-rooms, private messaging and even online voice messaging.

The traditional MPOG industry is highly fragmented with almost no dominant market leaders. Many of the available offerings are from small outfits with only a handful of hobbyists and enthusiasts providing their products free. In comparison with other online consumer industries, the MPOG industry is characterized by a high level of customer 'stickiness' and a total absence of physical delivery logistics. The nature of interactive online games is that customers tend to spend a lot of time on the website playing the games with other players. The rate at which online games become obsolete is slow. Many classical Chinese games (e.g. Mahjong) are still very popular today. There are very few competitors in the Chinese MPOG industry and the firm considers that their actions are highly predictable.

Environmental issues were analyzed to identify potential drivers of innovation, e.g. levels of competition, uncertainty, etc. Price competition presents the most severe competitive threats to Net Fun as its competitors often charge substantially less (or do not charge at all). Differentiation is mainly based on product quality and levels of service. Customer demands are relatively predictable and are growing particularly in view of the rapidly expanding Internet population in China.

Key Business Drivers and Threats

Product quality and customer loyalty are crucial for the business to succeed! (Peggy Chan).

There are many free online games for customers to choose from in the market. To convince customers to pay for online games, Net Fun needs to provide additional value. The quality of the products has to be superior to those available for free. While most free Chinese online games are rather simple planner or word games, Net Fun is starting to offer 3-D animated games. In addition, the firm provides virtual community building functions (e.g. chat-rooms and voice channels) and activities (e.g. regular game competitions), adding extra value to subscribers and at the same time helping to cultivate customer loyalty.

Marketing strategy also plays a critical role. The firm cannot afford to waste huge sums of money on conventional advertising with uncertain outcomes. Rather, the firm focuses on road shows and cross-referral marketing programs with other firms having large established customer bases (e.g. credit card companies and ISPs). In addition, the firm also puts in much effort in marketing bulk membership purchase schemes to other companies, with some success.

The major difficulty in managing an online game company is the management of its human resources.

Our best designers and technologists are creative and devoted people but they do not understand projects have deadlines and products need to comply with industrial level quality assurance! (Peggy Chan).

The greatest threats facing the firm and industry would be international competitors from the offline games industry entering the MPOG market. There are many strong players in the traditional offline games industry. Global companies such as Sony and Sega are already showing signs of preparing to enter the MPOG market through building online functions into their newest game consoles. Backed by enormous financial, technical and human resources, and a very large existing global customer base, these companies would become formidable competitors.

Innovation Factors and Processes

The most important factors that led to the establishment of Net Fun and its subsequent innovations were:

1. The personal interests of the original founders—they were themselves game designers and enthusiasts.
2. The founders' 'gut feeling' (in 1994) that the Internet would pick up in Hong Kong and there would be a market for Chinese MPOGs.
3. The new principal's vision of doing this business, her personal confidence in the new business model and in her ability to turn the firm around through professional management.
4. The new principal's background. She has many years of experience as an IT professional and entrepreneur. She had successfully created and managed an IT consulting and software development company (Excel Technology International Holding Ltd), leading the company to public listing in the local stock market.

The main obstacle that Peggy had to overcome was to convince her staff to fully embrace the new subscription-based business model and at the same time ensure that the new model would be viable in a market with no tradition of paying subscriptions. Convincing her staff was not too difficult as the old advertising-based business model did not work and the firm was losing money. To ensure the viability of the subscription-based model was more risky. The firm reckoned that its MPOG products had a definite technology and cultural (i.e. they are indigenous games) edge over its competitors and many of its customers would eventually stay with the firm after the initial shock of having to pay for their games. It turned out that a sufficient number of customers did stay with the firm to make its operations viable. The firm even managed to recruit enough new customers to enable it to return a modest profit. Steering the firm's culture from an *ad hoc* casual to a more professional one also turned out to be very challenging.

The innovation processes were:

1. Games designers and enthusiasts formed Net Fun out of personal interest
2. Introduced first Chinese virtual games community platform: *Cyber City*
3. Launched several free indigenous MPOGs on the *Cyber City* platform
4. Advertising-based business model did not work and the firm lost substantial money
5. Firm changed ownership and new Director came in
6. Changed business model, charging subscription fees and built marketing alliances
7. Enhanced product features, launched 3-D MPOGs
8. Returned to profitability

Website Development and Operational Issues

As Net Fun was staffed essentially by creative and technology enthusiasts, the firm decided to build everything in-house. Most of the development effort was focused on product development (i.e. the MPOGs and the *Cyber City* platform). The website development and other IT systems were relatively straightforward as the firm did not have to deal with physical products (i.e. no need to handle inventories, supply chain, or delivery logistics). Online payment support was outsourced to another firm specializing in online payments. The development of *Cyber City* took one year to complete. The development of each game took between two weeks to five months to complete, depending on the complexity involved.

Operational issues were few and far between. Unlike other online stores, the firm did not need to deal with the highly seasonal demand fluctuations common in the B2C industry. Demand from and the usage pattern of the firm's customers were highly predictable. The firm had installed tracking software logging the online behavior of its customers for capacity planning, product development and marketing purposes.

Website Features

Evaluation of the website (see Table 5.1) results in a modest CEC score of 63%. Company and product information were well provided. Customer services functions were well developed too, although the site did not include any convenient links to other relevant websites that may be useful to its customers. Purchasing and subscription functions could be enhanced by improving security, simplifying the payment process, and making the details of the transactions more transparent to customers. Ease of use could be improved too as the site had no search engine or site map and some navigational buttons did not work. Customers would also benefit from more innovations in services and technology. Although multi-media technology was employed (the site offered a *Shock* version), there was no individual website customization and no easy channel for enhanced customer feedback (e.g. games reviews). Currently there is 100% integration for all business systems and operations.

The system is considered by the firm to be a success. The system is reliable. The system is also the business. Success measures are profit, revenue and customer growth.

Customer Details

Net Fun's customer profile is predominantly in the 15−25 age group. Over 80% of the customers are local Chinese. The remaining customers are from overseas with a Chinese cultural background. There is a clear male dominance in the customer base and all customers are frequent Internet users. The firm holds regular MPOG competitions and asks participants for feedback on their games through e-mail. The firm also logs customers' online usage pattern and behavior for statistical analysis, although no formal satisfaction survey has been carried out.

The firm reckons that the most important reasons for customers to subscribe to the firm are its unique and high-quality products and the existence of a well-established virtual user community. After the initial loss of customers when the subscription fee was imposed, the firm has since lost very few customers, implying a high degree of customer loyalty. The firm believes this level of customer loyalty is a clear indication of customer satisfaction.

The Future

Net Fun sees the biggest challenges for firms wanting to become Internet retailers are:

- finding a long-term viable revenue model;
- building customer loyalty; and
- getting supply chains and logistics right, especially for online stores selling physical products.

In the near future, the firm plans to expand to the online education and entertainment ('edutainment') market through new product development and strategic partnerships with relevant firms. It also intends to expand to the mainland China market and the Taiwan market for MPOGs.

Further advice for other firms seeking to develop an Internet service is not to copy blindly from cases elsewhere. Hong Kong is geographically small and culturally unique and successful models in the United States are often not applicable in Hong Kong. Online stores need to be very specific about products, markets and customers and tailor their offerings accordingly. Product differentiation is critical. Online stores must present an attractive value proposition in the context of what their online and offline competitors can offer.

Conclusion

The Net Fun experience emphasizes the importance of product differentiation and focusing on market niches where a firm has an inherent competitive advantage. It is also a vivid example of how an online firm can switch successfully from an advertising-based revenue model to one based on subscription, relying on unique value-added products and services not easily available from competitors. It also stresses the importance of relevant managerial experience in the management team, and the need to figure out a marketing strategy capable of leveraging the uniqueness of a certain given online operation.

WINGONET: (wingonet.com)

Introduction

The Wing On Department Stores Group (Wing On) was established in 1907. After nine decades of department store business in Hong Kong, it has established itself as a local household name with seven outlets in Hong Kong providing a total of over half a million square feet of shopping space. Wing On is probably the first major department store in Hong Kong to set up an online store. The online store, wingonet.com, was launched in August 1998, after a couple of years of planning and preparation. Since then the online store has been experiencing double-digit annual growth in sales revenue, contributing some HK$90 million (US$11.5 million) to the total sales of the group currently. The number of products carried by the online store has also increased from 200 to 2000 during the last three years. Despite its sizable sales volume, the online store has a full-time staff of only one!

Although listed in the Hong Kong stock market with an average annual turnover of over HK$2 billion (US$256 million) in the last five years, Wing On is still very much family owned with much of its shares still owned by the Kwok family, which founded the company. The top management responsibility of the company rests with the Executive Committee of the Board composed of Mr Karl Kwok (Chairman), Mr Lester Kwok (Deputy Chairman), Mr Mark Kwok, Dr Kwok Man Cho, and Miss Adriana Chan. All the members of the Executive Committee were educated in the United States. Karl has an MBA from the Wharton School and Lester has an economics degree from Stanford University, for example. Although the family is typically Chinese in terms of cultural background, the leadership of the company has to some extent embraced Western management thinking and displayed a keen awareness of business trends in the Western world.

The explosive growth of B2C companies in the United States around 1995 and 1996 had caught the imagination of the top management of the company. Intrigued by the potential of e-commerce in Hong Kong, the company started feasibility studies in 1996 to see whether B2C operations would present the right opportunity for the company's business in Hong Kong. Around 1997/1998 the Internet had picked up momentum in Hong Kong with subscribers exceeding one million for the first time. The company realized that the time had arrived and the environmental conditions for B2C operations were mature. The decision to build the online store was made. A project team was formed and within one year, wingonet.com went live online. The value proposition was to merge Wing On's 90-year service tradition with the latest cyber-shopping technology to provide enjoyable and convenient shopping to its customers on the Internet.

Business Model

The company treats its online store as simply an additional channel for its goods and services. Although the online store is expected to attract some new customers in addition to Wing On's traditional ones, the role of the online store is mainly to supplement the company's well-established and sizable physical outlets. The business model is one of 'click and mortar', with the 'mortar' part playing a dominant role. The online store uses a business model akin to conventional catalog shopping, with enhanced interactivity and customer service levels enabled by the Internet. Channel conflicts are carefully minimized. Synergies are exploited wherever possible. Only selected products thought to be particularly suitable for online sales are sold on the online store. However, Internet discounts are sometimes given to selected products. Wing On's well-established brand name is drawn on to leverage its online store. The online store is integrated with Wing On main website. Customers of the online store are made aware in no uncertain terms that they are shopping at a Wing On department store.

Implementing the Business Model

The business model was implemented in just a few months. The online store shared all its back-end support operations, from supply chain through inventory management to logistics and customer services, with the physical stores. Apart from taking orders through the Internet, all the business processes of the online store were fully integrated with those of the physical stores. An outside Application Service Provider (ASP) was hired to carry out the implementation of the website and its ongoing operational maintenance. One full-time staff member in-house was given the responsibility to monitor the website operations, track business sales and irregular business activities (e.g. false orders), coordinate seasonal product launches, and liaise with the ASP to ensure the proper functioning of the website and that the necessary website features updates were made as needed.

The company chose very carefully the types of products sold on its online store. Out of the 10 000 products types sold in the physical stores, only about 2000 were made available on the online store. The company thought its customers would be confused if they were faced with too many products and navigation around the online store would become overly tedious. Unlike in the physical stores, products sold online are accompanied by detailed product information. The product selection on the online store was changed regularly to maintain a degree of freshness to the customers.

Ease of ordering from and navigating around the online store were two of the most important considerations in the implementation of the store. Credit card payments were accepted. Such payments would be verified by the company and followed by a confirmation telephone call to customers, informing them of the time and date of delivery. Purchase orders would then be entered into the company's normal ordering system in the same way as purchases made in the physical stores requiring a delivery service. The online store would also accept orders from overseas but would only deliver to locations in Hong Kong. In addition to selling through its own net shop (www.wingonet.com), the company also had a

Chinese only version of its online store hosted in Yahoo's Chinese shopping mall (i.e. Yahoo!Shopping at www.yahoo.com).

There were a few business concerns about the project. It was unclear if the size of the current online shopping market was sufficiently large to enable the range of potential product categories to be sold profitably. The volatile development cycle of e-commerce was a concern because it made the estimation of the optimal time to enter the market very difficult. By using a 'click-and-mortar' strategy (with the dominant 'mortar' part of it well established), the company minimized the risks of its online store. The payment system was also a business concern. The online store accepted credit card payment only, and the company had to deal with incidents of fake orders (i.e. invalid credit card numbers), which appeared to be on the increase. The online store was funded internally as a project to explore a new channel and enhance customer service. Quick profitability was not a top priority.

Industry, Competitor and Environmental Analysis

Wingonet.com operates as an online department store—a classic retail operation. In the retail industry, customer services, product quality and price attractiveness are all very important. Department stores need to be highly aware of market trends and to be able quickly to adapt to these trends in the context of the specific customer types that they serve. Department stores usually carry a large number of different types of products with quick turnovers, they need to use IT systems intensively for transaction support, inventory management, data analysis for managerial decision support and the provision of good customer services. It is also indispensable for stores to better understand their customers' buying behavior.

The rate at which products become obsolete in this industry is quite fast but the actions of competitors are often quite predictable. Wing On, like other local department stores both online and offline, closely monitors the activities of its competitors. As the local economy has been consolidating in the last couple of years, the overall demand for consumer goods has fallen and customers have become a lot more cost conscious. Price competition in the industry is high. The spending power of local consumers has dropped significantly since the major Asian financial crisis of 1998. There is also an increasing trend by Hong Kong consumers to travel to mainland China for cheaper shopping as cross-border traffic becomes more and more convenient. Thus less money is being spent in Hong Kong. Profit margins in the entire department store industry in Hong Kong have been under much pressure, forcing many department stores to explore new business models in order to cut costs and become more efficient. E-business models are starting to be introduced across the entire value chain. Wing On is starting to go directly to manufacturers for their supplies instead of through buying agents. To some extent, these market factors have also driven the company to start its exploration of online selling. To date, the company has not seen any significant competition coming from overseas department stores (online or offline) as they often do not have a sufficiently good knowledge of the specific tastes and buying behavior of local customers, which is very important for the success of a department store.

Key Business Drivers and Threats

Product quality and service levels are always the key business drivers (Maria Bong, General Manager).

The company paid a lot of attention to the selection of products for its online store, trying to anticipate the type of products that its customers would prefer to purchase online (as against its many conveniently located physical stores). The greatest immediate threat facing the firm and the department store industry as a whole is the softening of local demand as the result of a weakening economy and the fast increasing levels of cross-border shopping activities from local customers enabled by easy access to substitute shops in the Chinese mainland. The annual turnover of Wing On has dropped from HK$2.662 billion (US$341 million) in 1996 to HK$1.741 billion (US$223 million) in 1999, for example.

Innovation Factors and Processes

The most important factors that led to this project were:

1. Senior management's US background and awareness of e-commerce trends.
2. Market pressure on the firm to develop new business models to cut costs and increase sales.
3. Senior management's assessment that conditions for Internet shopping in Hong Kong were mature enough for the firm's online store.
4. Senior management's belief that the Internet would continue to proliferate, offering immense opportunities for e-commerce.
5. The firm's culture of using IT to support operations and improve customer services.

A few barriers the firm had to overcome for the project to be a success were identified. First of all was the lack of experience in implementing an online store and the firm's assessment that there were too few relevant (local) cases to benchmark on or learn from. Then there was the difficulty of positioning the online store correctly in the context of the company's extensive physical stores, bearing in mind potential channel conflicts. Online customer behavior was largely unknown too. Integrating the workflow and business processes of the online store with the physical stores also presented a challenge. There was a certain level of resistance (arising out of fear of the unknown) from the existing workforce against the activities of the online store in the beginning, which required a certain amount of education and training effort to overcome. As the development of the website was outsourced to an ASP, effective coordination with the ASP turned out to be a challenge as there was a sizable gap in background, expectation and language used between the IT people from the ASP and the management people of Wing On.

The innovation processes were:

1.   Senior management became aware of e-shopping trends developing in the United States
2.   Internal feasibility study for an online store started
3.   The search for new business models became intensified as pressure on the local market mounted after the Asian financial crisis in 1998
4.   Senior management determined that local conditions were ripe for online stores
5.   Senior management gave the go-ahead for the project
6.   Senior management decided to outsource website development
7.   Senior management appointed a coordinating person to oversee development
8.   Integration of online and offline business processes and workflows
9.   Commenced online business

Website Development and Operational Issues

As the company's own in-house IT team did not have any experience of developing an online store, website development and hosting were outsourced to an ASP. After carefully examining several candidate firms on the criteria of their financial background, prior relevant experience, existing client lists, examples of prior websites developed, and former clients' comments, the company chose a firm that it believed could deliver the best results. It took six months to implement the online store. In the beginning the company was only mildly satisfied as there was a fairly big communication gap between Wing On's management and the IT team of the outsourced firm. This gap gradually narrowed and the company was eventually quite satisfied with the end results.

There were a few operational issues. At first, there were only 200 items sold on the online store, which the company soon found out to be insufficient. Navigation around the online store was as easy as expected. There were also occasional server problems but the ASP did not report them to Wing On's management, leaving the company to figure out in the dark why sometimes sale activities dipped significantly for no apparent reasons. On occasions the company would need to mount marketing campaigns on the web quickly, but the ASP was sometimes not able to implement these campaigns fast enough on the online store. The implementation of the online store has undergone continuous revision once every couple of months or so since it started up, with a major re-launch 18 months after the online store first went live. Ease of ordering and navigation were the two most important criteria guiding the implementation of the online store.

Website Features

Evaluation of the website (see Table 5.1) shows a relatively high score (80%) on the CEC scale. Transaction and customer-related functions are all well developed, achieving full scores on transaction features, customer services, and ease of use. A couple of innovations in services and technology (e.g. delivery tracking and the use of customer suggestion forms) are noted but more could be done. For example, website customization for individual customers could be supported. Multi-media animation could be added judiciously to draw customer attention to important items. Website evaluation also suggests that more details on the company and its operations would be well regarded by customers.

Although the business processes of the online store were fully integrated with the physical stores, it was treated as a separate Wing On store and the website was a stand-alone system not connected to the other IT systems of the company. Manual processes were needed to transfer online orders to the IT systems of the physical stores for order fulfillment using the company's existing systems.

The system is considered by the firm to be a success. Maria says,

> It meets our requirements on the ease of ordering and navigation, price, turnaround time (i.e. lead time for making revisions), and the page loading time was good from the customer's perspective.

Customer Perspectives

Wingonet.com's customers are mainly Chinese professionals below the age of 45. There is a roughly equal split between male and female customers. (With their physical stores, the split is around 35:65.) Customers tend to be frequent Internet users and they use e-mail frequently to communicate with the company, often making good suggestions to the company. Although the online store only delivers locally, up to one-third of its orders (during peak seasons such as Christmas) originate from Chinese living aboard in North America, Australia, New Zealand, and the United Kingdom.

The firm believes that its reputation for reliability, product quality, reasonable price, and good levels of customer services are the main factors driving customers to shop with wingonet.com. The firm also thinks that the convenience of its many physical outlets acts as an inhibitor to its online store. However, an analysis of customer data has shown that many of wingonet.com's customers are not regular shoppers at its physical outlets.

The firm believes their customers are quite satisfied in general. Although no formal satisfaction survey has been carried out, there are many repeat purchases and friendly customer comments received through the online store, implying a certain level of customer satisfaction.

The Future

Wingonet.com sees the biggest challenges to firms in the future use of the Internet retailing as:

1. Getting both the external and internal business processes right. All business processes from customer targeting and communication, supply chain through to back-office logistics need to be very effective and seamlessly integrated.
2. Getting the right mix between the physical and the online channels. (The survival of a pure online channel is very difficult).
3. Getting staff trained up and developed in serving the new online shopping culture.

In the near future the company plans to introduce cross-merchandising activities with other business partners. The company also plans to enhance its marketing activities to increase the 'presence' of the online store among its target customers.

Conclusion

The wingonet.com experience shows how a traditional mainstream retail player can successfully develop an online channel both as an additional revenue stream and as a means to deliver enhanced customer services. The importance of leveraging on a strong traditional brand reputation is emphasized. The importance of ease of use for an online store is emphasized. Senior management's commitment and vision are also crucial for the success of the project.

CHAPTER CONCLUSION

The firms profiled illustrate a variety of successful implementations of Internet retailing that have been developed from a diverse set of motivations. A more complete examination of all innovation factors may be seen in Chapter 9.

Drivers

The most important factors that led to these projects were (not in significant order):

-   The principals' extensive knowledge, experience and capability in the business area (Ambassador, DVD, ebabyasia, Net Fun, Wing On) or the Internet (DVD, ebabyasia).
-   The principal was inspired by existing Internet operations (Ambassador, ebabyasia).
-   The principal's perception of a business opportunity through online retailing (all).

- Market pressure on the firm to develop new business models to cut costs and increase sales (Wing On).
- The principal's analysis that their products were suitable for selling through the Internet with likely customer acceptance of Internet purchasing (Ambassador, DVD, ebabyasia, Wing On).
- The firm's culture of using IT to support operations and improve customer services (Wing On).
- Back-end operations for the online shop were already in place, hence additional costs were marginal (Ambassador).
- The identification of the online store as part of a multi-channel retailing strategy (Ambassador).
- Initial pilot implementation resulted in sales orders (Ambassador).

Inhibitors

Major obstacles and barriers included:

- Securing supplies of quality products and services at a low cost (ebabyasia).
- The firm did not have a significant IT capability (Ambassador). Lack of experience in implementing an online store and the firm's assessment that there were too few relevant (local) cases to learn from (Wing On).
- Development complications. A sizable gap in background, expectation and language used between the IT people from the external website developer and client management (Wing On).
- The need to re-educate employees on how to operate an Internet business and to re-train them so that they can use the necessary Internet and computer tools to do their new jobs effectively (Ambassador, ebabyasia). Employee skepticism about a new and untried business model (from advertising to subscription) needed to be overcome (Net Fun). Employee uncertainty and resistance (Wing On).
- The firm's culture. Steering the firm's culture from an ad hoc casual to a more professional one (Net Fun).
- The payment system. Initially the firm had to rely on offline payment processing methods that were costly (DVD) or initially having high charges for online purchase payment processing (ebabyasia).
- The critical mass of customers willing to purchase online was unknown or initially limited (DVD, Wing On). This was largely due to lack of trust (DVD). The critical mass of customers willing to pay subscriptions was unknown but substantially below the current level of customers (Net Fun).
- Contrary to popular belief, the convenience of physical shopping in a highly populated city such as Hong Kong is not thought by the firm as an inhibitor of online shopping (Ambassador).
- Ensuring synergy between online and offline operations and avoiding channel conflict (ebabyasia, Wing On).

6
Internet Retailing in the United Kingdom

BOB GALLIERS AND ANNE WIGGINS

INTRODUCTION

In order to provide something of a window on the current state of e-commerce in the United Kingdom, we have selected five case companies that led the way in their respective industries. Before describing them in more detail, however, we first provide some background contextual detail for Internet retailing in the United Kingdom—in terms of detailed government policy infrastructure, stated enablers and inhibitors, and the effects of the technology shares crash of April 2000. In this way we can better understand the relative competitive position of UK companies with respect to other leading countries in relation to e-commerce generally and Internet retailing in particular.

The UK government strongly advocates the development of a 'legal, regulatory and fiscal environment' to facilitate its goal of the United Kingdom becoming the best place in the world to conduct e-commerce by 2002. Believing online business success to be critical to the future competitiveness of UK businesses, the government established its agenda in *Our Information Age: the Government's Vision* in mid-1998. To date, this has been followed by three further major government policy statements.

Crucially, the government recognizes that its e-commerce agenda can be delivered only in partnership with industry. As a consequence, the government Department of Trade and Industry (DTI) collaborates with the private sector in order to ensure that UK companies are in a position to recognize and exploit the opportunities available. To this end, the government has appointed both an e-envoy and an e-minister to ensure that the concerns of 'e-companies', or all companies that operate online, are heard and acted on within government.

Another key mechanism is the Information Age Partnership—a forum for dialogue between the public and private sectors involving the UK's IT, communications, electronics and creative content industries. In addition, many private sector companies of all sizes are working with the government-led *UK Online for Business*.

The United Kingdom is well placed to make the most of the opportunities that do exist. It has a world-class IT and communications infrastructure and digital services companies, including a highly sophisticated wireless device market, relatively low telecommunications costs, and a regulatory structure that facilitates one of the most important and competitive financial marketplaces. In addition, London is the European centre for venture capital. Consumer acceptance is higher than in many other European countries. Mass surveys (e.g. NetValue 2000) indicate that 30% of households are connected to the Internet and the profile of a 'typical' UK Internet user to be male (58%) and mature (35–49 years is the largest category with 32%, although 50% of users are aged less than 35 years).

The stumbling blocks to achieving the vision are slow broadband development and e-commerce taxation. Whilst the government acknowledges the strategic importance of the wide availability of inexpensive bandwidth, the reality is that broadband development in Britain is growing less swiftly than either businesses, consumers, or the government had anticipated or would like. The delay is widely reported to be due to the endemic and entrenched anti-competitiveness of British Telecom and a lack of intervention by the government. And there is, of course, always a tension between safeguarding tax revenues and helping new business. While the United States, for example, has placed a moratorium on new e-commerce taxes, Britain's tax breaks are of limited value to e-commerce companies and have an emphasis on preventing tax avoidance rather than promoting and encouraging enterprise.

Despite these problems, there remains enormous scope for extending both the business-to-consumer (B2C) and business-to-business (B2B) e-commerce markets in the United Kingdom. The most popular online purchases in the United Kingdom in 2000 (in descending order) were: leisure and travel products; software, hardware and other computer-related products; books; CDs; and groceries. Fletcher Research, the UK arm of Forrester Research, in its report *UK Online Retail: From Minority to Mainstream* (Forrester Research 2000b), predicts that online consumer spending in the United Kingdom will rise from US$2.6 billion in 2000 to US$30 billion by 2005.

Notwithstanding such optimistic forecasts, however, a number of high-profile UK internet ventures suffered highly public falls in the technology shares crash which began in April 2000. Some, such as the fashion site boo.com, and the health and beauty site ClickMango, are once again trading, but under new ownership. These resuscitated sites, almost without exception, have given up their former business models and strategies in exchange for a more restrained approach to product or service provision. For instance, boo.com no longer stocks and sells products; instead, it is now an online fashion guide with links to recommended retailers. And ClickMango is to be reincarnated as a brand of health and beauty products sold through shops—the most traditional retail outlet of all.

Such scenarios are typical. These companies invested enormous sums of money in building up public relations (PR) and awareness of their brands. While the actual business models were not sufficiently strong to keep the entity running in the original format, brand awareness has been established, and value lies therein for the new owners. Certainly, the business models of such companies have been evaluated and validated by significantly more cautious investors. One positive outcome of this is that most of the companies continuing to operate online, or who started business since the technology shares crash, have emerged as less extravagant, more robust, more disciplined and more tightly focused.

The technology shares crash has also affected large corporations. A number of traditional businesses, such as Pearson, Marks & Spencer and the Royal Bank of Scotland, were dissolving or extracting themselves from online initiatives they had previously committed themselves to, or were cutting their investment in their online divisions, not least in order to address hostile market reaction. For example, Pearson, the publishing group which includes the *Financial Times* and *The Economist* in its aegis, is planning to invest just £40–£50 million in the coming financial year on the group's combined Internet services, whereas in the annual return submitted in March 2001, £40 million was spent on marketing alone for the ft.com website.

Many UK businesses—including the case studies that follow—have decided that for strategic reasons, and in particular the need to remain competitive, they have to trade through e-commerce, and have therefore stopped trying to justify their investment on a quantitative financial basis. In its *Business in the Information Age International Benchmarking Study 2000*, (DTI 2000) the DTI claims that 70% of businesses currently use e-commerce alongside conventional business methods, and that many of the businesses that have not yet begun to use e-commerce plan to do so in the future. These figures indicate that the level of e-commerce activity is strong in the United Kingdom.

With the majority of UK businesses currently online in some capacity, the focus of attention has now switched to how businesses use their online connections. At present, very few businesses are totally reliant on e-commerce. While applications such as e-mail and online marketing are relatively widespread, online activities that require an increasing level of interaction and technical complexity have lower levels of adoption. DTI figures indicate that UK businesses tend to be farther up the e-commerce adoption ladder in dealing with their suppliers than they are on the customer side. For example, while 88% of UK businesses use e-mail every day, 66% have a marketing website, and 57% either allow their customers to order online or order online from their suppliers. About 34% either allow their corporate customers to make payment online or pay their suppliers online, but only 13% enable their retail customers to make payments online.

These percentages are clearly not high enough if the United Kingdom is to become 'the best place in the world to conduct e-commerce', whether this is to be by 2002, or later. According to Jupiter MMXI, a US-based thinktank, six of the seven most frequently visited websites in Britain, including `amazon.co.uk` and `yahoo.co.uk`, are American. As the leading websites obtain the highest advertising revenues, the United Kingdom clearly needs to foster more of its own successful e-commerce companies, such as those described below.

Overview of Cases

The five selected case studies represent the most popular online retail industry sectors in the United Kingdom—computer-related products, books, online food and groceries, and leisure and travel services.

Action was an immediate success when, in 1972, it began to sell printer consumables. Subsequently, increasing numbers of product lines were introduced. The company then, as now, aimed 'to be the leading reseller of brand leading computer equipment at the lowest possible prices'. Action is now the UK's number one mail-order or catalogue reseller of IT products, but it also fully integrates its entire product portfolio into a number of e-procurement systems.

The Internet has caused a revolution in publishing. **Blackwell's**, established in 1879, the world's largest independently held academic publisher of books, journals and academic software, and the oldest, and—ostensibly—one of the most traditional, of the UK chain booksellers, has been quietly spearheading a revolution. Launching one month before a then-unheard of start-up called Amazon, Blackwell's was the first of the UK chain booksellers to trade online.

Each of the companies within the **easyGroup** (`easyJet.com`, `easyEverything.com`, `easyRentacar.com`, and `easyValue.com`) adopts its founder's mission to take the 'complexity and hidden costs' out of the business sector it operates in. Concentrating on businesses that have become complacent and inefficient, the easyGroup operates primarily online, which enables it to pass on savings to its customers. Indeed, re-thinking business really seems to be the easyGroup's focus!

Lobster wants to be 'the Harrod's Food Hall of Cyberspace' and 'the gastronome's virtual answer'. By so doing it aims to change the way its customers shop for fine foods and wines. The company caters to a niche market with sophisticated tastes. It is, effectively, an online delicatessen targeting those with a discerning palate who either do not have the time to visit or are not in the vicinity of a shop selling, for example, Iranian caviar or freshly cooked lobsters, but want them. To that end, Lobster focuses on delivering only those products that one would never find stocked in a typical supermarket.

The strategy behind travel company **Thomas Cook** relaunching its online operations in 1999 as `thomascook.com` centres on the premise that the company provides its existing and potential customers with a one-stop travel portal 'they can trust'. Although the company's traditional competitors have, in the main, decided to go for new branding and/or multiple branded sites, Thomas Cook sees its brand name as being intrinsic both to the company's proposition and to everything it stands for. Since the launch of the company's initial website in 1995, significant online sales volumes have been transacted online. The thomascook.com website is now performing on a par with the most successful branches in the UK shops network, although the vast majority of people booking via the website are new customers of the company.

ACTION—'THE DEFINITIVE B2B CATALOGUE' (www.action.com)

Introduction

Action was an immediate success when it began to sell printer consumables and office supplies through its catalogues, and consequently increasing numbers of product lines were introduced. The company then, as now, aimed 'to be the leading reseller of brand leading computer equipment at the lowest possible prices'. Action is now the UK's number one mail-order or catalogue reseller of IT products, but it also fully integrates its entire product portfolio into a number of e-procurement systems.

The core business strategy of the IT reseller Action Computer Supplies Holdings Plc has been to build a profitable high growth online retailing company based on the proposition that experienced IT users—its customers—are increasingly able to specify precisely the products and services they require. The company, which employs approximately 650 staff, was founded in 1972, and is based in Alperton, London, with its warehouse in Buckingham, and its logistics operations housed in Southall. Six other major locations exist throughout the United Kingdom and Spain, the company's European base.

Action's philosophy is based on the fact that its customers can self-sufficiently manage the computer systems within their businesses, and that they expect to choose from a wide range of products and services with low prices, reliable delivery and simple order placing. The company executes this philosophy through what it calls 'buy-side' systems, which differ from 'normal' websites in that they are sponsored, subscribed to or owned by Action's corporate customers.

Action provides its corporate customers with versions of their website specific to them. This can involve specialist or pre-configured product lines unique to each customer, specific special offers, or a customized set of 'front-end screens'.

It seems that this approach is well suited to the needs of organizations that have their own IT infrastructure and want to be able to deal with a single efficient source of supply for a wide range of products and services to diverse locations. Action's account management approach ensures that the process is understood and agreed at all levels within both organizations, while the company's ability to customize its online communication and transactional systems enables it to match the specific requirements of these large customers. An IT system (the Masterpack system) was installed in March 2000 better to deal with this, and towards the end of 2000, the company was already seeing the benefits of a single system enabling unified processes across the company. These benefits include an improved ability to communicate information to customers, the ability to operate much more rapidly and efficiently, and a closer integration between the website and 'back office' systems.

The company's customer base of buy-side sites continues to grow, with a further 3425 customer sites added throughout 2000, and the total business customer sites equating to one in six UK businesses today. So comprehensive is the business that Phil Sbrana-Browning, Action's e-Commerce Systems Manager, claims that orders are being processed on average every two minutes, with approximately 80% of products delivered the following weekday. By August 2000 the company's turnover was just under £270 million, yet Action is considered to be a 'small-to-medium' company in its market.

Business Model

Action adopts the following mission statement: 'Action is a leading online participant in the business-to-business supply chain. It aims to provide directly, and through its partners, the widest range of IT products, services and supply chain solutions to all sizes of businesses.'

Action has built its reputation on providing its customers with the widest selection of brand leading products at the lowest prices, with the company's online sales amounting to nearly a third of its total UK sales in 2000. The company's catalogue and website pages contain over 29 000 leading brand products including hardware, software, networking, data communications and supplies, in addition to over 150 services from consulting to on-site PC repairs, break/fix maintenance, on-site resource, configuration and product roll outs. In addition, the company offers comprehensive free no-obligation pre- and post-sales technical information.

As a long-established catalogue company, Action was prepared for lower pricing and an online shopfront, and was not troubled by the customer fulfilment and after-sales problems that have dogged many online resellers. 'We've come out of the mail order business, which means we've been delivering this way—with same-day shipping and so on—for 18 years', Sbrana-Browning said. 'All we did was take our infrastructure and put a new web front on it.'

Implementing the Business Model

Action takes a commission from the manufacturer on every item it sells on any of its sites. The company's active range, Sbrana-Browning asserts, is the 'widest in the UK' but its electronic approach to data capture and communication means that it is able to expand this range still further, particularly with products that are only merchandised electronically. Thereby Action can justify the lower costs of providing product information electronically on a much wider range of less-frequently ordered products than can be achieved using conventional publishing —hence the company can grow the range without increasing the size of its paper catalogues. By automatically loading product information from suppliers, Action is able to present a wider range to their customers at relatively little incremental cost.

Sbrana-Browning has also overseen the introduction of advanced configuration tools and online compatibility guides that will better enable customers to select and buy the correct product(s) from this wider range. Although Action's printed catalogue is revised every 60 days, the main (and all subsidiary) websites are updated hourly. Action gives customers time-critical information via personalized e-mail, combined with links to the relevant section of its individually configured websites, which contain a database with complete descriptions, photographs, up-to-date pricing and current stock availability for every product.

Customers can both place an order and track its status online as it progresses through Action's system and that of its carriers, while customer-specific pricing agreements are handled automatically by the system and applied to customer orders. All post-sales services are carried out by Action, but in fact are seen to be by the subsidiary site it was purchased through.

A typical example of Action's order fulfilment process is as follows:

- The buy-side system is either sponsored, subscribed to or owned by Action's customers.
- A customer using a specific buy-side site selects and places an order for a product on that website.
- The website captures the order, verifies the credit card or debits an account, and thereby accepts payment.
- If the item is not included in the warehouse stock, a duplicate order of that product goes to the supplier or manufacturer of that product for them to deliver the item to Action. The customer order number, name and address are all featured on the delivery note, so that Action is able easily to match the product to the order.
- The item is packaged and despatched by an in-house courier.
- The purchaser pays on strict 30-day commercial terms if the item was not paid for by credit card.
- The distributor is paid on strict 30-day commercial terms.

Integrated computer systems enable Action to move rapidly and present a seamless operation to its customers across multiple suppliers, and allows the company to monitor each stage of the operation in a model that works identically for both B2C and B2B applications.

Industry, Competitor and Environmental Analysis

It is not a good time to be an online IT reseller. Most computer and technology companies are warning of lower than expected revenues because of continued weakness in the US economy and fears of an economic slowdown in Europe. After an unprecedented boom, IT companies and their suppliers are now in the midst of an unprecedented bust. Many corporate customers appear to have frozen their technology spending until further notice. Dead or dying dotcom companies are selling off their hardly-used equipment at steep discounts. In addition, many customers are constantly adjusting their budgets, often cancelling orders at the last moment, while still other corporate customers are realizing that they spent far too much on technology in the recent past, and are slashing their technology budgets.

These problems affect Action. However, Sbrana-Browning is confident that there will be a recovery from this 'buyers' strike' late in 2001, due to price cuts in Intel's latest high-end Pentium 4 microprocessor and the introduction of Microsoft's next Windows operating system. But he does reluctantly admit that the company is likely to see less profit in the 'near future'.

Key Business Drivers and Threats

The company's major challenges include combating a weakening market in order to ensure that it remains the industry leader in terms of both customer satisfaction and low-cost operation. Sbrana-Browning identifies Action's key business driver as selling the right product at the right price—if profit margins drop below 4%, it will become difficult to sustain the business. He identifies Action's key business threats as being dis-intermediation and determining ways to add value to customers to ensure that Action will remain successful, as margins grow increasingly slimmer.

Action was a large and established catalogue firm with a broad corporate clientele before it launched its online operations. Therefore, many of the systems and practices it needed were already in place. Compared with local competitors in its league, Action has a larger product range and more sales but fewer operating costs, because it combines them with a robust catalogue business.

Although the company monitors its competitors, it considers their actions to be established and predictable. However, the rate of product obsolescence is extremely high, with approximately one-third of the number of products changing in any given month. But the company is fortunate that, in the minds of its customers, it is not considered to be similar to the legions of unsuccessful Internet companies.

Innovation Factors and Processes

Sbrana-Browning considers that the implementation of Action's website has been an 'organic, informal' process. It was initially a case of 'try and see' and 'if it doesn't work, let's tweak it'. Since the beginning of 2000, however, there has been an increasing tendency to justify expenditure.

In 1995 Action began to produce CDs of its catalogue, and distributed these alongside its printed catalogue. The original ideal and business model remains aligned with the catalogue company, to which the primary website (including its subsidiaries) is still seen as a complementary channel.

The initial use of CDs was not as successful as had been anticipated, but the company persevered, and in May 1997 introduced special price initiatives for customers who linked from the CD to the company's website when purchasing. From this point on, online sales began to take off. Sbrana-Browning estimates that 50% of the company's B2C business is derived from its corporate clientele, who when making computer purchasing decisions at home, chose Action, as they do at work.

A major barrier to online success was the company's initial failure to successfully harness the benefits of online trading, perhaps due to the lack of an appropriate model. The company went through multiple adaptations of the website before 'getting the technology right'. The other primary barrier was converting the company's customers from phone/fax ordering to online ordering.

Sbrana-Browning identified the major threat to the company today as disintermediation, where customers direct-buy from manufacturers rather than go through a reseller. The innovation processes were:

- The identification of CDs as an alternative retail opportunity, leading on from the company's catalogues
- The production of CDs and analysis of why customers were not using them
- The recognition, with the development of the Internet as a mass selling tool, that it would be more cost-effective for the company to convert catalogue users to online users
- The introduction of special CD/online prices
- The success of special online pricing let to subsidiary/subscription websites

The major business concern about 'tackling' the Internet as a new channel was the company's lack of experience in that area. The company, however, had a growing, successful and highly profitable business that could fund experimentation. Therefore the company had the time and money to 'dabble' until it located the model that worked.

Website Development and Operational Issues

Although Action had been 'online' since May 1997, Sbrana-Browning considers the January 1998 website to be the first 'true' website, not least because it was comprehensive and robust, and because it worked with all browsers. As Action already had a large workforce covering various operations, the divisions of the company were restructured in order to ensure that 'no aspect' of the web operations was outsourced. However, the company did consult strategic partners who assisted with 'the more complicated' technology issues. Table 6.1 shows that Action's website supports the firm's focus on low price and broad product range. The product details, transaction capability, ease of use and customer services are well developed, although further details on the firm and more innovative customer services would be beneficial.

The decision to launch online operations was business-driven. The first live implementation of Internet trading took four months, and proved 'reasonably' satisfactory. However, there were, for several years, ongoing and extremely costly difficulties trying to integrate the back-end with the website, and separating and streamlining the systems within the company. The migration from NT to a Linux platform on a five-server cluster, for instance, proved fraught with unanticipated operational problems and issues, and took nine months.

From the outset, the level of customer satisfaction has been measured by a monthly survey, a policy inherited from the company's catalogue-only days. Regular monthly customer panels analyse customers' requirements, the results of which are distributed to every department. Action's online trading has been considered a success as determined by its having grown within four years to a third of the business.

The Future

Outside of the company's overriding goal to become 'truly pan-European', Sbrana-Browning considers that the company will focus its efforts on improving personal and after-sales services in order to dissuade customers from disintermediation. The company will initiate new services via other channels, such as wireless application protocol (WAP) and interactive TV (iTV). His advice for firms seeking to develop Internet services is to 'set a requirement against a marketing strategy to induce passing on lower costs'.

Conclusion

The experience of Action clearly demonstrates that the implementation of an online sales channel into an already established company, even with the appropriate infrastructure in place, is not always straightforward or immediately successful. The ability to experiment with and to revise the business model in tune with a company's operations and its customers' expectations and feedback is a crucial, though expensive and often overlooked, luxury.

BLACKWELL LTD—'QUIETLY SPEARHEADING A DIGITAL REVOLUTION' (www.blackwells.com/www.headfiller.com)

Introduction

The Internet has caused a revolution in publishing, and Blackwell's, established in 1879, the world's largest independently held academic publisher of books, journals and academic software, and the oldest and—ostensibly—one of the most traditional of the UK's chain booksellers, has been quietly spearheading this revolution. Launching one month before a then-unheard of startup called Amazon, Blackwell's was the first of the UK chain booksellers to trade online.

Still a family-owned business, Oxford-based Blackwell Ltd, has a turnover in excess of £200 million per annum, and employs more than 2000 people within its divisions:

- Blackwell Publishers
- Blackwell Science
- Blackwell's Bookshops (a UK chain of over 70 shops, including university bookshops, the Heffer's bookshop in Cambridge, and specialist travel, art, poster and music shops in Oxford)
- Blackwell's Book Services (a global leader in book distribution to academic libraries)
- Blackwell's Online (incorporating Blackwell's Online Bookshop, Heffer's Online Bookshop, Headfiller, and Blackwell's Reading Lists)
- Swets Blackwell (global subscription agent and information service which works in collaboration with 60 000 academic, medical, corporate and government libraries and information centres and 65 000 publishers worldwide)

In June 1995, Blackwell's Bookshops launched its first website, effectively 'tacking on' a new front end to its already established and successful mail order business. Growing user demand saw the revision of this site, the establishment of the division Blackwell's Online, and the launch of sites servicing other sections of the group, culminating in the launch of Headfiller (which targets a student audience), to coincide with the 2000/2001 academic year. It is intended that Headfiller's database will eventually incorporate the entire Blackwell group. In tune with this intention, Blackwell's is set to reclarify if not redefine the purpose of each section of the group.

Business Model

The key to the success of Blackwell's is 'timely information and timely fulfilment of customer requirements', according to Alan Leitch, MD of Blackwell Retail. Leitch says that Blackwell's aims to offer the same standards of service and information both on- and offline, and labels this 'multi-channel choice'. This multi-channel equation is complicated by the fact that, while it has strong and long-established links with businesses and institutions, the company also services customers directly. To integrate these aspects of the business, Blackwell's is planning a number of initiatives that will see all its websites working together with the bookshops. Online customers have the option of using the bookstores as collection points, and the two retail vehicles work together on buying back textbooks.

When an order is placed on any of the group's websites, the book required is automatically located either in the warehouse or in one of the stores. If the book is not in stock, it is placed on order. When it arrives, it is identified either as an Internet, mail order or store order, and sent to the appropriate destination within

24 hours. This implementation is a common model for retailers incorporating a mail order division, and Blackwell's was held in good stead by having already fine-tuned these processes in its substantial mail order operation before it went online.

Blackwell's bookshops, most of which are formally attached to or are near to academic institutions, teaching hospitals, and the corporate business community, have built much of their reputation on having knowledgeable, committed and helpful staff. Leitch predicts that in the future Blackwell's intends to keep its number of bookshops static, and will become even more selective in choosing store placements, in order to focus on inventing newer business models.

Industry, Competitor and Environmental Analysis

Leitch believes that there have been three phases of significant change in UK book retailing market and customer expectations. These have changed the face—and the cost—for consumers and retailers alike:

- Phase 1, between 1984 and 1990, saw the growth of, and competition between, the large UK book chains Blackwell's, Waterstone's, Dillon's, and W.H. Smith. As a direct result of this competition, Leitch believes that book-sellers in the UK became 'more professional' retailers.
- Phase 2 took place in the early 1990s, alongside the massification of tertiary education in the United Kingdom. This extended the ready market for Blackwell's core retail and publishing businesses, and the company's canny response saw their turnover increase by 50% during this period.
- Phase 3, which has taken place over the five years between 1995 and 2000, saw not only the ending of the Net Book Agreement (a cartel that had fixed minimum cover prices and ensured that titles could not be discounted within six months of publication), but also the consolidation of book chainsellers and the insurgence of the US lifestyle bookshops, but also the advent of the Internet.

Customers now simply expect more, and at better value. And despite the fact that book sales in the United Kingdom have fallen from £2.1 billion in 1990 to £1.9 billion in 1999, UK book buyers are able to purchase at prices considerably lower than what they would have paid several years ago. During the same period, UK bookshops have had to improve the service and facilities they provide in offline bookshops.

The ending of the Net Book Agreement in 1995 removed a core element of competition, eradicated the publishers' control of the UK market, and made books cheaper for customers. As the large book chains consolidate, they have been able to force publishers into conceding ever-bigger discounts: whereas 20 years ago UK bookshops would buy from publishers at, typically, a 35% discount on the cover price, the norm today is 50% on hardbacks and 60% on paperbacks. This reduction in the price of books is compounded by the growth of online retailing, which cuts down the numbers of customers walking into bookshops. Therefore price has become an even greater major marketing tool than ever before. And in addition to making the price of books much more transparent, the Internet retailers also speed up delivery. The impact of the Internet on the industry should not be underestimated, and Leitch believes that the advent of the Internet and online retailing has been 'the single most influential factor' in the reinvention of consumers' expectations.

Key Business Drivers and Threats

Leitch identifies Blackwell's key business success factor as 'ensuring that the profit margins are able to sustain operations'. Similarly, he is adamant that cash flow must support the activities of normal business 'across all channels'. He considers the greatest threat facing Blackwell's to be the increasing pressure on margin cost from meeting increased customer expectations.

Although amazon.co.uk, after only eight months of trading, supplanted Blackwell's as the third largest UK bookseller, Leitch claims that Amazon is not, in fact, Blackwell's direct competitor, as Blackwell's focuses on the academic and professional segments of the market. He does, however, perceive the emergence of new forms of delivery, such as e-books, to be potential threats, and acknowledges that just a 5% market shift to, say, e-books, would have a significant commercial impact on the industry.

To address these real and potential threats, Blackwell's has become involved with enterprises such as the Heron Project, which aims to improve and consolidate the delivery of information by increasing the accessibility of electronic library services. Other enterprises that Blackwell's is involved in are the International Electric Commerce Research Centre (www.iecrc.org), and the company's own Innovation Forum, a research and development unit that analyses issues such as e-learning to ascertain how they might impact on the company.

Headfiller was, according to Leitch, '100% business driven', and arose out of a 'major rethink' of Blackwell's e-business capabilities and strategies. He stresses that Headfiller's ability to enable students to search for the books recommended on the reading lists of the specific courses at participating academic and corporate institutions is a major strategic advantage of the site, which is expected to redirect anywhere between 1% and 5% of the current market in that area.

Leitch perceives potential barriers to the success of online projects as being:

- an inability to adequately fund the project(s);
- a lack of a robust IT infrastructure;
- a lack of appropriate specialist skills; and
- not taking precautions to ensure a smooth internal conversion.

He admits that while there was a 'huge' debate over the adoption of the brand Headfiller, the consensus held that it need not dilute the parent brand. But Blackwell's has experienced resistance as the store staff, particularly, have felt threatened. To address their fears, the company's management has made a particular and concerted attempt to facilitate the inter-relationship between off- and online retailing, which was, as Leitch admits, perhaps 'an artificial way of moving money within departments'. Despite these efforts, many floor staff, while understanding the strategic benefits of the launch and potential of Headfiller, remain concerned about its possible negative effects on the stores. They fear that Blackwell's will need to close branches in order to accommodate the site. The main—indeed the only— inhibitor to the company's online success that Leitch could identify was the skill-set and mindset of staff; by implication, the culture set of the company.

Innovation Factors and Processes

Philip Blackwell, the company's CEO, however, is a passionate champion of the Internet. He believes that 'this is a time of unprecedented change and enormous opportunity'. Issues within the company concerning the adoption of technology and the Internet, therefore, are approached at the management level not from the vantage point of what and to what extent to spend time and resources on developing the company's Internet business, but rather on finding the balance between the company's current core and online businesses. Philip Blackwell, along with Leitch, firmly believes that online sales will become the company's core business in the future, and to this end he established the company's Innovation Forum to explore and espouse technological change—an innovative move in itself for a company that has tended historically to be 'discreet rather than aggressive'.

Possessing an MBA from London Business School, Philip Blackwell was Director of Customer Relationship Management and E-Business at Cap Gemini Ernst & Young before taking up the post of CEO in the company his great-grandfather founded. He was also a non-executive director of the company for many years before becoming its CEO, and as such was a driving force behind the launch of Blackwell's first version website. His passion explains in large part how this traditional firm became so pioneering.

Leitch recognizes the paramount factors that led to the launch of Blackwell's online operations in 1995, and to the company remaining so Internet-driven, as being: the opportunity to extend market reach, the need to fulfil customer expectations, and the need to keep the brand relevant. The innovation processes of the company are identified by Leitch as being:

- Review of current capability
- Assessment of future market needs
- Business scoping
- General appraisal
- Board approval
- Business specification
- IT development
- Marketing and branding
- Launch

These processes indicate that management decisions within the company are approached and understood strategically at the highest levels, and that there is a defined and formal process to undergo before these decisions are implemented.

Leitch identified the business concerns about the decision to launch Headfiller as being:

- Channel conflict/brand management
- Securing the amount of investment required
- Allocating the relevant resources and skills
- Ensuring fulfilment solutions

Website Development and Operational Issues

Currently there are two technical teams within the company: one devoted exclusively to Headfiller, the other to all Blackwell's other online portals. It is intended that these inhouse teams will merge, and that they will be responsible for the company's existing and future portals. The initial Headfiller website development, however, was outsourced to Cap Gemini Ernst & Young.

From sign-off to its launch in Autumn 2000, Headfiller took 22 weeks, by which time it had cost £5 million, ex-marketing. Blackwell's has committed around £10 million to developing the site over a three-year period, including an initial marketing spend of over £1 million. A ground force of 100 student brand managers is being employed at key universities across the country to use promotional materials and viral marketing to spread the word about the site.

Launched in time for the 2000/2001 academic year, the Headfiller site offers discounts of up to 30%, credits on future purchases, and a scheme that allows students to sell their books back at the end of the academic term. Blackwell's in general, Headfiller included, has established cross-revenue partnership arrangements with travel, CD and lifestyle companies such as Virgin, Boxman, Blackstar and STA Travel in order to ensure each site's sustainability. In addition to course reading lists, Headfiller currently offers new and second-hand textbooks, CDs, DVDs, videos, computer games, posters and a range of other products including views on study materials and writing study guides from subject-based student site editors. From a basis of textbook provision, Headfiller aims to develop a service that goes beyond what the campus bookshop can offer, and Headfiller intends to develop digital coursepacks, giving lecturers the ability to detail particular articles and chapters from books that should be read. Blackwell's is also looking to expand Headfiller into the United States, Australia and Asia.

The blackwells.com website features the Sunday Times Bestseller List, a search facility which enables people to find books reviewed on the media when the title is not known, a rare and antiquarian section, an affiliates scheme, and, like all the Blackwell's online sites, free postage and packing to anywhere in the United Kingdom. Table 6.1 shows that Blackwell's website generally supports the firm's focus on niche marketing, service, low price and broad product range. The transaction capability, customer services and ease of use are reasonably well developed, although further details on the firm, products and more innovative customer services would be beneficial.

The Future

Global parity pricing in the publishing industry would undoubtedly impact on the company's online business, but for the foreseeable future Blackwell's has made the decision not to run primarily price-led sites. Leitch states that the company's target for its online sales worldwide is £30 million within 'a few years'. He acknowledges, however, that some of this will be cannibalization of existing business, that some of this business will be transacted at low margins, and that at some stage the company will have to be restructured in order to deliver on the potential for multi-channel choice.

Conclusion

Upon reflection, Leitch considers that the main thing Blackwell's would do differently would be to address the possibility of 'channel conflict' before it became an issue within the company. He recommends that other firms launching Internet services 'not let it become an IT project', urging them instead to look to integrate 'synergies, efficiencies and IT links within all areas' of their existing operations, and to build their Internet service around that.

Nevertheless, Blackwell's certainly appears to have been driven by tactical objectives in launching and running its various Internet services, and, in general, this case study yields the not unimportant indication that the motivation to engage in e-commerce is moving upwards in the management structure, resulting in a more top-down pressure within firms for e-commerce implementation.

EASYGROUP—'RE-ENGINEERING BUSINESS PROCESS'

(www.easygroup.com/www.easyjet.com/www.easyrentacar.com/www.easyvalue.com)

Introduction

Each of the companies within the easyGroup (easyjet.com, easyeverything.com, easyrentacar.com, and easyvalue.com) adopts its founder's mission to take the 'complexity and hidden costs' out of the business sector it operates in. Concentrating on businesses that have become complacent and inefficient, the easyGroup operates primarily online, which enables it to pass on savings to its customers. Indeed, re-thinking business really seems to be the easyGroup's focus!

The easyGroup companies are inextricably linked in the public's imagination with the group's founder and CEO, Stelios Haji-Ioannou, known as Stelios. Of Cypriot origin, he was born and raised in Athens, Greece. After studying in the United Kingdom at the London School of Economics and at the City University Business School, he returned to Greece to join his father's shipping firm as CEO at 23 years of age. He went on to found the Cyprus Marine Environment Protection Association in 1991, a year before launching his first commercial venture, Stelmar Tankers, with a fleet of 12 ships.

In 1995 Stelios, who describes himself as a 'serial entrepreneur', launched easyJet with a £5 million cash gift and £30 million loan from his father. In 1998 he formed the easyGroup as a holding company to explore new ventures extending the 'easy' brand and to capitalize on the expansion of the Internet (a phenomenon about which Stelios was initially suspicious). easyEverything launched in 1999, and was followed by both easyRentacar.com and easyValue in 2000.

The easyGroup, which James Rothnie, the Groups' Director of Corporate Affairs, describes as 'a business incubator', remains privately owned by Stelios, employs over 2000 people and had a turnover in excess of £350 million in the financial year to September 2000.

All the companies within the easyGroup are predominantly Internet-based, as is the Group's promotions and marketing. And the Internet focus has paid off, as within a relatively short time period the Group has won a host of awards, including:

- easyGroup—voted e-company of the year by Future UK Internet Awards
- easyJet—voted Low Cost Airline of the Year by readers of *Business Traveller* magazine, Best Low Cost Airline by readers of the *Daily Telegraph* and *Sunday Telegraph* newspapers, and New Media Marketer of the Year by *Revolution* magazine
- Stelios—voted Businessman of the Year by the *Liverpool Daily Post*

Business Models

Rothnie explains that the Group's ethos is to 'create high demand/low margin businesses'. Each of the Group's companies incorporates an in-house revenue management system designed to generate high load factors at profitable average yields in combination with simplified business processes to maximize efficiency and reduce costs, both to the companies and to their customers.

The services encourage early payment (which provides cash-flow), while the online booking system 'outsources' much of the work to customers, and cuts front-end and operational costs. Utilizing the Internet as a low-cost sales channel also provides scaleability without a significant increase in multi-lingual telephone sales and call centre costs to accommodate growth. Operating online also reinforces the branding and positioning of the easyGroup as an e-commerce focused company.

There is no formal reporting structure between the businesses in the Group. There is also no parent–sibling relationship between them. Each company has independent control over its own finances, and runs its own business, without subsidizing the others.

easyJet

The European short-haul sector is one of the world's most competitive air travel markets. easyJet, a 'high utilization, no frills, low-cost' airline, offers high frequency services on short- and medium-haul point-to-point routes within Europe from its airport bases. easyJet was one of the only budget carriers when it launched in November 1995 after the deregulation of the European airline industry. By September 2000 the company had survived the rise of several direct low-cost competitors, and in that financial year had flown over 5.6 million passengers, generating pre-tax profits of £22.1 million from 31 routes to 18 destinations with a core fleet of 18 Boeing 737 aircraft. Load factors for the month of October 2000 were 85.3%, and online sales accounted for 75% of all sales. Rothnie claims that the easyJet website gets, on average, half a million visitors a week.

The company seeks to continue to grow whilst maintaining profitability by combining low fares with sustainable lower operating costs. This is achieved by cutting out what Stelios calls 'unnecessary frills', by eliminating middlemen, by selling directly to passengers, and by using less congested and less expensive airports. Prices are closely linked to demand and the amount of time in advance that the ticket is booked. The goal is to maximize seat sales on every flight, which is essential for the company's core business, which relies on cost-effectiveness and punctuality. Stelios believes that six key strengths support the company's 'competitiveness, scaleability and sustainable growth':

- *A simple fare structure.* Only a single fare is offered at any one time for a specific flight, a pricing policy which the company believes offers value for money, although not necessarily the lowest, fares for any given route. All prices are based on one-way fares, only one class of seat is offered, the basic terms and conditions are the same, and all bookings can be transferred, subject to a small fee. easyJet encourages passengers to book online by offering a permanent discount to those who do so.
- *Low unit costs.* Unit costs are kept low by maintaining high aircraft utilization, by eliminating sales intermediaries, by focusing on Internet sales, by eliminating 'unnecessary service frills' such as refreshments, by operating a fleet of similar aircraft with a high density cabin layout, and by establishing long-term agreements with key suppliers.
- *Strong branding.* easyJet has established a strong brand in its key European markets through a high-profile marketing and advertising strategy incorporating the orange brand images. Stelios is often featured in the promotions.
- *A commitment to customer service.* The company aims to provide an image of being 'safe, professional, friendly and informal'. Accordingly, it retains control

over the key activities that involve dealing directly with customers, such as the sales and customer service activities in the call centre, website design and passenger handling.

- *A multi-base network.* easyJet's network strategy of providing dense point-to-point services reduces dependence on a single 'hub' and creates local competitive advantages at bases close to the airline's major target customer catchment areas.
- *A strong corporate culture.* This is what the company believes motivates employees, all of whom have access to a significant amount of information on the company.

In addition, the airline uses secondary airports, where it is paid to bring trade, rather than using the big hubs, which charge high landing charges. EasyJet's flotation in mid-November 2000 has enabled Stelios—who still retains a majority percentage of easyJet—to maximize the airline's growth potential by purchasing 32 new Boeing 737s.

easyEverything

The first easyEverything Internet cafe opened in London in June 1999. By the end of 2000, the chain of 'the world's largest Internet cafes' had grown to 18 cafés across Europe and the United States, all of which offer low-cost, 24 hours a day, 365 days a year Internet access. Rothnie claims that over one million customers use these Internet cafes every month.

easyRentacar

easyRentacar claims to be 'the world's first Internet-only car rental service'. Indeed, the booking system for easyRentacar is entirely online. Launched in April 2000, by December 2000 easyRentacar had 12 locations established across western Europe. By replicating the easyJet logic, Stelios believes the easyRentacar business can sustain low hiring costs by conducting the procurement procedure exclusively online; by using a uniform fleet of vehicles and not allowing customers to pre-order a specific model; by targeting easyJet passengers and those who live in city centres; and by choosing appropriate sites for such customers. Stelios is adamant that easyRentacar provides a choice for consumers 'who pay out of their own pockets and who will not be ripped off'. As with the other companies in the Group, price is dictated by demand. To that end, all customers pay a daily rental rate and a one-off preparation fee, but only those who drive more than 75 miles a day are required to pay the 20p a mile excess.

According to Stelios, the choice of Mercedes-Benz A-models reflects the easyGroup brand 'in the same way that easyJet uses brand new Boeing aircraft: we do not compromise on the hardware, we just use innovation to substantially reduce costs'.

The name of the company is displayed on the side doors and in the rear window of each vehicle, as Stelios believes that this form of advertising helps to reduce marketing costs. The formula seems to work, as expansion plans are in place to order a further 20 000 vehicles by 2002, and to grow to 30 rental sites across Europe by the end of 2001.

easyValue

easyValue.com offers price and availability comparisons for products bought from different online stores. The product categories at the time of the September 2000 launch were: books, CDs, DVDs, videos and video games. Electronics, personal organisers, property and life insurance have since been added, and further additions are to be introduced at a rate of around two categories a month.

Revenue for the business will be generated by advertising and commissions from the featured online stores on a shared revenue basis, although Stelios has admitted that he remains 'uncertain' as to how easyValue will generate a sustainable profit.

Implementing the Business Model

Stelios admits that it is becoming problematic that the easyGroup is so closely integrated with his personality. He acknowledges that at some stage he will have to step back, and the businesses will have to deal with their customers through their departments rather than through him.

Another, less positive challenge Stelios is increasingly having to confront is the fact that, whilst customers are prepared to forgo 'frills' in return for lower prices, they are not prepared to be taken for granted, and that the public relations costs of not appeasing customers when they are inconvenienced are enormous. But he remains surprisingly sanguine about such situations. One example occurred in December 2000, when easyJet's rival, the British Airways-owned Go, capitalized on press reports about horrendous easyJet cancellations and delays and thousands of furious, stranded easyJet passengers. In response, Stelios authorized an advertising campaign with headlines such as: 'If their own low-cost airline is so bloody brilliant why does easyJet win all the customer awards?'

Another such example occurred, also in late 2000, when easyRentacar customers found their credit cards had been charged hefty fines for 'damage' to the car they had hired—payments they had not authorized for damage they could not remember inflicting. Hundreds of complaints were made to consumer associations, and vicious reports appeared in the British press. Although easyRentacar now offers insurance, and inspects the cars in the customer's presence, Stelios seems genuinely surprised by the outcry, admitting only that the company 'underestimated how risk-averse our customers were' and that 'people want to pay something up-front and nothing else'.

Industry, Competitor and Environmental Analysis

The business approach throughout the divisions of the easyGroup appears to be to select mass markets with high cost structures with the potential for significant cost reductions, to re-engineer the business processes and to offer low-cost value-added services in a combination that ensures a profitable average yield.

Rothnie surmises that the rate at which products and services become obsolete in the industries in which the easyGroup operates is minimal to non-existent, despite the fact that the actions of the company's competitors are rarely predictable. He ascertains that while there is little threat to the Group's companies as a result of price competition, supply or competitors' services, there is a moderate threat of declining demand for easyEverything, and a high threat to the Group overall due to quality competition from competitors.

However, easyJet's high aircraft utilization makes it especially vulnerable to delays. The business is also subject to strong seasonal variations, and because a substantial portion of airline travel for business or holiday is discretionary, the industry tends to suffer during economic downturns. It is therefore likely that both easyJet and easyRentacar would be affected by a slowdown in the economy, but they could also potentially gain business as passengers trade down for a better priced deal.

easyJet is now positioned as the second low-cost European airline, after RyanAir, but it has the highest share of online bookings, at over 90%, compared with RyanAir's 60%. Low-fare flights account for just under 3% of scheduled traffic in Europe, compared with 22% in America, but the market is growing by 25% a year.

Key Business Drivers and Threats

Rothnie identifies the easyGroup's key business driver as locating, establishing and maintaining high demand/low margin businesses, while the key threat to the Group would be for the company to become 'complacent' and forget its core value of 'outsourcing the work to the customers'.

Innovation Factors and Processes

easyJet was founded as a result of a shipping accident in 1991 involving a tanker in Stelios's father's company. As CEO of the company at the time, Stelios was held accountable and faced a number of criminal charges, including manslaughter. The ensuing legal battle motivated Stelios to build a business that people 'liked'. Despite the fact that a year later he began his own shipping company, Stelios was thinking increasingly about starting his own airline, and finally did so after being inspired by the Southwest Airlines' low-cost business model whilst on a trip to the United States. Texas-based Southwest Airlines was the first United States airline to exploit US deregulation in 1978. Its no-frills business operates short, point-to-point flights between secondary airports and has a fleet made of one type of aircraft (also the Boeing 737) to reduce costs.

Rothnie identifies the primary factor leading to easyGroup's e-commerce adoption as being Stelios's recognition that the Internet is an ideal direct sales and distribution network, as well as an effective way to utilize the company's technology. The innovation process towards the adoption of e-commerce began in 1995, when easyJet launched a static website with a bookings phone number. A growing realization of the benefits of operating online led to the company reprogramming the website in 1997 to make it more interactive, and completely online sales were launched in 1998. The website has been continually adapted ever since.

The major barriers to be overcome for online projects to be a success were identified by Rothnie as being:

- a lack of education for both customers and staff that the Internet is integral to the business and is part of the corporate creed, and
- the ability of the company to recognize, acquire, and maintain the appropriate technology

Website Development and Operational Issues

According to Rothnie, all aspects of the easyGroup's Internet system were developed entirely in-house, and 'every body and every aspect had to adapt as the projects themselves did!'. The decision-making processes have all been informal—the approach is always to 'try and see', but such is the level of integration between the Internet and business systems that the company is able to move swiftly: easyJet took three months from making the decision to sell online to being able to do so, while easyRentacar took six months from conception to launch.

Technical glitches have inevitably occurred, but, according to Rothnie, 'nothing serious has occurred that has threatened the integrity of any part of the company's operations'. He claims that the general business approval processes, 'jurisdiction-based legal, bureaucratic and administrative and licensing problems' in countries where the Group has launched have caused much greater challenges.

Table 6.1 shows that easyJet's website has some support for the firm's focus on low price operations. The product details category rated at the highest level but transaction capability, customer services and ease of use were rated at lower levels than in other companies. Further efforts in these areas and more innovative customer services would be beneficial.

The Future

Rothnie sees the biggest challenges to firms in the future use of the Internet as a retail channel to be ensuring that they have enough customer incentive to achieve market penetration, and ensuring that they implement the correct internal reconstruction. Additional products and services, all on a high-quality no-frills basis, are to be introduced to easyGroup businesses in the future. These include roof racks

Table 6.1 Evaluation of selected UK websites

Firms	Company information/5	Product/ services information/5	Transactions/5	Customer services/5	Ease of use/5	Innovation/5	Total/30	CEC scale ⓒ (%)
Action	2	5	4	5	4	1	21	70
Blackwell	2	3	4	4	4	0	17	57
easyJet	4	5	3	2	3	0	17	57
Lobster	1	2	4	3	4	1	15	50
Thomas Cook	3	5	3	2	4	0	17	57

for easyRentacar, and web cams and sophisticated software in the easyEverything Internet cafes.

New ventures planned to be introduced in the future include easyMoney, which will provide online financial services, and `easy.com`, a free private web-based e-mail system. There are also discussions for easyHotels located at easyJet destinations.

Conclusion

Truth is surely stranger than fiction, for who would have thought of a plotline where a Greek shipping billionaire's son begins a consumer-championing airline so that people would like him? But, in doing so, Stelios has established a highly profitable company, based on the premise that 'the best incentive is always price—a customer's desire for a bargain usually overrides everything else'.

Stelios is emphatic that the only thing he would have done differently is to have made easyJet a 100% online company from 'day one'. His advice for other firms seeking to operate online is, 'don't delay!'.

LOBSTER—'THE GASTRONOME'S VIRTUAL ANSWER'
(`www.lobster.co.uk`)

Introduction

Lobster wants to be 'the Harrod's Food Hall of Cyberspace' and 'the gastronome's virtual answer', and by so doing to change the way its customers shop for fine foods and wines. The company caters to a niche market with sophisticated tastes—it is, effectively, an online delicatessen targeting those with a discerning palate who either do not have the time to visit or are not in the vicinity of a shop selling, for example, Iranian caviar or freshly cooked lobsters, but want them. To that end, Lobster focuses on delivering only those products that one would never find stocked in a typical supermarket.

Lobster, which launched in December 1999, is a small, privately owned online gourmet food provider with annual revenue 'in the mid-six figures'. The company employs just three full-time and four part-time permanent staff. Lobster's founder and MD, Alex Fitzgibbons, insists that in addition to its wide range, the company will search for other, specific products for customers, and will always endeavour to provide customers with 'a better personal service' than they could ever experience in a shop. And, with same-day delivery in London, and next-day delivery throughout the rest of the United Kingdom, Lobster's customers can get what they want quickly.

Business Model

Although Lobster is an online company servicing a niche market, the 'fundamental, age-old retailing principle(s) and concepts remain the same', according to Fitzgibbons, who believes that many of the e-commerce companies who did not survive the technology stock market crash had become obsessed with overturning these principles and concepts. Fitzgibbons, however, has been adamant since launching Lobster that 'the margin must cover the costs'.

Because the company deals with high-quality foodstuffs that customers cannot see, smell or examine, online retailing does present certain disadvantages for Lobster that are not applicable for retailing other goods online. However, the company has an advantage over, for example, an offline gourmet delicatessen, which will have considerably more wastage than Lobster, which is able to order stock daily to fulfil its orders.

Despite the fact that he and his team had expected that the bulk of the company's customers would be London based, with access to gourmet foods offline, but without the time to go out and buy them, but the result has, in fact, been the opposite. The bulk of Lobster's orders are delivered nationwide, to customers with the time to buy gourmet foods, but without access to them. This did not pose a logistical problem for Lobster as the company outsources its distribution and delivery systems, a deal that enables it to offer a flat rate for guaranteed next-day delivery throughout the United Kingdom without incurring the costs of setting up and maintaining a delivery fleet. While Fitzgibbons concedes that Lobster's market has not grown as quickly as he thought it would, he stresses that the 'unpredictabilities' that existed when the business began (such as establishing short-lived alliances with the wrong companies) have all been 'rationalized'.

Fitzgibbons began Lobster with the intention that it should be a long-term company, and therefore ensured that growth did not exceed demand or cashflow. He also feels very strongly that getting the timing right for building a business is fundamental, that 'if the timing isn't right you can be put out of business' and credits the fact that the company has not yet faced an infrastructure burnout to 'planning ahead'.

Since its launch, Lobster has concentrated its operation exclusively in the United Kingdom. Fitzgibbons intends for Lobster to 'crack the UK market' before introducing overseas deliveries on to its agenda. However, many of the site's customers are the British expatriate community in Hong Kong and the Middle East, who buy gifts from Lobster for their friends and family in the United Kingdom. Fitzgibbons feels that there is not the same 'rationale for price and ease of purchase' for potential customers in European countries such as France, Germany and Italy, as many of the products Lobster sells are widely available there. Finally, Fitzgibbons feels that Lobster's decision to deliver only within the United Kingdom reduces the company's risk of credit card fraud exposure.

Implementing the Business Model

All aspects of the website and many other aspects of the company's operations are outsourced, which adds somewhat to the cost but has 'so many benefits', not the least of which is flexibility. Fitzgibbons finds outsourcing much cheaper than having the infrastructure for the staff and facilities on retainer. Fitzgibbons has 'no idea' whether or not similar levels of outsourcing is a characteristic of other e-tailers selling high value goods, but the aspects of Lobster's business that will 'never' be outsourced are the selection, the storage and the packaging of the products it sells. Interestingly enough, these are the very aspects other companies tend most to outsource, but according to Fitzgibbons the product is 'so key' as to be 'inconceivable' that others should handle it.

Christmas is undoubtedly a concentrated period for gourmet food sellers, and the build-up, especially in online retailing operations, comes later, and with a slower build-up. Offline, Christmas sales and fulfilment might be spread over a six-week period, but for Lobster they are concentrated in the last two weeks of December. In fact, the same volume of business was transacted by Lobster in December 2000 as in the previous eleven months combined, although many customers' had pre-ordered goods to be delivered on specific dates during the season. According to Fitzgibbons, the company's infrastructure and fulfilment was 'successfully and sensibly' scaled to cope with the Christmas 'onslaught'. Unfortunately, when the volume of deliveries increased exponentially in the lead-up to the Christmas/New Year period, it proved more than the delivery company could cope with, despite accurate projections having been supplied to them. This meant that other last-minute measures had to be taken, but despite these efforts, 1.4% of orders missed their delivery. Fulfilment is the hidden side of the business.

Lobster became cashflow positive in December 2000, and was able to forecast a small profit—a notable achievement for an online company at a time when many are floundering, if still operating at all. In addition, the company was able to transact an 'encouraging' number of sales in the early months of 2001 following the Christmas/New Year period.

Although it is a very small company, there is a formal, disciplined structure of accountability and corporate governance at Lobster. Clear monthly, quarterly and annual budgets are developed, as are five-year financial forecasts, but strategic planning is 'informal and organic', taking place as and when necessary. The company has not needed to undertake formal strategic business planning since it raised the initial capital to start the business. Fitzgibbons takes the majority of decisions, including those pertinent to the day-to-day operations of the company. However, a board meeting is held every month, and 75% shareholder approval is needed for major decisions.

By the end of its first year, Lobster had spent only £50 000—25% of its turn-over—on advertising and marketing. However, £15 000 of this was spent on online advertising, which Fitzgibbons considers to have been 'completely wasted'. The marketing budget allocated for the Christmas 2000 season was only 4% of the turnover achieved, whereas it is usually 'just under' 10% of each month's turnover.

The company has, however, generated a considerable amount of positive PR. And with such a small advertising and marketing budget, word of mouth is critical. A typical new customer is a former recipient of a Lobster gift who is converted to purchasing from Lobster himself or herself. Since 40% of goods ordered from Lobster are gifts, the company is provided with a large proportion of 'double opportunities' for future sales.

Industry, Competitor and Environmental Analysis

The UK online gourmet and luxury products market is 'by no means closed', but Fitzgibbons feels that it would be difficult for any similar new businesses to begin to compete with Lobster. It remains positioned in a niche market, but despite the fact that the established gourmet food sellers do not yet have the management in place to fully exploit their online potential, Fitzgibbons intends for Lobster to be 'well established' in that market by the time they do. Fitzgibbons was surprised that the process of converting a browser to a purchaser was much slower than media reports had suggested, and labels this 'the gap between the hype and the actual'.

Lobster's more traditional and long-established gourmet food competitors, who include such retailing luminaries as Harrod's and Fortnum & Mason, were handling online retailing 'so badly' that Lobster was able to seize the opportunity 'much more easily' than they had anticipated.

Key Business Drivers and Threats

The key business drivers, according to Fitzgibbons, are 'the products, the IT, and the fulfilment procedure'. The IT must work, so that orders can successfully be taken, and the products—the food—have to be of the highest quality, well packaged, and delivered on time.

Price competition poses little threat to the company. However, quality is 'key', and Lobster is vigilant about the quality and condition of its products. Scarcity and declining demand pose less threat to the company than do local competitors, while international competitors pose even less threat. The demands and tastes of Lobster's customers are highly predictable, and the company has found that it does not need to alter its marketing practices in response to competition.

Lobster monitors its competitors' activities in an ongoing, informal way. Fitzgibbons considers their actions to be moderately predictable, but the company aims to offer a higher and more personalized level of service than its competitors.

Fitzgibbons considers the main handicap of online trading to be the availability of too much data, which makes it extremely difficult to step back and see 'the bigger picture'. Acutely conscious of the constant danger of losing his instinct, he feels that the more data he examines, the less 'fleet of foot' he becomes, and is constantly on guard against this. Fitzgibbons determines customer satisfaction by the conversion rate of browsers to buyers, by customer feedback, and by the percentage of customers who have a seamless order-to-completion experience.

Although he considers that Lobster has been a success, he prefers to calculate what he labels the company's 'success milestones', which have included meeting targets, becoming cashflow profitable, and 'getting the marketing mix right'.

Innovation Factors and Processes

Lobster was a '100% business-driven idea', according to Fitzgibbons, whose primary motive was to start a niche business—the channel for the business became apparent later. His interest in gourmet food in combination with how ineffectively other companies were retailing these products online in the United Kingdom culminated in the idea for Lobster. And as the plans for the company took shape, Fitzgibbons consciously chose to fund the company with a private backer rather than through a venture capital company. He found his backer, Rocco Forte (scion of the Trusthouse Forte hotel chain), and launched Lobster at the height of the Internet boom. Despite the distractions of the media and the hype at the time, Fitzgibbons saw Lobster as a slow-growth, long-term business.

Indeed, a key factor in Lobster's success seems to be Fitzgibbons himself. He was raised in the United Kingdom but studied in the United States before returning to work at Nintendo for three years, where he was responsible for retail marketing. He then went on to work for the retail marketing division of the Early Learning Centre, where he set up and ran its heavily retail-focused website.

Lobster launched in early December 1999. That the company was able to transform rapidly and effectively from concept to realization Fitzgibbons attributes to the fact that there was from the outset a clear business proposition, a single private investor and—initially at least—a small group of suppliers. After raising the initial £230 000 Fitzgibbons has been able to operate the company without a further influx of cash, due in part because Forte provides corporate credibility, which helped to separate Lobster from other startup dotcoms. In return, he expects the discipline expected of a much larger company. Even so, Fitzgibbons admits that he often had to 'cut corners' rather than use 'best practice procedures'.

Website Development and Operational Issues

Every aspect of Lobster's Internet development and operations has been outsourced, albeit under strict supervision, for the Internet aspect of this business *is* the business. Navigation and design are intended to be the strong points of the Lobster site. Although the same design has been used since the launch, new features are added as the company's range of products and services grows and in accordance with seasonal offerings.

Development began in mid-October 1999, and the site launched in early December 1999, with a pre-Christmas launch as the focus. There was a 100-day slip between intended launch and actual launch, which was 'hair-raising', as it was 'uncomfortably close' to Christmas. Nevertheless, outside of 'the usual hiccups' there were no major problems with the IT aspects of launching the site.

Since that time, Fitzgibbons claims there have been no 'noteworthy or major' operational problems with the equipment, integration problems, or backup equipment and procedures, as these matters are all outsourced. The Internet ordering system is fully integrated with the company's other IT systems, all of which are adapted from off-the-shelf packages.

Lobster constantly adds new products, recipes, menus and ready-to-go dinners through features sections such as *Recipes, Menus* and *Guest Chef*, in which the company has linked up with some famous chefs to present recipes sorted into categories, each of which is subdivided. The recipes, which are added to constantly, can be printed out, and come with serving suggestions. The ingredients available from Lobster are highlighted in these recipes, and can be added to a shopping basket. There is also an unedited chat, question-and-answer section of the site which customers have found invaluable.

Table 6.1 shows that Lobster's website has some support for the firm's focus on a niche market, customer service, broad range and low price operations. The transaction capability and ease of use were well developed and customer services were reasonably developed. The company and product details categories were rated at lower levels than in other companies. Further efforts in these areas and more of the innovative customer services would be beneficial for Lobster.

The Future

One future possibility for the company is for it to align itself or merge with another company, but Fitzgibbons definitely plans to increase Lobster's range of organic foods and to extend its range to include luxury gift products, such as cigars. In addition, he anticipates having to continue to battle against 'the British apathy about shopping online'.

Conclusion

Fitzgibbons expects that what he labels the 'carnage' of online companies over the last year is likely to result in making it more difficult for entrepreneurs to acquire funding for their business ideas. If Fitzgibbons was launching Lobster today, he feels that it would be a 'much tighter' business with a more defined range. His advice for firms launching operations is to 'stay niche', to treat online businesses essentially the same as any other retail business, while approaching selling 'from an e-tail point of view' and to keep costs within an 'absolutely comfortable' margin. He considers 'time and access' to be the 'great calls to purchase'.

THOMAS COOK—'MULTI-CHANNEL CHOICE'

(www.thomascook.com)

Introduction

The strategy behind travel company Thomas Cook relaunching its online operations in 1999 as thomascook.com centres on the premises that the company provides its existing and potential customers with a one-stop travel portal 'they can trust'. Although the company's traditional competitors have, in the main, decided to go for new branding and/or multiple branded sites, Thomas Cook sees its brand name as being intrinsic both to the company's proposition and to everything it stands for. Since the launch of the company's initial website in 1995, significant sales volumes have been transacted online. The thomascook.com website is now performing on a par with the most successful branches in the UK shops network, although the vast majority of people booking via the website are new customers to the company.

When Thomas Cook launched its first Internet site, Thomas Cook Online, in 1995, it was the first UK retail travel agency to offer customers a way to buy holidays, traveller's cheques and foreign currency, travel guides, holiday insurance and request flight availability on a selection of flights, over the Internet. Building on this early success, in late 1999 the company significantly increased its online investment in order to achieve a leadership position in the UK online travel market. The site was rethought, revamped, rebranded as thomascook.com, and relaunched to offer a complete online travel service.

Andrew Windsor, MD of thomascook.com, believes that the online businesses that will survive will be those able to combine a strong brand name with a multi-channel offering to customers. He is convinced that most customers would prefer to conduct online transactions with companies that have a visible and established high street presence, a description that certainly fits Thomas Cook. The Thomas Cook group services 3.5 million passengers annually, employs over 16 000 staff and operates throughout a network of 1050 locations in the United Kingdom and overseas.

Business Model

The thomascook.com operation is truly multi-channel—indeed, at the time of writing, it was the only UK travel company offering its services and taking bookings and payments across five distribution platforms: shops, phone, Internet, WAP enabled mobile phones, and iTV.

Windsor is convinced that iTV will be 'huge' for thomascook.com, since most UK homes already have a TV, and as many as a third of them already have iTV capability. Accordingly, thomascook.com has struck deals with all the UK iTV companies. Initial results show that the company's iTV customers are 'quite different' to its Internet customers, but whilst the content remains the same across all channels, the 'customer journey' and experience is still different across different media.

The company's experience has been that whilst many customers refer to the various thomascook.com channels during the holiday planning process, almost all feel the need to speak to someone before handing over money in the booking process. By understanding its customers in such detail, Windsor claims, the company can ensure its propositions are 'well targeted', and that the company will continue to keep its 'finger on the pulse' as consumers learn and patterns change as technology evolves.

thomascook.com set itself apart from other dotcom companies, according to Windsor, by not 'just jumping in, spending millions on TV advertising, and hoping that would be enough'. Instead, a lot of time and effort was spent negotiating a solid base of online affiliations and strategic partnerships with companies such as Freeserve, Lastminute and Excite. The company also invested in building its understanding of consumer perceptions and behaviour. Only when it was able to offer a wider range of products, an online booking capability, and a new user experience, did Thomas Cook begin to promote the thomascook.com site.

By taking the time to understand the type of visitors the site would be attracting, what these visitors would look for, and weighing this information against what their competitors were doing, thomascook.com was able to deliver the appropriate user experience when visitors came to their site. The company's research highlighted, for example, that there was a strong female bias to the visitors to the website—the opposite experience of most other websites. One explanation for this is that women are usually the key drivers when it comes to booking holidays, and this has carried through to researching and choosing holidays online.

The company's efforts to meet its customers' demands have paid dividends, as by the end of the calendar year 2000 the site was attracting more visitors than any other dedicated travel site in the United Kingdom, according to Neilson Netratings. In mid-2001 *The Sunday Times* rated the site the fifth best travel site in the United Kingdom, and the best UK high street brand trading online.

Implementing the Business Model

Windsor states that the company wants customers 'to think travel, think Thomas Cook, think online travel, think thomascook.com', acknowledging that in order to achieve this, the company needs to be able to provide 'a complete and personal one-stop travel shop service' across all channels.

The company aims to offer a uniform and seamless customer experience across all distribution and communication channels, and to add value at every point, from suggestions on where to go next to an easy order process for repeat bookers, by 'opening a dialogue' with its customers. To this end, the customer acquisition and retention teams work closely together to introduce and run customer promotions to encourage visitors to register with thomascook.com. This is considered the starting point for opening the company's 'dialogue' with its customers so that they can begin to communicate through personalized e-mail updates. And as the company gains a better understanding of the needs of individual customers, it will be better able to encourage these customers to continue to do business with them.

To this end, a strong relationship also exists between thomascook.com and Thomas Cook Direct. In fact, three-quarters of the customers who find their holiday through thomascook.com book them through one of Thomas Cook

Direct's centres. Around 42% of customers book their flights online, with the remainder booking them through Thomas Cook Direct, which has a dedicated team handling calls from thomascook.com. Interestingly, 84% of thomascook.com's customers have not used Thomas Cook travel shops regularly in the past, so the level of cannibalization across the company's business channels appears to be minimal. thomascook.com seems to have attracted new customers who may previously have seen Thomas Cook as too traditional to meet their needs.

Industry, Competitor and Environmental Analysis

The UK travel business is a highly consolidated seasonal business with low margin returns. Four major players control 75% of the European short haul mass travel and holiday market. However, there are few to no barriers to entry (as highlighted by the early and sustained success of the easyJet case study!) and the online travel industry in the United Kingdom is growing at a fast rate. According to Forrester Research, 1.6 million Britons spent £592 million booking holidays online during 2000. They estimate that figure will rise to 5.7 million Britons spending £3.7 billion by 2005, which would mean that 14% of holidays, and 45% of flights would be booked and paid for online at that time.

The online travel market, therefore, is a fiercely competitive environment, and market forces dictate that a site's aesthetic design and technological infrastructure should constantly be changed and refined, and that the product range be continually increased to attract the attention and trust of customers quickly to dissuade them from going elsewhere. However, Windsor firmly believes that the strength of the Thomas Cook brand was and remains a key strategic 'weapon'. He feels that here thomascook.com has an advantage over many of its competitors, as it is a travel name, not a flight name or a package holiday name. It therefore has an opportunity to capture and hold a significantly wider, and more profitable, market.

Key Business Drivers and Threats

Windsor identifies thomascook.com's key business drivers as being: product quality, price, service and loyalty, and cost control/productivity. He considers the greatest threat to the UK travel industry to be the increasing ability of customers to go directly to the product providers (the hotel, car hire company or airline) rather than intermediate through travel operators.

Innovation Factors and Processes

The need to 'differentiate and lead' led to a formal strategic review of Thomas Cook's e-commerce position, while shareholder belief enabled the company to act on the recommendations made by this review.

The innovation processes, which led to the launch of thomascook.com, were highly formalized (although the concept was initially discussed informally). A strategic review was authorized by a small group of senior management. The reviewers made formal recommendations to the senior management operating board, who in turn made formal recommendations to the supervisory board (shareholders). A decision was made and the programme undertaken, but regular, ongoing reviews are held at both management and shareholder board levels to monitor the maintenance and development of thomascook.com.

Barriers to the implementation of the thomascook.com relaunch included the company's need to overcome its fear of the potential cannibalization of business from other segments of the Thomas Cook group. The company also needed to allocate considerable funds to the project, which meant that other projects had to be either downsized or eliminated. And the company has a low appetite for risk, which meant that the senior management needed to be convinced beyond reasonable doubt that the project would be successful.

Nevertheless, the company has committed to investing £100 million into building thomascook.com over a five-year period to 2005. The rationalization for this large commitment at a time when many other companies are scaling back their Internet expenditure is that it is considered essential to the success of the future of the Thomas Cook group to transform the business in line with customer expectations and purchasing trends.

Website Development and Operational Issues

Much of the site development, and all of the digitization of content assets, was developed in-house, to mixed success. While some aspects were considered excellent, some did not work, and others were received poorly by customers. However, a mixed response also met the aspects of development that had been outsourced. From start of development to first live implementation, the process of relaunching the site as thomascook.com took six months. There were many difficulties, including (but not limited to) resource/skill constraints, poor delivery, and integrating the new system into the company's existing legacy systems. Such problems meant that the project was not launched according to schedule. Ongoing adaptations have met with different challenges, but again, the success rate has been what Windsor labels a 'mixed bag'. Despite these problems, he categorically considers thomascook.com to be a success.

A team of 60 staff are devoted to developing and maintaining thomascook.com. Believing that most travel sites are designed around their product ranges, not around their customers' needs, they want thomascook.com to be different. To that end, they generally scorn fancy graphics and lengthy downloads in their aim to make the site easy and 'intuitive' to operate.

The company measures success by analysing sales growth and customer satisfaction, while customer satisfaction is calculated by measuring timescales, cost functionality and user response, by determining the rate of converting browsers into buyers, and by establishing revenue against the cost per customer. thomascook.com offers around six million holiday combinations split into six subsites—sun, flights, snow, last minute, short breaks, and escapes.

Table 6.1 shows that thomascook.com's website has some support for the firm's focus on customer service, broad product range, and low prices. The product details were developed at the highest level and ease of use was also rated highly, but transaction capability and customer services were rated at lower levels than in other companies. Even though Thomas Cook is currently retaining a large percentage of customers who search online for information on holidays then book offline, the firm should not assume that this situation is sustainable. Further efforts in these lower rating categories, more company details and more innovative customer services would be beneficial.

The Future

Thomas Cook took the decision to operate thomascook.com as a separate but integrated business, as at some stage in the future the company intends to seek external investment in the form of partnership or capital to ensure that the site can develop without cannibalizing funds or resources from its parent company. However, the company goes to great pains to ensure that the website—and all other channels—functions as a core part of the Thomas Cook brand.

The thomascook.com team works closely with Thomas Cook Retail to ensure that the ideal of a seamless customer experience across channels becomes a reality. But the team is also aware that the company will have to keep ahead of the competition, and that means increasing its product breadth. For instance, at the end of 2000, although the thomascook.com website offered flights from hundreds of airlines, the vast majority of holidays on the site were offered through Thomas Cook owned charter airline JMC.

There are also a number of opportunities for international expansion. In early 2001, thomascook.ca was launched in conjunction with Thomas Cook Canada, and Thomas Cook is looking to replicate this model in Ireland and other countries in the foreseeable future. By harnessing the strengths of its integrated travel business, and by continuing to innovate and develop its e-commerce agenda, Thomas Cook aims to become the number one customer-led travel company in the United Kingdom and Ireland by 2003. However, the 'ultimate goal', says Windsor, is for thomascook.com to be the 'leading online travel agent in the world!'.

Conclusion

The thomascook.com case study illustrates the increasing importance of research and careful planning to ensure a focused business model before launching an online operation, even if an online business is designed to complement and to work in tandem with an existing offline business. A clear vision is necessary to capture the relevant market sector, especially in a fiercely competitive environment, and successful maintenance and management with the core business are crucial to ensure cross-promotion, ongoing support and integration across channels. Thomas Cook recognized that its brand name gave it a strategic advantage, and seized the opportunity to capitalize on it. However, future growth is not guaranteed, and so the company aims to expand the ranges it offers and extend the brand internationally.

Windsor feels that, if Thomas Cook were relaunching thomascook.com today, the firm would move 'much more quickly', get as much external expertise as possible, and would not build the technology in-house. He is adamant, however, that traditional bricks-and-mortar companies intending to launch e-commerce operations should not delay.

Chapter Conclusion

It is becoming increasingly obvious that many e-commerce companies are working out models that enable them to use the Internet and traditional channels of business in concert to the greatest strategic advantage. Certainly, this is the case for the United Kingdom as most of the case companies we have studied, except Lobster (a startup pure-player), combine off- and online business activities. These case studies provide examples of how a variety of different off- and online business models used in tandem can successfully be put into effect.

In general, the case studies yielded significant indications that the source of motivation to engage in e-commerce is moving upwards in the management structure, resulting in more top-down pressure within firms for e-commerce implementation. Nevertheless, most of the Internet activities described in the studies appear to have been driven primarily by tactical objectives (efficiency and cost reduction) with the emergent business/IT strategy models envisaged by Claudio Ciborra and others (Ciborra 1994) developing subsequently.

The participating case studies all recognized the potential strategic opportunities offered by embracing e-business, especially once they were all operating online to some degree. And once online, they sought to realize these opportunities, which included growing their market share; surpassing competitors (e.g. Lobster aims to provide a greater level of personal service than its customers would be able to find in a store); transforming their organizations (e.g. easyJet has automated its procedures to the extent that the bulk of them are conducted online—in effect, Internet applications have enabled the company to outsource much of the administrative work to its customers); and personalising customer relationships. Each of these companies has recognized that it is now better able to identify and retain its most profitable customers, find its most valuable customer segments, and understand its customers' specific needs by co-ordinating its off- and online channels.

Set against these drivers of e-commerce adoption are several inhibitors, which for the UK companies include fear of change, fear of operating costs, lack of accurate and appropriate models, poor operational knowledge of e-commerce, the need for staff education (which has proved critical for Blackwell's), and the need for customer education (which has proved especially critical for easyJet). For example, easyJet has had to pointedly demonstrate to its customers how purchasing online would benefit them, and has encouraged them to do so by offering discounts to online purchasers.

These UK case companies have measured business benefits from their e-commerce initiatives in terms of customer satisfaction, revenue preservation, revenue generation and cost savings. They also all recognize that their current competitive advantages are likely to be short-lived, and therefore intend to keep innovating into other channels, such as WAP and iTV.

Drivers

On the basis of the experiences communicated by the principals of these case study companies, it would seem that the following attributes are crucial to successful adoption of e-commerce:

- Recognition of and support from senior management for the Internet's strategic implications was essential as otherwise the necessary funds and other resources would not be available
- Recognizing and employing effective strategies to launch, adapt and maintain online operations
- Relevant analysis of the strategic opportunities the Internet facilitated
- Comprehensive integration of the Internet into the companies' core activities, which provided opportunities for further transformation

Tactically, when these case companies looked to introduce online trading, they were looking to achieve at least one of the following benefits:

- To provide additional channels to market
- To gain new and retain existing customers
- To increase agility, or responsiveness, and the ability to react to changing market conditions, which would in turn increase competitive advantage and market share
- To increase efficiencies and reduce overheads and costs per transaction

The principals in these companies felt that online trading was an ideal sales and distribution network, and that it would be an efficient way of utilizing their existing technology (except in the case of Lobster, a startup). They also felt that many of the systems and practices they needed to operate effectively online were already in place before making the decision to launch online operations, and believed that they would be subject to fewer operating costs than their competitors. This has proved not to be the case in any of the companies. In addition, Blackwell's and Thomas Cook specifically viewed the launch of online operations as an opportunity to extend market reach, at the same time fulfilling customer expectations and keeping their brands relevant.

Inhibitors

The most important barriers to be overcome were reported as being:

- The lack of appropriate business models to guide and direct these companies
- Getting approval for the investment and adoption costs
- Recognizing, sourcing and allocating the relevant resources and skills
- Customer education (especially pertinent for Action, easyJet and Thomas Cook)
- The culture of the company (especially relevant for easyJet and Blackwell's)
- Channel conflict/brand management issues (have particularly affected Thomas Cook and Blackwell's).

Inhibitors arising after operations commenced were:

- Disintermediation
- The necessity to revise and expand the initial business models and strategies employed
- Unreliable strategic partners
- Operating costs (although many of the costs are not technology investment costs as such, but human resource issues), staff training/re-training and the costs of acquiring new employees with new skills
- The lack of assessment methodologies to gauge the costs of e-commerce relative to its performance
- Determining ways to add value as margins grow slimmer (affects all the case studies, but Action, Blackwell's and Thomas Cook most profoundly)
- The emergence of new forms of delivery (a potential but severe threat to Blackwell's)
- Complacency (the easyGroup considers this to be its greatest threat).

Security risks were not cited as inhibitors pre- or post-implementation of online trading by any of the case studies save Lobster, who were concerned about the risk of exposure to credit card fraud.

It is possible from a close examination of these case companies to see that businesses are—as Porter (2001) suggests they should—making their e-business strategy their business strategy by ensuring that their online activities are central to their operations and by moving closer to full integration. Perhaps this is the key lesson to be gleaned from the UK study. An in-depth analysis of Internet innovation in all the featured countries, and how the factors inter-relate, is the focus of Chapter 9.

7
Internet Retailing in the United States

DON LLOYD COOK, BENZ JACOB, JAN PRIES-HEJE,
SANDEEP PURAO AND JONATHAN WAREHAM

INTRODUCTION

The United States has seen a dramatic rise and decline in the growth of new e-commerce startups, stock market evaluations and public perceptions concerning the long-term viability of e-commerce, that culminated in the crash of US technology shares in April of 2000. With the threat of a recession lurking in the Spring of 2001, the atmosphere surrounding e-commerce has dauntingly spun from euphoric to pessimistic in the course of a single year.

Yet e-commerce is still alive and well in the United States. At the time writing, over 50% of US citizens use the Internet and the figure is expected to reach 65% by the end of 2001. Internet users are now equally divided between male and female. About 75% of all Internet users are 18–29 years old, suggesting that prospects are good for the future of the market as these young, e-commerce savvy consumers reach their high income years in their 30s and 40s. And despite the market crash in April 2000 and the reduced expectations for online retailing in the Christmas season, fourth-quarter 2000 online retail sales were up by 67% from the previous year. While this relative growth is impressive, it is overshadowed by the potential. Of the over 856 billion dollars of retailing volume for the fourth-quarter, only 1% was online (excluding equities and airline tickets). So, as this aftermath of post-crash pessimism settles, the opportunities for massive expansion into online retailing remain enticing (US Department of Commerce 2000).

However, this potential will not be harvested by the archetypal dotcom startup fueled by a few good ideas, investor exuberance and Internet media hype. Many of these startups grew on the belief that they could succeed on the aggregation and intermediation of information alone, disowning the business risk and operational headaches associated with inventories, warehouses, and transportation. However, this parable has been completely discredited as companies like Amazon, when competing with established players such as Barnes and Noble, acknowledged that managing disparate, virtual inventories could not yield the massive volume discounts obtainable through a conventional wholesaler and retailer of physical inventories.

Thus, in the United States, we see two complementary trends that characterize the economy's evolution into a second phase of e-commerce. The first is the group of surviving first-generation e-commerce entities that have begun to acquire— either through alignments, organic growth, or acquisition—traditional business functions including warehouses, hybrid click-and-mortar sales channels, and logistics capabilities. This is exemplified by Amazon, who recently stated its intentions to align operations with the massive US retailer Wal-Mart. The second trend is characterized by established industry players who choose to augment existing sales, marketing, and logistics infrastructures with complementary electronic channels and customer support venues such as UPS, Sears, or HomeDepot. Firms are now recognizing that websites are easy to build and emulate, and that novelty in a market is a poor substitute for a well-managed, traditional industry player performing a needed function in the economy.

Overview of Cases

The choice of firms for this chapter is very much representative of this movement to the second phase. Our selection criteria explicitly aimed to identify a breadth of both 'old-' and 'new-economy' players that demonstrated an exemplary command of a given e-commerce domain be it information aggregation, the 'online experience', fulfillment and delivery, or overall after-sales service. Thus, in this portfolio, we see both startups that are confronted with a need to re-position and evolve in the current, post dotcom euphoric environment. These include HomeToDo, Outpost and WebVan. We also see established industry players such as UPS that are complementing existing business operations with e-commerce with UPS Online Tools and UPS Returns on the Web.

HomeToDo grew as an electronic marketplace matching service contractors with homeowners needing small to medium home maintenance projects completed. Significant user adoption challenges forced this startup to rethink its business model entirely, focusing more on offline functions and services. The company has successfully re-engineered its first business model and is now prepared to move back online with a new portfolio of services intended to bring them to profitability in 2001.

Outpost distinguished itself from many of its dotcom brethren by focusing on customer service and satisfaction, international business, and the assumption that it would eventually have to generate operating profits in order to survive. The company feels that it has 'identified the right marketing mix to acquire the "right" customers at a sensible price'. This company demonstrates how to endure in a business sector characterized by high levels of competition.

UPS Online Tools depicts how a 90-year-old established firm can rethink its operations and successfully develop an e-business initiative that complements and extends its core business. This highly regarded shipper of parcels and goods has developed a set of electronic tools that can be docked into any online retailing business application and seamlessly integrate with UPS's transportation, pricing, and tracking functions.

But development did not stop with UPS Online Tools. The **UPS Returns on the Web** program was piloted by online e-tailer buy.com. They confronted the problem of how to handle consumer returns of items in a way that is affordable and efficient from a business perspective and that still makes the customer as comfortable and confident as possible. UPS had some very new ideas for the dotcom world and in helping to solve one company's problem; it created a new cutting-edge business for itself.

Webvan was launched to address the need to deliver merchandise, especially groceries, to the homeowner. The original value proposition was pure: have no storefronts, maintain a citywide warehouse with sophisticated technology to expedite picking and assembling of orders as needed, and optimize the delivery schedules. Changes in observed demand and delivery patterns, and the need to search for supplementary revenue streams, have led to an adjusted implementation that continues to evolve.

HOMETODO—'FIX UP YOUR HOUSE' (hometodo.com)

Introduction

Hometodo.com was launched by two friends who had previously built a successful business selling pizzas at Duke University. Drawing on their own experience with home maintenance and the Atlanta home improvement marketplace, they launched a site where homeowners and service providers could interact, bid, and transact on specific jobs. However, reaching out to a highly fragmented market to attract homeowners and complexities in remotely costing projects proved to be insurmountable problems. As the year 2000 ushered in a more skeptical venture capital market, HomeToDo was forced quickly to rethink its approach. Today, HomeToDo garners data from home inspection reports and uses this information to create a customized advertising tool for service providers. At a time when many e-tailers are failing due to cash-burn, this company has sought to survive by reassessment of its options and a complete redevelopment of its business model to provide a low-cost, value-added service.

Scott Inman, a founder of hometodo.com, had recurring problems with his three-bedroom home in Atlanta. 'Every single year, about November, I decided it's time to take care of it', he says. Each year, it took more time and effort than he wanted. He contacted David Gendell, his room-mate from Duke University, where the two had previously built a successful business selling pizzas to hungry students. The two friends realized that they each spent $4000–$5000 annually on home maintenance and qualified home maintainers were often very difficult to find and retain.

Inman and Gendell founded hometodo.com in August of 1999, with the intent of creating a marketplace where homeowners can match up with service providers in a more convenient, effective manner than they do today. Most service providers spend up to 20%–30% of their time in sales and marketing, meeting homeowners, and calculating estimates. If these processes could be streamlined through the use of a provider-to-consumer portal focusing on the recurring tasks of home improvement, then both service providers and home-owners could harvest significant value.

HomeToDo was born through a round of venture capital investment (US$US1.6 million) in October of 1999. Homeowners filled out a description of their home and project, and HomeToDo sent this to its pool of contractors for bidding on the project. Each project submitted received up to four specific quotes provided by contractors online. The customer then selected one of the contractors and transacted directly with them.

HomeToDo's value to the consumer was the ability to solicit competing bids quickly and effectively from a pool of pre-screened service providers, thus significantly reducing the effort needed quickly to retain qualified contractors for a project. The online marketplace offered value to the service provider by aggregating a great deal of dispersed demand, funneling homeowners towards the provider without sales and marketing overheads.

After launching the first operational version of the site on 20 February 2000, the company added other metropolitan areas: Charlotte, Raleigh-Durham, Winston-Salem and Greensboro, North Carolina; Orlando and Tampa, Florida; Washington DC; Boston, Seattle, and Houston.

However, despite the apparent logic of the value proposition, high costs and low levels of consumer acceptance led HomeToDo to realize that its business model was flawed and unsustainable. But it did not end up in bankruptcy like so many other dotcoms. The founders reviewed their experiences to find a more sustainable model. In the process, they have gone from a dotcom to a non-Internet operation and are now returning to the Internet with a new approach. The company grew to over 20 employees by the summer of 2000; in October of 2000 they downsized to half the staff. In late 2000 the new business model attracted an additional round of financing of US$800 000. The company expects to be profitable in 2001.

Industry, Competitor and Environmental Analysis

The market potential for facilitating home improvement transactions is massive. Most households spend over US$2000 annually on home improvement, where the total American market is estimated at US120 billion. The target market for this type of service is dispersed and fragmented.

HomeToDo's direct competitors are Improvenet, Service Magic, E*Bay, and Handyman-online. Where Improvenet has focused itself on large projects and complex contracts, Service Magic and Handyman-online are directly competing in the market for smaller jobs.

Business Model

HomeToDo's initial business model had no cost for homeowners. For the contractors, there were no lead fees, only win fees of 5% that were collected upon completion of the job. In order to control and collect this completion fee, HomeToDo needed to follow the transaction, as they only realized revenue on its completion. HomeToDo targeted simple, same-day activities as these were easily tracked. The site software allowed service providers to update job status and price, should that change. In addition, the tracking system developed into a Customer Relationship Management system for providers with 10 different status levels. When all jobs were completed, a survey was sent to the homeowner, where price, quality, and other delivery parameters were verified. All service providers gave their credit card number to HomeToDo, so when the job was completed, HomeToDo collected revenue directly from the credit card. Contractor contact information was not on site so neither provider nor customer could circumvent HomeToDo to avoid the win fee.

However, this implementation of a marketplace business model was flawed. It required change in the manner in which homeowners solicit offers of home maintenance tasks. The firm underestimated the expense of broadcasting this message and educating a highly fragmented market with low transaction volumes. Repairers faced difficulties in providing fixed price quotations for complex tasks and the firm had a high overhead in tracking the jobs. Income levels in the first operating year proved to be inadequate.

Redeveloping the Business Model

HomeToDo therefore sought to eliminate the online marketplace. In the course of prospecting alternative income streams, HomeToDo embarked upon establishing relationships with home inspectors. In the United States, each time a home is sold an independent home inspector will spend roughly 3–6 hours preparing an itemized list assessing all structural components of the house in order to educate and protect the buyer. HomeToDo realized that this information was a highly valuable asset that could be marketed to service providers.

HomeToDo's new business model is based on buying this data from home inspectors and preparing a customized home maintenance brochure for the home-owner. Upon written acceptance from the purchaser of the home, the inspector releases the inspection report to HomeToDo in exchange for a small payment. HomeToDo aggregates and organizes all the information about the house in its database. From this database, HomeToDo prepares a 'personal home planner' where the new homeowner receives a document that not only details the current problems with the house, but presents this data with the contact information of HomeToDo's authorized service providers for that particular task in home's immediate area. Service providers pay HomeToDo an advertising fee.

User acceptance of this personal home planner has been over 90%. It costs the homeowner nothing, and provides them with access to pre-screened contractors, reducing the effort they need to complete the tasks highlighted in the home inspection report. The service providers are also happy to pay the advertising fee, as the placement is focused towards a potential client with a qualified need. In addition to tasks presently defined in the home inspection report as needed improvements, HomeToDo also aggregates data on the condition of the roof, appliances, and heating and air conditioning systems. Hence, although service may not be needed on these items in the current year, information about a roof or heater that may need replacing in the future can be sold to service providers. Not only is HomeToDo generating revenue on the initial presentation of the inspection report to the homeowner, it is cultivating an asset that will continue to provide revenue in the future.

Key Business Drivers and Threats

The three critical business factors are customers, suppliers, and the firm's contribution. The initial business model foundered on the costs of attracting customers. The new model has low-cost access to homeowners with specified requirements and pre-qualified, competent service providers able to meet those requirements. The service providers offer competitive bids for each specified job. While price reduction is one important dimension, an even more important customer value proposition may be risk reduction.

HomeToDo identifies qualified, trustworthy contractors through a rating system hosted on the website. When a job is complete, HomeToDo sends the homeowner a survey instrument that asks a number of factors about the contractor. The data are compiled and posted by HomeToDo. In addition, HomeToDo will only invite service providers into its network that pass a thorough screening process with the intent of identifying providers with a high level of repeat business and protecting consumers against service providers who have displayed a pattern of fraudulence, neglect, or poor business practices. It has been necessary to exclude several providers from the system, either due to poor user evaluations or to other breaches of accepted business conduct.

The issue of disintermediating HomeToDo has not been a significant threat, as they offer a $US1000/30-day guarantee, and dispute resolution. The home improvement industry is notorious for contractor disputes, so the HomeToDo 'quality promise' is pushed hard to ensure its value to both contractor and consumers. The firm has also additional information services on its website including data on general maintenance price levels, consumer education, and market information.

One of the greatest anticipated risks in launching HomeToDo was acceptance amongst the service providers. While it was not assumed that most contractors were very proficient with the use of information technology, it turned out that many of the providers had Internet access as a function of their accounting systems, and they often maintained brochure-wear websites. 'We were astounded with just how easy it was to convince the contractors to participate', said Gendell.

However, greater difficulties were encountered in the misalignment of expectations concerning job size and task complexity. Gendell states,

> You can create a matrix according to complexity. Low complexity would be air conditioner machine maintenance. High complexity would include air conditioner replacement. Most homeowners do not know what their units are or what the capacity level is. Thus, bidding on this relatively expensive and risky task is not a simple matter. However, most vendors have become much better at bidding online through time.

Hence, service provider acceptance proved to be much greater than originally expected. The problem of complexity of certain tasks has been overcome in the new business model through use of the home inspectors' reports that provide specified job requirements.

Once the initial problems of user acquisition and user acceptance were overcome, homeowners quickly became assimilated to this new method of soliciting offers on their projects. Of the 6000+ registered users on the system, HomeToDo averaged over one transaction per year, with over 40% return business.

However, the problems of user acceptance proved much more formidable than those of service provider acceptance. These challenges were the high cost of reaching, educating, and convincing homeowners of the value of using HomeToDo's online marketplace and the complexity of conducting sales and negotiation processes online. Many tasks are somewhat more complex than the homeowner anticipates, and resolving this complexity into an agreeable solution is normally moderated in the traditional sales process.

In its second incarnation, HomeToDo avoided both of these problems. Independent inspectors provided exact details of maintenance required. Service providers proved to be willing to pay a fee to the intermediary since it lowered their costs of acquiring new business. HomeToDo's contribution was in adding value by aggregating inspectors' reports, pre-qualifying repairers, linking capable service supply with specific service demand, offering guarantees of service and dispute mediation.

Innovation Factors and Processes

The most important factors that led to this project were:

1. The principals' entrepreneurial spirit and personal history of starting numerous businesses.
2. The principals' longstanding friendship, education (MBAs from Harvard and Duke University), and professional background with a strong emphasis on operational management.
3. The identification of the market inefficiencies in the private home maintenance market.
4. The ability of the principals to recruit talented individuals with track records from the Atlanta venture capital community and branded consumer goods industries (e.g. a senior brand manager from Coca-Cola).
5. A solid track record of operational skill. All of the senior management has had extensive operating experience with companies in the food, banking, medical, and consumer goods industries.
6. Willingness to re-evaluate their failing business plan and secure a more profitable approach even though it required the firm to move temporarily out of the online market.

The innovation processes were:

1. Inspiration from other Internet startups.
2. Resigned previous employment.
3. Examining Internet-based business opportunities.
4. Identified need for a marketplace for simple, one-day projects.
5. Prepared business and strategic plans.
6. Raised first round of funding from venture capital community.
7. Specified, designed, and had website developed. Arranged for hosting.
8. Commenced business.
9. Evaluated and re-developed business model
10. Raised second round of venture capital
11. Commenced new business

Website Development and Operational Issues

The website is programmed in JavaScript outsourced to a third-party provider. The site development was outsourced in the beginning but was later brought in-house due to fact that the high level of evolution in the site stressed the communication and coordination channels of the relationship. The JavaScript application runs on top of an Oracle database on the back end. Now that the web site is relatively mature, the HomeToDo management views the development and operational website issues as minimal.

Website Features

A significant barrier to user acceptance is simply the user's lack of knowledge concerning the complexity and cost of a specific task. For example, users who would like standard annual maintenance on a heating system may have expectations of paying only a certain amount. HomeToDo's website has an education section to help homeowners overcome this problem.

Owing to the fact that transaction capability has been eliminated in the new version of the business model, the website lacks many of the features that one normally attributes to best in class, commerce-enabled websites. Table 7.1 shows that in addition to lack of transaction capability, information on the company and the range of services provided is incomplete. The levels of customer service and ease of use are reasonable but there is ample room for improvement of the website through use of innovative customer-oriented services.

Customer Demographics

The typical user of HomeToDo has purchased a home with a value of US$150 000 or more. They are willing to spend US$300 on a home inspection. This means that they are typically upwardly mobile with dual incomes and limited time. The customers are represented by an equal distribution of males and females between 30 and 50 years of age.

The Future

Is HomeToDo still an e-commerce entity? It is to the degree that all the personal home planners are available to the homeowners online in addition to the physical copy. Moreover, they continue to provide service provider screening and consumer education online. Even though they have eliminated online brokering of maintenance tasks, they remain an aggregator and broker of information. Fundamentally, their value proposition is one of coordination and risk reduction for the homeowner, and market focus and customer qualification for the service providers. HomeToDo now expects to be profitable in the spring of 2001.

Conclusion

Through the winter of 2000/2001, with the national technology markets confronted with the threat of a nationwide recession, many Internet-based businesses have been forced to close their doors. Hometodo.com is not an exception to this phenomenon. Struggling with the problems of a fragmented and inflexible user base, HomeToDo was forced to acknowledge that the marketing expense and adoption resistance would prevent their online marketplace from ever achieving profitability. In response, HomeToDo has affectively re-leveraged its asset base of pre-qualified service providers and cultivated a database of highly detailed information on new home purchases. Through the 'personal home planner', HomeToDo has developed a totally customized venue for highly qualified and focused advertising space that will ensure its profitability in the next generation of e-commerce enterprises. The success of this re-position can be attributed to the principals' entrepreneurial spirit, tenacity, and solid foundation of operational management that ensured the competent execution of the original business plan and its re-invention.

OUTPOST—'CUSTOMER SATISFACTION AS A PATH TO PROFITABILITY' (outpost.com)

Introduction

Outpost.com was launched in 1995 under the guidance of founder Daryl Peck and has emerged as a leading seller of consumer computer products. Outpost is an online retailer specializing in consumer technology products. Early on outpost.com distinguished itself from many of its dotcom brethren by focusing on customer service and satisfaction, international business, and the assumption that it would eventually have to be profitable in order to survive. The dynamic nature of the online economy dictates that Outpost's future is by no means assured, but strategic partnerships with companies such as Tweeter, Brookstone, Apple, Compaq, and Sony as well as continued high marks for customer service and satisfaction may just give Outpost the edge over its e-tailing competition.

Daryl Peck was the founder and president of Inline Software, which primarily developed game and utility titles for Apple's MacIntosh platform. This led him into e-commerce, and in a manner that has since become the stuff of e-commerce legends. Not long after selling Inline, Peck found himself returning from the MacWorld Expo on a cross-country flight. He was reading a book called *The Internet Starter Kit for MacIntosh* which inspired him to venture online for the first time later that night. Cyberian Outpost was launched five months later for the princely sum of US$28 000. Outpost.com was one of the early pure-play ventures into business-to-consumer (B2C) e-commerce in the technology sector, and the name recognition and customer loyalty it developed early on have helped it to survive the early shakeouts.

Peck started Cyberian Outpost (now better known as outpost.com) in May of 1995 with a product line of only 800 items, but by August the number had grown to 3000. By 1999 Outpost stocked about 150 000 products. As of the beginning of 2001, the company featured over 200 000 products, mainly associated with consumer technology. The original Outpost employee was Peck himself, but four years later the company had 160 employees and has since grown to employ almost 350 people. Although still operating at a net loss, Outpost's net sales have increased from US$22.7 million in fiscal 1998, to US$85.2 million in 1999, and finally to US$188.6 million in 2000. In the last quarter of fiscal 2000 Outpost produced over US$76 million in sales. The company expects to produce revenues equivalent to almost US$1 million per employee in fiscal 2001.

Business Model

Outpost.com started with a simple business model of providing high-quality consumer technology goods directly to consumers over the Internet. However, the mantra from the beginning has been customer satisfaction and fulfillment. The Outpost model was designed to provide an exceptional online shopping experience, including customer service, support, and logistics back-office resources to acquire and retain customers. Thus, Outpost's model focused on superior customer service as its key competitive advantage while maintaining a competitive price. Unlike many of its competitors, such as buy.com, Outpost has eschewed competing primarily on price.

Outpost also chose to differ from its competitors by maintaining high levels of inventory, with the accompanying inventory management costs. This allows Outpost to ship goods quickly to consumers. In 1999 Outpost moved its chief warehouse to Wilmington, Ohio, immediately adjacent to the main hub for Airborne Express as well as being close to shipper DHL. This proximity allows orders to be taken until almost midnight for next day delivery in most of the United States. Orders are assembled at the warehouse and taken directly to Airborne, which provides the e-tailer with substantial service discounts. Early on, free overnight delivery on any item was a key part of the Outpost strategy but this was predicated on the assumption that even a customer who placed a small order (say US$7, on which Outpost could not make a profit after paying for the free overnight shipping) would become a customer who would make progressively larger purchases. However, market research indicated that this projection frequently did not hold true. With orders under US$50 representing only 3% of revenues, Outpost made the decision to discontinue free overnight shipping for orders less than US$100. Overnight shipping is still considered to be an integral feature for catering to a consumer base that values near-immediate gratification. A related back-channel service allows a customer to pay a US$10 fee and have a return picked up from any location of their choice. Given the customer service focus of Outpost, it is perhaps not surprising that it has built its own customer service training facility and moved to offering 24/7 customer assistance.

Outpost has benefited from a relatively consistent business model although company executives have been quick to note that there have been many changes in the execution of that model and it has also grown into what it calls the 'e-business services industry by forming alliances with both online and traditional bricks-and-clicks retailers' (*Outpost.com Year 2000 Annual Report*). In creating these alliances with companies such as Wolf Camera, Tweeter, and Brookstone, Outpost has gained access to over a thousand physical retail stores owned by its partners.

The relationship provides these major retailers with an online presence without having to develop the capacity themselves, while allying themselves with a company associated with high levels of customer satisfaction. Additionally, the company has also created another division known as `outpostpro.com` through the purchase of business-to-business (B2B) reseller CMPExpress. This division focuses on sales B2B technology products to small-to-medium size businesses.

In comparison with many of the dotcoms that were evolving in the same period, Peck took Outpost in some unusual directions. For the first two-and-a-half years of its existence, Outpost operated without venture capital funding, then raised capital in private placements during 1998, the same year it completed its Initial Public Offering. Also, Outpost focused very heavily on international business and maintained both a warehouse and substantial product inventory in order to allow easy overnight shipping and quick drop shipments to overseas customers. Information was also provided in several foreign languages in order to facilitate purchases by overseas customers, most of which can be delivered within 36 hours.

Industry, Competitor and Environmental Issues

Outpost inhabits a fiercely competitive environment, namely that of online consumer electronics retailers. The industry itself is in considerable turmoil as many once-promising dotcoms scale back or shut down entirely. Likely and potential competitors include online e-tailers such as `buy.com`, `egghead.com`, direct marketers such as CDW, PC Connection, and MicroWarehouse, as well as more traditional retailers like Circuit City and CompUSA. Although demand for some consumer electronics products, particularly home computers, has softened somewhat, the segment remains a multi billion-dollar market. Outpost has a competitive advantage in offering a very large selection of inventory with the convenience of live customer service 24/7 and usually next-day delivery. Among the pure e-tailers, Outpost is arguably in a stronger position because its focus on customer satisfaction and fulfillment has resulted in a customer base that exceeds one million and it reports about four million website visits per month. Also impressive is the fact that in the third and fourth quarters of fiscal year 2000, more than 50% of sales were generated by repeat customers. During the three completed quarters of fiscal 2001, repeat business was tracked at 58%, 59% and 60%, respectively. The cost of acquiring new customers has dropped by almost 50% in the last two years. These factors may be related to a brand recognition advantage arising from being a first mover in the field.

The organizational culture, while still casual, has also changed as dotcom managers and investors become more demanding. Whereas Peck once spoke of obsessing about preserving a culture where the company's mascots, gerbils Dot and Com, roamed freely about the offices, current CEO Kate Vick talks about facing e-commerce challenges with 'sound business ideas from experienced people (Anders).' The management change started when original founder and creative genius Peck stepped down as CEO in 1999 and was replaced by Robert Bowman (education: Harvard, Wharton MBA), a former President and Chief Operating Officer of ITT Corporation. Bowman maintained the original business model but changed the marketing focus. Bowman left Outpost in 2000 to become President and Chief Operating Officer of MLB (Major League Baseball) Advanced Media, which includes `mlb.com`. The current CEO is Kate Vick, formerly Executive Vice President and Chief Financial Officer at Outpost. Prior to joining Outpost she headed her own management consulting firm and had managed the NYC Entrepreneurial Consulting Group for Ernst and Young. She has stated that she is committed to continuing Outpost's commitment to 'delivering topnotch customer service [rather] than rock-bottom prices' (Anders 2001).

Outpost's greatest threat may be whether it can survive until it reaches profitability. Although it has historically been narrowing its losses each quarter in recent years, losses in the fiscal fourth quarter of 2001 may have actually widened. However, the company is forecasting sales of US$500 million in fiscal 2002 and expects to reach profitability by the end of that fiscal year. Revenues for the fiscal fourth quarter were estimated to be between US$118 and US$120 million, representing over a US$70 million increase in sales from the same quarter in the previous year.

Key Business Drivers and Threats

What has to happen for Outpost to succeed? During a recent interview with the *Wall Street Journal*, CEO Kate Vick outlined several factors.

- More profitable orders as a result of eliminating free overnight delivery on items under US$100.
- Continuing to build a structure that is scalable and able to reach a profit.
- Gaining customers who will buy repeatedly from Outpost, and across their product line.
- Continuing to offer top-quality customer service and to compete on service rather than price.

The greatest threats facing the firm and industry are achieving profitability in an increasingly skeptical market. CEO Vick had noted that 'a lot of people who created business models premised on there being an ever-flowing spigot of new cash to fund top-line growth'. She sees Outpost's advantage in not having followed that model and always planning for eventual self-sustaining profitability. Even though the news has been replete with dotcom failures, there is reason for companies such as Outpost.com to stay hopeful. According to the US Department of Commerce, online retail shopping for the fourth quarter of 2000 is growing substantially, even in the face of a slowing economy.

Innovation Factors and Processes

The most important factors that led to this project were:

1. The principal's long involvement in the computing industry and his initial exposure to the Internet by a book entitled *The Internet Starter Kit for MacIntosh.*
2. The principal's view of a business opportunity for an Internet store with a specific focus—a large range of high-quality consumer technology products.
3. The development of a successful business model based on customer service and order fulfillment rather than on price that could lead to profitability.
4. Venture capital funding on proof of concept.

Operational drivers included the willingness and capability to adapt to changes in the market environment with changes in the marketing plan and the organizational culture.

The major barrier to be overcome in this very early implementation of Internet retailing (May 1995) was uncertainty about the viability of the concept and its implementation. The principal source of this uncertainty was that the level of acceptance by suppliers and consumers was unknown.

Major innovation processes included:

1. Awareness of the business potential.
2. The determination of a business idea for utilization of the Internet by a large-range online store with consumer technology products.
3. The principal's decision to focus on service and fulfillment rather than on price.
4. Self-funded initial implementation to prove viability of the business concept.
5. The development of a website that aimed to facilitate consumer use and provide a pleasant shopping experience.
6. The delay in seeking venture capital until a successful model had been demonstrated. An early informal decision process during the innovation stage of the business which gradually gave way to more formalized mechanisms and business plans during the implementation stage.
7. The focus on having the back-end resources and processes in place to promote customer satisfaction and fulfillment.
8. Adapting to changes in the market environment with changes in the marketing plan and the organizational culture.

Website Development and Operational Issues

The original `outpost.com` website was typical of early dot.coms, the site was created in-house using Perl, CGI scripts and HTML code. Standard text editors were used for coding and back-end work was handled by an Oracle database. This simple architecture was modified from 1995–1997 to add graphics (Adobe Illustrator and Adobe Photoshop) as in-house developers used C to rewrite the original code. A search engine was also added during this period. The year 1998 saw a move offsite to Exodus, a web-hosting service and a change in the core operating software used to run the site. Outpost moved to using Broad Vision's application servers and iContacts live support tools. (Metz 2000). Outpost has continued to handle website development internally, although hosting is now external.

Website Features

On the customer usability and experience side, Outpost has developed a website that offers shoppers multiple methods to search for goods and also clearly indicates the availability of items from inventory when the customer finds the desired product. The site itself is heavily tabbed and categorized to aid consumers in directing their searches. Searches can also be made by brand or product type and bounded by certain attributes, such as price range. Consumers can also often structure their searches by the type of shopping they are doing, such as gift buying. A search engine is also provided along with 'store map' architecture to aid consumers.

According to internal Customer Satisfaction Surveys nearly 9 out of 10 customers (including both visitors and purchasers) were 'extremely' or 'very' satisfied with the result of their visit to the Outpost website. However, critics have still found room for improvement. Forrester Research faulted Outpost for not having the ability to cancel orders online as well as non-acceptance of returns on most non-defective software products. Website information is completely integrated throughout the outpost.com organizations as well as being highly coordinated with the two primary shippers, Airborne Express and DHL.

The website evaluation (Table 7.1) indicates reasons for the reported high levels of customer satisfaction. The categories of corporate and product information, transaction capability, customer services and ease of use were each rated highly at 4/5. Only the area of improved customer services through innovation was rated poorly compared with other market leaders and presents an opportunity for immediate improvement.

Customer Surveys

Outpost.com has enjoyed widespread praise for its efforts in customer satisfaction and fulfillment. It has been awarded the number 1 PowerRanking in the Computing Industry by Forrester Research in 1999, 2000 and 2001. Outpost has also been named as one of the top shopping experiences on the web and a winner of the Circle of Excellence award by bizrate.com. Circle of Excellence award winners are required to have achieved outstanding ratings, based on at least 2000 completed buyer surveys from the merchant's site, in six categories: ease of ordering; product selection and availability; on-time delivery; customer support; overall satisfaction and loyalty; and repurchase intent.

Table 7.1 Evaluation of selected US websites

Firms	Company information/5	Product/ services information/5	Transactions/5	Customer service/5	Ease of use/5	Innovation/5	Total/30	CEC scale © (%)
HomeToDo	2	2	0	3	3	0	10	33
Outpost	4	4	4	4	4	1	21	70
UPS Tools	4	3	0	3	4	1	15	50
UPS/Returns/buy.com	2	2	5	5	4	1	19	63
Webvan	3	4	4	4	5	1	21	70

The Future

Outpost sees the most important factors for companies in Internet retailing as being:

1. Producing a superior shopping and customer service experience, including 24/7 customer service and simplified return policies.
2. Getting products rapidly to consumers, next day if possible because of the 'instant gratification' nature of many of its products.
3. Focusing on gaining quality customers and retaining them through a combination of selection, competitive pricing, and superior customer satisfaction and fulfillment. The company feels that it has 'identified the right marketing mix to acquire the "right" customers at a sensible price—we are not interested in acquiring customers who only shop at below-cost prices'.
4. Demonstrating that e-commerce retailing solutions are both scalable and subsequently profitable.

The lesson for other firms is that even in an online environment, they must differentiate themselves in areas important to consumers such as customer service. In an arena where we are asking customers to buy goods and services from purely online (and intangible) e-tailers, customer service provides a very real link to the consumer.

Conclusion

Outpost.com represents one of the most promising opportunities for online retailing to prove itself as viable in the B2C sphere. Its focus on product range and selection, customer service, fulfillment, and strategic alliances with main suppliers and shippers brings in much of the wisdom of conventional retailers. This concept is extended with a New Economy approach emphasizing a highly usable website, 24/7 live and online service and next day delivery for most items.

UPS'S ONLINE® TOOLS—'TIE INTO OUR NETWORK'

Introduction

UPS is proud to call itself the world's only 90-year-old e-commerce company. Leveraging its position as a highly reputed, worldwide parcel shipping enterprise, UPS has blossomed as the shipper-of-choice for much of the growth in door-to-door deliveries demanded by the explosion of e-commerce. UPS has recently taken the next step to ensure its position as the pulse of many e-commerce entities. On the basis of its renowned online tracking application, UPS has developed a full portfolio of online tools that e-commerce enterprises can easily integrate into their storefront applications, offering a seamless interface from any e-tailing website to UPS's worldwide logistics network.

UPS was founded on 28 August 1907, in Seattle, Washington. With its head-quarters currently in Atlanta, Georgia, the company boasted over US$29 billion in revenue generated by the delivery of 3.5 billion packages and documents, roughly 13 million packages each day. UPS offers delivery to more than 200 countries via its network of 359 000 employees, 1748 operating facilities, and a fleet of 238 aircraft complemented by an additional 384 chartered aircraft. For the eighteenth consecutive year, UPS (NYSE:UPS) has been rated 'America's Most Admired' mail, package and freight delivery company in a *Fortune* magazine survey. The honor follows a similar survey in 2000 in which UPS was selected the 'world's most admired' company in its industry.

In 1995, UPS received recognition for an application that permitted customers to track the exact location of any parcel they had sent. By mid-2001, ups.com was receiving four million tracking requests daily and 40 million hits to the site overall UPS recently developed application programming interfaces (APIs) that enables customers to link product shipments, services and information throughout the entire transaction chain. UPS Online® Tools makes it possible to add state-of-the-art shipping and logistics capabilities to any website or enterprise application, allowing trading partners and customers to access important logistics information from any e-commerce application.

This case depicts how a 90-year-old established firm can rethink its operations and successfully develop an e-business initiative that complements and extends its core business. In what follows we describe how these new tools can be used by B2B and B2C firms to help them establish a scalable fulfillment operation, how UPS has used e-business strategically to complement its core business, and the different approaches used by UPS to do so. This minicase illustrates that the impact of e-business is not just at the visible consumer interface. It emphasizes the critical roles of e-business in supply chains and order fulfillment.

Industry, Competitor and Environmental Analysis

The company's competitors include the postal services of the United States and other nations, various motor carriers, express companies, freight forwarders, air couriers, and others. Its major competitors include Federal Express, the United States Postal Service, Airborne Express, DHL Worldwide Express, Deutsche Post, and TNT Post Group. The parcel shipping sector of the industry is characterized by intensive competition and innovative applications of technology aimed at capturing a strategic advantage.

Business Model

The widespread deployment of UPS Online® Tools represents an emerging trend that will have great significance for the development of e-commerce applications and business models. The integration of installed, third-party APIs into host applications provides transparency across businesses, vendors, and contractors. After a customer is registersed and is licensed to use UPS Online® Tools, the tools can be integrated into the company's software application.

The economic incentive for this type of service is based on the fact that UPS offers free access to the tools. The direct gain for UPS is additional package volume. By providing UPS Tools, UPS ensures its place as the carrier of choice and effectively precludes its competitors from this supply chain operation. Consequently, there is not a separate business model for this initiative. It complements the existing corporate UPS business model.

While the tools are described as 'standard modules' by UPS, they are actually quite flexible. In general terms, the system integrator is permitted access to UPS's operational data at a very low level. However, each client may need a variety of specific calculations concerning weight, taxes, or other unique statistics that are only relevant to their type of business. Moreover, cosmetic preferences can be customized individually.

Key Business Drivers and Threats

The immediate advantage to UPS is that the tools drive additional volume through their business. The following analysis of business drivers and threats focuses on the use of UPS Tools by B2B and B2C firms that may encourage or inhibit widespread use of the Tools. Benefits for B2B and B2C firms converge on a number of themes, including:

- Improved customer service—order errors can be corrected at the point of entry, offering flexible shipping options and customizable tracking numbers.
- Additional website functionality—through a digitized shipping procedure, online customers can shop, ship and track from one location.
- Increased time on site—customers return to the provider's e-commerce site and remain there to check shipping status. This may facilitate impulse buying and marketing opportunities.
- Cost reduction—reduced returns, decreased customer support phone calls, and address entry errors.

The quotes below are taken from customer testimonials aggregated by UPS:

'The shipping and handling charges and rates are simplified.'
'Tracking was really easy to integrate into a website.'
'We provide better customer service because of the Tracking Tool.'
'Now we get rate comparisons and service selections before items get shipped.'
'One of the best features [of the Tools] was the simplicity.'
'The best feature is that they [the Tools] allow the customer to stay on my clients' website without leaving their shopping experience.'

'The fact that it works over the Internet and does not incur any extra telecommunications cost.'

'The ability to customize the look was a nice feature.'

Hence, in exchange for making UPS the shipper of choice, e-commerce sites can benefit from ease of integration, increased site stickiness, less manual customer support, and streamlined shipping processes. The major business threat lies in the capability of the service provider to deliver and limitations on future innovation due to the provider's reluctance to support the initiative. UPS' experience and capability address the first threat and intense competition in the industry reduces the likelihood of the second.

Innovation Factors and Processes

The most important factors that led to the development of this project were:

- The first UPS site was set up in 1994 as static business advertising.
- In mid-1995, UPS added the opportunity of tracking packages to its site to increase customer accessibility to UPS.
- Since then, ups.com activity has doubled every four to six months. UPS made a decision early on to expand its Internet functionality beyond ups.com. The company made deals with portals, such as InfoSeek and Yahoo!. It also offered an early version of UPS Online Tools called UPS Internet Tools, which allowed anyone to freely download UPS functionality into any website.
- Organic growth and popularity led to one million tracking requests daily in 1998.
- Software was developed and tested, and consultant business partners were selected and invited to participate in implementation of the Tools.

Thus, the motivating forces in this case have been a combination of vision, careful planning, exploration, and discovery of how the Internet could be used to complement to an already well-functioning business.

The innovation processes were:

- Inspiration from success of its interactive services offered through Compuserve and PRODIGY in 1994.
- Development and experimentation with interactive shipping functionality.
- Offered tracking function to customers via ups.com, UPS website portals, and downloadable tools.
- Growth in popularity encourages development of API modules to be installed on third-party machines for tracking and other shipping functions.
- Success of initial modules inspires expansion into additional services.

Website Features

UPS Online® Tools are easy-to-install APIs that execute common gateway inter-face (CGI) programs that reside on Internet servers at UPS. Two versions of the tools are available: HTML and XML. All of the tools are available in the XML version. The current portfolio of UPS Online® Tools includes tracking, proof of delivery information, rates and service selection, time in transit, address validation, and shipping. The businesses that use UPS Online® Tools may employ any combination of these modules into their applications.

Website Development and Operational Issues

The commitment to e-commerce and Internet applications led to the opening of a new development facility in Atlanta in May 2000. The Innoplex is a converted warehouse, large and flat, and intended to house about 700–1000 IT staff and business users. Co-location is part of UPS's strategy. Marketing and users are co-located here to promote people-to-people proximity and facilitate interaction, for increased speed and time to market:

> The marketing people, the business people and the IS people are housed in the same building on the same floor. They are all an integral part of the team. The project charter is created and developed here (Project Manager).

To date, the employees are mostly new, with some managers having transferred from other sites. The environment is informal: casual clothes, mobile furniture, and impromptu conference room facilities. All kinds of amenities are also in place: areas for casual interactions, a Cappuccino machine in the cafeteria, a net bar, a pool table, etc.

One of the major differences at this UPS site in comparison with other UPS software development sites is that projects are much shorter, typically six weeks in length. At the same time 15–20 projects are running in parallel. The biggest project has 12 people; average projects have less than 6. The primary reason for keeping the size small is to facilitate interaction. Projects are staffed by people who have different skills. 'In the past, there were defined roles and responsibil-ities—more specialization. Now tools make it easy to do multiple roles, there's a blurring of lines for roles, and that sometimes causes political confusion and havoc', says one of the managers we interviewed. One manager contrasted the old way of doing things with newer Internet development (see Table 7. 2).

UPS has a formal systems methodology in place, namely the Rational Unified Process, but its use is very *ad hoc* at this site because 'it works best when you have crisp, clear business requirements' which is typically *not* the case—'there are no clear business requirements in Internet projects' as the manager states. Because of the huge number of Internet hits UPS receives daily, scalability is a major issue. To cope, UPS has a larger number of mirrored Unix servers.

Table 7.2   *Comparing practices at UPS: past and present*

How software engineering was done before at other UPS sites	How software engineering is done today for Internet applications at this UPS site
18–24 months to deliver an application. Due to changing requirements, two-year projects could become four-year projects	Six weeks to finish a typical project
Used to operate this way: business groups identified opportunities → business requirements written → design implemented requirements	No time for 'focusing on long-term business architecture' and thinking over the business implications. instead they have a laundry list of ideas
Waterfall inspired methodology. Sequential and rigorous	Parallel iterative development. Requirements, design, and testing all done in parallel, not sequentially.
Sufficient time to think through the architectural implications	One standard architecture used every time to save time
Quality assurance (QA) team responsible for testing quality issues across projects	QA people are part of the project group. QA manager plays more of a training role, not an evaluative role. 'Quality should be built in, not tested in'

In comparison with its other pages, evaluation of the UPS Tools page results in a low rating, largely due to its lack of transactional capability (see Table 7.1). Since the nature of Tools (software requiring customization and integration with the legacy systems in other firms) is unlikely to ever result in a standardized, price-listed product, it is unlikely that a transactional capability will ever be implemented on the page. Likely areas that could be improved include more details on the products/services and improved and innovative customer services.

The Future

The biggest challenge for UPS is to keep up with the frantic Internet speed and keep an eye on the competitors:

> Competition is driving the speed. We are always looking to keep up with and ahead of the competition (Project Manager).

Conclusion

The UPS experience emphasizes the importance of driving revenue off an established business model—the transportation of goods and parcels. By giving away the software, UPS has cultivated a large network of online retailers that are committed to driving volume through UPS as their shipper of choice. UPS's vision of becoming the primary infrastructure of the electronic economy is demonstrated by the establishment of a dedicated e-commerce development facility in Atlanta—close to the UPS headquarters—where they continue to develop applications to integrate with the business processes of their clients. Its new approaches to software and website development described above will be of interest to a broad range of organizations.

The key factors that led to development of UPS Tools were: inspiration by its early success with online interactive services, as well as the experiences of amazon.com and other Internet pioneers, a willingness to explore the potential of the Internet for possible strategic advantage, and an opportunity to extend core business with a very specific business implementation. UPS's initial functionality on its website was to provide broader accessibility to the company and its services. The success of the tracking module encouraged incremental extension of core business modules to customer sites using this new channel. No initial inhibitors or barriers were identified.

UPS RETURNS ON THE WEB—'MANY HAPPY RETURNS'

Introduction

It is often said that the 'devil is in the details' and for many Internet B2Cs one of the biggest details has been how to handle the problems of customer returns when you do not have a physical store. Internet superstore buy.com was trying to solve this most difficult problem in a way that was affordable and efficient from a business perspective and that still made the customer as comfortable and confident as possible. For an online store that offers almost 950 000 products between itself and partner stores, this problem could dramatically affect a customer's favorable opinion of the store. For this unique reverse-logistics problem, buy.com turned to an 'old-line' company, United Parcel Service (UPS). In helping to solve one company's problem, it created a new cutting-edge business for itself as part of its strategy to develop business tools for the Internet.

UPS is a 90-year-old company that employs 359 000 people, has over 1.8 million shipping customers, does a daily delivery volume of 13.6 million packages and documents in more than 200 countries and territories, earning almost US$30 billion in revenue in 2000. Its resources are enormous (152 500 delivery vehicles and hundreds of aircraft), and it is dedicated to becoming an integral part of e-commerce. UPS Chairman and CEO Jim Kelly feels the Internet has created a shift of power from businesses to consumers, representing the death of old-fashioned 'push' model retailing. Kelly argues that the position of UPS is working in the confluence of these physical and virtual worlds, 'where wires and tires converge'. UPS has pursued this vision with products such as UPS Returns on the Web and Online Tools.

UPS has taken the Internet to heart in a very practical way. Zona Research estimated UPS shipped 55% of goods purchased online during the 2000 holiday season. Kelly's argument is for businesses, including UPS, to continue to succeed, they must make online systems and functions available to their customers where the *customers* want to do business, reversing the 'push' model of retailing. In 'pull' models, consumers look to the web for information on quality, price, and other attributes, and 'pull' goods they want from the inventories of different companies. Leadership from UPS upper management has ensured that the company has been very involved with the evolution of B2C e-commerce. UPS Returns on the Web is one of the most recent programs to be generated through this involvement.

Returns on the Web is a reverse channel program piloted by Internet e-tailer buy.com to address the thorny problem of ensuring that customer returns are handled promptly, efficiently, with a minimum of steps for the customer, and with a supportable cost structure. The system underwent testing in September 2000 at buy.com, which has reported excellent results. The goal now is for UPS to expand the use of Returns on the Web to B2Bs and other B2Cs, a process that is well under way.

Business Model

The goal was to provide a complete system comprised of an automated, browser-based, self-service solution that integrates the online returns process with the B2C company's back-end databases. This provides significant benefits for both consumers returning items purchased online and for the e-tailers who originally sold the goods. For consumers, it means an easy-to-use system: they contact the company's website where they are asked to fill out an online form that will provide information about the reason for the return of merchandise. The system enables the customer to print a UPS shipping label on their home printer and provides assistance (including maps) in locating UPS drop-off locations, as well as a tracking number. For merchants, the consumer's request for a UPS shipping label triggers an e-mail to the merchant on the item being returned, reasons for return, and when it might be expected.

The e-mail and shipping label will provide merchants with information that will aid them in quickly and efficiently routing the returned item to the correct department. For example, if a customer indicates an item is being returned because they 'changed their mind', the item might be sent to re-stocking, whereas if the customer indicates the item is defective (through integration with the merchant's back-end databases and associated information), the message will indicate this to the business and the label the customer prints off at home will indicate which manufacturer to return the item to under warranty. Returns on the Web also offers additional flexibility for merchants by allowing a variety of service options. Merchants can choose from guaranteed UPS Ground, Next Day Air, second Day Air, or 3 Day Select services. The ease of use of the system and corresponding benefits for consumers should strengthen consumers' overall confidence in e-commerce and Internet merchants.

Returns are a reality of doing business. E-businesses, like all business, inevitably come to a fork in the road where they must decide whether returns are a weakness or a strength. Are you going to ignore your returns and let them weaken your business by draining productivity and cash flow? Or, are you going to approach returns with the same innovation and enthusiasm as other parts of your business, turning the process into a unique experience for customers that sets you apart from your competitors? (Tim Geiken, vice-president, UPS e-commerce).

The UPS Returns on the Web program was originally developed for online e-tailer buy.com. Travis Fagan, vice-president of customer support at buy.com, feels the system is a natural for his company:

One of our business objectives is to invest in technology that enables our customers to self-service on our website. UPS Returns on the Web fits nicely into buy.com's customer support strategy of providing customers with great service at a reasonable cost. Every dollar we save with UPS Returns on the Web, we can invest in new projects and applications to better serve our customers as we grow.

The Returns initiative complements UPS's core business model. While generating revenue for UPS through its mainstream pick-up and delivery business it adds value for B2C *or* B2B firms and their customers and further encourages those firms to retain UPS as carrier of choice.

Industry, Competitor and Environmental Issues

UPS is a primary carrier, along with firms such as Federal Express and Airborne Express, used to deliver goods purchased from online companies. UPS has also been very active in the area of e-commerce logistics and brought its formidable logistic experience to bear in creating UPS Returns on the Web. This product represents the efforts of UPS to provide critical tools for B2C merchants who are concerned about efficiency and customer service.

Research from Jupiter Communications indicates that returning merchandise ranked fifth on a list of twelve sources of dissatisfaction among Internet shoppers. However, 40% of these respondents also said that if items could be returned easily they would buy more online. Andy Tibbs said data collected during the 1999 peak shopping season strongly indicated that 'the message from customers was loud and clear. If you don't get the returns [problems] fixed we're gone.'

Environmental issues for the firm include innovation driven by a very competitive market with very aggressive players such as Federal Express. Differentiation among the companies is based on the ability to provide flexible shipping arrangements, pricing differentials, increased coverage, ability to meet shipping deadlines, and the ability to provide value-added services over and above the core shipping functions, such as the ability for customers (or businesses) instantly to track the status of a shipment.

Key Business Drivers and Threats

What needs to go right for UPS Returns on the Web to succeed? Andy Tibbs answers quickly that 'it's already succeeding', but goes on to explain some of the strategies and tactical calculations (and assumptions) that will establish his case. Obviously, the system must function well for clients and customers and achieve a level of comfort for both (it handled almost two-thirds of the returns from buy.com during the 2000 holiday season). Secondly, demand for consumer products purchased through the web must continue to grow. The environment seems particularly good for this product since, even in the face of the failures of numerous highly publicized B2C dotcoms, online consumer shopping was up over 30% in the United States during 2000.

The main threat facing the firm is that UPS Returns on the Web will eventually face competition from similar products from rivals such as FedEx or Airborne Express. However, UPS Returns on the Web is already up and running and UPS itself is already the leading shipper for Internet B2C firms. This provides UPS with a significant first-mover advantage in the reverse-logistics side of a market where it is already one of the dominant players. Additionally, Returns on the Web is designed to integrate with an Internet company's existing shipping/ordering/inventory software so disruption to the customer is minimal. For strategic reasons UPS chose to rollout the software in September 2000, at the tail end of the traditional acquisition cycle for B2C firms, allowing UPS gradually to 'ramp up' sales and promotion of the software, and allowing for extra opportunities for improvement and adjustment based on feedback from early customers.

Innovation Factors and Processes

The most important factors that led to this project were:

1. 1995—The technology steering committee at UPS forecast that e-commerce would become a major part of the company's future.
2. 1996—The formation of an e-strategy (including Andy Tibbs) team to help develop a strategic vision and create e-commerce strategies at UPS.
3. Andy Tibbs becomes director of e-commerce at UPS.
4. 1998—UPS takes an equity stake in TanData, a Tulsa, Oklahoma, leading-edge developer of transportation software, including the Chain-Link^{TM} software used as a basis for Returns on the Web.
5. Data from online consumers in January 2000 (from the December 1999 Christmas season) indicated that effective returns were a critical issue for e-commerce, and showed the clear need for a solution that would streamline the process. This stimulated UPS to develop a shipping solution and this led to the development of UPS Returns on the Web.
6. Decided to rollout the product during a non-peak period allowing ample time for improvement based on customer feedback.

Also of interest are the innovation processes within UPS that allowed this project to come to fruition. In many ways, UPS was an 'old-line' delivery company that some felt was in danger of being overpowered by younger and presumably more agile rivals such as Federal Express. However, UPS chose to reinvent itself by actively seeking ways to expand its Internet business as more than just a delivery company.

These innovation processes were:

1. Early commitment to e-commerce.
2. Making e-commerce a part of the strategic plan at UPS.
3. Allowing capable executives to craft strategies into workable goals.
4. A willingness to work with innovative companies such as buy.com to develop unique software and shipping solutions.
5. Implementation in September 2000, deliberately providing ample time for fine-tuning prior to the Christmas peak period.

Web Development and Operational Issues

UPS used its strategic alliance with TanData to develop an existing Internet shipping solution, ChainLink^{TM}, as the platform for UPS Returns on the Web. The completely automated service utilizes third-party Active Server Pages (ASPs) which minimize problems associated with the extensive IT implementation that would otherwise be required. Thus, the company avoids many technical issues such as site and server maintenance, upgrades, and database management. When the consumer completes the return information it is forwarded to the merchant who is given instant information about the particular product being returned, why it is being returned, when it is expected, and where it needs to go when it is received. Each return-shipping label provides three information fields for recipients. One is the return merchandise authorization (RMA) number and the other two are reference order numbers providing information to help the merchant complete several tasks. The system triggers shipping charges automatically on receipt of the merchandise and provides for the consumer's account to be credited at the same time. It provides for a variety of customizable e-mails for consumers, vendors, returns depots, or manufacturers providing additional information about the product being returned. For example, if a product is still under warranty, the system can be configured so that it would produce a shipping label that would route the merchandise directly back to the manufacturer for repair, rather than requiring it to be shipped first to the seller, thence to the manufacturer. The benefits seem obvious to buy.com vice-president of operations, Tom Wright.

> If we're not taking [toll-free] calls that cost $6 to $8 each and returns are being processed in two or three days, it has to be more efficient.

Evaluation of the website (see Table 7.1) in this case required investigation of two websites from the tightly integrated firms, UPS and buy.com, that jointly provided the returns service. The evaluation revealed inconsistencies across the two websites in levels of details on the firms and the products/services offered. Transactional capabilities and customer services were rated at the highest levels and ease of use was very high. Implementations of innovative customer services on the website rather than in the actual operations is an area for improvement.

Customer Surveys

The early results at buy.com have proven to be very encouraging for UPS. Under its previous system, returns to buy.com took an average of five to seven days to get a RMA label into the hands of the customer. The new process using UPS Returns on the Web takes about four minutes and makes the automated service available 24/7 365 days a year. Returns on the Web handled about two-thirds of buy.com's holiday returns for the 2000 holiday season, making for a successful launch. Benefits to the clients include dramatically reducing the call volume to company service centers. Customers surveyed in the initial implementation have been reported to be very pleased with the ease of use and convenience of the system. The system is of particular value to pure-play B2Cs who do not have a physical location and companies wanting to increase their ability to track and process returns more efficiently.

The Future

UPS sees the biggest challenges as being:

1. Continuing to produce products that will add value to consumers and merchants as part of UPS's overall portfolio of services.
2. Making sure that products are scalable and flexible enough to meet the changing demands of customers.
3. Customer service is everything for a dotcom business and returns have to be handled correctly to maintain customer loyalty. Delivery alone is not enough.
4. Meeting the challenges faced by competitors such as FedEx and the US Postal Service that are attempting to enter this market and may wish to compete on price, flexibility and their existing relationships with many B2C firms.

Conclusions

UPS Returns on the Web illustrates how solutions must be found for problems that confront B2Cs in order for them to survive. A problem for many has been how to handle returned merchandise since customer service is often one of the key differentiating characteristics between online firms. UPS Returns on the Web represents a significant step in addressing the unique problems generated by

B2C dotcoms and it illustrates that there is much more to serving customers than simply putting up a website and selling goods. Since US$5 out of every US$100 of goods purchased online are returned, back-office logistics systems may mean as much to the long-term profitability of a B2C company in terms of retaining customers as more traditional customer satisfaction measures.

The single most important factor that led to this project was the adoption by UPS of a corporate vision to reinvent the firm through the application of e-commerce. This was in 1995 and came as a response to intense competition in the market, pioneering efforts by Internet firms and following success of UPS's web-based parcel tracking project. The specific drivers were clearly recognized customer needs or customer problems in UPS's core business areas.

Data from online consumers in January 2000 (from the December 1999 Christmas season) revealed that effective returns was a critical issue for e-commerce, and showed the clear need for a solution that would streamline the process. This stimulated UPS to develop a shipping solution and this led to the development of UPS Returns on the Web.

WEBVAN—'THE LAST MILE IN E-COMMERCE' (webvan.com)

Introduction

Webvan.com was launched in 1997 by Tom and Louis Borders. Louis had earlier revolutionized the book-selling business in the United States by devising sophisticated inventory management systems and artificial intelligence (AI) systems to manage bookstores. This technological edge over its competitors helped Borders Books to stock considerably more selection and to be more profitable than any other bookstores in the United States. Borders Books was acquired by K-Mart in 1992 for an undisclosed sum believed to be in the hundreds of millions of dollars.

Louis Borders, a mathematician from MIT, believed that deliveries to homes could be optimized with the use of appropriate models, leveraging the results of appropriate forecasting models. Coupled with their earlier success in the bookstore industry and enthusiasm for the Internet's potential, Webvan was launched to address the need to deliver merchandise, especially groceries, to the homeowner. Even though margins in the grocery industry were traditionally low, Louis Borders believed that he could increase margins by eliminating store costs. Instead of expensive storefronts in prominent locations with employees to manage several stores in one city, he envisioned one huge warehouse for a city and delivery trucks that would service an entire city area. With his vision he was able to raise US$120 million from investors such as Benchmark capital, Sequoia capital, Softbank and Yahoo before the company went public in 1999.

Changes in observed demand and delivery patterns and the need to search for supplementary revenue streams have led to an adjusted implementation that continues to evolve.

Business Model

Webvan was founded with very little or no market research. The belief of the founders was that 'if we build it, they will come'. Therefore, the focus was exclusively in building the most sophisticated and the biggest distribution center as fast as it could be done. This was not so much a carefully constructed business model as a vision to develop and control essential business infrastructure. The founders got support for their vision from leading venture capitalists and investors. The original idea was to build each warehouse to stock three million stock keeping units (SKUs) which was revised during the preliminary funding rounds to around 50 000 SKUs. To reach all major cities in the country before any one else did was another key driver for this strategy. There was no time to wait and prove the vision in one city. Webvan entered into a contract with Bechtel to build 26 distribution centers in three years at a cost of US$1 billion.

Webvan was conceived as 'the last mile' in e-commerce. Because regional telephone companies owned the last mile to the customer's home and any long distance company that wanted to provide service to the customer had to go through the regional company that owned the last mile, Webvan wanted to be the company that owned the right to deliver to the consumer's home. Therefore the company picked groceries, including perishable items, as the primary products it offered because the consumers purchased groceries more frequently than any other item. After consolidating its position in the online grocery business, Webvan wants to add other consumer items to its offering.

Webvan does not ship the products from an existing grocery retail store as some of the other grocery delivery companies did. Instead it buys the products from the same suppliers as traditional grocery chains do, such as major wholesalers and direct from the manufacturers. In most cases Webvan has been and is able to obtain similar price discounts as the established grocery chains.

The founding vision is beginning to be realized. Webvan has B2B revenue streams from partnerships with other B2C e-commerce companies to deliver its products to customers. These companies place inventory of their products at Webvan's warehouse and transfer the orders they take on their website to Webvan for delivery.

Implementing the Business Model

Customers have to register once on the webvan.com website with their address and credit card information. The next time they log on they will automatically be taken to the web store of the distribution center their city is serviced from. Customers can store a shopping list on the web store, which they can submit with or without changes to it. Once a shopping list is assembled it is easy to place an order. The web store will announce products on sale and new additions so that customers can make changes to their shopping list. Inventory is managed in real time so that if an item is out of stock, it will be marked as unavailable on the web store.

Once an order is placed on the web store, the order is downloaded to the distribution center server, where it undergoes processing. Standard package items will be allocated from inventory. Preparation orders will be issued for fill-to-order items. Such items will be prepared and stored in specially marked locations to be picked for particular orders. Sophisticated software systems determine how many containers are needed for an order and release marked containers for each order. The containers travel on the conveyor system to the order pickers who are stationed at each carousel location. Rotating carousels bring the product to the picker rather than the picker go to the product location to pick the items. The system is highly scalable. Each distribution center is currently designed for 8000 orders per day, which can be scaled up without much additional investment.

Inventory and order picking are managed using warehouse management software (WMS) systems integrated with back-office enterprise resource planning (ERP) applications and front-end e-commerce applications. Inventory in the web store is updated daily with real time inventory in the warehouse. Stock replenishment is ordered automatically when the inventory drops below a threshold limit. Products with expiry dates are lot controlled in the warehouse and are systematically removed before the expiry dates are approached.

Webvan built its first distribution center in Oakland, California, near the San Francisco Bay Area. It is a 350 000 ft^2 warehouse consisting of temperature-controlled food storage and preparation areas, huge carousel bins where products are stored and retrieved automatically and miles of conveyor belts on which the shopping containers travel across the distribution center filling the orders on their way to the truck departure area. Webvan designed its delivery system as a hub and spoke model, much like FedEx. At present Webvan has distribution centers in 10 major cities including Atlanta, Chicago, Dallas, Los Angeles, San Diego and Seattle.

Another element of Webvan's model is that it has its own fleet of delivery vehicles. Webvan leases its delivery trucks. The now familiar logo is often seen as these vans carry products to customers. The logo is painted with eye-catching colors and a big Webvan name on either side of the truck. This is also intended to make the customers feel safe to open the door to the delivery person. Webvan has taken extra care in hiring its couriers with extensive background checks and referrals and gives them intensive training in how to interact with customers. For example, couriers are prohibited from accepting tips from customers. Route-planning software determines the optimum truck route for each truck for each shift and prints out a route map for the driver. A customer's credit card is charged at the time of delivery and the delivery person can make adjustments to the invoiced amount for returned goods, if any. This service level is unmatched by other e-commerce retailers.

Webvan promises convenience to grocery shoppers—do the shopping without leaving your homes. Also, it offers twice the selection compared with a typical grocery store. The company promises delivery the following day within a one-hour window that the customer chooses. Delivery is free, provided the order value is US$75 or more. For orders less than US$75, it charges a fee of US$4.95. Webvan hopes to offset the additional cost of delivery from the savings it can generate from not having expensive storefronts. Break-even is expected to be at 3000 orders per day at US$100 per order. That represents only about 1% of the grocery business in a major metropolitan city and the company expects to break even in its major markets by the end of 2001. Webvan currently averages more than US$110 per order, so the target is well within reach. The pricing structure for deliveries has, however, changed somewhat over time. Initially, delivery was free regardless of the order value. When Webvan instituted a delivery fee of US$4.95 (for orders less than US$75), the order volume dropped by about 40%. It was determined, however, that this clearly eliminated only the low-volume orders. It was therefore decided to stick to the policy of charging the modest delivery fee for orders below US$75.

Industry, Competitor and Environmental Analysis

Webvan considers itself to be in the US retail industry, which is estimated to be US$2.5 trillion in size. Of that, the grocery industry is US$500 billion. The grocery industry is dominated by national chains such as Safeway, Kroger, Winn-Dixie, etc. Traditionally the grocery industry is highly competitive and the margins are razor thin. Gross operating margin in the industry is estimated to be 10%–12%. Food is one of the largest periodic household purchases. Webvan does not consider the bricks-and-mortar grocery stores to be its competition.

In the online grocery business it competes with online grocers such as peapod.com, streamline.com, shoplink.com, netgrocer.com, eGrocer.com and a few other niche players such as pinkdot.com, urbanfetch.com and kozmo.com. Peapod is perhaps the oldest grocery delivery company having started its business in 1989. Its model was to shop from the local grocery store after an order was received and deliver the products within a two-hour delivery window. After Webvan's debut with its own warehouses in 1999, Peapod also changed to a warehouse model. Streamline and Shoplink charge a monthly subscription fee and deliver a wide variety of products to their customers weekly, using either a portable cooler or a leased pre-installed refrigeration unit in the customer's garage. Netgrocer ships non-perishable goods from its New Jersey warehouse to anywhere in the contiguous US states using FedEx three-day delivery. eGrocer works with affiliated local grocery stores and, after collecting the orders online, passes them on to an affiliated grocery store where the order will be picked, packed and kept ready for pick up by the customer at a separate checkout counter or drive through window. It also delivers to collection centers such as office buildings, convenience stores or gas stations.

Niche players cover a small geographic area and deliver emergency orders of last minute or emergency items within a short time from placing the order, e.g. pizza delivery. In future competition could come from traditional grocery stores such as Safeway, Publix, Haris teeter, etc. who are building their own home delivery models. On the home delivery front Webvan competes with UPS or

FedEx by entering into delivery agreements with other online merchants such as eve.com, petsmart.com, etc. Online merchants store their products in Webvan warehouses and have Webvan deliver their products to their customers.

Key Business Drivers and Threats

The logistics of home delivery are very complex, requiring product range, quality and prompt and flexible fulfilment. Webvan offered to make deliveries in a 30-minute window (later changed to one hour) of the customer's choice. It had to limit the number of orders it could take from a certain area at a certain time based on the number of trucks and drivers available to service that area. In some areas of the city, customers could not place an order for delivery at the time they wanted, while in other areas there was unused capacity. Therefore, it lost orders in some areas while the deliveries were inefficient in other areas. Webvan changed the delivery window to one hour in an attempt to get around this problem. That meant customers should be prepared to wait for up to an hour to get their deliveries.

Another logistical problem is that delivery times are not evenly distributed. The trucks and drivers will be busy during the popular delivery windows and at other times most of the trucks would stand idle. In order to be efficient Webvan needed to be able to get enough trucks when the demand was high and have only the required number of trucks when the demand was low. This is a classic logistical optimization problem that Webvan has not yet resolved.

One of Webvan's biggest threats would be a failure to achieve its targeted profitability resulting from a slow-down in Internet purchasing by consumers or an inability to attract the delivery business of other online retailers. Faced with substantial fixed costs in its warehousing and distribution systems, the firm needs consistent increases in throughput from increased online sales—either by its own customers or from others. Since the technology crash in 2000, funding for expansion has to be generated internally rather than from equity and the company is not close to making a profit. The company's survival depends on its ability to generate cash internally in the near future and to cut the costs of loss-making operations.

Webvan suggests that one of its biggest challenges is consumer behavior. Most people are not organized enough to plan for their grocery purchases even a day ahead and to make sure that they will be available to receive the products when they arrive. They would rather run to the nearby grocery store when something is needed right away and pick up other items when they are there. The shopping experience on the website depends on a customer's connection type to the Internet and the processing speed of her PC. If she has a slow PC and a slow connection to the Internet, the download delay could become prohibitive. This is an issue that confronts all B2C retailers.

Innovation Factors and Processes

The key motivations for this business were the beliefs that consumers would be ordering everything through the Internet in the future and that it was possible to revolutionize even mundane industries such as groceries through the innovative application of technology. The background of the founder in successfully trans-forming the bookstore industry by applying information technology was critically important. The investment climate was such that unlimited cheap investment money was available at that time to fund mammoth projects if Internet based. The major reasons for the establishment of the firm were not at all related to issues within the grocery retailing industry. The major processes were:

1. A business opportunity was identified in relation to a vision for Internet order fulfilment.
2. The vision was accepted for funding to US$120 million by venture capitalists and Internet firms.
3. The firm issued public shareholding.
4. Contracts were let for construction of the distribution centers.
5. A website was developed and operations initiated.

Website Development and Operational Issues

The website is tied to the back-end systems at various points. First, the website contains scheduling windows, which have a capacity. As customers choose their delivery schedules, some windows may close as they reach capacity. Information about scheduled deliveries is grouped at two different cut-off times during the day. The first appears at 8 pm. Orders placed during the day are collected and a routing algorithm is applied to arrive at the most efficient delivery schedule. The software that does the routing is called RIMMS. Since there is one warehouse per city, the routing algorithm minimizes the cost of this one-source—many-deliveries problem subject to delivery requirements constraints. The second cut-off point, which results in similar scheduling, occurs at midnight. It is therefore possible for a customer to place an order by midnight for delivery the next day. For a morning delivery, however, it is necessary to order by 8 pm the previous day.

The actual picking of products is also controlled by software, called MOVE, bought from Optum and customized by Webvan. The financials are supported by software from Peoplesoft. The integration between systems, therefore, is close to 100%, but for pragmatic reasons it is not real time. For example, routing happens twice a day. The inventory updates take place once a day, and forecasting is carried out less often.

Website Features

Webvan's current web presence is comprehensive. It provides the customer with the choice of city-specific ordering, i.e. customized, by taking into account where the customer's home account is registered. A customer can maintain multiple lists to eliminate repeated data entry requirements and even set up periodic shopping lists or specialized shopping lists. The customer can update the shopping basket, which can be confirmed immediately as the inventory updates are directly tied to the website on a daily basis. The customer selects a delivery schedule along with the shopping list and confirms the purchase with a credit card. The website is streamlined, allows several cross-selling opportunities and allows the customer multiple chances to take advantage of specials and sales.

Website Evaluation

Webvan's website is easy to navigate. It features a split window with the major indices on the left side. Each selection will explode into a submenu. It is easy to navigate between windows. Items selected need not be saved when going between windows. Loading time is short, even though the pages are rich with graphics and pictures of the products. Functionality is robust. Checking out is easy. There is no need to enter payment information each time. Order confirmation with all the items and prices are displayed immediately, which can be printed. There is plenty of help available online. Gomez.com—an online website evaluation service—has consistently ranked Webvan top among the internet grocery providers. It rates sites for ease of use, customer confidence, onsite resources and relationship services. According to Gomez, 'Webvan's site remains the industry standard-bearer; the benchmark by which others set expectations'.

Formal evaluation of the website (see Table 7.1) supported the reviews of other firms. Ease of use was the highest rated element. The provision of product information, transaction capability and customer services were all rated highly. However, other website elements, notably company information and innovative customer services, were the areas most in need of improvement.

Customer Issues

Internal customer surveys report a high level of satisfaction with Webvan's service. Customers find the product quality to be excellent and the delivery on time and courteous. Webvan did not place a link on their website for customer surveys, unlike some others reported in this volume. It is therefore not possible to comment on specific customer demographics. On the basis of known customer profiles, however, we know that most Webvan-registered customers are women with an income to support the average order of US$110. The most commonly ordered items include regular groceries, pet foods, and general interest magazines. In rare cases, customers have ordered electronics, such as the Sony Playstation. Apparently, a large number of customers have ordered once but not a second time. This must be of concern to the firm since one of the reasons for selecting the grocery industry was its high volume of repeat sales.

The Future

The concept was timely in terms of enabling technology. The enthusiasm of the investors for this concept was so high that the company had a market valuation of US$8 billion shortly after it went public. The prospects for the company also looked so bright and pervasive. However, all that changed in a short time. Investors have left in droves and raising capital for building additional distribution centers is a daunting task. The money for expansion has to come from operations and the company is nowhere near making a profit. The company's survival depends on its ability to generate cash internally in the near future.

One approach is to charge a fee for all deliveries. People who value convenience and time more than the delivery fee will continue to use the service. But order volume could drop substantially to make the operation unviable. Another approach is to keep all delivery windows open to take in as many orders as possible for the entire delivery area and then optimize deliveries using artificial intelligence systems. The company could offer incentives to customers based on existing delivery schedules. A third approach would be to reduce the scope and focus on distribution centers that are closer to turning a profit. Recently the company has resorted to closing down under-performing distribution centers in order to reduce the cash-burn rate.

Advice for other firms seeking to develop an Internet service is not to under-estimate the importance of market research and planning. The perception was that if an Internet business was set up and discounts offered to customers then the business would succeed. Old fashioned marketing planning and financial controls are necessary for Internet businesses too.

Conclusion

Webvan's major innovation drivers were an identified opportunity to establish an entirely new type of infrastructure business, the founders' qualifications, entrepreneurial spirit and previous experience with business startups (particularly the technology-based industry transformation of book retailing) and the investment climate at the time that provided virtually unlimited funding for proposals of mammoth Internet-based projects from reputable entrepreneurs. There were no identified initial inhibitors or barriers, although after the technology crash in 2000 operational inhibitors arose over on-going funding for expansion and to cover operational losses.

In spite of a strong business vision and a comprehensive implementation, Webvan, like several others in the B2C e-commerce area in the United States, is facing problems. Difficulties with cash flow have been reported in a 2001 *Business Week* article. However, the firm is confident that the current storm will blow over and the business will flourish. The fundamentals are strong and the overall industry sector, groceries, is here to stay.

Webvan's experiences are a source of important lessons for others in the Internet world. A commitment to a very high level of fixed costs with distribution centers and delivery fleets, without focused market research, targeted markets, specific cost advantages and revenue streams, appears, in hindsight, to have been a very high-risk approach. The firm appears to have assumed constant demand and focused its efforts on building a fulfilment capability. The distribution centers have a daily capacity for 8000 orders or more but have a break-even point of 3000; that may indicate over-capitalization.

The downturn in the economy may have a particular impact on cash-rich, time-poor consumers who are attracted to Webvan's grocery business. Notwith-standing internal customer surveys showing high levels of customer satisfaction, the low levels of repeat business indicate problems with the firm's implementation.

Finally, some mention should be made of the difficulties in applying technology-based innovation across retail sectors—from books to groceries. Customers' demands cannot be assumed to be identical. The products are certainly different. Books are relatively stable commodities but groceries are more seasonal, vary in quality and are perishable.

Postscript: In July 2001, Webvan declared bankruptcy.

CHAPTER CONCLUSION

The US firms profiled illustrate the diversity of motivations and variety of implementations that can occur when successful Internet operations are combined with sound, yet creative business thinking. More detailed examination of the innovation factors is made in Chapter 9.

Drivers

Of the many factors that directly led to these Internet initiatives, the most important were:

- The experiences of Amazon and other Internet pioneers were an inspiration resulting in other startups or initiatives (HomeToDo, UPS)
- Perceived opportunity to establish an entirely new type of business (Webvan) or an opportunity to establish or extend a business with a very specific business model and implementation (HomeToDo, Outpost, UPS)
- The founders' qualifications, entrepreneurial spirit and previous experience with business startups (HomeToDo, Outpost, Webvan)
- The investment climate at the time provided virtually unlimited funds available for proposals of mammoth Internet-based projects from reputable entrepreneurs (Webvan)
- A willingness to explore the potential of the Internet for possible strategic advantage (all firms)
- Cost reductions. UPS's initial functionality on its website was to enable customers to track parcels. The costs of providing customer service staff for this function had become excessive. The success of the tracking module encouraged the incremental extension of core business modules to customer sites using this new channel (UPS)
- Corporate strategy in a traditional firm. In 1995 as a response to intense competition and following the success of the web-based customer tracking

project, UPS determined e-commerce to be the means of reinventing the firm from being just a delivery company. A high-level team of experienced executives was established to create an e-commerce vision, develop strategies and to translate these into workable goals. The specific drivers were clearly recognized customer needs or problems—for integrated deliveries and then for returns—in UPS's core business areas. UPS acquired a leading-edge transportation software company to help provide the capability and worked with innovative customers to refine and tailor its products.

Operational drivers included:

- The ability of the principals to recruit talented individuals with a solid track record of operational skill (HomeToDo)
- A willingness to re-evaluate its failing business model and secure a more profitable approach even though it required the firm to move temporarily out of the online market (HomeToDo)
- A willingness and capability to effectively modify the implementation of business plans as required by market experience (Outpost, UPS)

Inhibitors

The most important factors initially inhibiting the innovations included:

- Uncertainty about the Internet. The greatest obstacle to be overcome for the project to be a success was a lack of understanding of the Internet's viability (Outpost)
- Lack of knowledge, initially about how the Internet could best be used, then technical, design and skill issues (how to do it, what worked, acquiring the skills required!) (Outpost)
- Uncertainty about supplier and customer acceptance (Outpost) or a lack of acceptance by suppliers and consumers (HomeToDo)
- No initial inhibitors or barriers (Webvan). None identified (UPS).

Operational inhibitors included:

- The nature of the service. Greater difficulties than expected were encountered in the misalignment of customer and supplier expectations concerning home maintenance job size and task complexity. An agreeable solution is normally moderated in the traditional process of onsite negotiation (HomeToDo)
- Cost of attracting customers. The marketing costs required to attract customers exceeded expectations (HomeToDo)
- Ongoing funding for expansion and to cover operational losses (Webvan)

While these motivating and inhibiting factors were identified by the firms as being most important, any consideration of success in Internet retailing should also note the broader context.

8
Evaluating Websites and Surveying Customers Online

OVERVIEW

This chapter includes details of the development of the innovative research tools used in this project, including a website evaluation framework and an Internet-based consumer survey. These are practical tools for managers and researchers. Managers can use the website evaluation framework to assess their own and competitors' sites and to make benchmark comparisons with the successful sites published. Researchers from many disciplines can use the same framework to distinguish between implementations of the Internet in different organizations. Details of the findings from application of these tools with implications for business are included in Chapter 10. Findings and their implications for researchers are shown in Chapter 9.

Part 1:
Evaluating Commercial Web Sites:
Development and Application of a Framework[1]

STEVE ELLIOT AND NIELS BJØRN-ANDERSEN

INTRODUCTION

This framework attempts to integrate knowledge and experience on a complex topic from disparate sources—a range of reference disciplines and empirical practices. The objective was to identify features and facilities that currently comprise a successful commercial website. Much research into 'what works' on the Internet has a narrow focus, e.g. on product (brand and extrabrand attributes), product types, industries, adoption factors, user demographics, security, risk, web page design and usability features. Little research considers how all these diverse areas need to come together to enable a successful Internet-based customer service.

A set of features and functions is developed that comprise a current representation of an 'ideal' website. This framework can be used to compare sites, to identify a path for improvement of a site and to provide a context for research with a specific focus. The framework was tested against the sites of 100 firms in 10 industry sectors and then used to analyse the Internet websites of the international

[1] The research program in electronic commerce which led to the development of this framework has received support from the Danish Social Science Research Council, the Centre for Electronic Commerce at Copenhagen Business School, Log-in, and The KnowledgeLab UK. All funding is gratefully acknowledged.

firms examined in this book. Analysis of the evaluation results suggests that organizations are leaders or laggards in their use of the Internet not because of the nature of an industry or its products but due to decisions made within the firms.

Industry has embraced the concept of e-commerce. A world-wide survey of 500 large companies found that 90% of top managers considered the Internet will transform or have a big impact on the global marketplace by 2001. However, several studies (e.g. Andersen Consulting 1999, Brown and Chen 1999, Nambisan and Wang 1999) have shown that despite enthusiasm for e-commerce, a major impediment to its widespread adoption seems to be uncertainty within organizations as to how to address the challenges it presents.

The business-to-consumer (B2C) component of e-commerce is significant with industry expectations of its growth from 1998 to 2003 to be US$8 billion–US$108 billion. Consumers have also embraced the concept of Internet-based e-commerce, although with less enthusiasm than industry. Documented consumer concerns with use of the Internet for purchasing include privacy, security, functionality and ease of use (e.g. Jarvenpaa and Todd 1997, Farquhar, Langmann and Balfour 1998, Ho and Wu 1999, and Elliot and Fowell 2000).

This framework is intended to address industry uncertainties and consumer concerns with commercial Internet sites by developing a framework identifying the key features and facilities for B2C websites. The framework will enable an assessment of a firm's current Internet provision against a standard set of key characteristics. The intention was to provide a means of evaluating a firm's current website in comparison with other sites and to assist firms to identify a potential path for development of a consumer-oriented website from their current implementation. The framework is proposed as a mechanism for clearly identifying options, opportunities and their implications for website development, in order to place it on the agenda for senior management.

Any framework intended for evaluation of commercial websites is destined for criticism not only from those companies whose sites are evaluated less positively but also from scientific sources. In designing an evaluation framework, decisions must be made as to the purpose or outcomes intended from the evaluation process. Is it merely to identify who is doing what; to determine who is doing it best at present; to compare sites with best business practice at the time of the evaluation; or to help identify a path for future development of a firm's Internet presence? The potentially subjective nature of an evaluation process may be criticized as well.

In developing the website evaluation framework we acknowledge these issues. The aims of this framework are clearly stated. Steps were taken to address the issue of subjectivity. This part examines a range of design details (both theoretical and empirical) relevant to evaluations of websites and explores the rationale of these features. The resulting draft framework was tested against 100 sites and then revised. The outcome of this process is the proposed Centre for Electronic Commerce (CEC) website evaluation framework.

DEVELOPMENT APPROACH

The overall objective was to develop a means of evaluating websites in order to encourage improvements in website design and implementation. The aim of this evaluation design and development process was the specification of an instrument that is transparent, logical and consistent and is capable of reliable application across a broad range of websites. The framework also aimed to support longitudinal monitoring of developments in websites so that a firm could assess the changes in its website over time. This latter aim requires the framework to cater for a rapidly changing technical and organizational environment. A multi-phase approach was adopted that comprised:

- A wide-ranging literature review from consumer adoption factors through technology interfaces to website evaluations
- A review of leading sites that were selected from the literature, industry reports and media reports as being successful, being award winners, or being identified as innovative or successful in service provision such as to be of interest to other firms. Sites were predominantly of US origin (e.g. Amazon, Dell and eBay) but also included European sites such as British Airlines, British Telecom, Carlsberg, Lego, Lufthansa and Volvo-cars
- Identification of factors from research and industry literature, determination of factor classes as well as a proposed scoring methodology. These sources were used to establish theoretical and empirical construct validity
- Comparison of factors with published industry scoring/checking/evaluation studies to identify any omissions
- Piloting and review to assess the content validity and reliability of the framework
- Testing the evaluation framework against the commercial sites of 100 of the largest Danish companies. The scope of the evaluation was limited to publicly available areas of a site
- Evaluation of the sites by two assessors independently. Results were compared to check reliability of the instrument
- Review and write-up

The process of overlaying industry and academic research to identify factors proved useful in order to meet research objectives. First of all it could help firms to identify what could be done and to provide possible directions for how it is being done by other firms. Secondly, factors based on theory were identified and applied where industry practice may not have provided an adequate treatment of issues. The assessment of the 100 websites was undertaken in January 2000 by a team from the CBS Centre of Electronic Commerce.

FACTORS INFLUENCING CONSUMER ADOPTION OF ONLINE RETAILING

Since the area of Internet retailing is relatively new and theoretical development is at an early stage, an examination of theoretical contributions that may have relevance to successful website design also considered the more general issue of consumer adoption of innovations. The factors are initially presented with related research issues and then grouped into evaluation categories.

Early work by Bell, Keeney and Little (1975) suggests that the customer needs to be attracted to an innovation, and that 'attraction may be a function of the seller's advertising expenditure, the effectiveness of the advertising, the price of the product, the reputation of the company, the service given during and after purchase, the location of retail stores and much more'.

Boyd and Mason (1999) conducted a study in the United States of consumer evaluations of innovative consumer electronic products (e.g. digital cameras, HDTVs, video-phones). Based on Rogers' (1995) innovation decision processes, the authors propose a two-stage conceptual model of consumers' decision-making. The intention-forming stage of their model proposes three antecedents of consumer adoption: characteristics of the individual (e.g. personal needs), communications (e.g. advertising, publicity and distribution) and attractiveness of the product category (influenced by product, firm and market-related attributes). The second stage captures the brand-choice process.

Boyd and Mason found extrabrand attributes to be antecedents of attractiveness to customers, with the most significant attributes being (in order of importance): cost, key benefits (these two were the most important by far with a large gap down to) firm's reputation, availability of accessories/service, and poor reviews. These are followed by attributes like product complexity, relative advantage, favourable reviews, level of standardization, and alternatives. Then follows a variety of features like firms time in business, future enhancements, future price trends, and number of model choices. Least important were advertising expenditures and size of the firm (last). The authors confirm Bell, Keeney and Little's (1975) finding of the importance of attractiveness as an antecedent of adoption and the implications of attractiveness for firms:

> Managers can improve an innovation's chances of success by influencing the level of the factors they can change and knowing the implications of the factors they cannot change (Boyd and Mason 1999).

An indication that theory relating to adoption of innovations may be applicable to website design is partly through recognition of the characteristics of sites as extremely dependent on the 'look and feel' and partly through recognition of the changing nature of innovations over their life:

> A shortcoming of much research studying innovations is that the innovation is assumed to remain unchanged over its life. It is more realistic to recognise that the innovation changes over time and that, as a result, consumer perceptions and evaluations can also change (Boyd and Mason 1999).

The limited academic literature specifically dealing with Internet retailing is generally consistent with adoption studies, but with the addition of some web-based features. Ease of use and usability are recognized as being important factors in successful Internet-based commerce. Studies conducted by Nielsen (1999) with over 400 website users suggest usability may be the most important factor. The principles of web design might also be based on knowledge acquired in the development of successful user interfaces for information systems (IS). Recognizing the overwhelming amounts of information available to firms, suppliers and consumers, IS development experience suggests that unless the design of an IS user interface is inviting, encouraging, timely, informative and user friendly then it is unlikely to be successful (Taylor 1986). Many websites appear to have been developed without regard to such lessons.

A particular focus of academic research has been on Internet issues in the financial industry. Financial services differ from other industries in that products are mostly intangible; product and service are difficult to separate; and many products are used infrequently. Also, there is a paucity of research and guidance in understanding the drivers of overall customer satisfaction at the firm level. Satisfaction with product offerings is a primary driver of overall customer satisfaction. Quality of customer service (financial statements and IT-enabled services) is also important but of varying impact across different customer categories. Functionality had the largest impact on satisfaction with quality of automated service delivery:

> Customers seem to be receptive to the potential benefits offered by an electronic system, such as speed and convenience, provided it addressed all their trading needs and was easy to use (Krishnan et al. 1998).

Roth and Jackson (1995) suggest that the quality of customer interface in the banking industry positively influences service quality (where the interface includes all interactions between customer and service provider).

Notwithstanding the specific nature of the banking industry and its products, these significant factors for customer satisfaction appear to be more widely applicable to Internet retailing as a whole. Antecedents of general consumer satisfaction have been proposed. These include: logistical support (distribution and after-sales service), technological characteristics (upgraded technical platforms to provide improved customer service), information characteristics (accuracy, reliability and security of information), homepage presentation (high quality text, graphics, image and animation) and product characteristics (product features and pricing). A positive correlation was found between increased levels in the antecedents and increased customer satisfaction (Ho and Wu 1999).

A survey of 220 Texan consumers identified convenience as the most important factor in Internet shopping. Their reactions to factors were categorized as: product perceptions (price, variety, product details, richer descriptions), shopping experience (effort, compatibility), customer service (responsiveness), and perceived consumer risk (customer testimonials, security, ordering/payment alternatives) (Jarvenpaa and Todd 1997).

In addition to consumer and website factors, organization-level characteristics have been identified. A study of 137 Internet sites selling women's apparel identified the following attributes that influence store traffic and sales: merchandise, service (FAQs, policies), product promotion, convenience (help functions, navigation, shopping cart, ease of use), checkout processes (carts, ease of use, full transaction pricing), as well as store navigation (product search function, site maps, consistent navigation, no broken links) (Lohse and Spiller 1998).

Another perspective on organizational-level innovation is from management theory. O'Neill, Pouder and Buchholtz (1998) reviewed the field to identify factors influencing firm-level adoption of strategies. Their conclusions suggest three major influences: the environment, characteristics of the organization, and characteristics of the strategy itself. High levels of environmental uncertainty, high levels of efficiency (reflecting competent management of technology), receptivity to change and learning as well as simple strategies that do not challenge established norms are all conducive to organizational innovation. The converse also applies.

Behavioural studies present an alternate view of consumer adoption factors. Concerned that much research into Internet shopping has been based on the demographic characteristics of consumers, Ramaswami, Strader and Brett (1998) took a consumer behaviour perspective explaining Internet usage for shopping using an ability–motivation–opportunity (AMO) framework. The authors suggest that the major determinants of online buying are: consumers' ability to purchase online, their motivation to do so, and their opportunity to access online markets. Their surveys of 413 randomly selected but predominantly 'middle-market' households in Nashville, Tennessee, indicate:

- Consumer use of online channels for financial products is related to their current use of such channels for financial information search.
- Consumer willingness to use online channels is not related to their current use of such channels.
- None of the demographic variables was related to online usage for buying financial products.

This last result is important because most industry studies in this area have shown the propensity to explain online usage primarily in terms of demographic factors.

Managerial implications of the Ramaswami study are that while there may be little scope for direct service provider influence in ability and opportunity (the A and O of the AMO model), motivation may be influenced by monetary savings (e.g. lower prices and total costs of transactions). These findings also suggest that consumers who use the online channel for gathering financial information are more likely to be online buyers of financial products. The wider implication of this is that companies wanting to do business on the Internet would benefit from increased provision of current information on the firm and its products so as to attract potential customers seeking online information.

In summary, website-related factors may be categorised into:

- company information (e.g. corporate reputation, firm size, age) and market information (market size, competitive structure, distribution channels and an aggregation of individual company attributes);
- product information (key benefits, variety, complexity, switching costs, relative advantage, perceived risk);
- processing capability (functionality, convenience, security, costs, motivation);
- customer services (service levels, quality, distribution and after-sales service, responsiveness, privacy, motivation); and
- ease of use (website presentation, usability, technological platform, quality of customer interface, site navigation, customer abilities, differences between customers).

WEBSITE EVALUATIONS

Numerous practitioner reports and reviews have been published purporting to identify the 'good' (and 'bad') features of websites. Site reviews range from idiosyncratic opinion pieces [e.g. Alsop's (1999) 'How I judge if a website deserves my business' or Kirsner's (1999) 'The dirty dozen') to international surveys of successful sites and features (typically by major consultancy and service providers, e.g. Andersen Consulting 1999, LSE/Novell 1999).

To be effective, however, a framework for reviews and evaluations of websites should not be narrowly focused on individual perspectives and current implementations but should be more broadly based. Prior experience in relevant areas, often incorporated into theoretical models, may be considered, e.g. IS as a discipline has a considerable body of knowledge on successful development of user interfaces. Similarly, the necessity for integration of IS systems and their alignment with corporate strategies has been (belatedly) acknowledged as being applicable also to Internet activities (Blodgett 1999).

Since the Internet is anticipated to transform markets and industries (Benjamin and Wigand 1995) it is inevitable that a level of uncertainty exists in retailers as to how it can be utilized. Uncertainties include a lack of knowledge of Internet technologies, resources required to develop and implement websites, specific business objectives, website features and the value of website features to the business.

It is not only small firms that are experiencing these uncertainties:

> Once upon a time, Fortune 500 companies might have gotten onto the Net by [creating] a Web site with basic company information, logos, and (if it was really sophisticated) links to up-to-date stock information. These days, that just won't do. Even though its still unclear what really works, [traditional firms] are trying all kinds of ambitious ventures. This is a sign of healthy experimentation. Absent a rule book for e-business, companies are taking steps to uncover strategies that will work for them. (Brown and Chen 1999).

Regardless of their lack of knowledge it is seen to be of critical importance that firms establish an Internet presence to develop their experience, to explore business opportunities and to reduce their exposure to Internet competitors (Gallaugher 1999). This approach is not so different:

> So how are people going to survive in the so-called New Economy? Well, ultimately the same way they survived in the old economy—through relentless innovation, unparalleled service, and an attitude of genuine helpfulness, but delivered in new ways (Hamel and Sampler 1998).

Once retailers decide to venture into cyberspace their first task is to define the level of functionality to be supported on the website. The range of Internet retailing functions may be separated into two groups: information provision and full transaction processing (i.e. information, invitation to treat, offer, acceptance, payment, delivery (online or off-line) and customer support). Most websites are limited to provision of information.

Consumer requirements of websites are separate but equally important. As with industry, the Internet is expected to have a major impact on consumers.

> The Web will fundamentally change customer's expectations about convenience, speed, comparability, price and service (Hamel and Sampler 1998).

Farquhar, Langmann and Balfour (1998) identify 20 generic consumer requirements, including: ease of use, consistency in user interfaces, privacy, security, cost transparency, reliability, error tolerance, design for different types of customers, order confirmation, and system status information. Conversely, many studies identify problems with websites that may alienate customers, including: out-of-date information, inconsistent navigation, slow loading pages, virtual company with no physical address or contact numbers, poor responsiveness to e-mail or other queries, poor transaction processing, poor ease of use, and lack of integration of Internet services with the rest of the organization.

The LSE/Novell study analysed the websites of 100 of the largest international companies on seven dimensions and then compared them across industry sectors. This LSE/Novell study was released at a critical time in the development of the evaluation framework and its influence on the framework's design is acknowledged.

PROPOSED EVALUATION FRAMEWORK

On the basis of theoretical research and industry experience, a framework for the evaluation of websites has been proposed. The orientation of the framework is from a customer's perspective, investigating the extent, scope and comprehensiveness of the website. The framework aims to measure the extent to which a company has adopted 'all' business opportunities offered by the Internet.

Some website evaluations (e.g. Gomez scorecards) differentiate between different types of customers (e.g. one-stop shopper, first-time shopper, last-minute shopper of gifts) and rate the site from these differing perspectives. This level of analysis is difficult to usefully sustain across the broad range of industries and sectors for which the CEC framework was designed. Therefore, in developing the CEC framework we have chosen not to use this meta-classification, but have included the capability of a site to support different types of customers, by making this one of the sub-categories in the framework. The evaluation framework consists of six categories (as shown in Table 8.1) each with five elements.

The issue of evaluation scoring raises two points of contention. First, some website evaluation schemes have been published with aggregate scores for websites expressed as, for example, 76.45 or 75.55. Doubtless these scores are based on mathematically sound calculations. However, they imply a level of precision in website evaluation that in our opinion is insupportable. The purpose of such an expression of accuracy is, inevitably, to rank and compare sites but the difference between scores of 76.45, 76.25 or 75.55 may be of little practical relevance. An evaluation would support a more meaningful comparison of sites by analysing the ratings for different categories and elements, e.g. product information, customer service, etc.

Secondly, in producing an aggregated score one needs to decide on the weighting of the individual categories. For example, should product information be given different weighting in a scoring system to transaction processing or ease of use? If so, by how much should it be different? Discussions about differing levels of importance for categories tend to distract attention from the main issue, namely the provision of a complete service to website customers. For this reason it was intended that the CEC framework should primarily focus on producing scores for each category since this would be more useful in identifying areas for improvement.

The CEC framework scores each element in a category on a binary basis. If the element is present 'at an acceptable level', then one point is awarded. If the element is not present, then no point is awarded. For example, a point is only awarded if the element 'product information' is present, the details are up to date, and they are comprehensive. This approach is consistent with the objective to assist improvement in website design and implementation. It also supports a less subjective level of scoring.

The binary approach to scoring, in some instances, may be too coarse. Indeed, in some situations it may be difficult to decide just how much is needed to assess that a website is fulfilling the requirement for say 'image-building'. A more elaborate assessment could have been developed using, for example, a five-point Lickert scale for each element. This scale could have been graded through the provision of concrete examples illustrating just what would be

Table 8.1 *Categories in the framework*

Company information and functions. This category reflects the necessity for organizations using the web to establish a corporate entity in the Internet market. The elements—corporate ownership, areas of products and operation and the contact or distributor details—directly support this issue. Firms that recognize that a website is more than a sales and product promotion vehicle frequently include other corporate functions, including news/press releases and recruitment opportunities. Each element in this category has the additional requirement for the details to be up to date and comprehensive.

Product/service information and promotion. This deals with information about the range of products and services currently provided (including pricing and promotions) and new products or services planned for the future. Each element in this category has the additional requirement for the details to be up to date and comprehensive.

Transaction processing. This provides an assessment of the extent to which the site supports full transaction processing (i.e. buying and selling online) with everything needed online for completing as large a part of the transaction as possible. This category is also intended to encourage information-only sites to move to online servicing and for transaction processing sites to offer a more complete service.

Customer services. This identifies the range of facilities available from a full service website, including sales assistance; corporate policies on issues such as security and returns; procedures if problems arise; customized services such as loyalty schemes; and a broader approach to customer service by including links to other relevant sites.

Ease of use. This assesses the usability of the site, which could be considered the least objective of the evaluation categories. The binary scoring approach and the double evaluation process (see below) are designed to reduce the level of subjectivity. The site information issue reflects the level of difficulty encountered by the evaluators in finding information (particularly for the first two categories) and having it presented promptly. The last three elements assess the site's usability for a range of different users of the site.

Innovation in services and technology. This reflects the necessity for firms to find new ways of doing business in an environment of rapidly changing customer expectations. The focus of the category is not innovation for innovation's sake but how innovation is applied to enhance customer relationships. It is expected that the examples for each element will vary over time, perhaps on an annual basis, but the focus on enhanced customer service in the area of order processing, feedback, community building or customization of the website will remain. The final element, novel and effective use of multi-media, is intended to further encourage exploration of new and effective ways to use these technologies.

necessary to achieve point 2 on the scale. Unfortunately, such a level of detail is inconsistent with the objective of having an evaluation framework capable of repeated application over time, e.g. every year. The more specific the measure, the greater the necessity to revise the scoring methods prior to each evaluation cycle. Each variation in an evaluation framework reduces the reliability of the instrument.

Reliability of the framework with all its 30 elements was established through a prior agreement on benchmarks by a limited number of assessors and through multiple independent assessments of sites in a pilot study.

TESTING THE EVALUATION FRAMEWORK

The framework was tested by its application to the websites of 100 diverse firms. A commercial company, Log-in,[2] provided the website addresses of the 10 largest Danish companies within each of 10 major business sectors. The firms ranged in size from medium to large. Diversity in size and industrial sector was sought to test the capability of the framework and to reflect a variety of levels of website activity across different companies and industries. The 10 sectors are shown in Table 8.2. It is important to note that there are no 'pure-players' among the 100 companies. They were selected in order to illustrate the extent to which traditional companies are meeting the requirements of the e-economy.

The website of each firm was evaluated independently by two assessors and the results compared. Where differences arose, the two assessors had to agree on a joint assessment. As expected, some differences occurred in the assessors' evaluation of the same website—sometimes even up to several points in each category. Despite the binary evaluation system and the attempt to make the criteria as objective as possible, the final evaluation of a site will always depend on a certain level of subjectivity. For example, how much information is needed to get a point for 'More detailed product/service specifications', do online sales of merchandising count as 'online purchasing' (it was decided that only the online sale of a company's core product would), and when is the use of multimedia 'novel and effective'? It cannot be contested that the overall objectivity of the research is improved by adding more independent reviews of the same website, since the number of reviewers increases the number of perceptions of what a website needs in order to earn its points. However, our pilot study also showed that even though a more detailed description of the benchmarks needed to earn a point for each element potentially would enhance the probability of arriving at the same assessment, such a detailed description would at the same time compromise its flexibility across business sectors.

As a result of the evaluation the definition of two of the elements were slightly modified. The third revision as a result of the test was more significant. It was originally intended that the CEC framework would not produce an aggregated total score. However, when advised of their rating senior management in firms strongly expressed a preference for a means of easily comparing firms, sectors and the market as a whole. Accordingly, even though the framework was not initially designed to develop such an aggregated score, it could be used for that purpose so long as one bears in mind that there is a certain element of adding apples and oranges. The scoring was extended to provide a CEC scale. This rating is determined by aggregating the scores for each category giving five marks for each of six categories for a maximum of 30. This value is then transformed to a rating measured as a percentage of an optimal score, e.g. the financial/insurance sector

---

[2] Log-in is a company specializing in business communication on the Internet that presents an annual 'Golden @ award' to the best Danish website.

Table 8.2 *Results of testing the framework*

Industry sectors	Company information/5	Product/ services information/5	Transactions/5	Customer services/5	Ease of use/5	Innovation/5	Total/30	CEC scale © (%)
Automobile	3.2	3.8	0.0	1.9	3.5	0.7	13.1	44
Consumer goods	3.8	1.4	0.3	0.7	3.1	1.0	10.3	34
Financial/insurance	4.9	3.1	2.5	2.5	3.0	1.6	17.6	59
Food industries	3.3	1.0	0.0	0.9	3.2	0.6	9.0	30
Newspapers and magazines	3.1	2.8	0.8	1.6	2.9	1.2	12.4	41
Pharmaceutical	3.6	1.6	1.4	2.1	2.6	0.4	11.7	39
Retailing	2.7	2.0	1.5	2.1	2.7	0.6	11.6	39
Supplies	4.2	2.6	0.5	1.9	2.6	0.8	12.6	42
Telephones/data	4.5	3.3	0.7	1.8	3.0	0.9	14.2	47
Transports and logistics	4.0	3.3	1.2	2.5	3.2	1.1	15.3	51
Average	**3.7**	**2.5**	**0.9**	**1.8**	**3.0**	**0.9**	**12.8**	**43**

has a total of 17.6 and a score on the CEC scale © of 59% (17.6/30 * 100% = 58.67% rounded up to a whole number = 59%). No weighting is applied to any category.

Examination of the data in Table 8.2 shows substantial differences between sectors. It is important to note that firm size within sector was the criterion for a firm's inclusion in the project. The firms were not evaluated as representing 'best in class'. The purpose of the framework is as a tool to enable self-assessment of a firm's website.

While companies across the board seem to have little problem in fulfilling almost four out of five requirements for 'company info', and are meeting 'ease of use' requirements, they were by and large very poor on 'conducting transactions' and on what we have termed 'innovation'. The customer service category also had considerable scope for improvement.

In summary one might say that the vast majority of the websites are at the level of the 'business card,' providing some information on the company and its products/services, with a reasonable ease of use. However, very few are providing possibilities for conducting transactions and providing services on the net. Paradoxically, while e-commerce represents innovation and structural change, what is being offered is not very innovative—just minor variations on limited themes.

A closer study of the differences between the business sectors reveals that financial institutions are noticeably ahead of the other sectors. This is to be expected. The possibility for reducing transaction costs in financial institutions makes it especially attractive for banks to move their business from the branch to the Internet. The business sector with the lowest evaluation for its websites is the food sector. Apparently, information on processed food products is not considered to be of interest to consumers and customer service seems to be poor!

Finally and surprisingly, the consumer goods category (including companies like Ecco shoos, Bang & Olufsen, Brantex, and Ikea) received a low evaluation. Only one site (Lego) was rated in the top 15 of all companies. Since the Internet provides a business opportunity to engage more closely with customers it had been expected that the consumer goods sector would have been more active in this arena. Analysis of the data in Table 8.2 as a whole indicates that the framework's scoring scheme could reflect the diversity of sites and industries. Industry sectors that could be expected to have performed well (e.g. financial/insurance) did score well. The converse, industries that could be expected to score poorly, was not as clearly illustrated. The anticipated emphasis in websites on information provision was confirmed in the scoring with the highest averages in categories being in information and ease of use.

One key aspect of the framework was not tested, namely the capability for firms to assess changes in their website over time. The framework's post-test review considered this aspect to have been satisfactorily addressed but recognized that testing of web-site changes remained outstanding. The CEC website evaluation framework overview, and detail, are shown in Tables 8.3 and 8.4, respectively.

Table 8.3 Website evaluation framework overview

Company info + functions	Product/service information and promotion	Buy/sell transactions	Customer services	Ease of use	Innovation in services and technology
1 Ownership, company mission statement, financial performance	General product/service groups	Supports online purchasing	Sales assistance, e.g. FAQs	Layout and design (easy to read, consistent, not distracting, intuitively easy to understand, creative design)	Enhanced customer services —orders (e.g. decision support, order status, delivery tracking, flexibility in delivery after order, etc.)
2 Operations and product/service area	More detailed product/service specifications, e.g. quality, performance, etc.	Security (policy/lock on transaction data not just on credit cards)	Customer policies, e.g. privacy, warranties, purchase exchanges	Site map or search engine	Enhanced customer services —feedback (e.g. customer input/reviews)
3 Image building, e.g. company news, press releases (must be less than one month old)	Pricing	Simplified processes, e.g. shopping trolley, two-click purchasing	After-sales procedures (e.g. returns/repair/exchange/help/problem FAQs)	Navigation, intuitively easy to find what one needs from the website. Site information easily and promptly accessible	Enhanced customer services —communities (development of communities with users, e.g. games, quizzes, prizes but also chat)
4 Contact details or list of distributors	Promotions on special products/services	Oneline payment + capacity for alternative payments	Customized services, e.g. loyalty scheme, membership or user 'clubs'	Site readily located by major search engines	Enhanced customer services —website customization for individual customers
5 Richer set of company-relevant functions, e.g. recruitment, etc.	Details on new or future products/services	Details of full transaction cost + order confirmation + delivery time/mode + trust assurance	Broader approach to customer services, e.g. links to other relevant sites	Caters for a range of users, e.g. graphics/text, novice/experienced, business/consumer, and different languages	Novel and effective use of multi-media (e.g. audio/video/animations)

Table 8.4   Evaluation detail

Company info + functions	Product/service information and promotion	Buy/sell transactions	Customer services	Ease of use	Innovation in services and technology
1 Ownership, company mission statement, financial performance Award: 1 for 2/3[a,b]	General product/service groups Award: 1 or 0[a]	Supports online purchasing Award: 1 or 0	Sales assistance, e.g. FAQs Award: 1 or 0	Layout and design (easy to read, consistent, not distracting) Award: 1 or 0	Enhanced customer services—orders (e.g. decision support, order status, delivery tracking, flexibility in delivery after order, etc.) Award: 1 if one is there
2 Operations + product/service areas Award: 1 for 2/2[a]	More detailed product specifications, e.g. quality performance, etc. Award: 1 or 0[a]	Security (policy/lock on transaction data, not just on credit cards) Award: 1 or 0	Customer policies, e.g. privacy, warranties, purchases exchanges Award: 1 for 2/3	Site map or search engine Award: 1 for 1/2	Enhanced customer services—feedback (e.g. customer input/reviews) Award: 1 or 0
3 Image building, e.g. company news, press releases (must be less than on month old) Award: 1 for 1/2	Pricing Award: 1 or 0[a]	Simplified processes, e.g. shopping trolley, two-click purchasing Award: 1 to 0	After-sales procedures (e.g. returns/repair/exchange/help/problem FAQs) Award: 1 or 0	Navigation easy. Site information easily and promptly accessible Award: 1 or 0	Enhanced customer services—communities (development of communities with users, e.g. games, quizzes, prizes but also chat) Award: 1 or 0
4 Contact details or list of distributors Award: 1 for 1/2	Promotions on special products/services Award: 1 or 0[a]	Online payment + capacity for alternative payments Award: 1 for 2/2	Customized services, e.g. loyalty scheme, memberships or user 'clubs' Award: 1 or 0	Website should be found readily by at least one of the major search engines Award: 1 or 0	Enhanced customer services—website customization for individual customers Award: 1 or 0
5 Richer set of company-relevant functions, e.g. recruitment, etc. Award: 1 to 0[a]	Details on new or future products/services Award: 1 or 0[a]	Details of full transaction costs + order confirmation + delivery time/mode + trust assurance Award: 1 for 3/4	Broader approach to customer services, e.g. links to other relevant sites Award: 1 or 0	Caters for a range of users, e.g. graphics/text, novice/experienced, business/consumer, different languages Award: 1 for at least two	Novel and effective use of multi-media (e.g. audio/video/animations) Award: 1 or 0

[a] Details must be comprehensive + timely or no points awarded.
[b] Award one point if two of the three criteria are present.

APPLICATION OF THE EVALUATION FRAMEWORK TO INTERNET RETAILING

Since the framework was tested and revised through an inter-sectoral analysis of Danish companies it may not have been internationally applicable nor appropriate for Internet retailing. Also, it may have presented difficulties for the accurate and reliable identification of significant distinguishing characteristics in websites. However, the study demonstrated that the framework was internationally applicable to Internet retailers and no difficulty was identified in its application. Some of the outcomes of the evaluations shown in Table 8.5 are striking and warrant further explanation.

The range of scores from 33% to 87% shows the capacity of the framework to distinguish between the websites of firms with different implementations.

The firms selected are successful e-tailers, often with award winning sites, so how could some scores be so much lower than others? Interestingly, both top and bottom scoring websites were award winners. The explanations are more to do with the award systems than websites. The basis for an award may be on grounds that have not been reflected in the CEC framework. For example, the LSE/Novell (2000) evaluation looked at the websites of the fastest growing international firms, or in its 1999 evaluation LSE/Novell assessed the websites of the largest international firms. Other awards are based on online traffic (e.g. hits or page impressions) or general popularity polls. Since the CEC framework is designed to reflect capability across the complete transaction experience rather than one specific facet of the organization, none of these factors (growth rates, market capitalization, traffic or popularity) is assessed. An alternative explanation is that websites are particularly dynamic and while they may have been a leading site once they may be no longer at this level.

The CEC scales in general are also generally low when compared with the 'ideal' website. This may indicate that there remains considerable scope for improvement in current websites.

Product information and ease of use are the best rated categories and innovation (not unexpectedly) is worst. While relentless innovation is often identified as a key to success in e-business, action is another matter. Unfortunately, company information is poorly dealt with by firms. The message that customers want to know who they are dealing with does not seem to have permeated sufficiently through corporate offices. The ratings for customer services are also disappointing since one distinctive characteristic of the Internet is its capability to provide mass customization and improved levels of customer service.

Startups are consistently rated higher than the Internet ventures of traditional firms. Only two of the top ten sites are from traditional firms. This underlines the significance of the path to Internet expansion by traditional firms through the acquisition of a well-performing startup. The 2000–2001 equity market decline facilitated this process and several of the more successful startups on this table were taken over in 2001.

Table 8.5 *International comparison of website characteristics*

Firms	Company information/5	Product/ services information/5	Transactions/5	Customer services/5	Ease of use/5	Innovation/5	Total/30	CEC- scale © (%)
Australia								
Chaos Music	3	5	5	5	4	2	24	80
Dymocks	2	5	5	5	5	0	22	73
E-Store	3	4	5	2	3	0	17	57
GreenGrocer	2	5	5	4	4	0	20	67
WINEPLANET	5	5	4	4	5	3	26	87
Denmark								
Haburi	3	5	5	3	4	2	22	73
Ravenholm	4	4	3	0	5	1	17	57
Rejsefeber	1	5	5	3	5	2	21	70
Saxo	3	5	3	3	5	0	19	63
Velux	2	2	3	1	1	1	10	33
Greece								
Beauty Shop	2	5	5	4	4	0	20	67
Best-e (oops.gr)	4	3	4	4	3	2	20	67
E-shop	2	4	5	3	3	2	19	63
Papasotiriou	2	3	5	3	4	1	18	60
Plaisio	5	4	5	3	4	0	21	70
Hong Kong, China								
Ambassador	3	4	3	3	4	0	17	57
DVDShelf	4	4	5	5	5	2	25	83
Ebabyasia	4	4	5	4	5	4	26	87
Net Fun	4	4	2	4	3	2	19	63
Wing On	3	4	5	5	5	2	24	80

Table 8.5 Continued

Firms	Company information/5	Product/ services information/5	Transactions/5	Customer services/5	Ease of use/5	Innovation/5	Total/30	CEC-scale © (%)
United Kingdom								
Action	2	5	4	5	4	1	21	70
Blackwell	2	3	4	4	4	0	17	57
easyJet	4	5	3	2	3	0	17	57
Lobster	1	2	4	3	4	1	15	50
Thomas Cook	3	5	3	2	4	0	17	57
United States								
HomeToDo	2	2	0	3	3	0	10	33
Outpost	4	4	4	4	4	1	21	70
UPS Tools	4	3	0	3	4	1	15	50
UPS Returns/ buy.com	2	2	5	5	4	1	19	63
Webvan	3	4	4	4	5	1	21	70
Averages	**3.0**	**4.0**	**3.9**	**3.4**	**4.0**	**1.1**	**19.4**	**65**

Although four of the countries are among the international leaders in e-commerce, no comparative analysis at a national level has been attempted. The firms and websites were selected as being successful examples of Internet retailers in their country likely to be of interest to an international audience. Since selection was not based on being the best in each country (whatever that means and however it could be determined) it would be unreasonable to draw international conclusions from the table. In some cases, particularly the United States with Amazon and eBay, well publicized examples of Internet retailers were deliberately not selected to avoid possible reader fatigue.

CONCLUSIONS ON WEBSITE EVALUATIONS

This section describes the development and application of the CEC website evaluation framework that enables a firm to compare the functions and features in its current website with those of an 'ideal' site. Grounded in theory and best practice, the framework's contribution is as a means of assistance to practitioners who recognize the critical importance of the Internet but remain unsure how best to implement a corporate Internet strategy. Uncertainty in senior management about how to proceed with e-commerce has been reported as a major inhibitor to its more widespread implementation. The CEC evaluation framework may be used as a means to clearly identify for senior management the implementation options and issues that lead to the development of a consumer-oriented, innovative Internet service.

The framework was tested by application to 100 companies in 10 diverse industries. Analysis of the outcomes suggests that successful implementation of Internet-based B2C e-commerce is due not to the characteristics of industry or product but to decisions made within firms. The industry sector rating closest to 'ideal' has digital products and services and so may have been expected to rate highly. However, the second highest rating industry has physical products. Industries rating poorly included retailing, consumer goods and food industries even though there are world-class examples in these industries of Internet-based commerce.

The CEC website evaluation framework was then applied to Internet retailing websites in Greece, Hong Kong (China), the six countries in this study, Australia, Denmark, the United Kingdom and the United States. Websites in the three English-language countries were evaluated by the same team to ensure consistency of application. Consistency was also maintained in the Danish evaluations since the Danish and Australian teams jointly developed the framework and collaborated to ensure alignment in its subsequent application. Consistency in the Greek and Hong Kong evaluations was established through detailed discussion of the framework and review of outcomes.

Questions about reliability arise when evaluation frameworks and customer surveys (see below) are translated. Uncertainties are introduced due to the difficulty in ensuring that the translation accurately and completely captures the question or benchmark item. This does not negate the potential utility of the translated instrument for a country; it only introduces uncertainty about the reliability of the application and the validity of the results *when compared across countries.*

Finally, our objective in developing the CEC website evaluation framework was to obtain a means of assessing web implementations that would be transparent, logical, consistent and sufficiently robust to be reliably applied across a broad range of websites over time. It worked well for this international study and we can see no reason why practitioners and researchers should not, with due acknowledgement, apply the framework for their own benefit.

Acknowledgements. We are grateful to Anders Mørup-Petersen for his contributions to a preliminary version of this part of the chapter, and to Jade Kahn, Ann Ohlson and the team at the Centre for Electronic Commerce in Copenhagen Business School for their assistance in applying the evaluation framework.

Part 2:
Internet Customer Surveys
STEVE ELLIOT

INTRODUCTION

Industry has embraced the concept of e-commerce but remains uncertain as to how to address the challenges it presents. Partly this is due to the unknown impact that e-commerce will have on business and partly because the problems confronting industry require the organizations and the industry to transform themselves in order to implement this new way of conducting business. Much attention is focused internally on organizational structure, systems and the skills required to implement e-commerce. In the midst of this upheaval it is easy for firms to lose sight of a most important focus, their customers.

This part deals with the development of an Internet questionnaire used to clearly identify a firm's customer profile, its experiences with the Internet in general and with the firm's site in particular, and the outcomes of customers' experiences. While the focus in this part is firmly on the consumer, the research project as a whole emphasizes the critical necessity for managers and researchers to view e-business ventures holistically. It is not losing sight of the customer that is the problem, but rather failing to recognize that all aspects of the initiative must be considered equally.

RESEARCH DESIGN

As can be seen in more detail in the research chapter (Chapter 9), the scope of this project is to:

1. establish key factors that promote or inhibit the adoption of implementations of Internet-based retail e-commerce;

2. identify relationships between the factors and their relative importance; and
3. establish key factors that promote or inhibit similar implementations in different countries.

Factors were examined at the level of the innovation; each major participant in the transaction process (i.e. providers and consumers); and the market or environment. This section deals with consumers' perspectives, particularly relating to research questions 3, 4 and 5. The key research questions were:

1. Which organizational factors influenced the provision of Internet-based retail services and how?
2. What characteristics of the implementations influenced the proposal and acceptance of that innovation?
3. What drives their consumers to, or inhibits them from, performing Internet-based transactions?
4. Which environmental factors influence adoption and how?
5. What international/cultural differences arise from the study, and can generalizations be made from these?

Research question 3 is addressed through application of a standard Internet instrument to a self-selected sample of purchasers from (not visitors to) each website. A selected sample approach is proposed as it most appropriately examines the research unit of analysis—the Internet implementation in a specific firm. An alternative approach of mass market surveying in order to obtain a sample for the particular firms being examined was discounted due to the excessive costs, uncertainties and time delays in volume sampling.

The standard instrument was based on preliminary research. The instrument was developed specifically to be applied in an international environment and was piloted with peers and experienced/novice Internet users. Issues of validity and reliability of instrument as well as consistency of application were explicitly addressed. Research questions 4 and 5 were addressed by analysis of the instrument developed for question 3.

The survey instrument was prepared centrally and distributed to the local researchers in each country for implementation. The local researchers were responsible for the selection of samples; application of the instruments; data-entry of responses; analysis of the outcomes (in English): and forwarding of all details to the Project Manager for comparative analysis.

A multi-phase approach was adopted that comprised:

*   A wide-ranging literature review
*   A review of other surveys in relevant areas
*   Identification of factors from the research and industry literature, determination of factor classes and approach. These sources were used to support theoretical and empirical construct validity
*   Design and development of the instrument

- Piloting and review to assess the content validity and reliability of the instrument
- Design and development of an Internet-based implementation of the questions
- Piloting, testing and review of the Internet-based instrument
- Development of a database
- Implementation
- Development of automated analysis and reporting tools
- Review and write-up (based on Judd, Smith and Kidder 1991 and Leedy 1997)

FACTORS INFLUENCING CONSUMER ADOPTION OF ONLINE RETAILING

An overlap clearly exists between the categories and elements of the successful retail websites identified above and those categories and elements that motivate consumers to accept and utilize online purchasing. Much of the research is similarly overlapping. For convenience, a summary of consumer-related factors identified in research raised in the previous section relating to website factors is provided. Factors that have been previously found to influence consumer decision-making to undertake online purchasing are grouped below. Note that different studies produce different findings that may appear to be contradictory. The level of uncertainty existing about reasons for consumer adoption was an important reason for this holistic study of success factors in Internet retailing.

- Demographics, including characteristics of the individual such as age, gender, education, income (confirmatory—Boyd and Mason 1999, Forrester 2000a; disconfirmatory—Ramaswami, Strader and Brett 1998)
- Ability—consumer's ability to purchase online (Ramaswami, Strader and Brett 1998)
- Motivation—perceptions of benefits attracting consumers to purchase online that outweigh reasons for not purchasing online (Bell, Keeney and Little 1975, Jarvenpaa and Todd 1997, Ramaswami, Strader and Brett 1998, Boyd and Mason 1999, Krishnan et al. 1999)
- Opportunity—access to a PC, the Internet and online markets (Ramaswami, Strader and Brett 1998)
- Experience with the Internet, through e-mail, chat sessions, information searches, including ease of use and usability (Taylor 1986, Roth and Jackson 1995, Lohse and Spiller 1998, Ramaswami, Strader and Brett 1998, Krishnan et al. 1999, Nielsen 1999)
- Experience with Internet transactions—familiarity and satisfaction with the process helps consumers overcome concerns (Roth and Jackson 1995, Ramaswami, Strader and Brett 1998, Ho and Wu 1999)

Existing surveys also were examined. At times it seemed that every business journal or magazine contained another survey, so the challenge was to identify the more relevant and potentially applicable surveys to help address construct validity. Worthy of particular mention are two influential survey series in the United States and Australia.

The pioneering Internet survey series in the United States is from the Graphics, Visualization & Usability (GVU) Center at Georgia Institute of Technology. Commencing in 1994 the 10 surveys in the series to date are developing a detailed view of web adoption and usage, most recently with a focus on e-commerce activities. Questions vary from survey to survey, but most recently include such potential factors as demographics, geographic locations, prior experience, consumer intentions, products and services purchased, skill levels and technologies used. The GVU Surveys employ non-probabilistic sampling, i.e. respondents self-select in response to solicitations on website banner ads and in popular non-Internet media. Nine cash prizes of US$100 were randomly awarded to the tens of thousands of respondents.

In Australia (where this survey was developed, pre-tested and initially piloted), the largest and most comprehensive Internet usage survey is undertaken by www.consult P/L. This survey has more than 60 comprehensive questions covering such potential factors as demographics, Internet sites visited, shopping experiences, and related Internet use, e.g. online banking and stock trading. The survey is advertised by ISP banner advertisements on 200 local websites, e-mails, magazines, newspapers and radio. In return for completing the survey, some 240 prizes (including a latest model PC) were awarded randomly to 55 000 self-selected respondents.

Numerous reputable commercial surveys were also reviewed to ensure that a wide range of issues relevant to this study were considered, e.g. Forrester Research's survey with 80 000 US respondents (Forrester Research 2000a). This survey series monitors the impact of income, age, education, technology optimism, ethnic background and level of accessibility on Internet usage, as well as the sources of motivation and the nature of online purchases.

INSTRUMENT DEVELOPMENT

On the basis of theoretical research and industry experience, a framework for the instrument was proposed. This included five main areas of questions:

1. Consumer profile—tell us something about you (eight questions, e.g. age, gender)
2. Internet purchase profile (five questions, e.g. How many times have you previously purchased over the Internet?)
3. Internet purchases from this site (four questions e.g. How did you come to this site?)
4. Experiences (five questions, e.g. What was the most important factor in deciding to make a purchase from this site?)

5.   Outcomes (six questions, e.g. How satisfied are you with using this site for purchases?)

The full survey is shown at the end of this chapter. The order of questions was an issue. There was some discussion about placing demographic questions first or last. We decided to place them first so we could see who was completing the surveys or not. In the event it was not important as the vast majority of respondents answered all questions. The number of questions was deliberately kept small to reduce the incidence of respondent fatigue.

The questions were based on theory of adoption of innovations, issues specific to Internet retailing (e.g. mass surveys that suggest a standard demographic of male, educated, wealthy) and a cross-check of other surveys to ensure that significant issues were not overlooked. Some issues were ignored. For example, in the major www user survey series from Georgia Tech (GVU WWW User Surveys 1994–1998) there are questions on the respondent's ethnicity that were not included as national adoption issues were of interest but potential racial adoption issues were outside the scope of this study. Some related questions were included that were relevant to the research scope but were possibly of more interest to the service provider (e.g. How could our website be improved?) to assist in attracting participation.

The issue of the form of presentation of the instrument should be discussed. An Internet survey was selected since this was the medium of the study and appeared to reinforce the research objectives. Alternatives (e.g. focus groups, telephone surveys) were considered and excluded due to the cost and difficulty in having consistency in an international study since few if any market research firms were active in all of the countries of interest (which would raise concerns about validity and reliability).

Selected sampling versus broad community surveys were considered. This raised the issue of the importance of dealing with research questions requiring in-depth examination of specific success stories in Internet retailing as opposed to general population surveys that had already been recognized as being inadequate for determining success factors in Internet retailing. Self-selected, non-probabilistic sampling based on responses to a survey invitation located on the retailers' websites raised the issue of independence. The survey was clearly presented as an independent international university-based survey. Confidentiality and privacy were assured with amalgamated results returned to the firm but no individual responses identifiable. There is no direct evidence but we believe this was a factor in consumer acceptance.

The questions were deliberately presented in a format that reduced the appearance of large numbers of questions through use of pull-down menus for selection. Most responses were captured through frequency counts but free form text entry boxes were included to capture unanticipated issues or opinions in this exploratory research.

PILOTING

The instrument was developed specifically to be applied in an international environment and once the questionnaire had been developed, two forms of pretesting and piloting were undertaken: to review the content validity and reliability of the actual questions and then to assess the Internet-based instrument. Piloting occurred informally and formally with colleagues in Australia and at the Centre for Electronic Commerce at Copenhagen Business School and with a variety of experienced and novice Internet users. Issues of validity and reliability of the Internet instrument as well as consistency of application were explicitly addressed. Minor revisions in questions and their order were made.

IMPLEMENTATION

Instructions and aids to international teams were prepared. The reasons for the consumer survey and its importance to the overall study were provided for each project team. Instructions to firms on placement and technology overhead for each firm (minimal) were provided. The importance of presenting surveys only to customers who have purchased from the site immediately after they have purchased was emphasized. This was a factor that persuaded at least one firm to participate as it had previously commissioned a market research firm to survey visitors to its site and had been dissatisfied with the number of spurious and questionable responses. The rationale for the customer surveys that was provided to firms was as follows:

1. Contents. This survey has been developed and is being applied internationally to identify the most significant current issues in Internet retailing —types of customers, their use of the Internet and their experiences with the particular firm's website.
2. Survey targets. Only customers who have purchased from a participating firm's website can complete the survey. The results are specific to the firm, i.e. the results are not from thousands of web surfers worldwide but from the firm's own customers.
3. Anonymity. Responses are anonymous since they are held on an independent university server. This encourages customers to respond where they may be reluctant to do so for a company survey.
4. No obligation for customers. The request to complete the survey is as a polite inquiry (Would you like to give us some feedback?) after the purchase is complete. Customers decide to do so or not.
5. Survey completion time for the 28 questions will be variable. (However, with approximately 900 survey responses there was not a single complaint about the time taken to complete.)

6. Completion rates varied. Sites that advise us of their sales transaction rates while the survey is in operation indicate the survey completion rate is between 12% and 30% of customers completing purchases. Location of the feedback request is an important issue. We monitor the rate of submissions and if we notice a problem we advise the project team. One firm located the request at the bottom of the page which required customers to scroll down before they found it. Once we notified them of the problem they located it more prominently near the receipt number and the surveys were completed within a couple of days. No firm found it necessary to provide an incentive for customers to complete surveys. The incidence rate of mischievous responses is almost zero.
7. Numbers of surveys. We seek 100 responses from each site.
8. Overhead for the firm. There is no technical overhead as the surveys are loaded onto a database at the university. Privacy for customers and confidentiality are assured. Placing a feedback request on a web page takes about 5 minutes.
9. Details of the survey responses and analysis are returned to the firm but all responses are anonymous.
10. Value to participants. Firms participating in the project gain benefits from: international recognition of their status as a leading Internet retailer in their country; research into their activities that provides the opportunity to reflect on their own experiences; new insights that arise during interaction with the researchers; feedback (e.g. website evaluation and customer surveys) to the company from the process; and the capability directly to compare their activities with other leading firms nationally and internationally.

The issues raised are presented as circulated. One point warrants further explanation: the number of responses. We sought 100 responses from each site. Firms in three countries declined to cooperate with the request to locate an independent customer survey on their website. A frequently expressed concern was that the firms did not wish to alienate their customers. Perhaps the lack of a financial incentive or award for respondents was also a deterrent. The other 15 companies did agree but for a variety of reasons [e.g. seasonal products out of season, hardware or software failures (theirs or ours), too busy to install the link (this took about 5 minutes of their webmaster's time) and changes in management policy] many of these firms could not produce a minimum number of surveys.

Ultimately, only eight firms in two countries (Australia and Denmark) produced usable surveys. The minimum accepted for reporting was 39, the maximum was 250 with an average of 113 surveys per company. A total of 901 surveys were received. In other countries some indication of customer perspectives was obtained from internal company polling or from external polls that dealt with the specific firm.

A minor variation in the questionnaire was made for one site. This firm had a URL with .com rather than .com.au and also international clientele so we

National profile

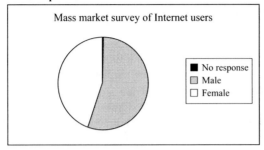

Online bookseller

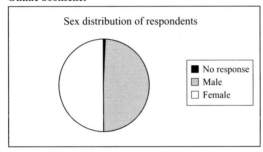

Online grocer

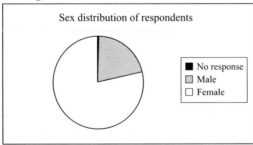

Online wine retailer

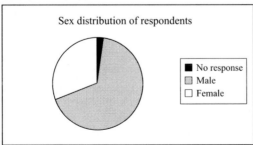

Figure 8.1 *Contrasting customer demographics*

needed to ask what country the customer was located in to identify different environmental issues.

Data collected were processed from Lotus Notes Internet forms into an Access database and then through Excel macros into a Word document for return to the companies. Manual analysis of free-form responses was performed by the research leader. The companies received graphs, frequencies, tables of responses to free form questions and cross question analyses. The difficulty in maintaining university server access at 24/7 levels for an extended period while surveys were being collected in different countries should be mentioned. Several hardware failures were experienced including one period of four weeks off the air (fortunately no surveys were active at this time).

The wealth of information gathered and the significance of particular factors revealed go to confirm the importance of a multi-methodology approach for information gathering in exploratory research. The free form text box showed that for one hapless customer the single most important factor in deciding to purchase groceries online was succinctly stated as: 'hunger—broken leg'. This simple response opens up a whole new line of research related to the convenience of online retailing for those who are temporarily or permanently housebound.

Of direct significance to business managers is the difference between the generic profile for Internet purchasers and that for a specific business. Figure 8.1 compares the gender profile for three firms with the national Internet user profile of 55% male. This simple variation from national norms illustrates an imperative for would-be successful Internet firms: know your customers.

CONCLUSIONS

This part describes the development and implementation of an internet customer questionnaire that provides consumer perspectives on 'what works' in Internet retailing. Based on theory and practice, the broad customer survey contributes by addressing uncertainties about what factors consumers find important in deciding to utilize online purchasing. Uncertainties arise due to the narrow focus of many studies that examine particular issues and, paradoxically, the breadth of mass-market surveys that reduce the complexities of individual consumers and Internet applications to averages.

An integral component of this research project is to examine each implementation holistically with environmental, organizational, innovation and consumer perspectives. Unfortunately, many firms that were keenly interested in the outcomes of this holistic study were concerned about potential strategic conflicts that may arise from independent surveys of their customers. While this is disappointing, the commercial sensitivity of the results of the survey must be acknowledged. The survey resulted in 901 responses from eight companies.

Analysis of the outcomes suggests that implementations of Internet-based B2C e-commerce that are based on a view of the customer that equates to an average demographic with average concerns about issues are destined for trouble. Many successful firms had customer demographic profiles that were contrary to the average Internet user profile. Also contrary to the concerns raised by the media, issues of security and privacy were not consumers' major concern. More details on the survey findings are shown in Chapter 9.

Finally, our objective in developing the internet customer questionnaire was to obtain a means of identifying consumer issues for specific firms in their implementations of e-commerce. The survey worked well for this international study and we can see no reason why practitioners and researchers should not, with due acknowledgement, apply it for their own benefit.

Acknowledgements. Shane Stephens' contributions to the Internet survey layout, database and the reporting are gratefully acknowledged. The project could not have been completed without his assistance. Thanks also to the many colleagues who reviewed the questionnaire design and its implementation and volunteered to 'test-drive' the prototypes.

Internet Customer Questionnaire

Consumer profile—Please tell us something about you:

C1. Age:
<1>   less than 18 years
<2>   18 to 20 years
<3>   21 to 30 years
<4>   31 to 45 years
<5>   46 to 60 years
<6>   more than 61 years of age

C2. Are you a male or a female?
<1>   Male
<2>   Female

C3. What is your main occupation?
<1>   student
<2>   manual worker
<3>   office worker
<4>   professional
<5>   home duties
<6>   unemployed
<7>   retired

C4. What is the highest level of education you have achieved?
<1>   did not complete high school
<2>   completed high school
<3>   completed trade qualifications
<4>   completed university

C5. Where do you live?
<1>   in a major city
<2>   in a city
<3>   in a town or village
<4>   in the country

C6. What is your approximate income compared with the national average income?
<1>   lower than national average income
<2>   average
<3>   above average
<4>   more than twice the national average

C7. How often do you access the Internet?
<1>   every day
<2>   at least three times each week
<3>   at least once each week
<4>   at least once each month
<5>   less than once each month

C8. Do you mostly access the Internet from?
<1>   home
<2>   friend's home
<3>   school, college or university
<4>   your work place
<5>   public building, e.g. library
<6>   commercial service, e.g. Internet cafe

Internet purchase profile

P1.   How many times have you previously purchased over the Internet?
   < 1 >   never
   < 2 >   1 time
   < 3 >   2–5 times
   < 4 >   6–10 times
   < 5 >   more than 11 times

P2.   When was the first time you purchased over the Internet?
   < 1 >   now
   < 2 >   this week
   < 3 >   this month
   < 4 >   in last year
   < 5 >   more than 1 year ago

P3.   Prior to this purchase, when was the last time you purchased over the Internet?
   < 1 >   this week
   < 2 >   this month
   < 3 >   in last year
   < 4 >   more than 1 year ago
   < 5 >   never

P4.   What types of products or services have you purchased over the Internet?
   [tick as many as you have purchased]
   < 1 >   computer products
   < 2 >   books
   < 3 >   travel
   < 4 >   music
   < 5 >   groceries
   < 6 >   flowers
   < 7 >   clothes
   < 8 >   tickets
   < 9 >   building products
   < 10 >   toys/gifts
   < 11 >   banking
   < 12 >   financial services/insurance
   < 13 >   others [please specify:]

P5.   Are your purchases over the Internet for?
   < 1 >   your own use
   < 2 >   for your work
   < 3 >   both

Internet purchases from this site

S1.   How did you come to this site?
   < 1 >   search engine
   < 2 >   someone told me
   < 3 >   prior knowledge of company
   < 4 >   advertisement on another website
   < 5 >   link from another website
   < 6 >   this is the website my firm uses for these types of purchases

S2.   How many times did you visit this site before you decided to purchase?
    < 1 >   1 time
    < 2 >   2–3 times
    < 3 >   4–9 times
    < 4 >   more than 10 times

S3.   What was your intention when you visited this site?
    < 1 >   general interest in browsing
    < 2 >   comparing prices
    < 3 >   purchase a specific product
    < 4 >   purchase a product but not sure which one

S4.   How many days from your first visit to the first purchase at this site?
    < 1 >   same day
    < 2 >   2 -5 days
    < 3 >   6–10 days
    < 4 >   more than 11 days

S5.   How many times have you previously purchased from this site?
    < 1 >   never
    < 2 >   1 time
    < 3 >   2–5 times
    < 4 >   6–10 times
    < 5 >   more than 11 times

Experiences

E1.   What was the single most important factor in deciding to make a purchase from this site?
    < 1 >   convenience—being able to buy at any time of day
    < 2 >   range of products
    < 3 >   availability of products
    < 4 >   price
    < 5 >   total cost of purchase
    < 6 >   ease of use of the site
    < 7 >   level of service provided
    < 8 >   provisions for security and privacy
    < 9 >   trusted name of the firm
    < 10 >   other [please specify:]

E2.   What was the second most important factor in deciding to make a purchase from this site?
    < 1 >   convenience—being able to buy at any time of day
    < 2 >   range of products
    < 3 >   availability of products
    < 4 >   price
    < 5 >   total cost of purchase
    < 6 >   ease of use of the site
    < 7 >   level of service provided
    < 8 >   provisions for security and privacy
    < 9 >   trusted name of the firm
    < 10 >   other [please specify:]
    < 11 >   no other factors

E3.   What was the greatest barrier or obstacle you had to overcome to make this purchase?
   < 1 >   finding the site
   < 2 >   finding your way around the site
   < 3 >   completing the purchase procedures
   < 4 >   concern about security/privacy
   < 5 >   uncertainty about products/services
   < 6 >   uncertainty about total cost of purchase
   < 7 >   concern about delivery
   < 8 >   other [please specify:]

E4.   What was the next largest barrier or obstacle you had to overcome to make this purchase?
   < 1 >   finding the site
   < 2 >   finding your way around the site
   < 3 >   completing the purchase procedures
   < 4 >   concern about security/privacy
   < 5 >   uncertainty about products/services
   < 6 >   uncertainty about total cost of purchase
   < 7 >   concern about delivery
   < 8 >   other [please specify:]
   < 9 >   no other barriers or obstacles

E5.   How easy was it to make a purchase from this site?
   < 1 >   very easy
   < 2 >   easy
   < 3 >   neither easy nor difficult
   < 4 >   difficult
   < 5 >   very difficult

Outcomes

O1.   How satisfied are you with using the Internet for purchases?
   < 1 >   very satisfied
   < 2 >   satisfied
   < 3 >   neither
   < 4 >   dissatisfied
   < 5 >   very dissatisfied

O2.   How satisfied are you with using this site for purchases?
   < 1 >   very satisfied
   < 2 >   satisfied
   < 3 >   neither
   < 4 >   dissatisfied
   < 5 >   very dissatisfied

O3.   Would you purchase similar products or services from this site in future?
   < 1 >   definitely
   < 2 >   possibly
   < 3 >   probably not
   < 4 >   definitely not

O4.   Would you purchase similar products or services from other sites in future?
   < 1 >   definitely
   < 2 >   possibly
   < 3 >   probably not
   < 4 >   definitely not

Q5. Would you recommend this site to a friend who wanted to purchase?
     < 1 >   definitely
     < 2 >   possibly
     < 3 >   probably not
     < 4 >   definitely not

Q6. Do you have any suggestions on how the site could be improved?
[Check as many as you consider necessary]
     < 1 >   range of products
     < 3 >   availability of products
     < 4 >   price
     < 5 >   total cost of purchase
     < 6 >   ease of use of the site
     < 7 >   levels of service provided
     < 8 >   provisions for security and privacy
     < 9 >   finding the site
     < 10 >   finding your way around the site
     < 11 >   completing the purchase procedures
     < 12 >   more details about products/services
     < 13 >   more details about delivery
     < 14 >   speed of loading
     < 15 >   other [please specify:]

Thank you for taking the time to help us improve our services.
© S.R. Elliot, UNSW, Sydney Australia, 1999.

9
Research Model and Theoretical Implications

STEVE ELLIOT

OVERVIEW

This chapter is concerned with establishing the research framework for this international study of success factors in Internet retailing. The focus of the research model is adoption decision-making at a strategic, organizational level in the context of e-business. The chapter is in four sections. The first section reviews current theory in adoption and proposes a general research model for e-commerce. The second section outlines the specific research scope and questions for the international study. The third looks at findings of the study and the fourth considers the theoretical implications of the research findings.

ADOPTION MODELS FOR BUSINESS-TO-CONSUMER ELECTRONIC COMMERCE

Introduction

Electronic commerce (e-commerce) presents the potential opportunity for strikingly different business ventures as well as radically new ways to run existing businesses. New technologies may be harnessed by organizations to help them to achieve competitive advantage; to transform relationships with customers, suppliers and business partners; to empower global business; and to redesign their organizations. In short, e-commerce may result in fundamental changes to current business practice.

Industry has embraced the concept of e-commerce. A worldwide survey of 500 large companies in 1999 found that 90% of top managers considered the Internet will transform or have a big impact on the global marketplace by 2001 (*Economist* 1999, reporting surveys by *The Economist*, Booz, Allen and Hamilton, and Forrester Research). The business-to-consumer (B2C) component of e-commerce is significant with expectations of its growth from 1998 to 2003 to be US$8 billion–US$108 billion. Despite industry enthusiasm for e-commerce, a major impediment to its widespread adoption is seen to be uncertainty within organizations as to how to address the challenges it presents.

Uncertainty about how and why organizations and individuals decide to adopt (or not to adopt) e-commerce exists also at a theoretical level. In June 1998, the noted author and researcher P.G.W. Keen acknowledged that while considerable research had been conducted into particular aspects of e-commerce, researchers remain unsure about many of the broader issues. Keen called for more holistic approaches to the research of particular implementations of e-commerce and to consider innovations in more detail.

In response, this section seeks to review current theory relating to technology adoption and to identify a more holistic and integrated approach to research in B2C e-commerce. A conceptual research framework aimed at supporting a more integrated research approach to the field is proposed that may better assist organizations faced with the multi-faceted challenges relating to the adoption of e-commerce.

Terminology

An innovation is 'an idea, practice or object that is perceived as new by an individual or other unit of adoption' (Rogers 1995). Organizational innovation is broadly seen to be 'the adoption of an idea or behavior that is new to the organization adopting it' (Daft 1978). An innovator is a first or early adopter of an innovation within an organizational population. Diffusion of an innovation is 'the pattern of its adoption by an organizational population over time' (Swanson, 1994). Innovation at a strategic level is that which assists a firm realize the goals and objectives of the organization as a whole.

Research Scope for E-Commerce

E-commerce provides a rich field for academic research. Studies have included: technology platforms; business challenges; management approaches; emergent organizational forms; and social and macro-economic impacts (Avgerou, Siemer and Bjørn-Andersen 1999). As an example of the current diversity of research, the 2001 IFIP TC8 Electronic Commerce Conference (Elliot, Andersen, Swatman and Reich 2001) presented investigations into business models and strategies, legislation, management of implementations in health care and logistics, knowledge management and decision-making, technologies, organizational impacts, social impacts and constructs (e.g. trust).

This level of variety, representative of research in the field, indicates both diversity and the degree of fragmentation. The danger of misinterpretation of a phenomenon by researchers undertaking narrow investigations into e-commerce has been highlighted by Keen (1998). The diversity of research interests could be seen as reflecting a level of confusion and lack of coherence in business that has occurred as a result of the rapid growth of e-commerce (Whinston et al. 1996). An alternate view is that the research areas mirror the richness and importance of this phenomenon that is predicted to have a strategic and structural impact on business (Malone, Yates and Benjamin 1989, Information Infrastructure Task Force 1993, Benjamin and Wigand 1995).

An integrated model would appear inherently suitable for research of a complex domain that is, itself, described in terms of frameworks. Zwass (1998) recognizes three meta-levels as necessary to analyze the impact of e-commerce: systems— infrastructure (hardware, software and telecommunications required to deliver services over the web); essential services (including messaging and settlement of business transactions); and delivery of products and services to consumers and business partners.

In an attempt to document the different conceptual issues relating to e-commerce, five conceptual approaches have been identified: transaction cost theory; marketing; diffusion; information retrieval; and strategic networking (Wigand 1997).

1. Transaction costs represent the post-production costs of a firm, i.e. the costs of coordination between buyers and sellers. Transaction costs comprise search costs (searching for products, buyers and sellers), contracting costs (setting up and carrying out the contract), monitoring costs (ensuring the contract is carried out), and adaptation costs (ongoing maintenance through-out the life of the contract). Separate transaction costs may be allocated to manufacturers, wholesalers, retailers and consumers. The choice of transaction depends on several factors, including the interests of different participants to the transaction and the level of uncertainty in describing the transaction.

2. The marketing efforts of the firm. Marketing activities may be customer, product or profit oriented. The essential tasks are to: identify a target customer type; determine customer desires; design products and services to meet these desires; present products and services to customers; persuade customers to purchase; and identify future products, services and applica-tions.

3. The diffusion of innovations among members or a social system, over time. Wigand utilizes Rogers' (1995) approach that the rate of diffusion is deter-mined by the characteristics of the innovation (e.g. relative advantage, compatibility, complexity, trialability and observability).

4. Retrieval of information from systems. Recognizing the overwhelming amounts of information available to firms, suppliers and consumers,

Wigand suggests that unless the design of an information systems user interface is 'inviting, encouraging, timely, informative and user friendly' then it is unlikely to be successful.

5.   Lastly, strategic networking, which is defined as an organizational form that enables network member firms to gain or sustain competitive advantage over those outside the network by optimizing transaction costs. Wigand considers trust to be an important mechanism that lowers transaction costs.

Wigand's approaches focus on firms and do not consider a full range of customer issues in e-commerce; however, they are significant as an attempt to identify issues of importance for research into e-commerce. This chapter is concerned with examinations of e-commerce as an innovation. Particular focus is given to the strategic challenges to organizations, to management and to consumers arising from its adoption.

Innovation Theory

Research into information system (IS) innovation has been conducted at the individual, departmental and organizational levels. Innovations studied include: personal work stations; spreadsheets; information centers; information technology (IT) outsourcing; database management systems; automatic teller machines (ATMs); and electronic supermarket scanners. The focus in these studies has been predominantly on innovation by individuals within organizations. Much of the innovation literature is actually concerned with diffusion of the innovation throughout an organization rather than initial adoption into an organization, i.e. innovation at a strategic level. The literature dealing with the adoption of technological innovation includes two major areas: intention-based models (which focus on behavioral aspects of innovators) and innovation models (focusing on innovation characteristics and processes).

Extensive research has been conducted on the applicability of intention-based models of innovation, which are grounded in theories of social psychology. These models include the Theory of Reasoned Action (Ajzen and Fishbein 1980) and the Theory of Planned Behavior (Ajzen 1991). Of primary interest is the Technology Acceptance Model (TAM) (Davis, 1989). Simply stated, TAM contends that the sole determinant of use of technology is the intention of the user, which is based on perceptions of the ease of use of the technology, and of its usefulness. This model has been independently tested and commended for its parsimony and applicability. A major disadvantage is that TAM excludes the possibility of influence from institutional, social and personal control factors (King et al. 1994, Taylor and Todd 1995). The implications of these omissions are considered below. Kwon and Zmud's (1987) proposed Five Forces model of innovation and Scott-Morton's (1991) MIT90's framework both acknowledge the significance of environmental issues.

A major influence in the innovation literature is the work of E.M. Rogers. Rogers locates adoption factors in individual, organizational and environmental groupings and sees the capability to distinguish between innovations of critical necessity to identify why some innovations are successful and some are not. 'The usefulness of research on the attributes of innovations is mainly to predict their future rate of adoption and use.' Rogers (1995) suggests that the bulk of research conducted on innovations has been concerned with the identification of differences between adopter groups with comparatively little regard for differences in characteristics of innovations. He provides a typology of characteristics for use in evaluation of an innovation: relative advantage; compatibility; complexity; and trialability. All are considered influential in innovation and adoption.

Rogers' earlier focus was on individual employee (as opposed to organization-wide) adoption of innovations, but his 1995 work identifies the attributes of innovations, adoption processes and adoption decision approaches for organizations. Rogers contends that the driver of the processes is the necessity to solve business problems, and later stages in this model cannot be undertaken until the earlier stages have been settled (Rogers 1995, p. 391). He sees the crucial agenda-setting stage as requiring an extended period, often several years, and considers that 'Innovations are not initiated on the spur of the moment, nor by a single dramatic incident, nor by a single entrepreneur'. While Rogers does examine organizational characteristics such as attitude toward the individual leader, internal organizational characteristics and external characteristics of the organization, he does not address the influence of organizational issues such as adequacy of resources available, the nature and culture of the organization, and the qualities of the organization's leadership, other than attitude to change.

Rogers' work has been criticized for producing dimensions 'as universally relevant as possible' but which were so abstract that they may not be easily applied (Boyd and Mason 1999). In a separate study, Rogers' attributes, processes and approaches have been compared with implementations of smart-card-based e-commerce and, in general, found not to reflect the levels of complexity and diversity found in practice (Elliot and Loebbecke 2000). Rogers' attributes of innovations were unable to distinguish between different implementations of smart-card payment systems. His perceptions of compatibility and complexity as adoption issues may not be considered significant to an organization with the potential for strategic advantage from an innovation. Conversely, other individual adopters within the same innovation may ignore issues of strategic advantage altogether, e.g. consumers may consider only ease of use and utility.

The theory of the adoption of IS has been mostly concerned with intra-organizational adoption rather than at the inter-organizational level necessary for e-commerce. Traditionally, organizations have needed to concern themselves only with their own requirements for Information Systems. Increasingly, however, pressures from e-commerce necessitate that these intra-organizational systems are closely integrated between, and capable of operation across, several organizations. The implications of inter-organizational systems on the adoption and diffusion of IT are a substantial increase in complexity at planning, requirements definition, design, development and implementation stages. Pressures to conform to external requirements may result in a period of externally imposed radical change to current practice. Operationally, inter-organizational systems represent a completely new set of challenges for both technical and business staff.

While current adoption theory has focused on individual adoption decision-makers (and for a single innovation treated the adopter as a single entity), Elliot and Loebbecke suggest that in some instances, notably inter-organizational inno-vations, this may not be applicable. Within a single innovation, individuals with very different roles and objectives are involved and these individuals may be in conflict. This potential for conflict between adoption factors raises the importance of further empirical investigation of multi-organizational adoption.

Environmental issues are those external to the organization and innovation. Kwon and Zmud's (1987) paper explains that these issues may be national (e.g. relating to the market or local legal structures) or international (e.g. trade restrictions applying to certain products and countries or international regula-tions). Market-related issues include uncertainty, concentration and competition. Internet retail applications are often international in their effect, i.e. they are not restricted to local markets and purchasers may be attracted from other countries. The necessity for increased attention to contextual and cultural factors has been identified by several authors (e.g. Benbasat and Zmud 1999, Walsham and Sahay 1999, and Lyytinen and Damsgaard 2001).

Calls have been made for convergence of the major areas of adoption theory: innovation and intention. Moore and Benbasat (1996) developed a tool for the study of initial adoption of innovations by individuals in organizations. This tool integrated the intentions-based models and innovations literature, including the Theory of Reasoned Action and the perceived characteristics of innovations.

Management Models

Another perspective on organizational-level innovation is from management theory. O'Neill, Pouder and Buchholtz (1998) review the literature to identify factors influencing the firm-level adoption of strategies and then test the results. Their conclusions suggest three major influences: the environment, the character-istics of the organization, and the characteristics of the strategy itself. High levels of environmental uncertainty, high levels of efficiency (reflecting competent man-agement of technology), receptivity to change and learning and simple strategies that do not challenge established norms were all found to be conducive to organizational innovation. The converse is also seen to apply.

Management theory as a whole has been criticized for assuming equivalence in international markets (Rosenzweig 1994). Criticism of adoption theory for similar reasons would appear justified, since the two major theoretical influences, innova-tion models and intention-based models, largely ignore environmental issues.

The practical significance of these external or environmental factors can be noted from world events. In December 1999, the European Union Commission released a 10-point action plan to exploit the potential of the information society. Proposals included:

> recognition of the urgent need for a clearly defined legal framework, including the information a trader must give a customer, what advertising e-mails must say about the sender, discounts and other promotions as well as the limits on liability of intermediaries for unlawful material on their web sites. The draft directive aims to remove obstacles to the growth and competitiveness of e-commerce within the EU (Hargreaves, 1999).

Consumer Adoption Models

Adoption theory is mute in an area that appears to be of critical importance to e-commerce: the consumer (Keen 1998, Krishnan et al. 1999). The role of consumers in the adoption of B2C e-commerce appears significant from both the empirical and theoretical perspectives. The importance of consumers' attitudes to the successful adoption of e-commerce has been documented in several studies (e.g. Jarvenpaa and Todd 1997, Ho and Wu 1999) but has little incorporation into adoption theory.

Reference must be made to the discipline of marketing for consideration of consumer issues relating to the adoption of new technological products (Venkatesh and Brown, 2001). On the basis of a US study of consumer evaluations of innovative consumer electronic products (e.g. digital cameras, HDTV, videophone) Boyd and Mason (1999) propose a two-stage conceptual model of how consumers' evaluation of product category attractiveness affects adoption decision-making. The first stage of their model (intention forming) proposes three key antecedents of consumer adoption: characteristics of the individual (e.g. personal needs), communications (e.g. advertising, publicity and distribution) and attractiveness of the product category (influenced by product, firm and market-related attributes). These antecedents are referred to collectively as extra-brand attributes. The second stage captures the brand-choice process. These two stages relate to Rogers, (1995) decision and implementation stages of the innovation decision process. A key contribution is the importance of attractiveness as an antecedent of adoption and the implications of attractiveness for firms. 'Managers can improve an innovation's chances of success by influencing the level of the factors they can change and knowing the implications of the factors they cannot change.'

Consumers have been found to rely on categories of information when evaluating innovations: product information (specific implementations adapted from Rogers' abstract dimensions, e.g. key benefits, variety, complexity, switching costs, relative advantage, perceived risk); company information (e.g. corporate reputation, firm size, age) and market information (market size, competitive structure, distribution channels and an aggregation of individual firm attributes) (Moore 1995, Boyd and Mason 1999). Bell, Keeney and Little (1975) suggest that

> attraction may be a function of the seller's advertising expenditure and effectiveness, the price of his product, the reputation of the company; the service given during and after purchase, the location of retail stores and much more.

The Bell, Keeney and Little (1975), Moore (1995) and Boyd and Mason (1999) studies of consumer attributes also highlight product and innovation attributes (e.g. price/cost, key benefits, variety, complexity, switching costs, relative advantage, perceived risk); company information (e.g. corporate reputation, firm size, age) and market information (market size, competitive structure, distribution channels and an aggregation of individual firm attributes). Boyd and Mason (1999) also highlight a frequently overlooked issue of changing consumer perceptions in line with product development. Much research studying innovations assumes that innovations remain unchanged over their life. They suggest a more realistic approach recognizes that the innovations change over time and, as a result, consumer perceptions and evaluations can also be expected to change. Extrabrand attributes were found, in order of importance, to be: cost, key benefits (these two are most important by far, then a gap down to) a firm's reputation, availability of accessories and service, poor reviews, product complexity, relative advantage, favorable reviews, level of standardization, alternatives. Then come a variety of features: how long a firm has been in business, future enhancements, future price trends, number of model choices. Least important were advertising expenditures and size of firms (last).

Satisfaction with product offerings has been found to be a primary driver of overall customer satisfaction. Quality of customer service (financial statements and IT-enabled services) is also important but of varying impact across different customer categories. Functionality had the largest impact on satisfaction with quality of automated service delivery—'Customers seem to be receptive to the potential benefits offered by an electronic system, such as speed and convenience, provided it addressed all their trading needs and was easy to use' Krishnan et al. (1999) in confirmation of the Roth and Jackson (1995) earlier study. One danger in generalizing from studies is that products and services are not homogeneous. For example, financial services have been recognized to differ from other industries: products are mostly intangible; product and service are difficult to separate; and products are used infrequently (e.g. on maturity rather than daily).

An alternative approach to consumer adoption issues by Ramaswami, Strader and Brett (1998) applies the ability—motivation—opportunity (AMO) model to consumer behavior in e-commerce. The contention is that consumers' abilities to purchase online, their motivation to do so, and having a reasonable opportunity to access online markets, are determinants of actual online buying.

Integration

An examination of the literature was made in search of a more representative research framework. Two models that incorporate the significance of environmental issues were identified: Kwon and Zmud's (1987) proposed Five Forces model of innovation, and, of perhaps lesser direct relevance, Scott-Morton's (1991) MIT90's framework of forces supporting organizational transformation. Kwon and Zmud's model includes innovation, organizational, and environmental factors.

An attempt was made to integrate the disparate theoretical areas discussed above into something more representative of industry practice. The integrated structure is based on an extension of Kwon and Zmud's (1987) model. The extensions proposed are also intended to address identified shortcomings in the theoretical models: more detailed innovation characteristics; organizational and inter-organizational roles/functions; the environmental factors cultural and international; and consumer issues. An integrative adoption model for B2C e-commerce consisting of the factors shown in Table 9.1 is proposed. The purpose of this model is to provide a contextual reference for practitioners and researchers who find the focus of their work to be too narrowly on specific aspects of e-commerce (Figure 9.1).

Discussion

An objective of this study was to determine a theoretical framework for further research into B2C e-commerce. Three issues prompted this review. First, acknowledgment of a significant impediment to adoption of e-commerce as a result of organizational uncertainty about how properly to address its challenges. Secondly, widespread reluctance by individual consumers to participate in B2C e-commerce. Finally, a call for more holistic approaches to research of particular implementations of e-commerce.

In response, this section has reviewed current theory relating to the adoption of innovation to identify a more holistic and integrated approach to research in B2C e-commerce. A conceptual research framework is proposed that aims to support a more integrated research approach to the field and that may better assist organizations faced with the multi-faceted challenges relating to the adoption of e-commerce.

Conclusions regarding the utility of current adoption theory as applied to B2C e-commerce may be reached. Significant factors identified during the review do not appear to be adequately reflected in current theory. These factors include environmental, consumer, inter-organizational and international factors. Based on the structure of Kwon and Zmud's (1987) model, extensions have been proposed in an attempt to more closely reflect current practice in theoretical models of adoption. The outcome, an integrative adoption model for B2C e-commerce, draws from IS, management and marketing disciplines. This model is

Table 9.1   *Factors in an integrative adoption model for B2C e-commerce*

Environmental
- Market (uncertainty, competition, concentration)
- Inter-organizational imperatives
- Legal
- Cultural and international

(*Sources:* Kwon and Zmud 1987, King et al. 1994, Rosenzweig 1994, Rogers 1995, O'Neill, Pouder and Buchholtz 1998, Hargreaves 1999, Elliot and Loebbecke 2000)

Organizational
- Individual employee (education, tenure, etc.)
- Structural (specialization, formalization)
- Task (uncertainty, autonomy, variety, etc.)
- Roles/functions (inter-organizational)

(*Sources:* Rogers 1995, O'Neill, Pouder and Buchholtz 1998, Elliot and Loebbecke 2000)

Innovation
- Compatibility, complexity, relative advantage, trialability, observability, usefulness, ease of use
- Distinguishing characteristics/features and perceived costs/benefits for each

(*Sources:* Davis 1989, Mathieson 1991, King et al. 1994, Swanson 1994, Taylor and Todd 1995, O'Neill, Pouder and Buchholtz 1998, Boyd and Mason 1999, Krishnan et al. 1999, Elliot and Loebbecke 2000)

[*Note:* There is a need to recognize the dangers in generalizing about innovations, i.e. innovative products and services are not homogeneous (Krishnan et al. 1999).]

Consumer
Benefits and costs to consumers are obvious determinants of success in retailing. Prior studies indicate that purchasers considered the major benefits of Internet shopping to include:
- Increased customization, e.g. 'capability to treat customers as individuals'.
- Convenience in purchasing 'anytime, from anywhere, to anywhere'.
- Increased range of products.
- Responsiveness in product delivery, e.g. 'instantaneous distribution of digital products and services'
- Cost savings through lower prices

Major consumer concerns leading to unsatisfactory experiences include
- Security
- Ease of use
- Poor levels of service
- Costs
- Product delivered did not meet expectations (Jarvenpaa and Todd 1997, Moreno and McCormack 1998, Krantz 1998, Elliot and Fowell 2000, Ernst and Young 2001)
- Consumers' abilities to purchase online, their motivation to do so, and the opportunity to access on-line markets

Note that innovations change over time and, as a result, consumer perceptions and evaluations can also be expected to change.

(*Sources:* Bell, Keeney and Little 1975, Moore 1995, Roth and Jackson 1995, Jarvenpaa and Todd 1996, Farquhar, Langmann and Balfour 1998, Elliot and Fowell 1999, Ho and Wu 1999, Keen 1998, Ramaswami, Strader and Brett 1998, Boyd and Mason 1999, Krishnan et al. 1999)

Figure 9.1   *Initial integrative adoption model for B2C e-commerce*

intended as a framework to guide further exploration of the adoption of B2C e-commerce.

Acknowledgment. A preliminary version of this material was presented at the Australian Conference on Information Systems 1998.

RESEARCH MODEL FOR THE INTERNATIONAL STUDY

The international study of success factors for Internet retailing is based on the general research model, the integrative adoption model for B2C e-commerce, proposed above. Background details, including theoretical and empirical justification for the research area, are examined in the previous section and are not repeated here. This section provides the focus for this specific study.

Project Aim, Scope and Key Research Questions

The aim of this project was to address the documented uncertainties of business and consumers with Internet retailing by examining factors leading to the success of leading examples of B2C e-commerce in each of six economies. The countries represent a broad range of environments to identify issues that may be specific to a particular market. The firms have been selected as significant examples of Internet retailing in industry sectors recognized as leaders in the use of the Internet, including travel, books, music CDs, technology sales, gifts, groceries and general merchandise (e.g. by the GVA, Forrester and www.consult research series). The scope of this project was to:

- establish key factors that promote or inhibit the adoption of implementations of Internet-based retail e-commerce;
- identify relationships between the factors and their relative importance; and

- establish key factors that promote or inhibit similar implementations in different countries.

Factors were examined at the level of: the innovation; each major participant in the transaction process (i.e. providers and consumers); and the market or environment. All components of the transaction cycle were examined, from information provision to payment and exchange. To the fullest extent consistent with the research aims, diversity was sought in the implementations. The key research questions were:

1. Which organizational factors influenced the provision of Internet-based retail services and how?
2. What characteristics of the implementations influenced proposal and acceptance of that innovation?
3. What drives their consumers to, or inhibits them from, performing Internet-based transactions?
4. Which environmental factors influence adoption and how?
5. What international/cultural differences arise from the study, and can generalizations be made from these?

Research Methodology

This project aims to extend current theoretical and empirical understanding of the drivers of and inhibitors to B2C e-commerce by producing generalizable findings of a very high level of quality as a result of rigorous research. This research is exploratory. The research questions are broadly based and require a multiple methodology research approach to address the separate areas of research: provider, innovation, consumer and environmental factors. The unit of analysis is the implementation by firms of an Internet retailing facility. A major strength of this project is that factors influencing the four perspectives on each implementation were assessed in a single, consistent and integrated study.

Provider Issues

This area addresses research questions 1, 4 and 5:

1. Which organizational factors influenced the provision of Internet-based retail services and how?
4. Which environmental factors influence adoption and how?
5. What international/cultural differences arise from the study, and can generalizations be made from these?

These research questions acknowledge the commercial imperatives required to implement a new retail channel. It is recognized that providers' actions may also influence consumer requirements. A series of mini case studies would address these research questions in five implementations in each country. Sites were selected as being significant implementations of Internet retailing in each country.

A qualitative approach was proposed. In order to capture business, technology and implementation experiences from the service-providing organization, target subjects included: the CEO; the organization's sponsor for the Internet retail project; the Internet retail project manager; and the manager with responsibility for IT. The interview topics were prepared and piloted in Australia and distributed to the local researchers in each country for review. The researcher in each participating country was responsible for: the selection of sites; the application of the instruments (in a mini case study of each firm); data-entry of responses; analysis of the outcomes (in English); and preparation of the case studies. The qualitative approach was seen as essential to enable a detailed understanding of differences in organizations and operating environments and to identify any anomalies in the different implementations. Research questions 4 and 5 were addressed by analysis of the research outcomes for questions 1 and 3.

Innovation Issues

This area addresses research question 2:

2. What characteristics of the innovations examined influence acceptance of that innovative implementation?

The IS innovations literature (e.g. Rogers 1995, Kwon and Zmud 1987, Moore and Benbasat 1996, Elliot 1998, and Elliot and Loebbecke 2000) identify elements of IS innovations which may influence its adoption or rejection. These include: compatibility, complexity, relative advantage, characteristics/features, and perceived costs/benefits. A qualitative research approach was considered necessary to address this question. Target subjects included: the CEO, those responsible for the Internet retail project and consumers. A separate website evaluation framework was developed and utilized to support comparative analysis of each firm's Internet site (see also Chapter 8 and Elliot, Mørup-Petersen and Bjørn-Andersen 2000).

Consumer Issues

This area addresses research questions 3, 4 and 5:

3. What drives their consumers to, or inhibits them from, performing Internet-based transactions?
4. Which environmental factors influence adoption and how?
5. What international/cultural differences arise from the study, and how can we generalize from these?

Research question 3 was addressed through primary and secondary research. A selected sample approach was proposed for primary research since the cost, uncertainty and time delays in volume sampling were considered excessive. With a potentially low incidence of customers for particular retailers in the general population, a completely random approach could require a very large sample size to obtain a minimum number of relevant responses. The research approach was to apply a standard instrument to a sample of consumers of products/services for each service provider in the study. The assistance of the provider in facilitating access to its customers was sought. The target sample size was a minimum of 100 consumers with purchase experience from each firm's Internet site, although this was varied in some instances due to events. Specific input was to be obtained also from consumer and regulatory bodies (as available). Research questions 4 and 5 were addressed by analysis of the research outcomes for questions 1, 2 and 3. As may be seen in Chapter 8, the survey instrument was prepared and piloted centrally. Issues of validity and reliability of instrument as well as consistency of application were explicitly addressed.

Environmental Issues

This area addresses research questions 4 and 5:

4.　Which environmental factors influence adoption and how?
5.　What international/cultural differences arise from the study, and how can we generalize from these?

Research questions 4 and 5 were addressed by analysis of the research outcomes for questions 1, 2 and 3. These research questions acknowledge the impact of environmental factors that may differ between countries. Factors may be local or generalizable. Analysis of environmental factors and comparisons between findings in each country were intended to support identification of significant environmental drivers and inhibitors.

Research Implementation

Implementation of this project took some time. The research design was developed from a research program initiated in 1995. The integrated research model was developed in 1997 and presented for comment at a conference in 1998. The model's positive reception and a seed funding grant from the KnowledgeLab in the United Kingdom enabled the project implementation to proceed. Refining the research model and research design and project planning took the balance of 1998 and early 1999.

Securing the participation and support of the project teams in each country occurred during 1999. In most countries this was relatively straightforward due to personal contacts. As with many e-commerce ventures, timing and environmental issues were paramount. It was extremely fortunate that the project was proposed at a time of such intense interest in the topic that the internationally regarded researchers were both willing and able to take an active role. This was particularly important since each team needed to secure its own funding.

The qualitative company questions and the consumer survey were developed and trialled centrally. The development of the web evaluation occurred during my sabbatical in 1999 at the Centre for Electronic Commerce at the Copenhagen Business School in Denmark. The consumer survey instrument was designed to be processed and analyzed with minimal manual intervention with responses captured in Lotus Notes form, stored in an Access database, graphed in Excel and presented to the organization in Word documents. The setup was challenging and the level of manual involvement proved to be greater than desirable. Attempts to translate the standard Internet-based survey into Greek experienced many software problems and were ultimately abandoned. A separate survey in Greek was developed. The instrument was presented on paper; the results were processed manually and then translated into English.

Many organizations were initially (and understandably) reluctant to place independent consumer surveys on their websites. In the United Kingdom, organizations expressed enthusiasm for the surveys but over a six month period none managed to implement the links on its website. In the United States, the firms resisted the surveys due to a variety of concerns: that customers were over-surveyed, or would be reluctant to complete a survey without reward, or since internal surveys had been completed recently, or to be effective the surveys would need to be placed on partner websites and that this would not be possible.

Although difficulties were experienced with implementing the customer surveys they remain a critical component of this research design. The importance of obtaining rich, multiple perspectives of the factors leading to success in organizational innovations cannot be over-stated. It is particularly important to gather customer feedback on customer-focused innovations.

RESEARCH FINDINGS OF THE INTERNATIONAL STUDY

This study sought answers to five research questions:

1. Which organizational factors influenced the provision of Internet-based retail services and how?
2. What characteristics of the implementations influenced proposal and acceptance of that innovation?
3. What drives their consumers to, or inhibits them from, performing Internet-based transactions?
4. Which environmental factors influence adoption and how?
5. What international/cultural differences arise from the study, and can generalizations be made from these?

The findings of the study are considered initially as a combined group of major factors across all categories and then looks at all factors identified within each of the research categories. Examples have been provided of the firms experiencing particular factors.

Factors Influencing Adoption

Major Drivers

Drivers have been categorized as initial and on-going. The order of listing is not significant. Initial drivers included:

1. The example of Internet pioneers. The experiences of Amazon and other Internet pioneers were both a threat that directly influenced a bookseller to establish an Internet operation and an inspiration resulting in other startups or initiatives (Dymocks, GreenGrocer, HomeToDo, Ravenholm, UPS, Velux).
2. A perceived business opportunity (E-Store, GreenGrocer, Haburi, HomeToDo, Outpost, UPS, Webvan, WINEPLANET) or other opportunity (Chaos).
3. A business threat to a traditional company (Dymocks).
4. The characteristics of the founders. The founders had experience and understanding of a business role for the Internet beyond novelty (Chaos, Dymocks, E-Store, GreenGrocer, Haburi and WINEPLANET). The founders' qualifications, entrepreneurial spirit and previous experience with business startups (HomeToDo, Outpost, Webvan). The founders' clear vision of a viable business venture (Haburi, Rejsefeber) or an organization's clear vision and purpose (UPS, Velux). The founders initially had a bright idea, not necessarily directly based on business (Chaos, Saxo).
5. The founders or executive managers had a willingness to explore the potential of the Internet for possible strategic advantage (all firms). Determination to succeed was a strong driver of the process (Haburi, Rejsefeber, Velux).
6. Cost reductions. UPS's initial functionality on its website was to enable customers to track parcels. The costs of providing customer service staff for this function had become excessive. The success of the tracking module encouraged the incremental extension of core business modules to customer sites using this new channel (UPS). One of Ravenholm's justifications was to reduce the costs of its printed catalogue.
7. Funding. The investment climate at the time readily provided initial funding (all except Haburi) or virtually unlimited funds for proposals of mammoth Internet-based projects from reputable entrepreneurs (Webvan). After the market crash produced reluctance in investors to support Internet ventures Haburi required extremely rigorous business planning and preparation to obtain initial funding.

In summary, the initial drivers were awareness, a clearly stated objective, the capabilities of the founders (or executives) and a benign investment climate. On-going factors that enabled successful implementation of the ventures were:

1. The acceptance by suppliers and customers (most startups, particularly Chaos, E-Store, Haburi, HomeToDo, Rejsefeber, Webvan, WINEPLANET).
2. The ability to secure or generate on-going funding (all firms).
3. The founders' determination to re-evaluate their failing business model or business situation and secure a more profitable approach even if radical measures were necessary (HomeToDo, Rejsefeber, Saxo). The willingness and capability to effectively modify business strategies and implementation based on feed-back from customers and market experience—unlike many dotcoms that failed due to a lack of market responsiveness to their initial offering (Chaos, GreenGrocer, Haburi, Outpost, Ravenholm, Rejsefeber, Saxo, UPS, Velux, WINEPLANET).
4. A corporate strategy in a traditional firm. UPS determined e-commerce to be the means of reinventing the firm from being just a delivery company. Note that a corporate strategy was not a factor for traditional firms Dymocks and the acquirer of Saxo.
5. The ability of the principals to recruit talented individuals with a solid track record of operational skill (HomeToDo).

Major Inhibitors

Initial barriers that needed to be overcome included (not in significant order):

1. Uncertainty about the Internet. The greatest obstacle to be overcome for the project to be a success was a lack of understanding of the Internet's viability (Outpost) or strategic implications at board level and with major business partners (Dymocks). Lack of knowledge about how the Internet could be used most effectively (all of the earlier adopters—Chaos, Dymocks, E-Store, GreenGrocer, Outpost, Ravenholm, Saxo, Velux, WINEPLANET).
2. Uncertainty about adequate levels of acceptance by suppliers and/or consumers of an innovative Internet-based business (Outpost in 1995, Haburi in 2000).
3. Lack of skills—particularly technical, design, development and operations skills (what worked on a website, how to do it, how best to maintain skills and capabilities when technologies were rapidly developing) (Chaos, Dymocks, E-Store, GreenGrocer, Outpost, Ravenholm, Saxo, Velux, WINEPLANET but not Haburi (established 2000)). Lack of business management skills in specific areas (Ravenholm, Saxo).
4. Lack of finance/funding (Chaos, Dymocks, Haburi, HomeToDo, Outpost, WINEPLANET).
5. No initial inhibitors or barriers (Webvan) or none identified (UPS).

In summary, the major initial inhibitors were uncertainty, lack of skills and lack of funding. Two firms (a startup and a traditional firm) reported no initial barriers to their implementations. These firms both had a clear vision and relevant prior experience (with technology-based business innovation and with web-based operations). Perhaps as a result of the levels of uncertainty and experimentation with what worked best, unpredicted outcomes frequently occurred that sometimes led to re-evaluation of the business approaches. Barriers that arose during implementation and critically threatened success were:

1. Resistance at various levels was experienced. This ranged from suppliers declining to provide products to purely online operations (Chaos) through supplier skepticism and reluctance to deliver directly to customers (E-Store, WINEPLANET) to a general lack of acceptance by suppliers and/or consumers (e.g. HomeToDo, Webvan). GreenGrocer had to enter into partnerships to obtain access to premium produce. Channel conflicts arose, directly between Dymocks and its franchisees and indirectly with WINEPLANET where traditional retailers reduced their stocks of a major wine producer's products after it had purchased 25% of the online firm. Concern about possible channel conflicts limited the scope of the Internet innovation for Velux and Saxo (initially).
2. Difficulties with implementation of business strategies. The firm rapidly outgrew its original target market (WINEPLANET). Greater difficulties than expected were encountered in the misalignment of customer and supplier expectations concerning home maintenance job size and task complexity (HomeToDo). Lack of clear linkage between corporate business strategies and the Internet venture (Velux).
3. Lack of breadth in business skills with too much focus on marketing and not being aware of the range of other business skills necessary to run an Internet business. This was especially the case for the two companies originally included in the Danish study (Gubi and Toycity) that both failed.
4. Operational issues. These included the necessity to bring core functions in-house due to unsatisfactory experiences (GreenGrocer) and the outsourcing of core functions to obtain best practice levels of performance (Chaos). Technical difficulties in developing, implementing and operating the website and systems (Haburi, Ravenholm, Rejsefeber, Saxo, Velux). Failure to maintain an on-going program of website and system innovation at some stage in the process (Ravenholm, Saxo). Lack of assigned responsibility for the Internet within the firm (Velux).
5. Attracting customers. Marketing costs required to attract customers exceeded expectations (most firms). Difficulty in attracting a critical mass of customers (Gubi and Toycity are prime examples but also Haburi, Saxo).
6. On-going funding for expansion and to cover operational losses (Webvan). Difficulty in obtaining a second round of financing (Gubi, Toycity, Haburi, Saxo).

7. Infrastructure. Early adopters of the Internet in Greece were plagued by frequent failures of the telecommunications networks (Plaisio).

Analysis of All Factors Across Categories

Having identified the major drivers and inhibitors, the next step was to overlay all factors across the research model (i.e. environmental issues, consumer, innovation and organization). This would help to identify the significance of multiple factors and assess the importance of a broader rather than narrower focus in investigating the organizational adoption of technology-based innovations.

Environmental Factors

It is easy to ignore the all-pervasive influence of environmental factors, but they can be as important to innovation as water is to fish. Without it they cannot survive. In many cases the founders of the Internet startups saw business opportunities without an awareness of the changeable economic climate that supported such ventures. It only became apparent after the stock market crashes in 2000/2001 and the downturn in the global economy that the benign environment for investment and investors' positive view of Internet ventures were both temporary occurrences. Only one of the firms examined (Haburi) sought startup funding after the crash but many sought a second round funding. All had difficulties. So too did many other firms that had previously assumed access to funding was a constant rather than being a variable factor. Their Internet ventures failed.

Environmental factors included:

1. Financial and other support for innovation (universally applicable). The investment climate provided easy access to initial funding (all ventures except Haburi) or virtually unlimited funds for proposals of mammoth Internet-based projects from reputable entrepreneurs (Webvan). After the market crash produced reluctance in investors to support Internet ventures, Haburi required extremely rigorous business planning and preparation to obtain initial funding. The existence of incubator/innovation environments assisted establishment and funding (Haburi, even after the market crash, Ravenholm, Velux, Rejsefeber, Saxo). The examples of Internet pioneers and government pronouncements supporting the Internet economy (Australia, Denmark, the United Kingdom, the United States) provided a positive environment for Internet ventures.

2. Uncertainty about the Internet and how it could be used most effectively (universally applicable to earlier adopters in a market)—particularly uncertainties about website developments, the skills required, the technologies and how to create and operate an Internet retail business (e.g. Chaos,

Dymocks, E-Store, GreenGrocer, Outpost, Ravenholm, Saxo, Velux, WINEPLANET).

3.   Consumer acceptance (universally applicable but to varying degrees). Some countries were earlier adopters of the Internet and had comparatively high levels of Internet usage (Australia, Denmark, the United Kingdom and the United States) while others were low (Greece and Hong Kong, China). Demographics differed between countries. For example, the United States had 75% of all Internet users aged below 30 years and was equally balanced between male and female. The United Kingdom had 50% Internet users aged less than 35 years and 42% female. Denmark had 53% of Internet users more than 35 years old with only 38% female. Australia had 62% of users over 30 years and 45% female. The impact of differing consumer demographics was unclear but may have significance for ventures targeted at specific age or gender markets. Antecedents of consumer acceptance included the widespread availability of relatively easy to use Internet technology and the availability of products and services of interest to consumers. A sustained period of global economic growth was further assisted by encouraging retail consumption. The 2000/2001 downturn in the global economy had the affect of constraining retail purchases by customers of both traditional and online stores and is a factor in the complex issue of customer retention.

4.   Inter-organizational imperatives (universally applicable but to varying degrees)—the necessity to modify or revise a firm's intentions or business approach to incorporate requirements from other organizations. This is dependent on the degree of integration with other organizations for mission critical business processes. Tight integration is where other organizations are critical for performance of at least some day-to-day core business functions. Without exception, but to varying degrees, all Internet retailers examined were tightly integrated with other organizations; see the examples in Table 9.2.

5.   Market factors (applicability variable). The size of the markets in differing countries were a potential factor. A small market could have encouraged multi-business model approaches not based on the novelty of the Internet that proved to be more resilient in the global economic downturn (Australia) and a large market that was familiar with purchasing remotely by telephone or by mail order catalogue (the United States) may have more easily adopted online shopping. However, once a market contained a sufficient mass of Internet-savvy customers to support a variety of online retailing the comparative size of the market appeared to have little overall significance, although the small size of their specific target market was a limiting factor for some firms. Several firms adopted a strategy of international expansion to overcome limitations in the size of their local market.

6.   Industry and competitive factors (applicability variable). The rate at which products/services became obsolete in the music industry was extremely high (Chaos). For Dymocks the threat of external competition from Amazon was

Table 9.2 Examples of core operational functions undertaken by external organizations

Firms	Telecom- munications/ ISP	Ordering website hosting	Purchasing	Warehouse/ supply	Delivery	Customer services, e.g. returns
Australia						
Chaos	✓			✓	✓	
Dymocks	✓	✓		✓	✓	
E-Store	✓			✓	✓	
GreenGrocer	✓		✓			
WINEPLANET	✓			✓		
United States						
HomeToDo	✓			✓		
Outpost	✓	✓		✓	✓	✓
Webvan	✓			✓ᵃ	✓ᵃ	
UPS	✓				✓	
UPS Returns	✓				✓	✓

ᵃ Webvan provides warehousing and delivery for other B2C firms.

the sole driver. In UPS, intense competition was an important factor. Conversely, industry and competitor analyses indicated little motivation for innovation except as a potential business opportunity (Ambassador, E-Store, GreenGrocer, Haburi, HomeToDo, Outpost, Saxo, Velux, Webvan, WINEPLANET). Supplier resistance and channel conflict were major concerns to some firms (e.g. Chaos, E-Store, HomeToDo, Velux, Wing On).

7. Legal issues (applicability variable). Legal issues were important mainly in their absence. While several governments stated their support for Internet activities, apart from Denmark there was little real national support. Governments also erected few inhibitors, although restrictions on online pornography (Australia) and gambling (Australia, the United States) were applicable. In one case, WINEPLANET, the absence of state and county-based restrictions on liquor sales such as are common in the Unied States enabled the venture quickly to cater for a national market.

8. The infrastructure necessary to support online retailing is taken for granted in many countries. The importance of infrastructure as an adoption factor was shown when early adopters of the Internet in Greece were plagued by frequent failures of the telecommunications networks—hardly an encouragement to use the Internet for purchasing. However, the lack of reliability in power supplies to many regions of the state of California (that developed to crisis levels in 2000 and 2001) and the subsequent impact on delivering reliable levels of service by Internet retailers (among others) reminds us of the mission-critical importance of infrastructure in all countries. Other components of infrastructure include financial (a viable means of payment for online purchases) and delivery (of purchased products). Several countries, including many developing countries, rely on currency for payment and

have little access to credit or debit cards that can support online purchases. An alternative is for consumers to pay on delivery but this reduces the low cost attractiveness of the e-store business model. Similarly, the availability of a low-cost, efficient and reliable delivery capability is an often overlooked essential component of online purchasing.

9. The International and cultural issues were determined through analysis of the research findings. This study returned a limited view of international/ cultural drivers and inhibitors, perhaps due to its focus on successful examples of e-business. The most significant issue arising from this analysis is a surprising degree of alignment between the implementation experiences of firms in different countries. One possible cultural issue was identified, namely a strong preference for undertaking commercial transactions face-to-face and a consequent reluctance to use the Internet for business purposes. While this reluctance was noted in several countries it may have been more significant as an indicator of resistance to change than as a cultural factor. It was noted particularly in Greece and Hong Kong by the early online retailers. Lower levels of Internet penetration in some countries were noted as an inhibitor to international expansion, e.g. by DVDshelf.com, which supplies Chinese films worldwide.

Organizational Factors

Organizational factors included:

1. The characteristics of the founders/executives (universally applicable for startups, variable applicability for traditional firms). Characteristics include qualifications, background and relevant prior experience. This is important for startups (e.g. Chaos, E-Store, Haburi, HomeToDo, Outpost, Webvan). It was of lesser importance for traditional firms moving into an online operation with no clear strategy (Dymocks), whereas in firms with a clear vision and purpose it appeared to be significant (UPS's Director of e-commerce). Founders or executive managers had a willingness to explore the potential of the Internet for possible strategic advantage (all firms) and a determination to succeed by re-evaluating and modifying their business approaches when faced with market or operational difficulties (most firms). Committed and capable executive management teams for initial implementation were also important.

2. A perceived business threat or opportunity (near universal applicability). Perceptions were frequently but not exclusively provoked or inspired by Internet pioneers. UPS faced a business threat of intense competition; Dymocks a threat from Amazon; Chaos sought industry restructure.

3. Uncertainty and a lack of skills (near universal applicability in earlier adopters). Founders and executives were unsure about the exact nature of the

perceived Internet opportunity and the skills required to exploit it. Some startups lacked the breadth of business skills required.

4. A business strategy or culture (variable applicability). UPS developed its corporate strategy to incorporate Internet initiatives but Internet ventures in some traditional firms had no relationship with corporate strategy (e.g. Dymocks). Others lacked clear linkages between corporate business strategies and the Internet venture (Velux). Difficulties with the implementation of business strategies occurred, e.g. the firm rapidly outgrew its original target market (WINEPLANET) or the business was less suited to the Internet than expected (HomeToDo). Both UPS and Ravenholm sought to support business strategies by reducing operational costs through their Internet ventures. An organizational culture of innovation assisted the venture (Saxo, Velux).

5. Operational issues (variable applicability). These included a range of difficulties such as inadequate operational performance; technical problems in developing, implementing and operating the website and systems; management failure to assign responsibility for the Internet venture or to maintain an ongoing program of website and system innovation; and the costs and challenges of attracting a critical mass of customers. Most firms experienced operational problems to some extent.

6. Organizational structure and tasks (variable applicability). In startups the existing structure and tasks are not applicable as adoption factors. Structural factors were not generally seen to be significant in traditional firms except for Velux (where many different parts of the organization were involved in the initiative but no one had responsibility) and for Dymocks (an alignment between franchisees and the corporation in the initial stages meant this was not an initial factor, although it subsequently became one as litigation erupted between the parties over ownership of the Internet venture). In UPS the existing organizational structure and tasks were not an adoption factor since e-commerce implementation became an organization-wide commitment. Task uncertainty was endemic as all firms strove to understand what worked in a web world. Roles were of little importance in the setup stages but became crucial over time (in traditional firms, especially for Velux).

7. Work practices (variable applicability). The startup firms were characterized by informal work practices, except where specialized functions were outsourced to third-party firms. Formal business plans were required for some firms (GreenGrocer) particularly to attract external funding (Chaos, Haburi, WINEPLANET) but not others with internal funding (Dymocks, E-Store) or a persuasive vision (Webvan).

8. Inter-organizational roles and functions (universally applicable but to varying degrees). Without exception all Internet retailers examined were tightly integrated with other organizations in order to provide seamless levels of service; see the examples in Table 9.2. No online retailer provided its core business services without assistance from at least one other organization.

Innovation Factors

To better understand success in innovation, Rogers (1995) proposed that the innovation's distinguishing attributes be identified. The CEC web evaluation framework was developed for this purpose (see also Chapter 8). The unit of analysis for the innovations is the Internet venture, but specific attention is given to the characteristics of the website, its most visible and critical implementation. The website was also examined for consistency with the differentiating strategies of each firm. This is necessary since a website that has only basic features or has some essential features that are flawed or incomplete might be acceptable to customers if the firm has a lowest price strategy and provided the total cost of purchase is lower than competitors. It is the Internet equivalent of the low-cost, low-service supermarket that has narrow aisles crowded with open boxes of goods for shoppers to help themselves.

The research model required innovations to be analyzed across a range of issues including their compatibility, complexity, relative advantage, characteristics/features and perceived costs/benefits. Compatibility had little relevance since the innovations required totally new and radically different business processes and operations. Complexity was rated high, as was relative advantage on initial implementation, but this declined over time as competitors established new business processes. WINEPLANET's implementation provides an on-going competitive advantage with its ability quickly to analyze competitors' actions and full integration. The website characteristics are shown on Table 8.5. The website information and functions were critical to the success of all of these Internet ventures. However, the level of implementation of information and functions differed between firms.

Perceived costs/benefits of the websites *to the firms* were determined by comparison of the firms' differentiating strategies and highest rated website features, as shown on Table 9.3. The costs related to the provision of website features. Benefits to the firm were derived from the degree of alignment between those features provided on the website and the firm's differentiating business strategies. Comparison of the differentiating strategies and website features showed that the website features were generally consistent with their corporate strategies. Many firms erred on the side of caution and provided more features than absolutely necessary to support their strategy. Given the high levels of uncertainty surrounding the provision of Internet retailing, this is a prudent approach. Several firms advised that their differentiating strategies included customer services, but this category of functions was not well implemented on their websites. The CEC website evaluation framework enables ready comparison of strategies with features and the lack of inconsistency between them represents an opportunity cost that should be addressed.

Two firms in Table 8.5 stand out as having inadequate websites. HomeToDo and Velux received CEC scales of only 33%, i.e. they had only a third of the features of an ideal website. At the time of the research, HomeToDo was in

Table 9.3 Comparison of business strategy and highest rated website features

Company	Differentiation	Highest rating website categories (4 or 5)	Consistency?
Action	Brands, price	Products, transactions, service	Y
Blackwell	Niche market, product range, service, price	Transactions, service, ease of use	Y
Chaos	Products, service, price	Products, transactions, service, ease of use	Y
Dymocks	Price-competitive (but facing franchisee channel conflict), service	Products, transactions, service, ease of use	Y
easyJet	Price	Products	?
E-Store	Price, product range, quality products	Products, transactions (service & ease of use rated low)	Y
GreenGrocer	Product quality and service	Products, transactions, service, ease of use	Y
Haburi	Price, product and service	Products, transactions, ease of use	N
HomeToDo	Product, service (strategy in transition)	No categories rated highly	N
Lobster	Niche market, service, product range and prices	Transactions, ease of use	?
Outpost	Service, order fulfillment	Company, products, transactions, service, ease of use	Y
Ravenholm	Price, service	Company, products, ease of use	N
Rejsefeber	Price, service	Products, transactions, ease of use	N
Saxo	Dual B2C and B2B markets, price & service	Products, ease of use	N
Thomas Cook	Product, price, service	Products, ease of use	Y
UPS Returns	Integrated service levels across firms	Transactions, service, ease of use	Y
UPS Tools	Products (site not designed for transactions)	Company and ease of use	Y
Velux	Products, service	No categories rated highly	N
Webvan	Service (fulfillment specialist)	Products, transactions, service, ease of use	Y
WINEPLANET	Price, product range and service	Company, products, transactions, service, ease of use	Y

transition from one business model and strategy to another. The low rating and lack of consistency between the website and the business strategy captures and reflects this transition phase. Five years after initial implementation, Velux's website is only starting to support transactions. Customer service, ease of use and innovation are all rated poorly. In contrast to the corporate strategy to reach out to customers across the supply chain, provision of information on the company and its products are also poorly implemented. Velux could obtain much more benefit from its website but the lack of competitive pressure for online services in their industry provides little incentive to do so.

A higher level of cost/benefits also needs to be acknowledged. For traditional firms the Internet venture is just one component of their overall operations. In one situation (Saxo) the parent firm conceded that the venture was not supporting its organizational strategic goals and the venture was sold. In one other firm (Velux) the Internet venture was not seen to be adequately supporting the organization's core business and has been neglected. Otherwise, parent organizations have acknowledged the contribution of their Internet innovations by maintaining and expanding the Internet operations. At times, an adverse market response has been required to motivate the firms into action.

Consumer Factors

The research model identified perceived costs and benefits as the major factors for investigation in consumer decision-making to adopt online shopping. Tables 9.4 and 9.5 show benefit and cost factors from the customer surveys. In summary, the customers sought benefits from online shopping of (starting with the most important): convenience, price, availability, quality, product range, trusted name, and total cost of purchase (i.e. price plus delivery-related costs). The amalgamated barriers or costs that confronted consumers were: concerns about security, uncertainty about delivery, uncertainty about products and services, purchase procedures, and website usability. These factors were important for initial adoption and also for maintaining consumer preferences for purchasing from specific retailers.

These findings contrast with mass survey results that provide very different pictures. According to one mass survey, major concerns when using the Internet identified quality information (10% of responses), easy ordering (9.7%) and reliability (9.6%) as being important to more respondents than security (9.3%) (GVU's 10th User Survey, 1999). Another mass survey showed computer viruses (22%), response times (13%), junk e-mail/intrusive marketing (12%), security of financial details (12%), privacy of individual's details (11%), and the cost of Internet access (10%) (consult.com.au 2000). Other studies (e.g. by Gartner Group) report security and privacy concerns as being paramount.

Differences between mass market and targeted consumer surveys highlight the potential problems inherent when the complexities of individual consumers and Internet applications are reduced to numerical averages. Specific concerns may be

Table 9.4 *Benefits sought by consumers*

	Chaos	Dymocks	E-Store	GreenGrocer	WINEPLANET	Haburi	Rejsefeber	Saxo
Convenience	2	1	2	1	1	2	2	1
Price	1		1		3=	1	1	3
Availability	4	2	3		2			2
Quality				2				
Product range	3				3=	3	3	4
Trusted name		3						
Total cost of purchase	5							

Source: Customer surveys.

Table 9.5 *Barriers overcome by consumers*

Barriers	Chaos	Dymocks	E-Store	GreenGrocer	WINEPLANET	Haburi	Rejsefeber	Saxo
Security	1	2	2=	1	3	3	3	1
Delivery uncertainty		1		3	1	2	2	2
Purchase procedures			1		2			3
Product uncertainty	3	3	2=	2		1	1	
Usability	2							

Source: Customer surveys.

more important to specific groups of consumers than are apparent from the mass surveys. An Internet initiative needs to carefully research the perceived costs and benefits of its target market rather than rely on average perceptions. Further research is required to investigate these issues, but examples of the deep differences between target groups for different firms can be seen from an examination of demographic characteristics.

The findings in this study demonstrate that an examination of consumers' perceived costs/benefits provides only part of the explanation for successful adoption of Internet retailing. Further exploration was made of demographic factors and additional, non-motivational factors associated with the ability—motivation—opportunity (AMO) model.

Figure 8.1 illustrates the necessity for retailers to recognize the specific demographic characteristics of their target market. Contrasting the national profile for Internet users in just one area, gender, Figure 8.1 shows that while nationally 55% of users are male the profile for a range of online retailers varies from 66% male (wine merchant) through 50% male (bookseller) to 79% female (grocer). Gender is an obvious area of distinction and considerable and on-going market research is required for retailers to identify the characteristics of their target market. These findings are consistent with Boyd and Mason's (1999) study of the influence of extrabrand attributes (including the characteristics of the individual) in consumer adoption. Further analysis of the consumer survey responses is required to more fully understand the influence of particular personal characteristics.

While support was found for a demographically based distinction between customers, support was also found for behavioral views of consumer adoption. Ramaswami et al.'s ability-motivation-opportunity framework suggests that the major determinants of online buying are: the consumer's ability to purchase online, her motivation to do so, and her opportunity to access online markets.

Since all respondents gained access to the customer survey only after having completed purchases online, the ability factor was a prerequisite. Motivation includes cost/benefit factors already considered above. Respondents reported accessing the Internet predominantly from home or work but also from friends' homes, school, college or university, public buildings (e.g. libraries) and from commercial services like Internet cafes.

So, in response to the question 'Why do consumers purchase over the Internet?', this study confirms that issues separately identified by previous researchers as the predominant motivation for consumer adoption may have been influential. Of equal significance is the finding that none of the factors could be excluded as being influential. Consumers were distinguished by demographics, ability, motivation (cost/benefits) and opportunity. Further exploration is required but the clear implications from this research are that:

- a broad range of factors influences consumer adoption;
- factors may be of greater or lesser influence for consumers in different situations or at different times; and

- a business or research focus on one set of factors in isolation is unlikely to provide a complete and accurate understanding of the actual factors influencing consumer adoption of Internet retailing.

THEORETICAL IMPLICATIONS

The implications of this research project for business managers are shown in Chapter 10. The aim of this research was to assist firms facing uncertainty about B2C e-commerce by:

- establishing key factors that promote or inhibit the adoption of implementations of Internet-based retail e-commerce;
- identifying relationships between the factors and their relative importance; and
- establishing key factors that promote or inhibit similar implementations in different countries.

Uncertainty exists also about how well current theory can be applied to the adoption of e-commerce. Theory tends to consider elements of innovation in isolation and to assume constancy in other factors. Since e-commerce has a transforming effect on business processes, products, organizational structures and industries, any assumptions of constancy appear to be at odds with observation. Faced with documented uncertainty about e-commerce adoptions in theory and practice this exploratory research project has examined successful implementations of B2C e-commerce holistically. Multiple research methods have been applied to gain perspectives from the environment, the organization, the innovation and the customer. Rather than focus on one economy, the research has been conducted in six countries.

From a research perspective, the international study served to test the research model. The contribution of the research is in extensions of prior theory in innovation from being focused largely internally on individual innovation factors to a holistic examination of all factors influencing successful organizational-level innovations in B2C e-commerce. Specific contributions are in the breadth of factors (the consumer category) and the depth (more detailed examination of elements within each category). A further contribution arises from examination of the processes in organizational adoption of e-business innovation.

The limitations of this work should be considered in conjunction with the research findings. The research focus was on successful adopters but did not examine non-adopting firms or non-adopting consumers; only five implementations were examined in each of only six countries; the selection of the particular countries (a broader range of economies and developments in adoption of e-commerce could have been examined); and the currency of any research in an area developing as dynamically as e-commerce.

The research findings of this multi-method international study support the necessity for a holistic examination of all innovation factors. Individual characteristics of the innovation, organization, consumer or environment in isolation fail to explain the success of these ventures. Some of the research findings challenge prior theory. At the level of organizational adoption of innovation, Rogers (1995) contends that 'adoption doesn't occur as a result of a single dramatic incident nor by a single entrepreneur' and that innovation at an organizational level occurs only in response to a business problem. While some cases support these contentions the majority of cases did not. Many startups were initiated by a single entrepreneur (e.g. Chaos, easyJet, GreenGrocer). Several (but not all) traditional firms were confronted with a business problem that led to their Internet venture, but the most frequent reason given for the creation of Internet startups was in response to a perceived business opportunity. The stated drivers for the technology adoption model (TAM) specifically excluded environmental influences, which is totally at odds with the details on environmental issues identified above by this study as being influential in the adoption decision process.

Extensions to the E-Commerce Research Model—Factors

This international study was based on a proposed research model of e-commerce adoption (Table 9.1). Subsequent to the research, this model needs to be critically reviewed to consider the extent to which the model reflected the findings. All the categories required extension to incorporate factors identified in the research. A revised and extended research model, an integrated adoption model for B2C e-commerce, is the result (see Table 9.6).

A very significant outcome of the research was the finding that the categories of adoption factors were integrated. Not only are factors from all four categories critical to the success of the Internet venture but factors are applicable across categories, e.g. lack of business and technical management skills are applicable in both the organization and the innovation categories, and customer acceptance is important in the environmental, organizational and consumer categories. Examination of these factors in only one area would provide an inadequate understanding of the importance of the factor in the success of an Internet venture.

The environmental category was extended to include additional factors under the market element (i.e. the availability of funding, acceptance by suppliers and consumers, and the threat of channel conflict). The legal element was revised as an infrastructure element that included legal and regulatory factors and extended to incorporate the technical infrastructure required to support reliable Internet service levels.

The organizational category had extensive revisions to incorporate a strategic as opposed to operational orientation. New elements include: a strategic adopter (for organizational-level adoption, this includes the characteristics of the founder(s)/CEO/Champion, e.g. qualifications, relevant prior experience, capability to determine a business vision, willingness to explore the potential of the

Table 9.6 *An integrated adoption model for B2C e-commerce*

Environmental factors

- Market (uncertainty, competition, concentration, funding, acceptance, channel conflict)
- Inter-organizational imperatives (degree of integration of core business functions required across organizations)
- Infrastructure (legal, regulatory, technical, financial, delivery)
- Cultural and international

Organizational factors

- Strategic adopter (for organizational-level adoption, this includes the characteristics of the founder(s)/CEO/Champion, e.g. qualifications, relevant prior experience, capability to determine a business vision, willingness to explore the potential of the Internet, capability to review and revise business models and strategies in response to the market)
- Strategic motivation (inspiration from Internet pioneer, business threat or perceived opportunity)
- Business model(s) and strategies (realistic business models and effective business strategies)
- Skills (at the strategic, tactical and operational levels)
- Individual employee (education, tenure, etc.)
- Structural (specialization, formalization)
- Task (uncertainty, autonomy, variety, etc.)
- Roles/functions (inter-organizational)

Innovation factors

- Compatibility, complexity, relative advantage, trialability, observability, usefulness, ease of use
- Distinguishing characteristics/features (website characteristics based on the CEC web evaluation framework)
- Perceived costs/benefits (to the firms)

Consumer factors

The major benefit factors of Internet shopping include:

- Convenience in purchasing 'anytime, from anywhere, to anywhere'
- Cost savings through lower prices
- Availability of products
- Quality of products
- Increased range of products
- Responsiveness in product delivery, e.g. 'instantaneous distribution of digital products and services'.
- Increased customization, e.g. 'capability to treat customers as individuals'.

Major consumer concern factors leading to unsatisfactory experiences include:

- Security
- Uncertainty about delivery
- Uncertainty about products
- Purchase procedures/ease of use/usability
- Poor levels of service
- Costs

Additional consumer factors include the demographic profiles of customers for particular firms and products, consumers' abilities to purchase online and their opportunity to do so.

Internet, capability to review and revise business models and strategies in response to the market); strategic motivation (inspiration from the Internet pioneer, business threat or perceived opportunity); business model(s) and strategies (for successful innovation these need to be realistic business models and effective business strategies); and skills (at the strategic, tactical and operational levels as required for effective and efficient implementation of strategies).

The innovation category was extended in the distinguishing characteristics element to incorporate website characteristics based on the CEC web evaluation framework.

The benefits and costs to consumers would appear to be obvious determinants of success in retailing but consumer issues have received little attention in adoption theory. This study, in general, confirmed prior market research, although with different emphasis. The major benefits of Internet shopping include, in decreasing order: convenience in purchasing 'anytime, from anywhere, to anywhere', cost savings through lower prices, availability of products, quality of products, and increased range of products. Two other benefits identified in market research and other studies were not explicitly raised as desirable benefits but were mentioned in general responses: responsiveness in product delivery, e.g. 'instantaneous distribution of digital products and services' and increased customization, e.g. 'capability to treat customers as individuals'. Major consumer concerns leading to unsatisfactory experiences include: security, uncertainty about delivery, uncertainty about products, purchase procedures/ease of use/usability, poor levels of service, and costs.

Additional consumer elements were the consumers' abilities to purchase online, their opportunity to access online markets, and the demographic profile of the customers for particular firms. Note that innovations change over time and, as a result, consumer perceptions and evaluations can also be expected to change

E-Commerce Research Model—Processes

Theory on adoption processes suggests that the processes occur over time leading to the adoption decision and its implementation. Subsequently, this decision is refined and re-examined, often leading to re-invention of the innovation (Rogers 1995, Broadbent and Weill 1999). The innovation–decision process described by Rogers consists of five stages:

1. knowledge—the individual (or decision-making unit) is exposed to the innovation's existence and gains some understanding of how it functions;
2. persuasion—the individual (or decision-making unit) forms a favorable or unfavorable attitude toward the innovation;
3. decision—the individual (or decision-making unit) engages in activities that lead to a choice to adopt or reject the innovation;
4. implementation—the individual (or decision-making unit) puts an innovation into use; and

5. confirmation—the individual (or decision-making unit) seeks reinforcement for an innovation decision already made, but may reverse this decision if exposed to conflicting messages about the innovation.

Rogers also discusses the concepts of re-invention (the degree to which an innovation is changed or modified by a user in the process of its adoption and implementation) and discontinuance (a decision to reject after having previously adopted it). Rogers calls for further research into adoption processes to incorporate the temporal aspects of adoption.

The cases broadly supported Rogers' process theory with critical adoption decision-making factors being grouped as initial or on-going. Incremental planning and decision-making in support of the adoption occurred over considerable time with many reviews and revisions of the adoption decision taking place in response to market experience with the innovation. This study found that in most cases adoption decision-making was not a single event but occurred over an often extended period. While determinants of successful innovation may be partly based on the initial adoption factors, this project suggests that success is based also on implementation of the innovation. Distinction between the initial motivating factors and the actual and the implemented factors leading to success should be made.

Three different process models were identified: informal, formal and alternating. The models are an amalgamation of the experiences of firms but all steps were not necessarily undertaken by all firms or with the same emphasis. The alternating process model commenced informally and became progressively more formal as the necessity to secure external funding was reached, reverted to informal then became more formal in implementation due to shareholder requirements.

An informal innovation process model was utilized by some traditional firms, e.g. Dymocks, Plaisio and Ravenholm. The processes were:

1. Identifying a perceived business threat or opportunity
2. Informal discussions and investigations
3. Decision-making to proceed
4. No prepared statements of business plan, strategies or budget
5. Funding sourced internally
6. Implementation proceeding with internal IT development staff or outsourced
7. Little effort to integrate existing operations and Internet operations
8. Commencing business (processes 8–10 represent the implementation cycle).
9. On-going review, revision (radical or incremental) and re-development in response to experiences and market forces.
10. Additional funding (as required)

A formal innovation process model was adopted by most startups, particularly those requiring external funding (e.g. Greengrocer and Haburi) but also by traditional firms that saw the Internet innovation to be an integral part of their business strategy (e.g. Blackwell and UPS Returns). Table 10.3 shows a more complete representation of this model. The processes were:

1. Awareness of the business potential of Internet-based activities
2. Identifying a perceived business threat or opportunity
3. Investigating Internet-based business opportunities
4. Undertaking market research
5. Formal business and strategy planning
6. Formal decision-making to proceed
7. Securing funds
8. Identifying specific goals
9. Planning for implementation
10. Establishing a reliable, integrated, scaleable technology platform
11. Developing a fully functional website, making arrangements for hosting website
12. Establishing the capability for integrated logistics (e.g. purchasing, supply, warehousing, distribution) through in-house operations and/or strategic partnerships.
13. Initial promoting/marketing of the brand
14. Commencing business in pilot mode to test/revise according to market response and to fine tune operations in the low-demand period
15. Full implementation (processes 15–17 represent the implementation cycle)
16. Continual reviewing, revising (radically or incrementally) and re-developing in response to experiences and market forces.
17. Securing additional funding (as required)

An alternating innovation process model combined steps from the formal and informal models with formality being introduced by external influences typically related to funding. The initial aim of the innovation may not have been clearly determined or specified by the startups (e.g. Chaos, Saxo (initially)). Arguably, this model is relevant only to pioneers and the time for pioneering in Internet retailing has past. A contrary argument is that this model remains relevant since initiatives in different industries that have no prior experience with the Internet may go through a similar learning and experimental process. Many countries are still at a pioneering stage in their implementations of Internet retailing. The stages are:

1. Awareness of the potential of Internet-based activities
2. Identifying a perceived opportunity, not specifically business oriented.
3. Informal discussions and investigations
4. Decision-making to proceed
5. No prepared statements of business plan, strategies or budget

6. Funding sourced internally
7. Limited operations commence
8. Funding crisis or business opportunity identified
9. Formal business and strategy planning
10. External funding secured
11. Implementation proceeding with internal IT development staff or outsourced
12. Some effort to integrate Internet operations
13. Full implementation (processes 13–15 represent the implementation cycle)
14. Continual reviewing, revising (radically or incrementally) and re-developing in response to experiences and market forces
15. Securing additional funding (as required)

Integration of Factors and Processes

A major contribution of this study is in its illustration of the characteristics of successful adoption of innovations in Internet retailing. Case after case demonstrates that success requires the interaction of factors and processes over a considerable period of time. Different factors may be more or less influential and different processes applied depending on the actual firm and its situation. A simple analogy of a ball rolling between two points may illustrate the integration required between the various categories of innovation factors and the processes (see also Chapter 10).

A ball represents the innovation. Success is obtained by moving the ball along a path to the next milestone. The environment is the slope of the path—variously ranging from steeply inclined through level to gently declining. The drivers apply the momentum. Continuous application is required to start the ball rolling and to overcome friction, representing consumers. Friction is initially difficult to overcome but eases with the build-up in momentum. Of course, consumer rejection totally prevents the ball from rolling. The surface of the path may be smooth (few inhibitors) or rocky (many substantial inhibitors). The organization represents the mass of the ball. Larger organizations are harder to move but can go a long way once moving.

There are many different paths (processes) to the first milestone. Some have fewer obstructions than others. Some paths go nowhere. The innovator makes and maintains the ball, chooses the path and tries to coordinate the drivers in order to overcome the obstacles. Depending on an innovator's skill and experience the ball may be more or less well suited for the task in hand. Maintenance is required to repair the ball along the way as it is easily damaged by traveling over a rocky path. The ball does not roll evenly but is inherently unstable with a tendency to run off the path unless carefully nurtured. Many balls stall, get stuck, and are abandoned or crash and burn. These also create obstacles in the path. The innovator is not operating in isolation. There is actually a race between innovators to get their balls to each of the many milestones. Gold medals are awarded at each checkpoint, not necessarily to the first across the line.

This simple analogy could be enhanced with increasing levels of complexity (e.g. enhancing the innovation *en route*) but at this level serves to remind both innovators and researchers alike of the complexities of the task, the skills and experience required, and the absolute necessity for careful consideration of all potential factors and processes.

Much current research into e-business is rigorously designed but too narrowly focused. This study demonstrates the necessity for broadly based, exploratory research that examines Internet innovations holistically. At this stage in our understanding of this new phenomenon called e-business we simply do not know enough to limit our investigations to particular aspects of Internet adoption or to examine them without reference to their context. There is great necessity for effective research that is broadly based, exploratory and relevant to the wider community as it seeks to overcome the high levels of uncertainty about the Internet. It is also necessary that this research demonstrates academic rigor and helps to develop theory to more adequately explain e-business.

10
Conclusion

STEVE ELLIOT

OVERVIEW

The purpose of this book was to identify success factors in Internet retailing by examining successful online retailers in six countries. The book was based on a research project that aimed to:

- establish key factors that promote or inhibit the adoption of implementations of Internet-based retail e-commerce
- identify relationships between the factors and their relative importance and
- establish key factors that promote or inhibit similar implementations in different countries

As shown in Chapter 9, the research project identified these adoption factors and their relationships but found that these alone could not adequately explain success. Owing to the dynamic nature of Internet retailing, success in many cases relied not only on the foundation established in the adoption stage but also on constant attention to and revision of firms' business models and strategies.

This final chapter draws together the experiences of firms and other findings of the international research project. The next section reviews the major factors that led to successful establishment of Internet retailing startups or adoption of an Internet channel by traditional retailers. Analysis of all adoption factors is shown in Chapter 9. The third section looks at the range of business models and strategies implemented and compares firms in different countries selling similar products, books and technology. The fourth section looks at the processes involved in successful innovation. The fifth section considers the major factors for success in Internet retailing as a whole rather than just at the establishment/adoption stage. This section accumulates experiences and advice from the firms examined on what they see as the critical factors leading to on-going success in their business. The section integrates the factors and processes into a conceptual model of successful innovation and ongoing operation. The final section reaches conclusions on e-business retailing based on the international project and considers directions for further developments.

MAJOR ADOPTION FACTORS

An analysis of the firms in this study shows that those factors most critical to success in the adoption of Internet retailing included both drivers and inhibitors. A complete examination of these factors is shown in Chapter 9 with only the most important factors listed here. Adoption factors have been categorized as initial and on-going. Initial drivers of the Internet ventures included (in the order they arose):

1. The example of Internet pioneers
2. A perceived business opportunity
3. A business threat to a traditional company
4. The characteristics of the founders or executives, e.g. qualifications, skills and previous business or technology experience; also, a willingness to explore the potential of the Internet and a determination to succeed
5. The opportunity for cost reductions in existing operations
6. The availability of investment funding

In summary, the initial drivers were awareness, a clearly stated objective (opportunity or threat), the capabilities of the founders (or executives) and a benign investment climate. On-going factors that enabled successful implementation of the ventures were:

1. Sufficient levels of acceptance by suppliers and customers
2. On-going funding
3. The founders' willingness and capability to effectively modify business strategies and implementation based on feedback from customers and market experience—unlike many dotcoms that failed as a result of the market's rejection of their initial offering
4. Alignment with corporate strategy in a traditional firm
5. The ability of the principals to recruit talented individuals with a solid track record of operational skill

Initial barriers that needed to be overcome included (not in significant order):

1. Lack of knowledge about how the Internet could be used most effectively
2. Uncertainty about adequate levels of acceptance by suppliers and/or consumers
3. Lack of finance/funding
4. Lack of skills; technical, operations and business management

Two firms (a startup and a traditional firm) reported no initial barriers to their implementations. Both firms had a clear vision, relevant prior experience and ready access to funding. Perhaps as a result of the levels of uncertainty and experimentation with what worked best, unpredicted outcomes frequently occurred that necessitated re-evaluation of the business approaches. Barriers that arose during implementation and critically threatened success were:

1. Resistance at various levels, e.g. suppliers declining to provide products to purely online operations, supplier septicism and reluctance to deliver directly to customers, a general lack of acceptance by suppliers and/or consumers (initial and continuing) and channel conflicts.
2. Difficulties with implementation of business strategies or lack of clear linkage between corporate business strategies and the Internet venture.
3. Lack of breadth in business skills with too much focus on marketing and a lack of awareness of the range of other skills necessary to run an Internet business.
4. Operational issues, which varied according to the circumstances, e.g. one firm found it necessary to bring core functions in-house due to unsatisfactory experiences while another firm outsourced core functions to obtain best practice levels of performance. Technical difficulties arose in developing, implementing and operating the websites and systems. Some firms failed to maintain a continual program of website and system innovation.
5. Marketing costs required to attract customers exceeded expectations.
6. On-going funding for expansion and to cover operational losses.
7. Unreliable infrastructure, e.g. early adopters of the Internet in Greece were plagued by frequent failures of the telecommunications networks.

The diversity in these major factors influencing success in Internet retailing is striking. Success requires a complex interaction between organizational factors (e.g. business vision, models, strategies, skills and capabilities), environmental factors (e.g. funding, level of Internet acceptance, legislative support), the innovation (e.g. website features and functions and the technical capability to develop and operate a website), and consumers (e.g. targeted market, profile, acceptance, utilization and retention). The challenge for business lies not just in the complexity of factors required for success but also in the necessity for unceasing efforts to maintain the viability of a venture once it has been established.

BUSINESS MODELS AND STRATEGIES

Chapter 1 reviewed Timmers' models for business-to-consumer (B2C) e-commerce and displayed the business models apparent for each of the firms examined in Figure 1.2. Figure 10.1 shows that in addition to those models originally identified, many firms implemented secondary business models as they modified or expanded their business scope to improve their viability.

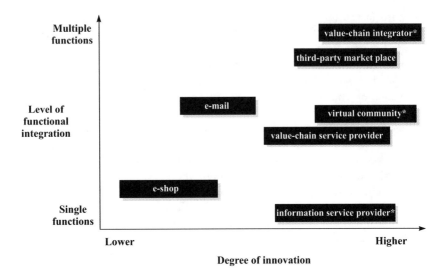

Figure 10.1 *Internet business models examined (* = secondary business model). Reproduced from* Electronic Commerce: Strategies and Models for Business-to-Business Trading, *Paul Timmers, © copyright 1999 by John Wiley & Sons, Ltd, Chichester, with permission*

One firm actually discarded its original business model in favour of another. The third-party market-place proved to be problematic for the US firm HomeToDo so it transformed its business into a value chain integrator and expanded its offerings to include information service provision for homeowners on household maintenance matters. The Australian startup Chaosmusic added value chain integration to its B2C business by generating packaged content from different sources for the business-to-business (B2B) market. Largely in the effort to retain customers, many firms extended their original business scope to include a virtual community business model.

The experiences of these firms show that while prerequisites for success are a clearly stated and understood Internet business model and realistic strategies for its implementation, ultimate success or failure is determined by the capability of the firm to customize both business model and strategies to effectively meet the changing requirements of the market.

Comparison of Firms Across Different Countries Selling the Same Product Types

Retailers of two types of products were selected for international comparison, books and technology. Both product types are commodities, i.e. they are so standardized that it would be possible for any or all of the online stores to sell the same product. Consequently, there is a reduced likelihood that differences between the implementations in different countries can be attributed to the products sold. The business model and strategies were analysed for each of the cases. The dominant business model was the e-shop.

Analysis of the online retailers' strategies across different countries (shown in Tables 10.1 and 10.2) reveals unanticipated insights. Irrespective of differing environmental factors between the countries (e.g. size of market, levels of competition, levels of consumer acceptance of the Internet, levels of government assistance, degree of support from legal structures and reliability of the communications infrastructure), differing organizational adoption processes, different product types (books and technology) and different consumer profiles, with only one exception the firms competed on price. With that one exception (Outpost adopted an exclusively service-based strategy) all firms had multiple competitive

Table 10.1   *Market differentiation of online bookstores by country*

Store	Startup/ traditional?	Market niche strategy?	Low-price strategy?	Service-levels strategy?	Product focus? range/brand
Blackwell, UK	Traditional	✓	✓	✓	Range
Dymocks,[a] Australia	Traditional		✓	✓	
Papasotiriou, Greece	Traditional	✓	✓		Range
Saxo,[b] Denmark	Startup		✓	✓	

[a] Dymocks had a defensive strategy but competed on price and service.
[b] Saxo had a dual market strategy, B2B was price-based, B2C service-based.

Table 10.2   *Market differentiation of online technology stores by country*

Store	Startup/ traditional?	Market niche strategy?	Low-price strategy?	Service-levels strategy?	Product focus? range/brand
Action, UK	Traditional		✓		Brand
E-Store, Australia	Startup		✓		Range and Brand
Outpost, US	Startup			✓	
Plaisio, Greece	Traditional		✓	✓	Range
Ravenholm, Denmark	Traditional		✓	✓	

strategies coupling low prices with service, a niche target market, a comprehensive range of products, or limited their products to those with market-leading brands.

An initial explanation for this behaviour could be the nature of the products— the tendency for commodities is always towards price-based competition. Examination of the range of firms and products in Table 9.3 reveals that approximately 30% of online retailers do not compete on price. However, three of those retailers have commoditizable product ranges (fresh food from GreenGrocer, technology products from Outpost and building products from Velux). This suggests the critical decision factor in determining business strategy is not the type of products but the organization's vision of its strategic positioning as a price, quality or service organization. The other firms that did not compete on price focused on the provision of services and competed on service levels.

A simple explanation for the focus on price competition could be that the low-cost potential of Internet-based operations supports a low-price strategy. An alternative explanation is that firms are at an early stage in their understanding of competing in the e-space and are limiting their competitive approaches. The exception, Outpost, made a conscious decision to compete on service levels. Other firms, such as GreenGrocer, also competed on product quality and service levels rather than price.

Further research is required to clarify if:

- a focus on price competition is just an initial stage of development in online business strategies;
- non-price strategies are sustainable in light of general customer expectations of lower prices for online products;
- customer expectations will develop over time to include general acceptance of service-based strategies; and
- exclusive focus on a niche consumer market seeking quality and service in specific product types is viable for online retailers.

INNOVATION PROCESSES

As described in Chapter 9, a formal innovation process model was adopted by most startups, particularly those requiring external funding. Traditional firms that saw the Internet innovation to be an integral part of their business strategy also used formal processes. Table 10.3 shows those processes. Some firms adopted informal or alternating models that by-passed several steps, particularly 4, 5, 6, 10 and 14. Note that processes may be undertaken at different stages to those indicated in the model, depending on the circumstances. For example, process 2, identifying a perceived business threat or opportunity, may arise as part of a general awareness building (i.e. the awareness stage) or may be part of a formal investigation of potential business opportunities (investigation stage). Similarly, market research may be a general review of market requirements (investigation

Table 10.3   *Internet innovation process model*

Stage	Processes
Awareness	1. Awareness of the business potential of Internet-based activities 2. Identifying a perceived business threat or opportunity
Investigation	3. Investigating Internet-based business opportunities
Planning	4. Undertaking market research 5. Formal business and strategy planning
Approval	6. Formal decision-making to proceed 7. Securing funds
Preparation	8. Identifying specific goals 9. Planning for implementation
Establishment	10. Establishing a reliable, integrated, scalable technology platform 11. Developing a fully functional website, making arrangements for hosting website 12. Establishing capability for integrated logistics e.g. purchasing, supply, warehousing, distribution) through in-house operations and/or strategic partnerships 13. Initial promoting/marketing of the brand
Preliminary implementation	14. Commencing business in pilot mode to test/revise according to market response and to fine-tune operations in low demand period
Implementation cycle	15. Full implementation 16. Continual reviewing, revising (radically or incrementally) and re-developing in response to experiences and market forces 17. Securing additional funding (as required)

stage) or a focused evaluation of the specific requirements of a market niche for the purpose of product planning (planning stage).

MAJOR SUCCESS FACTORS IN INTERNET RETAILING

In addition to an investigation of the major factors influencing successful adoption of the Internet, executives were asked to identify the overall determinants of success for online retailers. Since the overall factors include adoption issues there is some overlap between the sections. Advice from the retailers for other firms has also been incorporated, often as direct quotes. 'So what has to go right for the business to succeed? Seriously, everything!' This response, from GreenGrocer's Douglas Carlson, was echoed by nearly all firms. Market positioning (to find the site), order processing, payment, logistics, order fulfilment, delivery, returns and after-sales service must all work perfectly. Key business success factors are complex and inter-related. Specific success factors include:

- A viable business model for the whole organization. What is the value driver for customers from your Internet site, e.g. price, convenience, product range, mass customization, customer recommendations, community building? What is your source of competitive advantage? 'Do not underestimate the importance of market research and planning.' 'Old fashioned marketing planning and financial controls are necessary for Internet businesses too.'
- Be clear on priorities. 'You can't do everything.' 'Keep focused on the strategies and issues seen to be important to the firm.'
- Managing a holistic, integrated solution to business. There is the need to totally transform existing approaches to running a business to achieve the level of real-time integration required. 'Have realistic expectations, emphasize the importance of good management and implement vigorously.' 'Traditional firms facing the question to enter the Internet or not, have to think differently and be completely open to new ideas. They have to continuously question everything they currently do and ask themselves why and how they do this.'
- Secure adequate funds for expansion (but be careful not to inadvertently lose control of the venture).
- Understand your target market(s) and meet their needs. Focus on gaining quality customers and retaining them through your competitive advantages.
- Product type. Some products may seem more suited for business on the Internet, i.e. where the product is a standardized commodity and does not exhibit characteristics that require personal interaction (e.g. touch, feel, smell, taste or visual inspection) for selection. That is, the quality of the product is not variable inherently or between retailers and so is not considered a serious threat to consumers shopping remotely on the Internet. Examples of commoditizable products include books (Blackwell, Dymocks, Papasotiriou, Saxo), CD and DVD music (Chaos, DVDshelf), computers and consumer electronics (Action, E-store, Outpost, Plaisio, Ravenholm), tickets (Rejsefeber) and wine (WINEPLANET). However, products do not have to be commoditizable, e.g. fruit and vegetables (GreenGrocer, Webvan) or home maintenance (HomeToDo).
- Branding. Marketing to present the brand (startups). Having an established brand name (traditional firms) is a very powerful competitive advantage.
- Do the right things well. Part of the challenge in generating revenue is to have the right focus, i.e. a focus not solely on customer acquisition and marketing but looking more at customer fulfilment—actually providing the size and range of products and the services customers require.
- Supply is a constant challenge either due to suppliers declining to provide their products to online stores or distribution channels not being reliable.

- Website and fulfilment capability. Firms need to have a full service solution on their website. This means they need to 'jump into e-business with both feet'. Companies that do a test and a pilot are doomed to failure since a pilot cannot be both fully functional and fully integrated. Therefore a pilot is rarely successful. Companies often cancel the pilot comfortable with the knowledge that the Internet is not a success and are happy to get out of it. 'Build a structure with the capability to cost effectively provide products for customers attracted by value-added, Internet-enabled services that is scalable.' 'Eliminate areas that do not create value for the customers.' 'Keep your site fresh and different.' 'Personalize it for each customer.' 'How to do it better?' 'Be prepared to continually invest in innovation.' 'This all takes time and money.'
- Gain significant first-mover advantages. Some analysts suggest first-mover advantage to be a fallacy since second-movers learn from the pioneers' mistakes and rapidly overtake them. However, firms as diverse as Ambassador, Chaos, Haburi, Outpost, Webvan and UPS (Returns) identified the first-mover advantages of brand recognition (i.e. lower costs in attracting customers) and the opportunity to secure a market-leading presence before competitors react. Over time, the plethora of Internet firms is expected to consolidate into a few large and some small specialist firms. Firms need to avoid being caught in the mid-range of sizes where costs will be high. 'Find your market niche and attack it globally (i.e. don't be constrained geographically).'
- Learn from customers and their needs (gain feedback and provide timely response).
- Learn from competitors. 'We are always looking to keep up with and ahead of the competition.'
- Generate sales and produce profits. These may arise through minimization of fixed costs by outsourcing as many functions as possible. 'It is important to find the right balance between operational costs and revenues.'

The greatest threats to Internet retailers (excluding those to specific industries) are:

- An international competitor entering the local market or local competitors getting it right
- Having an Internet fulfilment approach that is not sufficiently scalable
- Competition—price is a major competitive threat to a firm with a business strategy of low-cost leadership
- A limitation on the firm's growth by the current size of the online market
- Channel conflict—two of the business strategies critical to one firm's future (i.e. customer relationship management and growth through franchising) are essentially incompatible
- Internet companies failing and lowering confidence in Internet-based retailing
- A downturn in the stock market and 'a lower share price that means the firm is vulnerable to takeover'
- Achieving profitability in an increasingly sceptical market
- Lack of innovation, because success is based on on-going developments

Although key business success factors are complex and inter-related, different business models may require an emphasis on different factors. For example, the Danish travel firm Rejsefeber has implemented two business models. A fully functional electronic mall requires the firm to arrange partnerships with suitable airlines and hotels able to provide products and services on demand. To be successful, Rejsefeber's partners must have appropriate products for its customers at competitive prices. The website offering full transaction processing for sale of these products needs to be usable, efficient and accessible as well as scalable at peak periods. Conversely, for the additional community services business model, the key success factors are for the site to be usable, responsive to questions and provide the capacity for consumers to post their holiday photographs.

Few, if any, of these factors are not equally applicable to any traditional business venture. In other words, the principles for business success remain constant. All that distinguishes the Internet from traditional business is the way those principles are implemented!

CONCEPTUAL MODEL OF SUCCESSFUL INNOVATION

A major contribution of this study is in its illustration of the characteristics of successful adoption of innovations in Internet retailing. Case after case demonstrates that success requires the interaction of factors and processes not only at the adoption stage but over a considerable period of time. Different factors may be more or less influential and different processes applied depending on the actual firm and its situation. A simple analogy of a ball rolling between two points has been used to illustrate the experiences of the firms examined that integration is required between the various categories of innovation factors and the processes (see Figures 10.2, 10.3 and 10.4). The conceptual model was introduced in Chapter 9.

CONCLUSIONS AND FURTHER DEVELOPMENTS

Arguably the most important message for both managers and researchers arising from the project is that success in Internet retailing, as with many other innovations, depends on the interaction of a broad range of factors and processes. Like explorers, innovators and researchers of innovation need to carefully consider all real and potential issues before they venture into the unknown. They must keep alert for the unexpected as they go.

Implications for business

Leading firms in Internet retailing are aware of how little is currently known about what works and what does not and have been very supportive of this research project. The rapid demise of Internet firms since early 2000 raised widespread

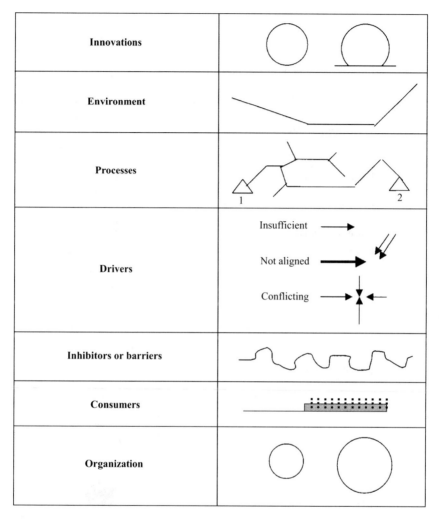

Innovations	
Environment	
Processes	
Drivers	
Inhibitors or barriers	
Consumers	
Organization	

Figure 10.2   *Elements in the rolling ball model*

concerns about the viability of business over the medium. Although much of the reporting was ill-informed, a general apprehension developed about Internet retailing that resulted in stock market falls and uncertainty about how Internet-based firms could best prepare for the future, and even questioned if there was a future.

By intensive examination of successful Internet retailers in six countries, this book addresses these concerns directly and shows how firms have achieved success on the Internet. Furthermore, it shows that the general principles of business apply equally to Internet-based business. Owing to the novelty of the Internet and the ready availability of funding arising from a sustained period of stock market growth during much of the 1990s, many new firms ignored those essential

Situations		
1	Insufficient forces or poor alignment of drivers	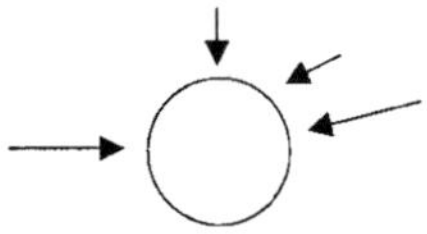
2	Innovation not suitable for all requirements	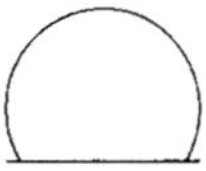
3	Inhibitors greater than drivers	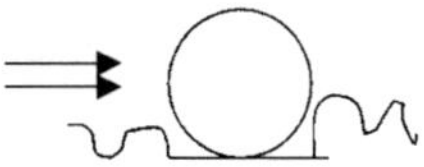
4	Innovation in a hostile environment	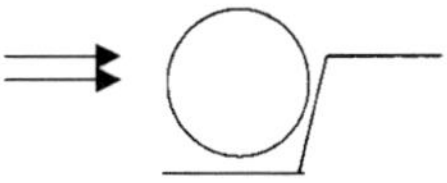
5	Organizational resistance to innovation	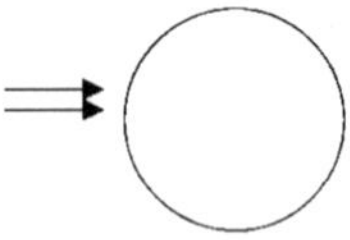
6	Inadequate planning and/or implementation processes	
7	Consumer resistance	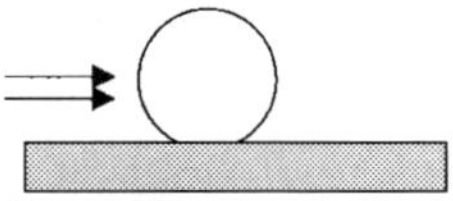
8	Insufficient maintenance of innovation	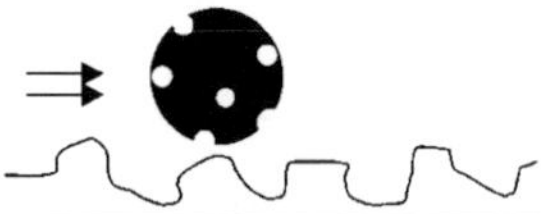
9	Multiple barriers	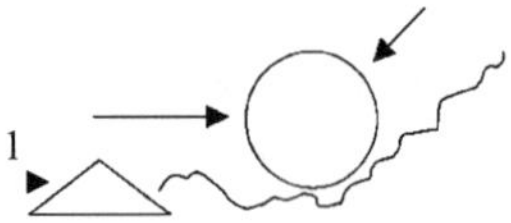
10	Innovation successful	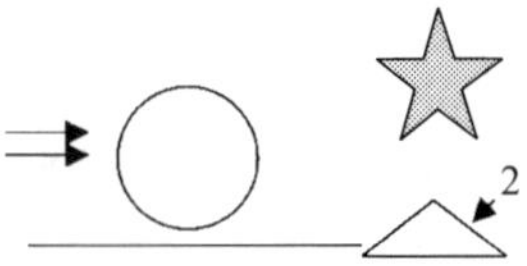

Figure 10.3   *Critical situations in successful innovations*

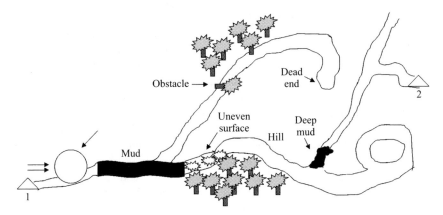

Figure 10.4   *Rolling Ball conceptual model of Internet innovation*

principles of business. These firms failed when, inevitably, the funds dried up and the novelty wore off.

While the principles of business are the same, the way those principles are applied to Internet-based business is radically different to traditional business practice. The types of differences and the ways they can be used to transform firms and industries are shown through the cases studies in each chapter. Tools to assist firms in their strategic planning and implementation of e-business are included in Chapter 8.

This chapter has shown the major factors and processes utilized by firms in successful adoption and operation of their Internet ventures. Success has been dependent not only on the initial adoption but on continual re-assessment of the alignment between market requirements and forces and the venture. The difference between success and failure depends on how effectively the firm can meet the market's changing requirements. A successful business does not just have to get it all right from the start but must keep on making the right decisions as external factors in particular strive to drive it off course. This often entails modification to the business strategies over time but may also require a complete rethink of the business models. In at least one case (HomeToDo) this entailed the startup withdrawing from online activities, refining a new business model, and then re-entering the online arena. In other situations it has resulted in a firm with first-mover advantage being punished by competitors for failing to keep up with the relentless waves of innovation.

The rolling ball conceptual model of Internet innovation illustrates this lesson: that success is an inherently unstable state requiring effective construction of the innovation to meet specific requirements and continual monitoring, modification and maintenance to maintain the suitability and momentum of the venture. The cases examined show how innovations fail when the innovation is inappropriate, the driving forces insufficient to maintain momentum, and the necessity for constant maintenance and modification is ignored.

Advice from the firms spells out the critical importance of an integrated, responsive operation. Traditional firms with a supply-push approach to the market focus on developing efficiencies within their standardized functional business units. The Internet enables efficiency in operations for firms that customize their offerings in response to market demands. This opportunity for mass customization can transform the structure of firms and industries and promote the use of specialized service providers in particular functional areas to obtain international levels of best practice. This potential is, however, extraordinarily difficult to realize. While there are no magic solutions to this challenge, the cases show how firms in different countries are working to realize this potential.

A more complete picture will only develop over time and some lessons will be specific to the circumstances of individual firms, but across all firms general areas of advice have emerged. To an extent beyond that required in traditional firms, everything counts in the success of an Internet business and everything has to run properly. The Internet enables very complex and detailed processes to be performed instantaneously across companies and countries. Consumer expectations have developed to expect these logistical miracles as a matter of course and customers will punish in the market any company that fails to deliver to this expectation. Therefore, successful online firms recognize that the answer to the question, 'What has to go right for the company to succeed?', is 'Seriously, everything!' Everything is relevant but some factors are more relevant than others for particular ventures. Each initiative must have a clearly understood business model and a realistic value proposition. Strategies to implement the model(s) need to be clearly stated and carefully constructed but the necessity to be flexible in response to specific market conditions is imperative.

In short, the most important lesson arising from this project is for firms to recognize that each Internet venture is unique. Even firms with the same business model in the same industry will have different strategic strengths and weaknesses so all elements of the plan will need to be carefully analysed to identify what is likely to impact success and to address the element specifically. Internet ventures that did not understand the inter-related factors that determine success and relied on a single issue (often novelty) have failed. Examples include: marketing good but logistics poor; logistics good but efforts unfocused by market research; and a bright business plan but an inability to implement the business practices as they were not appropriate for commoditization.

Much focus has been on products that could sell online. The argument is that some products are more suited for Internet retailing, e.g. digital products or those products that do not require personal interaction for purchase. Haburi, however, has shown that a low-cost factory outlet can sell personal and fashion products very successfully. Books are successfully sold online but books are not actually digital. The issue is more that books can be commoditized, i.e. standardized. Such a variety of products and services have been sold successfully over the Internet that the type of product no longer appears to be the critical issue.

For services, success appears to come from services that do not require personal interaction, e.g. note the experiences of HomeToDo. More emphasis should be made on the type of business process that can be standardized. Mass customization can come at the level of selection of specific services that address predetermined customer needs from a large collection of standardized services. In the future, doubtless the capability to provide more sophisticated customization will be developed, but currently this is as good as can be implemented.

Finally, firms offered some advice and cautions for newcomers to the Internet:

- Look at all the research available in your areas of interest to help develop your understanding and to identify what others find important or interesting in these areas.
- Be aware of differences between published research into any aspect of the Internet. Much research is conducted for a particular purpose that may not be identified but that may influence the results.
- Beware of generalized conclusions. These always require analysis to determine if the conclusions are relevant to particular implementations.
- Recognize the differences between firms and critically analyse those differences. One firm (E-store) has automated its analysis of competitor prices to help derive its competitors' business models and strategies so it can more effectively compete.
- Know your business.
- Know your customers and their requirements.
- Aim to use the Internet to add value, not just to reduce costs.

IMPLICATIONS FOR RESEARCHERS

Much research into 'what works' on the Internet has a narrow focus, e.g. on product (brand and extrabrand attributes), product types, industries, adoption factors, user demographics, security, risk, web page design, and usability features. Little research considers how all these diverse areas, and more, need to come together to enable a successful Internet-based customer service. Consequently, research into e-business has been criticized by Keen (1998) and others as being too narrowly focused.

This research project is unique in that it attempts to examine Internet retailing holistically (i.e. it looks at success factors from the environmental, customer, company and website perspectives) in six countries across three continents. The research model is shown in Figure 9.1. Subsequent to the research, this broadly based model was critically reviewed to consider the extent to which the model reflected the findings. All the categories of factors were found to be relevant to adoption of Internet retailing at an organizational level and, in addition, the range of factors within each category required extension to incorporate factors identified in the research. The conceptual model was introduced in Chapter 9.

A revised research model incorporating these revisions and extensions is proposed: an integrated adoption model for B2C e-commerce (see Table 9.6).

A very significant outcome of the research was the finding that the categories of adoption factors were tightly integrated. Not only were factors from all four categories found to be critical to the success of the Internet venture but factors were found to be applicable across categories. For example, lack of business and technical management skills are applicable in both the organization and innovation categories and customer acceptance is important in the environmental, organizational and consumer categories. Examination of these factors in only one area would provide an inadequate understanding of the importance of the factor in the success of an Internet venture.

An additional outcome of this research was the identified significance of innovation processes as an element in successful innovation. The cases broadly supported Rogers' process theory with critical adoption decision-making factors being grouped as initial or on-going. Incremental planning and decision-making in support of the adoption occurred over considerable time with many reviews and revisions of the adoption decision taking place in response to market experience with the innovation. This study found that in most cases adoption decision-making was not a single event but occurred over an often extended period. While determinants of successful innovation may be partly based on the initial adoption factors, this project suggests that success is based also on implementation of the innovation. Distinction between the initial motivating factors and the actual and the implemented factors leading to success should be made. A formal Internet innovation process model is proposed (see Table 10.3).

A major contribution of this study is its illustration of the characteristics of successful adoption of innovations in Internet retailing. Success requires the interaction of factors and processes over a considerable period of time. Different factors may be more or less influential and different processes applied depending on the actual firm and its situation. A simple analogy of a ball rolling between two points has been used to illustrate the integration required between the various categories of innovation factors and the processes. The rolling ball conceptual model (see Figures 10.2, 10.3 and 10.4) reminds innovators and researchers of the complexities of the task, the skills and experience required, and the absolute necessity for careful consideration of all potential factors and processes.

In conclusion, this study demonstrates the necessity for broadly based, rigorous, exploratory research that examines Internet innovations holistically. The objective of this research was to develop theory that will more adequately explain the potential of e-business and show how it may be realized. At this stage in our understanding of e-business we simply do not know enough to limit our investigations to particular aspects of Internet adoption and operation or to examine them without reference to their context. This book illustrates the importance of effective research that is relevant to the wider community as we seek to better understand how the Internet can transform business as we know it.

References

Ajzen, I. (1991) The Theory of Planned Behavior, *Organizational Behavior and Human Decision Processes*, **50**, 179–211.

Ajzen, I. and Fishbein, M. (1980) *Understanding Attitudes and Predicting Social Behavior*, Prentice-Hall, Englewood Cliffs.

Alsop, S. (1999) How I Judge if a Web Site Deserves My Business, *Fortune*, **140** (4), 16 August, 167–168.

Anders, J. (2001) Outpost CEO Sees Profits, No Layoffs for Dot-Com, *The Wall Street Journal*.

Andersen Consulting (1999) *eEurope Takes Off*, Andersen Consulting, London.

Avgerou, C., Siemer, J. and Bjørn-Andersen, N. (1999) The Academic Field of Information Systems in Europe, *European Journal of Information Systems*, **8**, 136–153.

Bell, D.E., Keeney, R.L. and Little, J.D.C. (1975) A Market Share Theorem, *Journal of Marketing Research*, May, 136–141.

Benbasat, I. and Zmud, R.W. (1999) Empirical Research in Information Systems: The Practice of Relevance, *MIS Quarterly*, **23** (1), March, 3–16.

Benjamin, R. and Wigand, R. (1995) Electronic Markets and Virtual Value Chains on the Information Superhighway, *Sloan Management Review*, Winter, 62–72.

Blodgett, M. (1999) The Bigger Picture, *CIO*, Section 1, 15 October, 69–75.

Boyd, T.C. and Mason, C.H. (1999) The Link Between Attractiveness of 'Extrabrand' Attributes and the Adoption of Innovations, *Academy of Marketing Science Journal*, **27** (3), 306–319.

Brown, E. and Chen, C. (1999) Big Business Meets the E-World, *Fortune*, **140** (9), August, 88–94.

Ciborra, C.U. (1994) From Thinking to Tinkering: The Grassroots of IT and Strategy, in: C.U. Ciborra and T. Jelassi, eds, *Strategic Information Systems: A European Perspective*, Wiley, Chichester.

Daft, R.L. (1978) A Dual-Core Model of Organizational Innovation, *Academy of Management Journal*, **21** (2), 193–216.

Davis, F.D. (1989) Perceived Usefulness, Perceived Ease of Use, and User Acceptance of Information Technology, *MIS Quarterly*, **3** (3), 319–340.

DTI (2000) *Business In The Information Age: International Benchmarking Study, 2000*, Department of Trade and Industry, London.

Economist (1999) Business and the Internet, 26 June, 1–34.

Elliot, S. (1998) Smart-Card Based Electronic Commerce: An Exploratory Study, in: R. Edmundson and D. Wilson, eds, *Proceedings of Australasian Conference on Information Systems '98*, Vol. 2, UNSW, Sydney, pp. 171–183.

Elliot, S. and Fowell, S. (2000) Expectations versus Reality: A Snapshot of Consumer Experiences with Internet Shopping, *International Journal of Information Management*, **20** (5), October, 323–336.

Elliot, S. and Loebbecke, C. (2000) Theoretical Implications of Adopting Interactive, Inter-organizational Innovations in Electronic Commerce, *Journal of Information Technology and People*, Special Issue on Adoption and Diffusion of IT, **13** (1), 46–66.

Elliot, S., Mørup-Petersen, A. and Bjørn-Andersen, N. (2000) Towards a Framework for Evaluation of Commercial Web Sites, in: S. Klein and B. O'Keefe eds, *Proceedings of the 13th International Electronic Commerce Conference*, Bled, Slovenia, 19–21 June.

Elliot, S.R., Andersen, K.V., Swatman, P. and Reich, S. eds (2001), Developing a Dynamic, Integrative, Multidisciplinary Research Agenda in E-Commerce/E-Business, *Proceedings of the IFIP TC8 Working Conference*, Salzburg, Austria, June, BICE Press, Ourimbah.

Ernst and Young (2001) *Online Retailing in Australia*, Ernst and Young, Sydney.

Farquhar, B., Langmann, G. and Balfour, A. (1998) Consumer Needs in Global Electronic Commerce, *Electronic Markets*, **8** (2), 9–12.

Forrester Research (2000a) The Truth About the Digital Divide, Forrester Research, at http://www.forrester.com/ER/Research/Brief/0,1317,9208,00.html

Forrester Research (2000b) *UK Online Retail: From Minority to Mainstream*, May, London.

Gallaugher, J. (1999) Challenging the New Conventional Wisdom of Net Commerce Strategies, *Communications of the ACM*, **42** (7), July, 17–29.

Gomez Web Site, www.gomez.com

GVA (1999) *10th User Survey*, at http://www.gvu.gatech.edu/user_surveys/survey-1998-10/tenthreport.html

Hamel, G. and Sampler, J. (1998) The E-Corporation, *Fortune*, **138** (11) 7 December.

Hargreaves, D. (1999) Prodi to Launch EU Drive on Internet, *Financial Times*, 8 December, 2.

Ho, C.F. and Wu, W.H. (1999) Antecedents of Customer Satisfaction on the Internet: An Empirical Study of On-Line Shopping, *Proceedings of the 32nd Hawaii International Conference on System Sciences*, IEEE Computer Society, Los Alamitos, California.

IDC (2000) Internet Commerce Market Model, **6** (3), International Data Corporation.

Information Infrastructure Task Force (1993) *The National Information Infrastructure: Agenda for Action*, US Government, Washington.

ITU (2000) *Yearbook of Statistics*, International Telecommunications Union, Geneva.

Jarvenpaa, S.L. and Todd, P.A. (1997) Consumer Reactions to Electronic Shopping on the World Wide Web, *International Journal of Electronic Commerce*, **1** (2), Winter, 59–88.

Judd, C., Smith, E.R. and Kidder, L.H. (1991) *Research Methods in Social Relations*, 6th edn., Holt-Reinhardt.

Keen, P.G.W. (1998) Puzzles and Dilemmas: An Agenda for Value Adding IS Research, Keynote Presentation at European Conference of IS, France, 5 June.

King, J.L., Gurbaxani, V., Kraemer, K.L., McFarlan, F.W., Raman, K.S. and Yap, C.S. (1994). Institutional Factors in Information Technology Innovation, *Information Systems Research*, **5** (2), 139–169.

Kirsner, S. (1999) The Dirty Dozen, *CIO Web Business*, 1 September, 22–25.

Krantz, M. (1998) Click Till You Drop, *Time Magazine*, **152** (3), 20 July, 34–37.

Krishnan, M.S., Ramaswamy, V., Meyer, M.C. and Damien, P. (1999) Customer Satisfaction for Financial Services: The Role of Products, Services and Information Technology, *Management Science*, **45** (9), September, 1194–1209.

Kwon, T.H. and Zmud, R.W. (1987) Unifying the Fragmented Models of Information Systems Implementation, in: R.J. Boland and R.A. Hirscheim eds, *Critical Issues in Information Systems Research*, Wiley, Chichester.

Leedy, P.D. (1997) *Practical Research Planning and Design*, 6th edn, Prentice-Hall, Englewood Cliffs.

Lohse, G.L. and Spiller, P. (1998) Electronic Shopping, *Communications of the ACM*, **41** (7), July, 81–87.

LSE/Novell (1999) *The 1999 Worldwide Web 100—Ranking the World's Largest 100 Firms on the Web*, London School of Economics, London.

LSE/Novell (2000) *The Web 2000 Top 100 Growth Report*, London School of Economics, London.

Lyytinen, K. and Damsgaard, J. (2001) What's Wrong with Diffusion of Innovation Theory?, in: M.A. Ardis and B.L. Marcolin, eds, *Diffusing Software Product and Process Innovations*, Kluwer Academic Publishers, Boston.

Mathieson, K. (1991) Predicting User Intentions: Comparing the Technology Acceptance Model with the Theory of Planned Behaviour, *Information Systems Research*, **2** (3), 173–191.

Metz, C. (2000) How They Built It: Outpost.com, *2DNet*, 8 February.

Moore, G.A. (1995) *Inside the Tornado*, Harper Business, New York.

Moore, G.C. and Benbasat, I. (1996) Integrating Diffusion of Innovations and Theory of Reasoned Action Models to Predict Utilization of IT by End-users, in: K. Kautz and J. Pries-Heje, eds, *Diffusion and Adoption of Technology*, Chapman & Hall, London.

Moreno, K. and McCormack, S. (1998) E-shopping, *Forbes*, **161** (3), 9 February, 40.

Nambisan, S. and Wang, Y.M. (1999) Roadblocks to Web Technology Adoption?, *Communications of the ACM*, **42** (1), January, 98–101.

NetValue (2000) *European Internet Statistics*, November, NetValue Paris, at http://
www.NetValue.com/corp/presse/index_frame.htm? fichier=
cp0016.htm

Nielsen, J. (1999) *Designing Web Usability: The Practice of Simplicity*, New Riders Publishing, USA.

O'Neill, H.M., Pouder, R.W. and Buchholtz, A.K. (1998) Patterns in the Diffusion of Strategies Across Organizations: Insights From the Innovation Diffusion Literature, *Academy of Management Review*, **23** (1), January, 98–114.

Porter, M.E. (2001) Strategy and the Internet, *Harvard Business Review*, March, 63–78.

Ramaswami, S.R., Strader, T. and Brett, K. (1998) Electronic Channel Customers for Financial Products: Test of Ability–Motivation–Opportunity Model, *Proceedings of the Association of Information Systems' Americas Conference*, August, 328–300.

Rogers, E.M. (1995) *Diffusion of Innovations*, The Free Press, New York.

Rosenzweig, P.M. (1994) When Can Management Science be Generalized Internationally? *Management Science*, **40** (1), 28–39.

Roth, A.V. and Jackson, W.E. (1995) Strategic Determinants of Service Quality and Performance: Evidence From the Banking Industry, *Management Science*, **41** (11), 1720–1733.

Scott Morton, M.S. ed. (1991). *The Corporation of the 1990s: Information Technology and Organizational Transformation*, Oxford University Press, New York.

Swanson, E.B. (1994) Information Systems' Innovation Among Organizations, *Management Science*, **40** (9), September, 1069–1092.

Taylor, R.S. (1986) *Value-Added Processes in Information Systems*, Ablex, Norwood.

Taylor, S. and Todd, P.A. (1995) Understanding Information Technology Usage: A Test of Competing Models, *Information Systems Research*, **6**, 144–176.

Timmers, P. (1999) *Electronic Commerce: Strategies and Models for Business-to-Business Trading*, Wiley, Chichester, p. 4.

US Department of Commerce (2000) *The Emerging Digital Economy II*, Economics and Statistics Administration, Office of Policy Development at http://ecommerce.gov, June.

Venkatesh, V. and Brown, S. (2001) A Longitudinal Investigation of Personal Computers in Homes: Adoption Determinants and Emerging Challenges, *MIS Quarterly*, **25** (1), March, 71–102.

Walsham, G. and Sahay, S. (1999) GIS for District-Level Administration in India: Problems and Opportunities, *MIS Quarterly*, **23** (1), March, 39–66.

Whinston, A.B., Applegate, L.M., Holsapple, C.W., Kalakota, R. and Rademacher, F.J. (1996) Electronic Commerce: Building Blocks of New Business Opportunity, *Journal of Organizational Computing and Electronic Commerce*, **6** (1), June, 1–10.

Wigand, R.T. (1997) Electronic Commerce: Definition, Theory and Context, *The Information Society*, **13**, 1–16.

www.consult (2000) 9th Australian Online Survey, www.consult.com.au/oz9_charts.shtml

Zwass, V. (1998) Structure and Macro-level Impacts of Electronic Commerce: From Technological Infrastructure to Electronic Marketplaces, in: K.E. Kendall ed. *Emerging Information Technologies*, Sage, Thousand Oaks, California.

Index

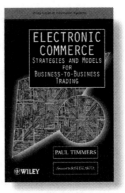

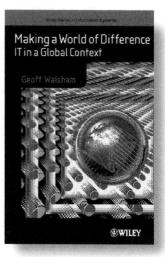